WITHDRAWN

ROME AND CHINA

A Study of Correlations in Historical Events

ROME AND CHINA

A Study of Correlations in
Historical Events

FREDERICK J. TEGGART

Berkeley, California
UNIVERSITY OF CALIFORNIA PRESS
1939

UNIVERSITY OF CALIFORNIA PRESS
BERKELEY, CALIFORNIA

❖

CAMBRIDGE UNIVERSITY PRESS
LONDON, ENGLAND

Printed in the United States of America
by Samuel T. Farquhar, University Printer

PREFACE

CONCERNING the reasons for the inquiry of which partial results are offered in the following pages, I may point out that thirty years ago I found myself confronted with the difficulty that, whereas in the opinion of scholars history was a science, the results achieved by historical inquiry were wholly unlike those characteristic either of physical or biological research. In this situation I felt compelled to make an exhaustive study of the expositions given by historians of their aims, and at the same time to familiarize myself with the actual procedure of scientific work in more than one field. These studies gave occasion, as time went on, for various publications,[1] and led in the end to the definite conclusion that, while historical scholars exercise the greatest care in acquiring and sifting the data of which they make use, they employ, in presenting their results, a form of statement which is in the tradition of literature and which has no relation to science. Consequently I took leave of the conventional discussions of history and science and asked myself the question whether historical data might not be utilized for other ends than the composition of historical narratives. It appeared, indeed, that since historical data constituted the record of human experience in its broader aspects, it was a matter of the highest importance to discover whether this experience might not be used for the purpose of gaining verifiable knowledge concerning "the way things work" in the world of human relations. And, further, since governments are dependent upon scholars for knowledge, it seemed of moment to determine whether historical scholars

---

[1] "The Circumstance or the Substance of History," *American Historical Review* (July, 1910) ; *Prolegomena to History* (University of California Press, 1916) ; *Processes of History* (Yale University Press, 1918) ; and *Theory of History* (Yale University Press, 1925).

[v]

(even though they had never attempted it) might not utilize their accumulated materials to elicit some form of dependable knowledge for the guidance of men of affairs.

The question thus posed presented serious difficulties. Nevertheless it became clear that the possibility of obtaining verifiable knowledge from historical data turned upon the acceptance of three requirements: first, that the aim of the historian should be, not the composition of a narrative, but the investigation of a problem; second, that the problem to be investigated should have reference to a class of events; third, that the procedure of the investigation should be based upon the comparison of events in different parts of the world or different areas.

To be put in operation, the type of inquiry just indicated required, as a first step, the discernment or discovery of a class of events and thus of a problem; and, further, it seemed desirable in an initial venture that the class and the problem to be selected for investigation should already have been recognized by historians. After careful exploration a case was found which exactly met the conditions. Historians have long recognized in the recurrent barbarian invasions of the Roman empire a group of events which might be isolated for purposes of description and discussion; they have acted on the assumption that the recurrence of the invasions set a problem which called for elucidation; and they have accepted the responsibility of formulating theories to account for the phenomena. To all appearance, therefore, historians had followed here the most obvious course of scientific inquiry. Nevertheless, when many histories which dealt with the subject had been examined, it became evident that in no single one of them had the explanatory theory adopted been derived from a study of the actual events. In all, indeed, the theories relied upon were suppositions, not inferences from an assemblage of known historical occurrences. Consequently a problem which had been fully accepted as pertaining to the field of history still remained open for investigation.

The recurrence of the barbarian invasions offered, then, a suitable problem for scientific inquiry. In accordance with the requirements specified above, it at once became necessary to assemble all data which might be supposed to have a bearing upon the occurrences in question. With this object in view, the procedure adopted was to set down, in chronological order, all known events, wars, and disturbances *in each separate kingdom* or region of the continent of Eurasia, for a period of five hundred years. The compilation of data for every country from Britain to Cambodia took the form of separate chronological lists, and the next, though long delayed, step in the investigation was to set these lists side by side and compare the occurrences in geographical order across the map of Eurasia. All this labor, it should be understood, had been undertaken on purely theoretical grounds; hence it was profoundly gratifying to find, when the work of comparing the details had been carried out, that the results were, beyond expectation, unmistakable and definite.

The evidence assembled in the pages following has reference only to the period from 58 B.C. to A.D. 107. Within these decades every barbarian uprising in Europe followed the outbreak of war either on the eastern frontiers of the Roman empire or in the "Western Regions" of the Chinese. Moreover, the correspondence in events was discovered to be so precise that, whereas wars in the Roman East were followed uniformly and always by outbreaks on the lower Danube and the Rhine, wars in the eastern T'ien Shan were followed uniformly and always by outbreaks on the Danube between Vienna and Budapest. In the period here referred to, invasions or uprisings occurred on the Roman frontiers in Europe on forty occasions. On nine of these occasions disturbances on the upper Danube followed wars at Guchen and Turfan, in the eastern T'ien Shan. On thirty-one occasions disturbances both on the Rumanian Danube and on the Rhine followed wars on the eastern frontiers of the Roman empire, more especially in Syria or Armenia. (The Roman records are poor,

yet for three occasions only, out of thirty-one, is information
lacking concerning occurrences on the lower Danube.) Even in
the briefest summary it must also be pointed out that, of the
wars in the Roman East, eighteen followed wars in Chinese Turkistan, so that, of the forty occasions on which outbreaks took
place in Europe, twenty-seven were traceable to the policy, or
rather changes of policy, of the Han government.

An illustration may, perhaps, make clear the relationship of
events. In A.D. 102 the great administrator Pan Ch'ao, who had
maintained Chinese power and prestige in the Tarim basin for
thirty years, was permitted to retire, and his departure was soon
followed by the outbreak of disturbances all the way from
Kan-su to the Pamirs. As a consequence, in the years 105–107
the Chinese were forced to withdraw from the "Western Regions."
Also, in the Near East, in 105–106 Pacorus, king of Parthia,
was overthrown, while contemporaneously Cornelius Palma
took possession of Petra and annexed Arabia. Again, in Europe,
in 106 Trajan invaded Dacia, and in 107 annexed it. More re-
motely, in or about 106–108 the Romans were forced to evacuate Scotland. In the same period, moreover, the Hsiung-nu
(Huns) took Guchen and Turfan from the Chinese (in 105),
and, in correspondence with this event, in 107 the barbarians
invaded Pannonia (i.e., Hungary west of the Danube).

The primary result of the investigation has, therefore, been to
establish (for the first time) the existence of *correlations in historical events*. The correlations, it should be understood, are in
themselves historical facts, though facts which have not hitherto
been brought to light, and in themselves are of great significance. That these facts have not previously been discerned is due
to the practice by which the history of each and every country is
treated in isolation by specialists. Up to the present moment the
procedure of comparing events throughout the Eurasian continent has not been brought to bear upon the study of historical
problems.

Now tests which have been applied give every indication that correlations in events are to be expected in the history of Eurasia, at least down to the end of the fifteenth century. Hence it seems of the utmost importance, for the understanding of human relations, that the undertaking which has here been set on foot should be prosecuted in a thorough and comprehensive manner. Clearly, in the strictly modern period, the pattern of world events outlined is not to be expected. Yet, in order to gain a position from which the actual changes brought about by European expansion overseas may be understood, it is essential that the course of events under the older system of overland commerce should be known in detail.

The establishment of correlations in historical events does not, indeed, solve the problem of the recurrent invasions in Central Europe, but it does define this problem in new and explicit terms. How, then, are we to account for the circumstance that Roman wars in Armenia occasioned barbarian uprisings on the lower Danube and the Rhine, and that Chinese wars in the T'ien Shan occasioned similar outbreaks in Hungary? Now, stated in this form, the problem assumed an unexpected aspect, and in an embarrassing manner called for inquiries of a sort not represented in the chronological data previously compiled. In other words, the focus of inquiry shifted from the critical examination of dates to an exploration of the possible linkages, considered geographically, between peoples situated in Armenia and in Rumania, separated as they were by the Black Sea, and between peoples situated in the T'ien Shan and in Hungary, separated as they were by Dzungaria, Western Siberia, Russia, and Poland. Into the perplexities and difficulties of these studies, which entailed scrutiny of Ptolemy's account of northern Eurasia, it is not necessary to enter in a prefatory statement. Suffice it to say that the outcome of this phase of the undertaking was the conclusion that the correspondence of wars in the East and invasions in the West was due to *interruptions of trade*.

At this point the opportunity must be taken to insist upon the urgent need for detailed and systematic study of the use and disuse of trade routes as contributory to an understanding of the relations of peoples throughout the world (and this statement applies to the twentieth no less than to the first century of the Christian era). Further, the need also is compelling for the close investigation of the effects produced by interruptions of trade and changes of routes not only on the barbarian tribes, but also on the greater political organizations. Thus the effects of wars which arose out of interruptions on the great "silk route" through Persia are plainly visible in the internal history of Rome. Cicero directed attention to the fact that war could not occur in the East without shaking the money market at Rome to its foundations, and seemingly there could be no better illustration of the interdependence of nations than the consideration that a decision of the Chinese government should have been responsible for a financial panic in the capital of the Roman empire.

As already stated, inquiry concerning the recurrent invasions of the northern barbarians was undertaken because these outbreaks represented a class of events which had long been recognized by historians. It has now been shown that the occurrences in Europe were closely related, in a majority of instances (twenty-seven out of forty), to wars in Hsin-chiang, the extensive western province of China, and thus an inquiry into a series of disturbances on the frontiers of the Roman empire has had the unexpected outcome of demonstrating the highly important place of China as a factor in the history of the remote West. But the effects of Chinese policies and wars were not restricted to Europe, and the invasions from which the inquiry set out represent one aspect only of the complexities which ensued upon changes within the Chinese empire. It follows, therefore, that if the history of Eurasia in general and of Europe in particular is to be understood, the history of China must be placed in the foreground. In the continuation of the investigation, this course will be adopted, and proper attention given to the conditions which found expression in Chinese policy. Thus, from a new point of departure, and by means of a comparison of histories, an effort will be made to account for the invasions of the third century by displaying the consequences for the world of the collapse of the Later Han dynasty.

It may possibly be thought at this point that the study of history cannot well be organized with reference solely to the incidence of barbarian attacks on a vanished empire. In other words, it may be imagined that, while one class of events has actually been detected, such a phenomenon is rare and cannot be taken as the basis of a historical science. It must be stated, therefore, that classes of events are in number practically unlimited, and are by no means restricted to the outbreak of wars.

As an example of a wholly different type, I may point to the great religious movements associated with the names of Zoroaster in Persia, Lao-tzŭ and Confucius in China, Mahavira (founder of Jainism) and Gautama Buddha in India, the prophets Ezekiel and Second Isaiah, Thales in Ionia, and Pythagoras in southern Italy. All these great personages belong to the sixth century B.C., and their appearance certainly constitutes a class of events. Yet, though the correspondence of these events has frequently been observed,[2] no serious effort has ever been made, so far as I have been able to discover, to treat the appearance of these great teachers—within a brief compass of time—as a problem which called for systematic investigation.[3] But with-

---

[2] Most recently by Professor Stanley A. Cook, *The Old Testament, an Interpretation* (Cambridge, 1936), 230.

[3] The suggestions which from time to time have been put forward in explanation of the occurrences serve merely to emphasize the fact that an inductive procedure has not been regarded as an essential condition in the investigation of an outstanding historical problem. See, for example, Adolf Brodbeck, *Zoroaster* (Leipzig, 1893), 21; Albrecht Wirth, *Der Gang der Weltgeschichte* (Gotha, 1913), 181; Hugo Rachel, *Geschichte der Völker und Kulturen* (2. Aufl., Berlin, 1922), 91; C. F. Lehmann-Haupt, "Geschichte des alten Orients," in L. M. Hartmann, *Weltgeschichte*, I (3. Aufl., Gotha, 1925), 217.

out this knowledge how are we to envisage or comprehend the workings of the human spirit? The history of human achievement, indeed, displays extraordinary variations of advance and subsidence. How are the outstanding advances of men at different times and places to be accounted for? Think of ancient Egypt and Babylonia. How are the great periods of supreme attainment to be accounted for? Think of Sophocles and Shakespeare. How are the cessations of effort to be accounted for? Think of the old antagonists Greece and Persia. On these questions men have speculated and have written many books. But no one has approached the questions with any semblance to the patient care exercised in the study of an atom of hydrogen, even though the systematic investigation of the problems hinted at lies well within the limits of possibility.

If, then, we are to comprehend "the way things work" in the world of human interests and activities, to ascertain the conditions under which men attain their highest capabilities, and to understand the hidden causes of the collapse of civilizations, it is imperative that we should make use of the procedure here described as the comparison of the experience of men in all the different parts of the world.

Finally, if we are not to be swamped by the dogma that Revolution is the Way of Progress, we must be prepared to exercise every possible effort to discover the actual conditions and the actual means under and through which human advancement has been effected. For the guidance of life we cannot, without reverting to the age of alchemy, accept any *a priori* philosophy of history. But the alternative to this acceptance is a wholehearted concentration, in the spirit of modern scientific work, on the study of World History, conceived as the comparison of histories for the elucidation of the problems of human existence.

FREDERICK J. TEGGART

Berkeley, California
August 1, 1938

ACKNOWLEDGMENTS

THE INVESTIGATION which is represented here by a first publication was made possible through the support given to it, first, by the Board of Research, and later, by the Institute of Social Sciences of the University of California. I desire to express my deep appreciation of the aid provided by these bodies, and in this relation to mention with cordiality the name of Professor A. O. Leuschner, long the chairman of the Board. In the actual work of bringing together data concerning occurrences throughout Eurasia for a period of five hundred years I was fortunate in receiving the continued and effective assistance of Miss Grace Dangberg, and it is a matter of sincere regret that during the last five or six years, when the materials assembled were being scrutinized and the statement of results was being prepared, her knowledge and coöperation were no longer available. My thanks are also due to Miss Leona Fassett, for the skill and pains which she has exercised in converting my written memoranda and manuscript into exemplary typescript. Further, I desire to thank Professor P. A. Boodberg, of the Department of Oriental Languages, for the sustained interest which he has taken in the investigation. I desire also to express my appreciation of the thought and care given to the final problems as the book passed into the printer's hands, by Mr. Harold A. Small, editor of the University of California Press.

F. J. T.

CONTENTS

[xv]

MAPS

The maps are designed only to supplement the text and are not consistent in the use of ancient and modern names.

Chapter I

CAESAR · AUGUSTUS · TIBERIUS

THE NORTHERN FRONTIERS of the Roman empire were invaded by barbarian peoples on many occasions, and numerous histories have been written which set forth what is known to have taken place in the vicinity of the Rhine and Danube when the barbarian tribes came in conflict with the Roman legions. Every scholar, moreover, who has composed a history of the world, a history of Rome, or a history of Medieval Europe has found it necessary to adopt some opinion in regard to the inception of these events. The need to account for the recurrence of the invasions has been fully recognized, and theories of different kinds have been formulated in explanation of the phenomena. In these histories and inquiries, however, the sources of information which have been relied upon have been those which relate to the history of Rome, and as a result the narratives and discussions have been dominated by an exclusive interest in the fortunes of the Roman empire. In the present investigation, on the contrary, an attempt has been made to show that the study of events in any national history may more effectively be approached through the observation of concurrent happenings in different parts of the world, and, more particularly, that the antecedents of occurrences on the frontiers of the Roman empire may be definitely determined by taking into consideration the course of events in the Near and the Far East. Accordingly, the inquiry into the background of the barbarian invasions has entailed a methodical use of Chinese, no less than of Roman, historical sources, and the results presented in the following pages have been arrived at by making comparison of disturbances recorded throughout Eurasia. The information obtained in this manner has been embodied in a number of separate studies, in each of which the presentation moves from earlier to later and consequently in direction from east to west. The first of the principal divisions of the inquiry embraces a period of approximately one hundred years, and in it attention is directed to the correspondence of events in the Roman East and in Europe.

I

Lucullus and Pompey in Asia Minor and Armenia.—In 74 B.C., Mithridates Eupator, king of Pontus and Bosporus,[1] seized Bithynia, which had recently been declared a Roman province. The Senate at once decided upon war and entrusted the conduct of operations to M. Aurelius Cotta and L. Licinius Lucullus. At the outset (in 73) Mithridates defeated Cotta, captured the Roman fleet in Chalcedon, and laid siege to Cyzicus. Lucullus, however, forced him to abandon the siege and destroyed the Pontic army during its retreat; moreover, in 72 he overcame Mithridates at Cabira, and in the years 72–70 completed the conquest of his dominions in Asia Minor.

Here it may be mentioned parenthetically that in 72–71 M. Terentius Varro Lucullus, brother of Lucius Lucullus and governor of Macedonia, put down an uprising of the Bessi, on the

---

[1] For the career of Mithridates, see Théodore Reinach, *Mithridate Eupator, roi de Pont* (Paris, 1890). Geyer, "Mithridates" (12), *RECA*, XV (1932), 2163–2205. The literary tradition uniformly has the spelling "Mithridates"; inscriptions have, with similar consistency, the spelling "Mithradates."

The history of the third Mithridatic war has been fully dealt with in recent publications. See J. G. C. Anderson, "Pompey's Campaign against Mithradates," *JRS*, 12 (1922), 99–105. T. R. Holmes, *The Roman Republic and the Founder of the Empire*, I (Oxford, 1923), 176–219, 398–433. Gelzer, "Licinius" (104), *RECA*, XIII (1926), 376–414. Felix Guse, "Die Feldzüge des dritten Mithradatischen Krieges in Pontos und Armenien," *Klio*, 20 (1926), 332–343. H. A. Ormerod and Max Cary, *CAH*, IX (1932), 356–371, 376–383, 390–396, 897–898. See also J. M. Cobban, "Lucullus and Pompey," in his *Senate and Provinces, 78–49 B.C.* (Cambridge, 1935), 99–137.

upper Maritsa, and continued the campaign as far as the Dobrudja and the coast of the Black Sea. It is also of interest that
in 72 or 71 Ariovistus, with a following of German tribesmen,
crossed the Rhine and took service with the Sequani in war
against the Aedui.

Meanwhile Mithridates had taken refuge in Armenia with his
son-in-law Tigranes the Great. In 69, therefore, Lucullus invaded Armenia, where he took the new city of Tigranocerta. In
68 he marched northward with the intention of seizing Artaxata,
the old capital of the country, but his army mutinied in the face
of the hardships encountered, and he was forced to retire; some
compensation for the misadventure was found, however, in the
capture of Nisibis. On the other hand, the check to the Roman
advance encouraged Mithridates to reënter Pontus; in 67, near
Zela, he defeated the Roman army commanded by C. Valerius
Triarius, and within the year recovered the greater part of his
kingdom. The disaffection of his troops forced Lucullus to remain inactive.

In 66 B.C., Pompey (Cn. Pompeius Magnus) was appointed
to take the place of Lucullus in command against Mithridates.
He promptly advanced from Cilicia into Pontus and there defeated Mithridates in the battle of Nicopolis; the Roman success
was facilitated by the coöperation of Phraates III of Parthia,
who attacked Tigranes of Armenia and thus prevented him from
bringing support to his ally. Pompey next invaded Armenia,
where he captured Artaxata without difficulty, and at the end of
the season's campaign went into winter quarters on the southern
border of Albania. In the spring of 65 he inflicted a defeat on
Artoces, king of the Iberians, and then crossed over westward
into Colchis. At the mouth of the river Phasis (Rion) he met the
Roman fleet, commanded by Servilius, and confided to it the
further pursuit of the king of Pontus; he himself turned eastward again to overrun Albania, but stopped short of his objective, the shores of the Caspian Sea.

1. BOSPORUS, ARMENIA, AND SYRIA.

Mithridates passed the winter (66–65) at Dioscurias, in Colchis, but the rapidity of Pompey's movements in 65 compelled him to retire still farther, through the Caucasus Mountains, to the kingdom of Bosporus.[2] Though on his arrival in his northern dominions he was opposed for a time by his son Machares, and though the coast of the Bosporan kingdom was effectively blockaded by the Roman fleet, Mithridates embarked upon the enterprise of invading Italy by way of the Danube and proceeded to raise a new army. In 63, however, his son Pharnaces joined a revolt against him, and Mithridates put an end to his own life. When news of this event reached Pompey, he recognized Pharnaces as king of Bosporus and as "friend and ally" of Rome, but limited the extent of his dominions, and even exempted the city of Phanagoria from his rule. Pompey also dismembered the kingdom of Pontus.

The campaigns of Lucullus and Pompey put an end to the political unity of the northern and southern coasts of the Black Sea (Bosporus and Pontus), and the blockade of the Bosporan ports similarly effected the disruption of the economic system of the Mithridatic empire. The dismemberment of this empire created an opportunity which was grasped by Burebista, under whose leadership Dacia became "la plus grande puissance barbare de l'Europe," though it would seem less than appreciative to regard as a barbarian a man who had "raised his people to such a height through training, sobriety, and obedience to his commands that within only a few years he had established a great empire and had subordinated to it most of the neighboring peoples."[3]

---

[2] On the kingdom of Bosporus and its history, see especially Basilius Latyschev, "Brevis conspectus historiae regni Bosporani," in his *Inscriptiones antiquae orae septentrionalis Ponti Euxini*, II (Petropoli, 1890). Brandis, "Bosporos" (3), *RECA*, III (1899), 757–789. E. H. Minns, *Scythians and Greeks* (Cambridge, 1913), 563–638. Max Ebert, *Südrussland im Altertum* (Bonn, 1921), 244–259. M. I. Rostovtzeff, *Iranians & Greeks in South Russia* (Oxford, 1922); *Skythien und der Bosporus*, I (Berlin, 1931).

[3] Strabo vii. 3. 11 (303–304).

The Romans in Syria, 64–58 B.C.—The activities of Pompey after the defeat of Mithridates likewise had consequences of lasting importance, for in 64 B.C. he annexed Syria, the last remnant of the Seleucid empire. The pacification of the newly acquired territory occupied, at first, the attention of the Roman commander, but he proceeded at the earliest possible moment (63) to Damascus and made preparations for an expedition against Petra, the desert stronghold which controlled the great trade route from the Red Sea. His march to Petra was interrupted, however, by rebellion in Judaea, and he was forced to employ his troops in the siege of Jerusalem. Pompey did not himself resume the interrupted campaign, but in 62 he sent M. Aemilius Scaurus, the first Roman governor of Syria, to take possession of the Nabataean capital. Nevertheless the city was not captured, for Aretas III, king of the Nabataeans, discovered a means of escape from the impending danger through the payment of a large sum of money.[4] At the end of 62 Pompey returned to Italy, and in 61 entered Rome in triumph.

The immediate successors of Scaurus in the governorship of Syria, L. Marcius Philippus (61–60) and Cn. Cornelius Lentulus Marcellinus (59–58), "each spent the whole of his two years in repelling the attacks of the neighboring Arabs"—possibly Nabataeans—and the situation had become so serious in 58 that the Senate decided "to appoint for Syria proconsuls,

[4] For the annexation of Syria, see Emil Schürer, *Geschichte des jüdischen Volkes im Zeitalter Jesu Christi,* I (3.–4. Aufl., Leipzig, 1901), 294–304. Josef Dobiáš, "Les premiers rapports des Romains avec les Parthes et l'occupation de la Syrie," *Archiv orientální,* 3 (1931), 215–256. Honigmann, "Syria," *RECA,* 2. Reihe, IV (1932), 1622.

For Pompey's campaign against Petra, see Plutarch *Pompey* 38, 41. Josephus *BJ* i. 6. 4 (131); *Antiq.* xiv. 3. 1–4 (34, 38, 46, 48). Appian *Mithr.* 106. Dio xxxvii. 15. 1–2. Florus i. 40 (29). Orosius vi. 6. 1. See also Wilcken, "Aretas" (3), *RECA,* II (1896), 673–674. Damascus had been occupied in 66 or 65 by L. Lollius and Q. Caecilius Metellus Scipio. Benziger, "Damaskos" (1), *RECA,* IV (1901), 2046. Münzer, "Lollius" (6), *RECA,* XIII (1927), 1376.

For the campaign of Scaurus, see Josephus *BJ* i. 8. 1 (159); *Antiq.* xiv. 5. 1 (80–81). Rohden, "Aemilius" (141), *RECA,* I (1894), 588. Albert Kammerer, *Pétra et la Nabatène* (Paris, 1929), 167–168.

with power to levy troops and engage in war like consuls."[5] Under this new arrangement Aulus Gabinius took office in 57 B.C.

Events in Europe, 64–58 B.C.—While the Romans were thus engaged in the East, conflicts were taking place in the regions of the lower and the upper Danube and among the German tribes. First, in 64 B.C., L. Manlius Torquatus, governor of Macedonia, gained notable successes in war for which (in 63) he was accorded the title of *imperator*. Again, in 62 B.C., C. Antonius Hybrida,[6] likewise governor of Macedonia, became involved in war with the Dardani and their neighbors, on the upper Vardar and the upper Morava, and Dio says that the army under Hybrida's command was driven out of the country by the tribesmen. In 61 the same general was even more unfortunate, for near Istrus, on the Black Sea, he was defeated and his army routed by the Bastarnae, who had crossed the Danube into the Dobrudja. Somewhat later, in 59, Gaius Octavius, father of the emperor Augustus and governor of Macedonia from 60 to 58, was engaged against the Bessi and other tribes on the Macedonian border, and defeated them in a "great battle."

Second, in or about 62 B.C., Burebista,[7] king of the Dacians, opposed Critasirus, king of the Boii and Taurisci, who had invaded the territory between the Theiss and the Danube. In 61 or 60 he overcame the Boii and Taurisci and "actually caused

<hr>

[5] Appian *Syr.* 51. Schürer, *Geschichte des jüdischen Volkes*, 304–305. On the troubles with the Arabs at the beginning of the Roman régime in Syria, see D. H. Müller, "Arabia," *RECA*, II (1896), 352–353.

[6] Livy *epit.* 103. Dio xxxviii. 10; li. 26. 5. Carl Patsch, *Beiträge zur Völkerkunde von Südosteuropa*, V (Wien, 1932. *SAWW*, 214), 38–40. In *RECA*, see Seeck, "Antonius" (19), I (1894), 2579–80; Ihm, "Bastarnae," III (1899), 111.

[7] On the kingdom of Burebista, see Strabo vii. 3. 5 (298), 11 (303–304) ; 5. 2 (313). Brandis, "Dacia," *RECA*, IV (1901), 1958–60; "Burebista," Supptbd. I (1903), 261–264. Camille Jullian, *Histoire de la Gaule*, III (Paris, 1909), 144–154. E. H. Minns, *Scythians and Greeks* (Cambridge, 1913), 123–124, 464. Vasile Pârvan, *Getica, o protoistorie a Daciei* (Bucureşti, 1926) ; *Dacia, an Outline of the Early Civilizations of the Carpatho-Danubian Countries* (Cambridge, 1928). P. Henry, "Une histoire des Gètes avant la conquête de la Dacie par les Romains," *Revue historique*, 156 (1927), 269–293. Patsch, *Beiträge zur Völkerkunde von Südosteuropa*, V, 42–51. See also Fluss, "Scordisci," *RECA*, 2. Reihe, II (1921), 835.

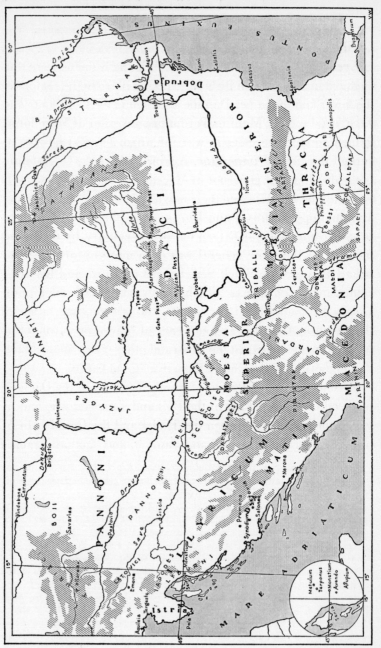

2. THE PEOPLES OF THE DANUBE AND THE BALKANS.

their complete disappearance,"[8] though some at least of the Boii crossed over into Noricum and laid siege to Noreia (Neumarkt in Styria). About the same time (61 or 60) the Helvetii, in Switzerland, set about making preparations to migrate westward. Also in 61 the Allobroges, situated between the Isère and the Rhone, who were neighbors of the Helvetii, rose in revolt against the Roman government; they were put down in 60 B.C. by C. Pomptinus.[9] Furthermore, in 61 Ariovistus completely crushed the Aedui at Magetobriga (the site is unknown), and thereafter turned against his employers, the Sequani, and prepared to establish himself permanently in Alsace.[10]

In or about 59, 32,000 of the Boii joined the Helvetii, and early in 58 the Helvetii, with a host (numbering, it is said, 368,000 persons) which included the Rauraci, the Tulingi, and the Latobrigi, as well as the Boii, set out with the intention of making a new settlement in Gaul.[11] It was this migration which Caesar encountered in the first campaign of the Gallic war, and the movement of the tribes was brought to an end by his victory

[8] Strabo vii. 3. 11 (304). Strabo gives no dates in relating the achievements of Burebista; his statements are such, however, as to imply that the war against the Boii occupied some length of time. The accepted date for the overthrow of the Boii is "ums J. 60 v. Chr.;" see, in *RECA*, Ihm, "Boii," III (1899), 631; Brandis, "Dacia," IV (1901),1959; Fluss,"Taurisci," 2. Reihe, V (1934), 8. See also Benedictus Niese, "Zur Geschichte der keltischen Wanderungen," *ZDA*, 42 (1898), 152–161: "Der Untergang der Boier."

For the possibility that Critasirus had formed "un grand empire," see Jullian, *Histoire de la Gaule*, III, 145 note 4. For the territorial dispute, see Strabo vii. 5. 2(313); on this Brandis says, *RECA*, Supptbd. I, 263: "vernichtete er die keltischen Boier und Taurisker, welche über die Donau bis an die Theiss vorgedrungen waren . . ." For the "desert" of the Boii, see Strabo vii. 1. 5 (292). Pliny *NH* iii. 146. Ptolemy ii. 14. 2.

[9] Caesar *BG* i. 2–3 (Helvetii), 5 (Boii), 6 (Allobroges). For the Allobroges, see also Livy *epit.* 103. Dio xxxvii. 47–48; xxxix. 65.

[10] For Ariovistus, see Caesar *BG* i. 30–54; vi. 12. Dio xxxviii. 34–50. Cicero *ad Att.* i. 19. Klebs, "Ariovistus," *RECA*, II (1896), 842–845. Jullian, *Histoire de la Gaule*, III, 149–159, 221–241. T. R. Holmes, *Caesar's Conquest of Gaul* (2d ed., Oxford, 1911), 57–68, 553–555, 635–657. Ludwig Schmidt, *Geschichte der deutschen Stämme*, II. 2 (Berlin, 1913), 144–153.

[11] Caesar *BG* i. 5–29. Jullian, *Histoire de la Gaule*, III, 193–220. Holmes, *Caesar's Conquest of Gaul*, 46–57, 613–634. Eugen Täubler, *Bellum Helveticum* (Zürich, 1924). Felix Stähelin, *Die Schweiz in römischer Zeit* (2. Aufl., Basel, 1931), 57–75.

near Bibracte (Mont Beuvray). In the peace enforced after the battle, Caesar permitted the Boii to remain in the territory of the Aedui, at the request of the latter, but compelled the survivors of the Helvetii to return to the territory they had abandoned in Switzerland. Less than three months later (58) Caesar defeated Ariovistus in the neighborhood of Vesontio.

Third, in Germany, it appears to have been between 62 and 60 that the Suebi attacked the Usipetes and Tencteri, for Caesar states that they had carried on war against these peoples for several years before they succeeded in driving them out in 58. In this last-mentioned year, 24,000 Harudes (Charudes ?) crossed into Gaul and harried the territory of the Aedui. Also in 58 the Suebi, in addition to the expulsion of the Usipetes and Tencteri, forced the submission of the Ubii, and, under the leadership of Nasua and Cimberius, appeared on the Rhine, at the mouth of the river Lahn, opposite the position of the Treveri.[12]

The foregoing particulars indicate that, at least in point of time, the upheavals in the Near East occasioned by the successes of Pompey and his conquest of the world from the Maeotis to the Red Sea (as Pliny describes it) were accompanied by wars in Central Europe, and the occurrences in the two regions were evidently of similar complexity. In presence, however, of such diversity, any attempt to suggest specific correspondences in the events would at the outset be unwarranted.

II

Romans and Parthians, 57–50 B.C.—In Syria, notwithstanding the continued hostility of the Arabs and the outbreak of serious disturbances within the province, more especially in Judaea, Aulus Gabinius began to make preparations for a campaign against the Parthians.

---

[12] For the activities of the German tribes, see Caesar *BG* i. 31, 37, 54; iv. 1–19. See also Schmidt, *Geschichte der deutschen Stämme*, II. 3 (1918), 405–410. Ihm, "Charudes," *RECA*, III (1899), 2194. Besnier, "Tencteri," *RECA*, 2. Reihe, V (1934), 490–492.

In Parthia, during the time of Philippus or of Lentulus (in or about 58), Phraates III was murdered by his sons Mithridates (III) and Orodes (II). Despite variances in the accounts of Justin, Dio Cassius, and Appian, it seems probable that Mithridates succeeded his father as king of Parthia, and that shortly afterwards he invaded Armenia (58?). Subsequently, however, Mithridates was driven out by Orodes and took refuge in Syria, where he appealed to Gabinius for support in an attempt to recover his kingdom.[1]

The appearance of Mithridates of Parthia provided Gabinius with a suitable pretext for an invasion, and in 56 B.C. he crossed the Euphrates. At this juncture, however, Gabinius received instructions from Pompey to restore Ptolemy XI Auletes to the throne of Egypt, and he withdrew his troops from Parthian territory. The governor of Syria carried out the Egyptian undertaking in the early months of 55 B.C., though during his absence from the province pirates plundered the people to such an extent that the taxes could not be collected.[2] Either before or after the expedition to Egypt, Gabinius made an attack upon the kingdom of the Nabataeans.

Meanwhile Mithridates, though deprived of the expected as-

---

[1] Justin xlii. 4. Dio xxxix. 56. Appian *Syr.* 51. See also Strabo xii. 3. 34 (558) ; xvii. 1. 11 (796). Josephus *BJ* i. 8. 7 (175, 178) ; *Antiq.* xiv. 6. 2, 4 (98, 103). Plutarch *Antony* 3. 2; *Cassius* 21. 7.

George Rawlinson, *The Sixth Great Oriental Monarchy* (London, 1873), 147–149. Alfred von Gutschmid, *Geschichte Irans* (Tübingen, 1888), 86–87. Ferdinand Justi, "Geschichte Irans," in *Grundriss der iranischen Philologie*, II (Strassburg, 1896–1904), 498. Heinrich Dressel, "Ein Tetradrachmon des Arsakiden Mithradates III," *Zeitschrift für Numismatik*, 33 (1922), 156–177. Clément Huart, *Ancient Persia and Iranian Civilization* (New York, 1927), 106. Geyer, "Mithridates" (23), *RECA*, XV (1932), 2211. W. W. Tarn, *CAH*, IX (1932), 604. R. H. McDowell, *Coins from Seleucia on the Tigris* (Ann Arbor, 1935. Univ. of Michigan Studies, Humanistic Series, vol. 37), 212–216.

[2] On the governorship of Gabinius, see the edition of Cicero's *De provinciis consularibus* by H. E. Butler and M. Cary (Oxford, 1924), 89–97. Emil Schürer, *Geschichte des jüdischen Volkes im Zeitalter Jesu Christi* (3.–4. Aufl., Leipzig, 1901), 305–306. Vonder Mühll, "Gabinius" (11), *RECA*, VII (1910), 427–428. For the disturbances in Syria in 56, Dio xxxix. 59. Josephus *Antiq.* xiv. 6. 2 (100) ; *BJ* i. 8. 7 (176).

sistance of a Roman army, returned to Mesopotamia and, in opposition to his brother, maintained himself in authority for some years (56–54). In the end he was overcome by the Parthian general Surenas and, on his surrender (54), was put to death by Orodes.

At the beginning of 54 B.C., M. Licinius Crassus took over the province of Syria. The new governor had previously declared his intention of making war on Parthia, and, as Plutarch says, "flew on the wings of hope as far as Bactria and India and the Outer Sea." Hence without delay he crossed the Euphrates, and with little or no opposition reached Nicephorium; at the end of the season's campaign, elated with his success, he returned to Syria, having taken no steps to press the advantage he had gained. Early in 53 B.C. he again crossed the Euphrates; on this occasion, however, he was attacked at Carrhae by the Parthians, under Surenas, with the result that the Roman army was completely routed and Crassus himself was slain.[3]

Orodes had sent Surenas to oppose the invasion of Crassus, while he himself proceeded against Artavasdes I of Armenia, who had offered assistance to the Romans. After Carrhae, indeed, the Parthians gained possession of the whole country east of the Euphrates (including Armenia), and in 52 they entered Syria. This preliminary incursion was successfully opposed by C. Cassius Longinus, who had taken over the province upon the death of Crassus, but in the summer of 51 B.C. the Parthians,

---

[3] Plutarch *Crassus* 16–33. Dio xl. 12–27. Appian *Syr.* 51; *BC* ii. 18. Josephus *BJ* i. 8. 8 (179) ; *Antiq.* xiv. 7. 1, 3 (105, 119). Velleius ii. 46. Justin xlii. 4. Livy *epit.* 106. Florus i. 46. Eutropius vi. 18. Orosius vi. 13. Rufus Festus 17.

Rawlinson, *The Sixth Great Oriental Monarchy*, 150–177. J. H. Schneiderwirth, *Die Parther* (Heiligenstadt, 1874), 52–67. Gutschmid, *Geschichte Irans*, 87–93. Pietro Manfrin, *La cavalleria dei Parthi nelle guerre contro i Romani* (Roma, 1893), 37–99. Kurt Regling, "Zur historischen Geographie des mesopotamischen Parallelogramms," *Klio*, 1 (1902), 443–476; "Crassus Partherkrieg," *Klio*, 7 (1907), 357–394. Paul Groebe, "Der Schlachttag von Karrhae," *Hermes*, 42 (1907), 315–322. Francis Smith, "Die Schlacht bei Carrhä," *Historische Zeitschrift*, 115 (1916), 237–262. Adolf Günther, *Beiträge zur Geschichte der Kriege zwischen Römern und Parthern* (Berlin, 1922), 14–38. Gelzer, "Licinius" (68), *RECA*, XIII (1926), 295–331. Tarn, *CAH*, IX (1932), 606–612.

under Pacorus, son of Orodes, and Osaces, returned in force and overran Syria up to the walls of Antioch. Here they were repulsed by Cassius, and shortly afterwards Osaces, the general in command, was killed by the Romans in an ambush. Pacorus remained in Syria during the winter (51–50), seemingly without molestation by M. Calpurnius Bibulus, the new governor, and only in the summer of 50 withdrew his cavalry across the Euphrates.[4]

Events in Europe, 57–50 B.C.—The fact that Cicero denounced both Gabinius and Piso in unmeasured terms for the disorder in their respective provinces serves to draw attention to the similarity of conditions in Syria and Macedonia from 57 to 55 B.C.

During his governorship of Macedonia, 57–55, L. Calpurnius Piso (consul in 58) was compelled to face simultaneous uprisings of the Dardani, Bessi, and Dentheletae, who overran the country and penetrated even as far as Thessalonica.[5] Further, Julius Caesar, whose jurisdiction extended over Illyricum as well as Gaul, visited the former province on two occasions only during his tenure of the governorship; of these the first was in the winter of 57–56, the second in the winter of 55–54. No specific reason is given for his action on the earlier occasion, but at the beginning of 54 his presence in Illyricum was made necessary by raids of the Pirustae (55), which may perhaps be regarded as an extension of the troubles in Macedonia.

In Dacia, after his war on the Boii, Burebista turned his attention eastward, and by 55 B.C. had reduced to submission the Greek cities on the coast of the Euxine (Black Sea) as far as

---

[4] For the Parthian invasion, see Cicero *ad fam.* ii. 10; xii. 19; xv. 1–4, 9; *ad Att.* v. 18, 20; vi. 1, 5. Dio xl. 28–30. Josephus *BJ* i. 8. 9 (180, 182) ; *Antiq.* xiv. 7. 3 (119, 122). Caesar *BC* iii. 31. Plutarch *Antony* v. 2. Livy *epit.* 108.

[5] Cicero *in Pisonem* 84, 96. Carl Patsch, *Beiträge zur Völkerkunde von Südosteuropa*, V (Wien, 1932), 41–42. On "Piso and his governorship of Macedonia," see the edition of Cicero's *De provinciis consularibus* by Butler and Cary, 82–89. See also Münzer, "Calpurnius" (90), *RECA*, III (1899), 1387–90. Geyer, "Makedonia," *RECA*, XIV (1928), 766.

Olbia;[6] this success implies that he had also overcome the peoples, including the Bastarnae, situated between the Carpathians and the Black Sea. Thereafter his dominions extended from Bohemia to the lower reaches of the river Dnieper, and from Carinthia to the mouth of the Danube.

In Gaul, during the year 57 B.C., Julius Caesar[7] prosecuted his conquest northward into the territory of the Belgae; in the summer of that year he overcame the Bellovaci, the most powerful of the Belgae, then the Nervii, and finally the Atuatuci. In 56 he subjugated the Veneti, in Brittany, but his campaign, later in the year, against the Morini and the Menapii was without significant results. Contemporaneously the Germans were restless, and at the beginning of 56 Caesar sent Titus Labienus into the country of the Treveri, in anticipation of an attempt by the Germans to cross the Rhine. In the winter of 56 the Usipetes and Tencteri[8] crossed the lower Rhine and quartered themselves on the Menapii. They had been dispossessed by the Suebi in 58, and meanwhile had been wandering "in many parts of Germany." In 55 the two tribes moved southward into the territory of the Eburones and Condrusi; here, however, they were opposed by Caesar, who seized the leaders while negotiations were in progress and annihilated the tribesmen in their encampment. It was in pursuit of a remnant of the same peoples that Caesar

---

[6] The date of this conquest is uncertain. Dio Chrysostom in his 36th Oration speaks of the capture of the Greek cities by the Getae as having occurred 150 years earlier. Though the speech was not written until A.D. 102–103, the 150 years should in all probability be reckoned back from the time of Dio's visit to Olbia, which would seem to have been in A.D. 95 or 96; the activity of Burebista on the coast of the Black Sea would fall then between *ca.* 56 and 47 B.C. Hans von Arnim, *Leben und Werke des Dio von Prusa* (Berlin, 1898), 301, 306. Schmid, "Dion" (18), *RECA*, V (1905), 855, 857, 872. E. H. Minns, *Scythians and Greeks* (Cambridge, 1913), 123, 464. Patsch, *Beiträge zur Völkerkunde von Südosteuropa*, V, 46–48.

[7] For the extensive literature on Caesar's conquest of Gaul, see Camille Jullian, *Histoire de la Gaule*, III (Paris, 1909), 149–152, 193–194, 221–222, and *The Cambridge Ancient History*, IX (1932), 944–946.

[8] Caesar *BG* iv. 4–19. Dio xxxix. 47–48. Jullian, *Histoire de la Gaule*, III, 323–330. T. R. Holmes, *Caesar's Conquest of Gaul* (2d ed., Oxford, 1911), 689–706. A. T. Walker, "Where Did Caesar Defeat the Usipetes and Tencteri?" *Classical Journal*, 17 (1921–22), 77–86.

made his first crossing of the Rhine. In the same year (55) he also made his first expedition to Britain.

Again, there were uprisings in Europe which parallel the hostilities on the Euphrates initiated by the activities of Crassus. For these years, 54–50 B.C., the information available concerning affairs in the Balkans is limited to that contained in the general statement of Suetonius that the Dacians poured into Pontus and Thrace, and of Strabo that Burebista plundered Thrace as far as Macedonia and Illyricum.[9] More specific accounts have been preserved in regard to outbreaks, in 52 and 51, in the region between the Save and the Adriatic.[10] In 52 the Iapodes overran Aquileia and sacked Tergeste (Trieste)—Appian says that they "drove back the Romans twice within the space of about twenty years" (before 35 B.C.), but the date of the second attack is not known. In 51 the Delmatae and other tribes took the city of Promona from the Liburni; when the latter appealed to Caesar, he sent word to those who were holding Promona that they should give it up to the Liburni, and when they refused, he sent against them a strong detachment, which, however, was totally destroyed by the Illyrians.

In the West, the years 54 to 52 witnessed the great uprisings in Gaul, first, under Ambiorix, and, second, under Vercingetorix. In the winter of 54, after Caesar's return from his second invasion of Britain, the peoples of northeastern Gaul rose, under the leadership of Ambiorix, one of the kings of the Eburones (on the Meuse). At the outset Ambiorix gained a marked success by overcoming the Roman force at Atuatuca, and it was not until the summer of 53 that the revolt was fully put down. During the conflict the Treveri received support from the Germans beyond the Rhine; hence, even before Ambiorix had been overcome, Caesar crossed the river, though this second expedition accomplished nothing of importance. On the other hand,

[9] Suetonius *Iulius* 44. 3. Strabo vii. 3. 11 (304).
[10] Caesar *BG* viii. 24. Appian *Illyr.* 12, 18.

the Sugambri (on the Ruhr), who had crossed over to join in the pillage of the territory of the Eburones, made a successful attack on the Roman camp at Atuatuca, and were able to withdraw with the booty they had collected. Very early in the year 52 the peoples of Central Gaul rose against the Romans, under the leadership of Vercingetorix of the Arverni. On the occasion of this widespread and formidable revolt Caesar was so hard pressed that he sent across the Rhine and enlisted German cavalry and foot-soldiers. Early in 51 the Belgae again rose, and this final effort to oppose Caesar was led by the Bellovaci, under Correus; the rising ended abruptly when Correus was killed.

It will be observed, then, that from 57 to 55 there were marked disturbances in Syria and on the Euphrates, that, correspondingly, there were significant uprisings on the borders of Macedonia and in Illyricum, and that, in the West, the German tribes gave evidence of unrest, the Usipetes and Tencteri actually invaded Gaul, and Caesar for the first time crossed the Rhine. Again, it is noticeable that when, between 54 and 51, the Romans, under Crassus, invaded the Parthian dominions and the Parthians in turn invaded Syria, there were disturbances on the borders of Macedonia and in Illyricum, while, in the West, the risings of Ambiorix and Vercingetorix taxed the energies of Caesar, the menace of the Germans led to his second crossing of the Rhine, and, in 52, his own plight forced him to enlist their aid against the Gauls.

III

The Romans in the East, 49–47 B.C.—The struggle between Caesar and Pompey (49–48 B.C.) involved the Roman world from Spain to Syria. In the latter region Q. Caecilius Metellus Pius Scipio used his authority as governor of Syria to collect money and troops for Pompey, his son-in-law. In his account of the civil war Caesar mentions the circumstance that Scipio, "having incurred some losses near Mount Amanus [between Syria and

Cilicia], styled himself imperator,"[1] but gives no further indication in regard to the enemies encountered. It may also be pointed out that, in making his preparations for war, Pompey sent C. Lucilius Hirrus on a mission to Orodes to enlist Parthian troops in his cause.[2]

The civil war opened the way for serious disturbances in another quarter. In 63 B.C., after the death of Mithridates Eupator, Pompey had recognized Pharnaces as king of Bosporus, but had narrowly restricted the extent of his dominions. "Just as soon," then, "as he learned that Pompey and Caesar were at variance," Pharnaces grasped the opportunity to regain in their entirety the possessions of his father.[3] With the aid of Spadines, king of the Aorsi, and Abeacus, king of the Siraci, he made himself master of the coast of the Maeotis (Sea of Azov), from Phanagoria, on the eastern side of the Straits of Kerch, to Tanais, on the river Don. Later, and about the time of the battle of Pharsalus (48), Pharnaces crossed over from Bosporus, took possession of Colchis, subjugated Lesser Armenia and parts of Cappadocia and Pontus, and defeated Caesar's lieutenant, Cn. Domitius Calvinus, at Nicopolis. Thereafter, when he had reduced Amisus, he marched rapidly into Bithynia and the province of Asia. At this point the fortunes of the Bosporan king underwent a radical change: first of all, Asander, who had been left at Panticapaeum in charge of the kingdom, declared his independence, and Pharnaces was forced to turn back in order to cope with his rebellious brother-in-law; then he had just reached

---

[1] Caesar *BC* iii. 31.

[2] Caesar *BC* iii. 82. Dio xli. 55. 3–4; xlii. 2. 5. Justin xlii. 4.

[3] Dio xlii. 9. 2; 45. 2. On the activities of Pharnaces, see Hirtius *Bell. Alex.* 34–41, 65–78. Dio xlii. 45–48; xliv. 46. 1; xlv. 29. 4. Plutarch *Caesar* 50. Appian *Mithr.* 120–121; *BC* ii. 91–92. Suetonius *Iulius* 35–37. Strabo xi. 2. 17 (498); xi. 5. 8 (506); xii. 3. 14 (547); xiii. 4. 3 (625). Livy *epit.* 112–113. Florus ii. 13. 61–63. Eutropius vi. 22. Walther Judeich, *Caesar im Orient* (Leipzig, 1885). Brandis, "Bosporos" (3), *RECA*, III (1899), 777–778. Groebe, "Iulius" (131), *RECA*, X (1917), 238–240. T. R. Holmes, *The Roman Republic*, III (Oxford, 1923), 509–514. M. E. Deutsch, "Veni, vidi, vici," *Philological Quarterly*, 4 (1925), 151–156. F. E. Adcock, "Nicopolis and Zela," *CAH*, IX (1932), 676–679.

Pontus when he received intelligence that Caesar was hurrying northward from Syria. Pharnaces faced about to meet the new danger, but, at Zela (47), was completely defeated.

After the battle of Zela, Pharnaces recrossed the Black Sea for the purpose of recovering control of Bosporus. With the assistance of "Scythians and Sarmatians" he established himself in Theodosia and Panticapaeum, but in the continuation of the struggle with Asander was killed. Meanwhile Caesar had conferred the kingdom of Bosporus upon Mithridates of Pergamum, who had rendered him important services at Alexandria. Mithridates collected an army and (in 47 or 46) sought to obtain possession of Bosporus; he, too, however, was defeated, and lost his life when he encountered Asander.[4]

Events in Europe, 49–47 B.C.—During the civil war (49–48 B.C.) the peoples on the borders of Macedonia were in a state of disturbance, but it is difficult to determine whether this condition preceded or followed their enlistment in the struggle, either on the side of Pompey or of Caesar. Pompey, indeed, was in a position to draw upon the peoples of the lower Danube for support, and Burebista also took his side. On the other hand, the Parthini were hostile to him, and in 48, when he withdrew from Dyrrhachium to engage in his last campaign, he found it necessary to leave M. Porcius Cato to hold them in check.[5]

---

[4] Wilcken, "Asandros" (4), *RECA*, II (1896), 1516–17. E. H. Minns, *Scythians and Greeks* (Cambridge, 1913), 589. Geyer, "Mithridates" (15), *RECA*, XV (1932), 2205–6.

After the defeat of Mithridates (46), Asander ruled over Bosporus until his death at a very advanced age in 17 B.C.; Strabo remarks, xi. 2. 11 (495), that he held possession of the region east of the Maeotis as far as the river Tanais (Don). At a time which is not definitely known he fortified the isthmus of Perekop—"he walled off the isthmus of the Chersonesus which is near Lake Maeotis," Strabo vii. 4. 6 (311)—to keep out the Scythians; as authority for this statement Strabo cites Hypsicrates, a writer who lived in the time of Julius Caesar, hence the action described may reasonably be assigned to the earlier years of Asander's reign. The vexed question of Asander's recognition by the Roman government is scarcely relevant to this inquiry.

In 46 B.C., Chersonesus (in the Crimea) sent a deputation to Caesar, with what object is not known. M. I. Rostovtzeff, "Caesar and the South of Russia," *JRS*, 7 (1917), 27–44.

[5] Dio xlii. 10. 1–2; see also xli. 49. 2. Caesar *BC* iii. 42.

In Illyricum, both before and after the battle of Pharsalus, war was carried on vigorously by the partisans of Caesar and Pompey.[6] In 49 C. Octavius, for Pompey, defeated C. Antonius; after this reverse Caesar sent Q. Cornificius, in the spring of 48, against the Delmatae, with whom Octavius was in alliance, and later in the year sent additional forces to Illyricum under the command of A. Gabinius. It may have been on their own initiative[7] that in the winter of 48–47 the Delmatae fell upon Gabinius, at Synodium, and destroyed the greater part of his army; the commander with difficulty escaped to Salonae, where shortly after he died. It was not, indeed, until the spring of 47 that Octavius was driven from the scene of action by P. Vatinius.

During these years the only reference to the peoples beyond the Rhine is that Caesar employed German cavalry against Pompey. In Gaul, however, at the beginning of 46 (February), there was an uprising of the Bellovaci, though nothing is known of the circumstances attending the outbreak beyond the fact that it was put down by Decimus Junius Brutus.[8]

IV

The Romans in the East, 46–42 B.C.—The defeat of Pompey at Pharsalus (48) did not at once bring to an end the resistance of his supporters.

While in the East and on his way to oppose Pharnaces (47), Caesar had appointed his kinsman Sextus Julius Caesar governor of Syria. Not long afterwards Q. Caecilius Bassus, an adherent of the Pompeian party, won over the legions under Sextus and precipitated a war which brought affairs in Syria into grave

---

[6] Hirtius *Bell. Alex.* 42–47. Caesar *BC* iii. 9. Appian *Illyr.* 12, 25, 27, 28; *BC* ii. 58–59. Dio xli. 40; xlii. 11. Livy *epit.* 110.

On the wars in Illyricum, see especially Gustav Zippel, *Die römische Herrschaft in Illyrien bis auf Augustus* (Leipzig, 1877). Judeich, *Caesar im Orient*, 158–164. Georg Veith, "Zu den Kämpfen der Caesarianer in Illyrien," in *Strena Buliciana* (Zagrebiae, 1924), 267–274.

[7] F. E. Adcock, *CAH*, IX (1932), 716, is of opinion that the tribes "wished to be rid of Rome once and for all."

[8] Livy *epit.* 114.

disorder (46 B.C.).[1] Bassus received reinforcements from the Arabs and the Parthians, and was thus able to hold out at Apamea, on the Orontes, against the armies, under C. Antistius Vetus, Q. Marcius Crispus, and L. Staius Murcus, which Caesar sent in succession against him. The situation is illuminated by Cicero in a letter to Atticus, written in 44. Balbus, he says, "has had a letter from Vetus, dated the last of December [45], saying that when Caecilius was besieged and already within his grasp, the Parthian Pacorus came with a large force, and so Caecilius was snatched from his hands and he lost many men."[2]

Toward the end of 44 B.C., P. Cornelius Dolabella proceeded to Syria to take over the province, which had been assigned to him by the Senate. In this action, however, he was forestalled by C. Cassius Longinus (one of the murderers of Caesar), who arrived in time to win over the opposing armies of Bassus and Murcus, and to gain the support of four legions which Cleopatra had sent from Egypt for service under Dolabella; Cassius also obtained the assistance of Parthian bowmen. Thus it came about, in 43, that Cassius successfully blockaded Dolabella in Laodicea and drove him to suicide.[3] Subsequently, after he had plundered the cities of Syria and Asia Minor, Cassius joined Marcus Brutus, and with him was defeated by Antony and Octavian at Philippi (42). Appian relates that a Parthian force, sent to aid Cassius and Brutus in 42, "ravaged Syria and many of the neighboring provinces as far as Ionia, and then returned home."[4]

---

[1] Dio xlvii. 26–27. Appian *BC* iii. 77; iv. 58. Josephus *BJ* i. 10. 10 (216–217); *Antiq.* xiv. 11. 1 (268–270). Strabo xvi. 2. 10 (752–753). Livy *epit.* 114. In *RECA*, see Münzer, "Caecilius" (36), III (1899), 1198–99, and "Iulius" (153), X (1917), 477–478.

[2] Cicero *ad Att.* xiv. 9.

[3] Dio xlv. 15. 2; xlvii. 28–31. Appian *BC* iii. 7–8, 24, 26, 63, 78; iv. 58–62. Josephus *BJ* i. 11. 1 (218–219); *Antiq.* xiv. 11. 2 (271–272). Strabo xvi. 2. 9 (752–753). Velleius ii. 69. Livy *epit.* 121. Orosius vi. 18. 12. Cicero *ad fam.* xii. 11–15. For Syria under Cassius, see Emil Schürer, *Geschichte des jüdischen Volkes im Zeitalter Jesu Christi* (3.–4. Aufl., Leipzig, 1901), 310–312. See also Fröhlich, "Cassius" (59), *RECA*, III (1899), 1732.

[4] Appian *BC* iv. 63.

Events in Europe, 46–42 B.C.—In the region of the lower
Danube, Burebista had taken the side of Pompey in 49–48.
There is no definite information concerning his activities after
that date, but his power and influence increased to an extent
which led Caesar to regard him as formidable and to resolve
upon the overthrow of the Dacian kingdom at the earliest possible moment.[5] In March, 44, a large army had already been
transferred across the Adriatic for this purpose, and Octavian
(later Augustus) had been sent in advance to Apollonia. In
Dacia, when the Italian merchants heard of Caesar's preparations, they hastily withdrew from the country.[6] On the other
hand, at the end of 45 or the beginning of 44, certain men rose
up against Burebista and deposed him,[7] and thereafter his dominions were divided among four or five kings.

After Burebista's death, uprisings and incursions on the borders of Macedonia are again referred to, and it might almost
be thought that the control exercised by a strong government
north and south of the Danube had afforded a measure of protection to the Roman frontier. In 44, rumors of an incursion
into Macedonia by the Getae were circulated at Rome.[8] More
definitely, in 43 M. Junius Brutus, who was in control of Macedonia, found it necessary to conduct an expedition against the
Bessi, on account of depredations which they had committed,
and was acclaimed imperator by his soldiers.[9]

In Illyricum, in 45 and 44 B.C., P. Vatinius, Caesar's appointee as governor of the province, was forced to carry on war
against the Delmatae; his success was such, indeed, that he was
saluted imperator by his soldiers and was granted the honor of
a triumph.[10] In 44, however, he suffered severe losses in a new

---

[5] Strabo vii. 3. 5 (298), 11 (304). Velleius ii. 59. 4. Suetonius *Iulius* 44; *Augustus*
8. Livy *epit.* 117. Appian *Illyr.* 13; *BC* ii. 110.

[6] Vasile Pârvan, *Dacia* (Cambridge, 1928), 138–139, 157.

[7] Strabo vii. 3. 11 (304). See also Suetonius *Augustus* 63. Florus ii. 28. Dio li.
22. 8. Plutarch *Antony* 63. 3.

[8] Appian *BC* iii. 25.   [9] Dio xlvii. 25. 1–2. Livy *epit.* 122.

[10] Cicero *ad fam.* v. 9–10. Appian *Illyr.* 13.

attack of the Delmatae, and shortly after Caesar's death surrendered his legions to M. Junius Brutus.

Farther west, in 44, the Raeti gave trouble, and L. Munatius
Plancus gained a victory over them for which he was awarded a
triumph.[11] Lucius Antonius also was granted the honor of a triumph for a victory which, in 42, he gained over "certain peoples in the Alps."[12]

No outbreak on the Rhine is reported between 45 and 42,
though in April, 44, Cicero received alarming news; a week
later, however, he was able to write to Atticus: "Balbus has better news about Gaul. Twenty-one days ago he had a letter that
the Germans and the tribes there, on hearing about [the death
of] Caesar, sent ambassadors to Aurelius, who was appointed
by Hirtius, saying that they would do as they were bidden."[13]
If to this remarkable statement the fact is added that after 52
peace on the Rhine was unbroken until 39–38, it will be seen
that the German cavalry[14] employed by Caesar served at one
and the same time to deplete the war bands of the peoples beyond the river and to provide hostages for the good conduct of
the tribesmen left at home.

v

Romans and Parthians, 40–38 B.C.—While engaged in making
preparations for war against Antony and Octavian, Cassius had
sent Q. Labienus to solicit assistance from Parthia. When the
Republican cause collapsed, in 42, Labienus was left stranded
at the Parthian court, but in 41 he succeeded in persuading
Orodes to undertake the conquest of Syria. Late in 41 or at
the beginning of 40, the army under Pacorus, son of Orodes,

---

[11] Hanslik, "Munatius" (30), *RECA*, XVI (1933), 546–547. The information
is derived from the inscription on the mausoleum of Plancus; on the other hand,
the *Fasti triumphales* monument records that the victory was obtained over the
Gauls (*ex Gallia*), and the priority of this authority is maintained by Ettore Pais,
Fasti triumphales (Roma, 1920), 285–287, 520.

[12] Dio xlviii. 4. 2–5. Dio is skeptical in regard to the achievement.

[13] Cicero *ad Att.* xiv. 4 and 9.

[14] For the service rendered by the Gallic and German cavalry, see F. E. Adcock,
CAH, IX (1932), 646.

and Labienus crossed the Euphrates,[1] and shortly thereafter defeated the governor of the province, Decidius Saxa. When they had taken possession of Syria, Labienus and Pacorus divided their forces: the latter turned southward into Palestine, the former occupied Cilicia and overran Asia Minor as far as Lydia and Ionia.

In the spring of 39 Antony sent P. Ventidius Bassus against Labienus and the Parthians, and in the campaign of that year Ventidius took Labienus by surprise, forced him to make a precipitate retreat, and inflicted upon him a defeat, near the borders of Cilicia, in which Labienus was killed. Within the year Ventidius recovered Cilicia, defeated the Parthians, and restored Roman government in Syria. In 38 Pacorus, who had assembled a new army, again crossed the Euphrates, but in an attack upon Ventidius near Gindarus he was defeated and killed. Later in the year Antony himself besieged and captured Samosata, where some of the fugitive Parthians had taken refuge with Antiochus of Commagene.

In 38/37 Orodes II was murdered by his son Phraates IV, and the deed was followed by widespread disturbances throughout the Parthian dominions.[2]

Events in Europe, 40–38 B.C.—In 40 B.C., L. Marcius Censorinus, with six legions, defeated the Parthini, who had invaded Macedonia.[3] Nevertheless, in 39 the Parthini again rose,

---

[1] Dio xliii. 51. 5; xlviii. 24–27, 39–41; xlix. 19–21. Appian *Syr.* viii. 51; *BC* v. 10, 65. Plutarch *Antony* 28, 30, 33, 34. Josephus *BJ* i. 13; 15. 2–3; 16. 6–7; *Antiq.* xiv. 13; 15. 5–9. Strabo xii. 8. 9 (574) ; xiv. 2. 24 (660) ; xvi. 1. 28 (748), 2. 8 (751). Velleius ii. 78. 1. Justin xlii. 4. Tacitus *Hist.* v. 9. Frontinus i. 1. 6. Livy *epit.* 127–128. Florus ii. 19. Orosius vi. 18. 23. Eutropius vii. 5. Rufus Festus 18.

George Rawlinson, *The Sixth Great Oriental Monarchy* (London, 1873), 186–192. J. H. Schneiderwirth, *Die Parther* (Heiligenstadt, 1874), 70–85. Alfred von Gutschmid, *Geschichte Irans* (Tübingen, 1888), 94–96. Pietro Manfrin, *La cavalleria dei Parthi* (Roma, 1893), 101–114. Adolf Günther, *Beiträge zur Geschichte der Kriege zwischen Römern und Parthern* (Berlin, 1922), 39–50. Münzer, "Labienus" (5), *RECA*, XII (1924), 258–260.

It may be noted that in 41 Antony sent a cavalry force to plunder Palmyra. Appian *BC* v. 9–10.

[2] Dio xlix. 23. 3–5. Plutarch *Antony* 37. 1. Justin xlii. 4–5.

[3] Münzer, "Marcius" (48), *RECA*, XIV (1930), 1554–55.

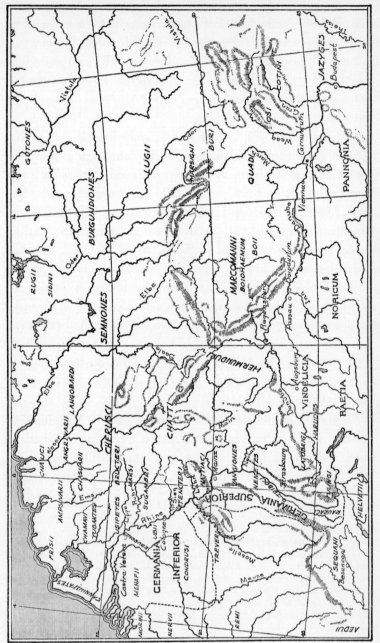

3. THE PEOPLES OF NORTHERN EUROPE.

and C. Asinius Pollio was sent against them with eleven legions.[4] Pollio reduced them to submission and also fought against the Dardani. Farther west, in 40, the Iapodes destroyed Pola.[5]

When Antony, in 39, started for the East, on account of the Parthian war, Octavian set out for Gaul, which was in a disturbed condition.[6] Before the end of the year the situation in Italy was such as to demand his return, and he left M. Vipsanius Agrippa to carry on war against the Aquitani, over whom he won a victory in 38. In the winter of the same year (38) Agrippa proceeded against German tribes who had invaded Roman territory; he drove them back, and in their pursuit was "the second of the Romans to cross the Rhine for war."[7] It may have been on this occasion that Agrippa installed the Ubii in lands on the left bank of the Rhine, in the vicinity of Cologne. "They were placed," Tacitus says, "in charge of the bank itself, after they had given proof of their loyalty, in order to block the way to others, not in order to be under supervision."[8]

VI

Romans and Parthians, 37–33 B.C.—In anticipation of war with Parthia, Antony, in 37 B.C., sent P. Canidius Crassus into Armenia. Crassus overcame the Armenians and forced Artavasdes I

---

[4] Dio xlviii. 41. 7. Florus ii. 25. Appian *BC* v. 75.

[5] M. P. Charlesworth, *CAH,* X (1934), 84.

[6] Appian *BC* v. 75.

[7] Appian *BC* v. 75, 92. Dio xlviii. 49. 2–3. Eutropius vii. 5. Rau, *RECA,* 2. Reihe, VI (1937), 2306, is of opinion that the Treveri were involved in the disturbances. On the career of Agrippa, see especially Rudolf Daniel, *M. Vipsanius Agrippa, eine Monographie* (Breslau, 1933), and Meyer Reinhold, *Marcus Agrippa, a Biography* (Geneva, N. Y., 1933).

[8] Tacitus *Germania* 28; *Ann.* xii. 27. Strabo iv. 3. 4 (194). The date of the translocation of the Ubii is not known; it may have been carried out either in 38 or in 19 B.C. For discussion of the question, see Victor Gardthausen, *Augustus und seine Zeit,* I (Leipzig, 1891), 660. Karl Winkelsesser, *De rebus divi Augusti auspiciis in Germania gestis quaestiones selectae* (Detmoldiae, 1901), 1–6. Camille Jullian, *Histoire de la Gaule,* IV (Paris, [1913]), 102 notes 2 and 6. Ludwig Schmidt, *Geschichte der deutschen Stämme,* II (Berlin, 1918), 157 note 4, 426 note 2. Eduard Norden, *Die germanische Urgeschichte in Tacitus Germania* (2. Abd., Leipzig, 1922), 386. Karl Schumacher, *Siedelungs- und Kulturgeschichte der Rheinlande,* II (Mainz, 1923), 7.

into an alliance. Early in 36 he also proceeded against the peoples south of the Caucasus; he defeated Pharnabazus, king of the Iberians, and with his assistance defeated Zober, king of the Albanians. In 36 Antony advanced from Zeugma northward to Carana (Erzerum), in Armenia, and then with an army of 100,000 men marched into Media Atropatene, where he laid siege to Phraaspa, the capital. On the road, however, Antony had become impatient, and had left Oppius Statianus to follow with the three hundred wagons which constituted his siege train; while, then, he was ineffectively engaged in besieging Phraaspa without artillery, the Parthians fell upon Oppius, and eventually the Roman army was forced to make a disastrous retreat.[1]

In 35 it became necessary for Antony to send Marcus Titius with legions from Syria against Sextus Pompeius, who, after his defeat by Octavian in Sicily, had established himself in Asia Minor; Titius captured Sextus in Phrygia and put him to death.[2]

In 34 Antony again led an army into Armenia; on this occasion he advanced to Artaxata, where he seized and imprisoned

---

[1] Plutarch *Antony* 37–52. Dio xlix. 24–33, 39–41, 44. Appian *BC* v. 75, 95, 132, 145. Josephus *BJ* i. 18. 5 (362–363) ; *Antiq.* xv. 4. 3 (104). Strabo xi. 13. 3 (523). Velleius ii. 82. Justin xlii. 5. Livy *epit.* 130–131. Florus ii. 20. Orosius vi. 19. 1–3. Eutropius vii. 6. Rufus Festus 18.

For description, photographs, and map of Phraaspa (Praaspa, Phraata), see "The Institute's Survey of Persian Architecture: Preliminary Report on Takht-i-Sulayman", *Bulletin of the American Institute for Iranian Art and Archaeology*, 5 (1937).

August Bürcklein, *Quellen und Chronologie der römisch-parthischen Feldzüge in den Jahren 713–718 d. St.* (Berlin, 1879). Johannes Kromayer, "Der Partherzug des Antonius", *Hermes*, 31 (1896), 70–104. Lucile Craven, *Antony's Oriental Policy until the Defeat of the Parthian Expedition* (Columbia, Mo., 1920. Univ. of Missouri Studies, III, no. 2). W. W. Tarn, "Antony's Legions", *Classical Quarterly*, 26 (1932), 75–81. See also George Rawlinson, *The Sixth Great Oriental Monarchy . . . Parthia* (London, 1873), 197–208. Alfred von Gutschmid, *Geschichte Irans* (Tübingen, 1888), 97–101. Emil Schürer, *Geschichte des jüdischen Volkes im Zeitalter Jesu Christi* (3.–4. Aufl., Leipzig, 1901), 312–316: "Syrien unter der Herrschaft des M. Antonius". Pascal Asdourian, *Die politischen Beziehungen zwischen Armenien und Rom* (Venedig, 1911), 58–64. Josef Sandalgian, *Histoire documentaire de l'Arménie*, II (Rome, 1917), 483–488. Adolf Günther, *Beiträge zur Geschichte der Kriege zwischen Römern und Parthern* (Berlin, 1922), 50–74. M. A. Levi, "La politica orientale di Antonio", in his *Ottaviano capoparte*, II (Firenze, [1933]), 97–138. W. W. Tarn, *CAH*, X (1934), 66–83, 906–912.

[2] Appian *BC* v. 133–144. Dio xlix. 17–18. Livy *epit.* 131.

Artavasdes, on whom he laid the blame for the failure of the
Parthian campaign. At the same time he welcomed the alliance
offered by the king of Media Atropatene. In 33 Antony returned
from Armenia and embarked upon the struggle with Octavian,
which ended in his defeat at Actium.

Events in Europe, 36–33 B.C.—In 36 B.C., Octavian had
brought to a conclusion his war with Sextus Pompeius, and in
the winter of 36–35, after a short visit to Rome, had returned
to Sicily with the intention of crossing over to Africa, when
he heard that the Salassi, Taurisci, Liburni, and Iapodes, who
for some time had been in a disturbed state, had now openly
revolted and were even plundering Italy. Octavian, therefore,
entrusted the African campaign to others and proceeded to
Illyricum.[3]

At the outset of the Illyrian war Octavian sent one force, under C. Antistius Vetus, against the Salassi,[4] and another, from

---

[3] On the Illyrian war, see Dio xlix. 34. 1–2; 35–38; 1. 28. Appian *Illyr.* 16–28;
BC v. 145. Suetonius *Augustus* 20. Velleius ii. 78. 2. Strabo iv. 6. 10 (207) ; vii. 5.
4–5 (315). Livy *epit.* 131–132. Florus ii. 23.

Gustav Zippel, *Die römische Herrschaft in Illyrien bis auf Augustus* (Leipzig,
1877). Henri Cons, *La province romaine de Dalmatie* (Paris, 1881), 136–149. Victor
Gardthausen, *Augustus und seine Zeit*, I (Leipzig, 1891), 317–330. Johannes Kro-
mayer, "Die illyrischen Feldzüge Octaviens," *Hermes*, 33 (1898), 1–13. Georg
Veith, *Die Feldzüge des C. Iulius Caesar Octavianus in Illyrien in den Jahren 35–33
v. Chr.* (Wien, 1914) ; "Metulum und Fluvius Frigidus," *JOAI*, 21–22 (1922–24),
Beiblatt, 479–494, 507–510; see also 495–508. Walter Schmid, "Der Feldzug Okta-
vians gegen die Japoden und die Einnahme Metulums," *Römisch-germanische
Kommission*, 15. *Bericht*, 1923–24 (Frankfurt a. M., 1925), 178–182. Dino Gribaudi,
"Synodium," *Rivista di filologia*, 53 (1925), 413–418. Carl Patsch, *Beiträge zur
Völkerkunde von Südosteuropa*, V (Wien, 1932), 55–62. Erich Swoboda, *Octavian
und Illyricum* (Wien, 1932), and see discussion by Ronald Syme, *JRS*, 23 (1933),
66–71. Nicola Vulić, "La guerre d'Octave en Illyrie, 35–33 av. Ch.," *Acropole*, 7
(1932), 115–122; "The Illyrian War of Octavian," *JRS*, 24 (1934), 163–167. Ronald
Syme, "Augustus and the South Slav Lands," *Revue internationale des études bal-
kaniques*, 3 (1937), 33–46.

[4] Appian *Illyr.* 17. Dio xlix. 38. 3 says that the Salassi were overcome in 34 by
M. Valerius Messalla Corvinus, but his campaign was in 28; at the time of Octavian's Illyrian war Antistius Vetus carried on war against the Salassi for two years.

On the Salassi, see Strabo iv. 6. 6–7 (204–205) ; their importance consisted primarily in the fact that, as Strabo says, "the road for all who pass over the mountains
from Italy runs [through their territory]." See also W. W. Hyde, *Roman Alpine
Routes* (Philadelphia, 1935. Memoirs of the American Philosophical Society, vol.
2), 57–64.

Aquileia, against the Taurisci, with instructions to occupy the country as far as Emona, while he himself advanced against the Iapodes by way of Tergeste and Senia. Monetium, Avendo, and Arupium, strongholds of the Iapodes east of Senia, admitted him without opposition. Terponus surrendered when a defeat had been inflicted upon the tribesmen. Metulum, their chief fortress, was taken after a struggle in which Octavian was wounded, and was destroyed. The fall of Metulum opened the way for an extension of the campaign into the valley of the Save. Here the first point of attack was Siscia, and although the Pannonians sent aid to the defenders, the place was taken, and was occupied by Roman troops under the command of Fufius Geminus.

In 34 Octavian, who was then in Gaul, received news that some of the newly conquered peoples, and also the Delmatae, had risen in revolt, and that the inhabitants of Siscia had expelled Geminus and his soldiers. By the time he had reached Siscia, however, Geminus had suppressed the uprising on the Save, and M. Vipsanius Agrippa had proceeded against the Dalmatians. Octavian thereupon turned southward into the country of the Delmatae, where he stormed Promona, captured Synodium, and laid siege to Setovia. After these successes he confided the conduct of the war to T. Statilius Taurus and returned to Rome. At the beginning of 33 Octavian returned to Dalmatia, and the war was brought to a close when the defenders of Setovia were forced by starvation to surrender.

The Illyrian campaigns of Octavian are described at some length by Roman historians to counterbalance the contemporaneous wars of Antony in the East. The parallel is carried to the point of suggesting that, just as the attack on Parthia was designed to carry into effect the plans of Caesar, so the advance into Illyricum was inspired by Caesar's determination to put an end to the empire of Burebista—even though Burebista's dominions had already been broken up in 44 and Octavian did not set foot in Dacia. The campaign of 35 B.C. was made necessary by a widespread uprising of peoples in close proximity to northern Italy. A point of more immediate importance than the reasons which induced Octavian to undertake the war is that the emphasis placed upon it (for political purposes) had the effect of throwing into the shade other occurrences of the time in Europe. It is highly significant that Octavian, after the campaign of 35, should have been obliged to cross the Alps in the winter of 35–34;[5] and since his other journeys to Gaul were all in response to invasions or uprisings, there is every reason to believe that some outbreak had threatened Gaul in the year 35. Again, though the evidence is also meager, it is probable that at or about the same time there were disturbances in the region of the lower Danube. It should be understood that the peoples who most frequently harassed the frontiers of Macedonia were the Bessi and the Bastarnae. Now, in his account of the Illyrian war, Appian refers to the possibility of war not merely with the Dacians but with the Bastarnae, and he speaks also of the Bessi as having offered their submission to Octavian.[6] The fact that Octavian should have contemplated an expedition against the Bastarnae while engaged in Illyricum may well be regarded, considering the circumstances, as evidence of disturbances in the region of the lower Danube. In 35 Macedonia was within the jurisdiction of Antony, though at the time he himself was fully occupied with his ventures against Parthia and Armenia. The references contained in Appian's narrative would seem to

---

[5] Dio xlix. 38. 2. Dio says that he "had set out to lead an expedition into Britain." It has been suggested that the name of the Britons was employed by Roman writers of the Augustan period for barbarians in general (as the word "Indians" in modern times). Georg Schleusner, *Die Reisen des Kaisers Augustus in Geschichte und Dichtung* (Barmen, 1903), 4.

[6] Appian *Illyr.* 16, 22, 23. Patsch, *Beiträge zur Völkerkunde von Südosteuropa*, V, 63–64. Patsch accepts the view that there was an uprising of Dacians and Sarmatians; he thinks that it had been instigated by Antony because Octavian had been secretly in communication with the Armenian king "for the purpose of injuring him" (Dio xlix. 41. 5) ; but this suggestion is scarcely necessary, since every Roman invasion of Armenia was followed by similar outbreaks.

indicate, then, that Octavian was concerned about the situation on the Macedonian frontier, even though it lay in Antony's territory, but that the two legions left to guard the frontier had been equal to its defense without his intervention.

VII

Parthians and Armenians, 32–24 B.C.—Antony's retirement from Armenia did not put an end to hostilities in the East. No sooner, indeed, had he turned westward than Phraates IV of Parthia and Artaxes (son of Artavasdes I) of Armenia attacked Artavasdes of Media Atropatene, Antony's ally, and though at first the Parthians suffered reverses, they nevertheless defeated Artavasdes and effected his capture (32?).[1]

Meanwhile opposition to Phraates had manifested itself in Parthia, and in 31 a usurper named Tiridates gained the upper hand and drove Phraates from the kingdom. In the following year (30) the dispossessed monarch, who had obtained aid from the Scythians, returned, and Tiridates II was forced to take refuge with Octavian in Syria.[2] On his side, Phraates at once proceeded to occupy Media Atropatene, and when this had been accomplished, he placed Artaxes on the Armenian throne (30). The new king inaugurated his reign by putting to death all the Romans found in Armenia.

---

[1] On affairs in Armenia and Parthia, see *Res gestae* 32. Dio xlix. 44; li. 16, 18. Plutarch *Antony* 53. 6. Josephus *Antiq.* xv. 4. 3 (105). Justin xlii. 5. 6. Tacitus *Ann.* ii. 3.

In 32–31 Herod of Judaea carried on war against the Nabataeans, at the instigation, it is said, of Cleopatra. Josephus *BJ* i. 19 (365–369, 380–385) ; *Antiq.* xv. 5 (110–126, 147–160). Walter Otto, "Herodes" (14), *RECA*, Supptbd. II (1913), 46. Albert Kammerer, *Pétra et la Nabatène* (Paris, 1929), 184–189.

[2] W. W. Tarn, "Tiridates II and the Young Phraates," *Mélanges Gustave Glotz*, II (Paris, 1932), 832, says: "The revolt *may* have begun in late autumn 32, but Phraates IV was not completely expelled from his kingdom until after June 31; in 30 he came back ... and before the end of 30 Tiridates and Artavasdes fled to Syria ..."

With reference to the return of Phraates in 27, see Tarn, 833–834: "The invasion took place not later than the summer of 27, and perhaps in 28 ... fighting was going on in 26, but by the summer of 25 Phraates was definitely victor ..." See also R. H. McDowell, *Coins from Seleucia on the Tigris* (Ann Arbor, Mich., 1935), 222.

Octavian took no immediate steps against Artaxes, though he appointed Artavasdes of Media Atropatene, who had escaped from the Parthians, as king of Armenia Minor. It must, however, have been with his cognizance and permission that, in 27 B.C., Tiridates II invaded Mesopotamia in a second attempt to drive out Phraates IV. He succeeded so far that he issued coins in 26 and 25, but was then forced to take refuge in Syria.

Contemporaneously (27–25) Amyntas, king of Galatia, was engaged in war with the Homanades, a warlike people situated in the Taurus Mountains; in 25 he was defeated, taken prisoner, and put to death by the mountaineers. Thereafter Augustus annexed the kingdom of Galatia.[3]

Also in 25 Augustus sent Aelius Gallus from Egypt on an expedition designed to effect the conquest of Arabia Felix. Gallus actually reached southwestern Arabia in 24, but accomplished nothing of importance, since the nature of the country and the lack of water forced him to retire.[4] There may have been some connection between the Roman invasion of Arabia and the circumstances which made it necessary, in 24, for M. Terentius Varro, governor of Syria, to proceed against Arab tribesmen who had attacked Damascus.[5]

Events in Europe, 31–23 B.C.—The last phase of the conflict between East and West—that between Antony and Cleopatra, on the one hand, and Octavian, on the other—was decided at the battle of Actium (31 B.C.). On this occasion also the peoples on the borders of Macedonia participated, and the Dacians took the side of Antony; in the campaign of Actium, however, they proved of no great assistance to him, "owing to strife among

---

[3] Strabo xii. 6. 3–5 (569). Dio liii. 26. 3. Eutropius vii. 10. 2. Sir W. M. Ramsay, "The Homanadeis and the Homanadensian War," *JRS*, 7 (1917), 232, 234. For the name "Homanades," see J. G. C. Anderson, *CAH*, X (1934), 270 note 4.

[4] Strabo xvi. 4. 22–24 (780–782) ; xvii. 1. 53 (819) . Dio liii. 29. 3–8. *Res gestae* 26. Pliny *NH* vi. 160–162. Josephus *Antiq.* xv. 9. 3 (317).

[5] Josephus *BJ* i. 20. 4 (398–399) ; *Antiq.* xv. 10. 1 (344–345). See also Strabo xvi. 2. 20 (756). Emil Schürer, *Geschichte des jüdischen Volkes im Zeitalter Jesu Christi,* I (3.–4. Aufl., Leipzig, 1901), 319–320. Max Fluss, "Terentius" (86), *RECA,* 2. Reihe, V (1934), 691–692.

themselves."[6] Cotiso, the most prominent of Burebista's successors, also crossed the Danube, but suffered defeat under circumstances which are not known.[7]

In 29 the Senate ordered that the gates of the temple of Janus should be closed, "implying that all their wars had entirely ceased," though there were "numerous disturbances going on in various regions."[8] The Bastarnae had crossed the Danube in 30, had overrun the territories of the Moesi, Triballi, and Dardani, and finally had crossed the Haemus and attacked the Dentheletae, whose king Sitas was an ally of Rome. Consequently, in 29 M. Licinius Crassus,[9] "chiefly out of fear for Macedonia," proceeded against the invaders with an army of four or five legions, and drove them back across the Balkan Mountains into Moesia. Here, though checked at first by the opposition of the Moesi, Crassus won a victory over the Bastarnae at the confluence of the Cebrus (Tzibritza) and Danube. He then turned against the Moesi and "subdued all except a very few," but late in the year his army suffered severely at the hands of the Thracians. In 28 the Bastarnae again crossed the Danube, but in a new attack upon Sitas and the Dentheletae were again defeated by Crassus. The Roman commander then "conceived a desire" to punish the Thracians, and subdued the Maedi and Serdi, "though not without difficulty." Thereafter he took occasion, at the expense of Dacian kings in the Dobrudja, to extend his conquests to the mouth of the Danube. In the same year (28) a new uprising of the Moesi was put down, and the subjugation of the region between Macedonia and the Danube was then completed.

[6] Dio li. 22. 8. Plutarch *Antony* 63 mentions Dicomes as a king of the Dacians who had promised to come to Antony's support.

[7] Horace *Carm.* iii. 8. 18. For different views concerning the defeat of Cotiso, see Brandis, "Dacia," *RECA*, IV (1901), 1960–61. Carl Patsch, *Beiträge zur Völkerkunde von Südosteuropa*, V (Wien, 1932), 70.

[8] Dio li. 20. 4–5.

[9] Dio li. 23–27. Livy *epit.* 134–135. Florus ii. 26. Patsch, *Beiträge zur Völkerkunde von Südosteuropa*, V, 69–82. In *RECA*, see Groag, "Licinius" (58), XIII (1926), 272–285; Geyer, "Makedonia," XIV (1928), 766; Fluss, "Moesia," XV (1932), 2370–71.

Contemporaneously, uprisings took place in Gaul, and hostilities broke out on the Rhine frontier. In or about 29 Gaius Carrinas subdued the Morini and other tribes of northeastern Gaul, and drove back the Suebi, "who had crossed the Rhine to wage war." At the same time M. Nonius Gallus put down an uprising of the Treveri, who had brought in the Germans to help them.[10] In 28 M. Valerius Messalla Corvinus won a victory over the Aquitani, in Gaul, and subsequently carried on a campaign against the Salassi.[11]

Notwithstanding these successes, the disturbances continued for some years, and the presence of Augustus[12] was required north of the Alps. It is said that in 27 and again in 26 he made preparations to cross over to Britain, but in fact he devoted himself during the years 26 and 25 to the subjugation of the Cantabri and Astures in Spain.[13] Also, in 25 he sent A. Terentius Varro Murena against the Salassi. Varro invaded their country at many points simultaneously, and put an end to their uprisings, for at the conclusion of his campaign he sold the men of military age into slavery.[14] In the same year (25) Marcus Vini-

---

[10] Dio li. 20. 5; 21. 5–6. Emil Ritterling, *Fasti des römischen Deutschland* (Wien, 1932), 3–4.

[11] Appian *Illyr.* 17. Strabo iv. 6. 7 (205). Groag, in Ritterling, *Fasti*, 4.

[12] In 27 B.C. the name Augustus was conferred upon Octavian by the Roman Senate.

On the reign of Augustus, see more particularly Victor Gardthausen, *Augustus und seine Zeit* (Leipzig, 1891–1904). Ettore de Ciccotti, "Augustus," *DER*, I (1895), 879–924. Otto Seeck, *Kaiser Augustus* (Bielefeld, 1902). J. B. Firth, *Augustus Caesar and the Organisation of the Empire of Rome* (New York, 1903). E. S. Shuckburgh, *Augustus: the Life and Times of the Founder of the Roman Empire* (London, 1903). Fitzler & Seeck, "Iulius" (132), *RECA*, X (1917), 275–381. T. R. Holmes, *The Architect of the Roman Empire* (Oxford, 1928–1931). *CAH*, X (1934), chs. i–xviii. Léon Homo, *Auguste* (Paris, 1935). G. P. Baker, *Augustus, the Golden Age of Rome* (New York, 1937). John Buchan, *Augustus* (Boston, 1937).

[13] For the preparations, see Dio liii. 22. 5; 25. 2. Livy *epit.* 134. Horace *Carm.* i. 35. 29–30; iii. 5. 1–4.

For the war in Spain, see David Magie, "Augustus' War in Spain," *Classical Philology*, 15 (1920), 323–339. Ronald Syme, "The Spanish War of Augustus," *AJP*, 55 (1934), 293–317.

[14] Dio liii. 25. 2–4. Strabo iv. 6. 7 (205–206). Fluss, "Terentius" (92), *RECA*, 2. Reihe, V (1934), 708.

cius crossed the Rhine—he was the third Roman commander to do so—and conducted a punitive expedition against some of the Germans because they had seized Roman traders and put them to death.[15] In 25 the temple of Janus was closed for the second time in the reign of Augustus.[16]

In 22 Marcus Primus was impeached before the Senate for having made war on the Odrysae, in Thrace, without authorization while governor of Macedonia.[17] Nothing further is known concerning the governorship of Primus, and nothing whatever of the circumstances which led up to his campaign, but it is usually assumed that the war occurred in 23.

VIII

The Roman East, 20 B.C.—From 22 to 19 B.C., Augustus was in Greece and the East, where he was engaged in the settlement of questions which had been left in abeyance since 30. He was gratified to recover from the Parthian king the standards lost by Crassus at Carrhae, and Phraates was satisfied, by giving up the trophies, to avoid the invasion of Parthia which he believed Augustus contemplated. Augustus at this time made a redistribution of territory among the client kingdoms on the Euphrates frontier. In addition, he sent Tiberius[1] into Armenia in 20 B.C., with an army drawn from the legions in Europe, to settle the outstanding account with Artaxes. The Armenian king had, however, been murdered before the arrival of Tiberius, who placed the crown upon the head of Tigranes II and brought the country again under Roman domination; later Augustus stated that he might just as well have made Armenia a province.

The Danube and Rhine frontiers, 19 B.C.—In 20 or 19 B.C. the Bessi, in the Balkan Mountains, rose against Rhescuporis,

---

[15] Dio liii. 26. 4. Ritterling, *Fasti des römischen Deutschland,* 4–5.

[16] Dio liii. 26. 5. [17] Dio liv. 3. 2.

[1] Dio liv. 9. 4–5. *Res gestae* 27. Suetonius *Tiberius* 9. 1; 14. 3. Velleius ii. 94. Strabo xii. 3. 29 (556); xvii. 1. 54 (821). Tacitus *Ann.* ii. 3. Josephus *Antiq.* xv. 4. 3 (105).

king of Thrace; they were put down by Marcus Lollius, acting in conjunction with Rhoemetalces, uncle and guardian of Rhescuporis.[2]

Toward the close of 19 the Pannonian war—as Velleius Paterculus puts it—was begun by Agrippa, in the consulate of Marcus Vinicius (October–December, 19 B.C.); it may be inferred that an incursion of tribesmen from beyond the river Save had become a source of alarm in Italy.[3]

At the same time the people in Gaul, as Dio says, "were not only quarreling among themselves, but also were being harassed by the Germans."[4] Augustus sent Agrippa to deal with the situation (possibly at the end of 20); he put a stop to the internal disorders and restored peace on the Rhine, and thereafter suppressed an uprising of the Cantabri in Spain.

IX

The kingdom of Bosporus, 17–14 B.C.—Whether, in his apportionment of kingdoms in the Roman East, Augustus appointed

---

[2] Dio liv. 20. 3. In *RECA*, see Ritterling, "Legio," XII (1924), 1229; Groag, "Lollius" (11), XIII (1927), 1380–81; Fluss, "Moesia," XV (1932), 2371. See also Carl Patsch, *Beiträge zur Völkerkunde von Südosteuropa*, V (Wien, 1932), 83.

[3] Velleius ii. 96. 2. The statement given above follows the text and translation of F. W. Shipley (Loeb ed., 1924), which differs materially from the version of the passage commonly accepted. According to the MS and the *editio princeps* (1520) of Velleius, the war was begun when Agrippa and Marcus Vinicius were consuls— for the details, see the edition of Friedrich Kritz (1848), 416–417—but since Agrippa at no time was consul with Vinicius, the reading involves an error of fact, and some emendation of the text becomes necessary. Vinicius was consul once only, in 19 B.C., hence Lipsius (1591) proposed the reading to which Shipley has returned, and which fits the historical circumstances. On the other hand, the emendation of Ruhnken (1779), which has been generally followed, implies that the Pannonian war was begun by Agrippa and Vinicius in 13 B.C., and gives rise to historical difficulties which have not been overcome: thus it overlooks the fact that the Pannonian war had already been going on, if not in 19, certainly in 16 and 14; it involves speculation over the possible relations in command of Agrippa and Vinicius; and it requires for its support the substitution of the name of Vinicius for that of Vinnius in the text of Florus (ii. 24), with the added implication that the consul of 19 was not only subordinate to Agrippa in 13, but also to Tiberius in 12 B.C.

[4] Dio liv. 11. 1–2. Emil Ritterling, *Fasti des römischen Deutschland* (Wien, 1932), 5. Rudolf Daniel, *M. Vipsanius Agrippa, eine Monographie* (Breslau, 1933), 84. Meyer Reinhold, *Marcus Agrippa, a Biography* (Geneva, N. Y., 1933), 88 note 70.

a certain Scribonius king of Bosporus must remain in doubt; according to Dio, Scribonius claimed descent from Mithridates Eupator and asserted that he had received the kingdom from Augustus, and the occasion for this disposition may have arisen when Asander (who was over ninety) entrusted his wife Dynamis with the regency. Be that as it may, disturbances of some sort broke out in 17 B.C., and Asander committed suicide when his subjects went over to Scribonius. After the death of the king, Dynamis remained in power (17/16), and then married Scribonius, who thus came to rule over Bosporus.[1] On the other hand, when Augustus heard of these occurrences, he sent Agrippa to deal with the situation (at the end of 17 or the beginning of 16).

In 16 B.C., Agrippa arrived in Asia Minor, and at once sent Polemo I of Pontus to the Crimea. On learning of this action, the people of Bosporus killed Scribonius, but they also resisted Polemo, out of fear that he might become their ruler, and Agrippa's deputy could not reduce them to submission (16–15). Agrippa himself was occupied, during 15, in Syria and Judaea; before the end of the year, however, the opposition to Polemo made it necessary for him to return to Ionia, where he made preparations for a campaign in Bosporus, and early in 14 he set out with a fleet for Sinope. The threat of an invasion induced the Bosporans to submit, and Agrippa settled the affairs of the kingdom by giving it to Polemo, in addition to his kingdom of Pontus, and by arranging a marriage between Polemo and Dynamis. Thus (in 14) "the revolt among the tribes of the

---

[1] On affairs in Bosporus from 17 to 8 B.C., see Dio liv. 24. 4–7. Strabo xi. 2. 3 (493), 11 (495), 18 (499); xii. 3. 29 (556). Josephus *Antiq.* xvi. 2. 1–2 (12–22). Lucian *Macrob.* 17. Eutropius vii. 9. Orosius vi. 21. 28. Orosius contributes the information that Agrippa recovered Roman standards which had been captured by Mithridates.

E. H. Minns, *Scythians and Greeks* (Cambridge, 1913), 591–595, 611. M. I. Rostovtzeff, "Queen Dynamis of Bosporus," *JHS*, 39 (1919), 88–109; *Iranians & Greeks in South Russia* (Oxford, 1922), 150–152. J. G. C. Anderson, *CAH*, X (1934), 267–269. In *RECA*, see Wilcken, "Asandros" (4), II (1896), 1517; Rohden, "Aspurgos," II (1896), 1739–40; Brandis, "Bosporos" (3), III (1899), 778–781; Stein, "Dynamis," V (1905), 1879–80; Stein, "Scribonius" (3), 2. Reihe, II (1921), 859–860.

Cimmerian Bosporus was quelled,"[2] and the scope of Agrippa's outlook, from Sinope, in effecting a settlement of affairs in the region of the Black Sea would seem to be reflected in the statement of Augustus that "our friendship was sought, through ambassadors, by the Bastarnae and Scythians, and by the kings of the Sarmatians who live on either side of the river Tanais, and by the king of the Albani and of the Hiberi (Iberi) and of the Medes."[3] In 13 B.C., Agrippa returned to Rome.

The Danube and Rhine frontiers, 16–14 B.C.—In 16 B.C., Sarmatians, presumably Bastarnae, crossed the Danube, but were driven back by "Lucius Gaius," possibly L. Tarius Rufus. The Dentheletae and Scordisci ravaged Macedonia (the measures, if any, taken against them have not been recorded). An uprising took place in Dalmatia. The Pannonians and Noricans invaded Istria; they were defeated by P. Silius Nerva, governor of Illyricum. The Raeti, situated between Noricum and Gaul, overran adjacent districts in Gaul and Italy and plundered travelers who made use of the Alpine passes. The Vindelici rose, and L. Calpurnius Piso proceeded against them from Gaul. The Camunni and Vennii (Venostes), Alpine tribes, took up arms against the Romans; they, too, were subdued by Silius.[4]

Beyond the Rhine, in 16, the Sugambri, Usipetes, and Tencteri seized some Romans and put them to death; then, under Maelo, king of the Sugambri, they crossed over into Gaul and inflicted a defeat upon Marcus Lollius in which the standards of

[2] Dio liv. 24. 4.

[3] *Res gestae* 31.

[4] For the invasions of 16, see Dio liv. 20.

For the name L. Tarius Rufus, see, in *RECA*, Ritterling, "Legio," XII (1924), 1229; Fluss, "Moesia," XV (1932), 2371; Groag, "Tarius" (3), 2. Reihe, IV (1932), 2321–22. See also Carl Patsch, *Beiträge zur Völkerkunde von Südosteuropa*, V (Wien, 1932), 91. For the activities of Silius Nerva, see Nagl, "Silius" (21), *RECA*, 2. Reihe, III (1927), 92–95. Erich Swoboda, "Zur Occupation Noricums," *Klio*, 28 (1935), 180–186. For the Raeti: Dio liv. 22. 1–2. For the Vindelici: Orosius vi. 21. 22; Edmund Groag, in Emil Ritterling, *Fasti des römischen Deutschland* (Wien, 1932), 7, suggests that the Piso mentioned may have been "wohl nur Unterlegat des Tiberius" in 15 B.C., but in *PIR* (2. ed., 1936), no. 289, identifies him with L. Calpurnius Piso pontifex, consul in 15.

the Fifth Legion were lost.[5] The defeat of Lollius was so alarming that Augustus, accompanied by Tiberius, hastened to Gaul, but on his appearance (it is said) the Sugambri and their allies retired and made peace. Tiberius was entrusted with the administration of *Gallia comata* (16–15), "which was in a state of unrest through the inroads of the barbarians and the dissensions of its chiefs."[6]

In 15 B.C., Augustus took decisive measures against the Raeti and Vindelici, and while Tiberius led an army against them from Gaul, Drusus attacked them from the side of Italy. The operations conducted by Tiberius were directed primarily against the Vindelici.[7]

In 14 B.C. the Pannonians again rose, and were again subdued; and it would seem to have been at this time that Tiberius overcame the Scordisci. Contemporaneously Cn. Cornelius Lentulus won distinction on the lower Danube by pressing back the Dacians (Getae) and Sarmatians (Bastarnae). Thus, by the end of 14 B.C., Agrippa in the East, and Augustus in the West, had succeeded, to all appearance, in restoring order on the northern frontiers.

The date of the wars carried on by Cornelius Lentulus constitutes a problem for which no generally accepted solution appears to be forthcoming, and hence the statement made above requires elaboration.

The last five books of Livy, as epitomized in the *Periochae*, dealt with the campaigns (138) of Tiberius and Drusus in Raetia, (139) of Drusus against the Germans, (140) of Piso against the Thracians and Drusus against the Germans, (141) of Drusus against the Germans and

---

[5] Dio liv. 19. 1; 20. 4–6. Suetonius *Augustus* 23. 1. Velleius ii. 97. 1. Tacitus *Ann.* i. 10. Julius Obsequens 71. On Maelo, *Res gestae* 32. Strabo vii. 1. 4 (291). Ronald Syme, "Some Notes on the Legions under Augustus," *JRS*, 23 (1933), 17–19, and *CAH*, X (1934), 360, follows Julius Asbach, *Bonner Jahrbücher*, 85 (1888), 15, in placing the defeat in 17 B.C.; but see Groag, "Lollius" (11), *RECA*, XIII (1927), 1382–83, and his later statement in Ritterling, *Fasti des römischen Deutschland*, 5–6.

[6] Suetonius *Tiberius* 9. 1. See also Dio liv. 19. 6; 21. 2. Groag, in Ritterling, *Fasti des römischen Deutschland*, 6–7.

[7] Dio liv. 22. Strabo iv. 6. 9 (206); vii. 1. 5 (292). *Res gestae* 26. Livy *epit.* 138. Velleius ii. 39. 3; 95. Suetonius *Tiberius* 9. 1–2. Florus ii. 22. Pliny *NH* iii. 136–137. Felix Stähelin, *Die Schweiz in römischer Zeit* (2. Aufl., Basel, 1931), 95–119.

Tiberius against the Dalmatians and Pannonians, and (142) of Drusus against the Germans, with his death and obsequies. In these books, then, Livy's narrative included the events on the Rhine and Danube for the years 15 to 9 B.C.

The information contained in the epitome of Livy is meager in the extreme, but it is well known that some additional details from his narrative have been preserved in the histories of Florus, Eutropius, Aurelius Victor, and Orosius. Now each of these epitomists, for the period represented by Livy (138–142), gives some list of peoples conquered by Augustus. Two of the lists—those of Florus (ii. 21) and Orosius (vi. 21. 14)—are identical, and include, first, the Norici, Illyrii, Pannonii, and Delmatae, and then, for the lower Danube, the Moesi, Thraces, Daci, and Sarmatae. It is clear, therefore, that the source from which these writers drew their information recorded a series of events, not in strict chronological sequence from 15 to 9 B.C., but in geographical order from west to east, from Noricum to Thrace and the mouth of the Danube.

It is probable that the four principal epitomists utilized not the actual text of Livy, but an early abridgment; and later writers carried the process of condensation even further. So, in Jerome, Prosper Tiro, and Syncellus, there appears a version, attributed to Eusebius, in which it is said that Tiberius overcame the Vindelici and all the peoples on the borders of Thrace. The statement, though many times removed from the original, still preserves the west–east arrangement of events; but in it abbreviation has been carried to such a length that conquests have been associated with the name of Tiberius which in the more extended accounts were attributed to other commanders.

The source drawn upon by the epitomists, whether the text of Livy or an abridgment, provided something more in the way of information than the bare names of a number of peoples, and each of them was in a position to insert in his restricted account an item or more not recorded by any of the others. Thus Florus (ii. 28–29) says that the Thracians were completely vanquished by Piso; that the Dacians were pushed back by Lentulus; and that the Sarmatians were debarred from access to the Danube by the same general. Tacitus (*Ann.* iv. 44), in speaking of the career of Lentulus, makes it clear that the Dacians mentioned by Florus were Getae; the Sarmatians were, in all probability, the Bastarnae. Orosius (vi. 21. 22), unlike Florus, omits all reference—except in his initial list—to the peoples of the lower Danube, but passes on (21. 28) to the fact that the Bosporani were overcome by Agrippa, an event which occurred in 14 B.C. It is not open to doubt that the reference of Orosius (and Eusebius) to the Bosporani came from Livy, for Eutropius (vii. 9), in the same context, adds to his enumeration of the peoples subjugated during this period "all the maritime cities of Pontus, and among them the most notable, Bosporus and Panticapaeum." The form of his statement suggests that the original author (Livy) had mentioned other places and peoples in the region of the Black Sea, and the inference is borne out by Aurelius Victor (*epit.* i. 7), who, in a passage which parallels that of Eutropius, contributes the information that the Getae and Bastarnae were compelled to make peace—*Getarum populos Basternasque lacessitos bellis ad concordia compulit.* But these troublesome Getae and Bastarnae who were forced into *concordia* were the Dacians (Getae) and Sarmatae (Bastarnae) who, according to Florus, were pushed back by Cornelius Lentulus, and the Bastarnae who, according to Augustus (*Res gestae* 31), sought "our friendship."

It would appear, then, that, in 14 B.C., Agrippa achieved a settlement of affairs in the region of the Black Sea; that through the agency of Polemo he crushed the uprising in Bosporus and established friendly relations with the kings on both sides of the river Don; and that through the instrumentality of Lentulus he brought to terms the hostile peoples beyond the lower Danube. The conclusion that the campaigns of Lentulus stood in immediate relation to the activities of Agrippa in 14 B.C. is in accord with the results which Patsch has arrived at by a wholly different form of argument.[8]

Difficulties also arise in relation to the activities of Tiberius from 14 to 12 B.C.

First, Dio states (liv. 24. 3) that in 14 a new uprising of the Pannonians was put down, but he does not mention the name of the Roman commander. According to Velleius (ii. 39. 3), Tiberius conquered the Scordisci, directly east of the Pannonians, and this conquest must have been effected in 15 or 14; since, then, Tiberius was engaged against the Vindelici in the earlier year, and since some Roman general was in command on the Save in the later, it may be inferred that Tiberius was in charge of operations against the Pannonians, and that he also proceeded against the Scordisci in 14 B.C.

Second, it is not questioned that Tiberius carried on war against the Pannonians in 12 B.C. Florus, however, says (ii. 24) that Augustus sent

[8] Patsch, *Beiträge zur Völkerkunde von Südosteuropa*, V, 91–94; see also Ronald Syme, "Lentulus and the Origin of Moesia," *JRS*, 24 (1934), 113–137.

Vinnius to subdue the Pannonians and that the person so named defeated them on the Save and the Drave. On the basis of this passage
(in conjunction with a particular reading of Velleius ii. 96. 2) there
has been introduced into histories of the empire the statement that "in
13 B.C. operations were begun against the Pannonians by Marcus Vinicius." While the classical historians are not communicative on the subject of the Pannonian war of 12 B.C., something in regard to Vinnius
still remains to be gleaned. Dio (liv. 31. 3) supplements his brief notice of the war with the remark that Tiberius "took away the enemy's
arms"—which seems a gratuitous piece of information. Florus, however, shows that Dio's statement is a curtailed version of a longer account when he says (ii. 24) that "the arms of the conquered enemy
were not burnt, as was the usual custom in war, but broken to pieces
and hurled into the current." The unusual reference to the weapons of
the enemy in these passages indicates clearly that the two authors drew
from the same source, though an action attributed to Tiberius by Dio is
associated by Florus with Vinnius. Despite the difference in the names,
it is obvious that the incident related refers to one and the same campaign—but to which author is credence to be accorded with respect to
the commander? Now an examination of the text of Florus brings to
light the singular fact that he does not once mention the name of Tiberius. In his version the war against the Raeti and Vindelici was carried
on by Drusus alone. In connection with the Pannonian, Dalmatian,
and German wars of the years 12 to 8, at the points in the narrative
where Tiberius becomes prominent, and where he is mentioned by Livy,
Velleius, Dio, and other historians, Florus brings in the names Vinnius,
Vibius, and Varus. Florus suppressed the name of Tiberius: he twice
omitted altogether events in which Tiberius was conspicuous and passed
on to those in which Vibius and Varus were actually concerned; once
he included the fact of the war (in Pannonia), but substituted for
Tiberius an individual otherwise unknown. Vinnius may conceivably
have been a secondary figure in the campaign of 12, as the Piso of
Orosius (vi. 21. 22) may have been in that of 15 B.C.; he was not
Marcus Vinicius.

X

The Roman East, 13–7 B.C.—In Bosporus, the union of Polemo
and Dynamis was of brief duration; subsequent events would
seem to indicate that Dynamis left the husband forced upon her
by Augustus and Agrippa and became the head of the party

opposed to him. Polemo was certainly unwelcome in Bosporus, and during his reign carried on a war which extended from the eastern coast of the Maeotis southward as far as Colchis; the nature of the conflict may be inferred from the statement that he sacked Tanais, on the Don, "because it would not obey him." In or about 9 B.C., Polemo attacked the Aspurgiani, who held the territory between Phanagoria and Gorgippia, but was defeated, taken prisoner, and put to death.[1] After the fall of Polemo, Dynamis returned to power in the kingdom, and the coinage attributed to her is continuous from 8 B.C. to A.D. 8. It seems clear, therefore, that after 8 B.C., Augustus acquiesced in the separation of Bosporus from Pontus and recognized the ruler who was acceptable to the Bosporan people.

Phraates IV of Parthia evidently had many difficulties to contend with during his long reign (37–2 B.C.). The fact that in 10 or 9 B.C. he handed over "all his sons and grandsons" to the custody of Augustus[2] suggests that he then feared or was engaged in civil war; there is, indeed, a hint that at some time between 12 and 9 B.C. he had to contend with a usurper named Mithridates.[3]

Late in 10 or at the beginning of 9 B.C., Herod, king of Judaea, invaded the kingdom of the Nabataeans.[4] Further, at some time between 12 B.C. and A.D. 1, seemingly between 10 and 7, possibly in 9 and 8 B.C., P. Sulpicius Quirinus carried on a war against the Homanades, in the region of the Taurus; he won the honors of a triumph, Tacitus says, for having stormed the fortresses—of which there were forty-four—in their territory.[5]

---

[1] For the literature, see § IX, note 1.

[2] *Res gestae* 32. Velleius ii. 94. 4. Strabo xvi. 1. 28 (748). Josephus *Antiq.* xviii. 2. 4 (42).

[3] Josephus *Antiq.* xvi. 8. 4 (253). Alfred von Gutschmid, *Geschichte Irans* (Tübingen, 1888), 116.

[4] Josephus *Antiq.* xvi. 9. 2 (283–299); 10. 8–9 (335–355). Emil Schürer, *Geschichte des jüdischen Volkes im Zeitalter Jesu Christi* (3.–4. Aufl., Leipzig, 1901), 373. Walter Otto, "Herodes" (14), *RECA*, Supptbd. II (1913), 125. Albert Kammerer, *Pétra et la Nabatène* (Paris, 1929), 209–211.

[5] Strabo xii. 6. 5 (569). Tacitus *Ann.* iii. 48. Pliny *NH* v. 23 (94). Sir W. M. Ram-

The Danube and Rhine frontiers, 13–7 B.C.—In 13 B.C. the
Bessi, led by "a priest of the Dionysus worshiped by that people," overran Thrace, killed Rhescuporis, the king, and drove
out Rhoemetalces, his uncle and guardian. At the same time the
Sialetae invaded Macedonia. On this occasion the Bessi directed
their attack eastward to the Thracian Chersonese (which was
the property of Agrippa), and, to oppose them, L. Calpurnius
Piso (consul 15 B.C.) was summoned from Asia Minor. Piso
proceeded against the Bessi, most probably in 12, and, though
defeated at first, as Dio says, continued his operations in Thrace
for three years. Eventually he "restored security to Asia and
peace to Macedonia."[6]

At the end of 13 the Pannonians rose, and the disturbance was
such as to make it necessary that Agrippa should hasten to Illyricum.[7] The war came to an abrupt end, and after a short absence Agrippa returned to Italy, where (in Campania) he died,
toward the end of March, in 12 B.C. A new outbreak, however,
caused Augustus in 12 to send Tiberius (who had been consul
in 13 B.C) to deal with the situation, and this he did by devastating the country of the Pannonians with the aid of the Scordisci,
and by selling most of the men of military age into slavery.[8] In
11 the Delmatae also rebelled, and Tiberius transferred the
greater part of his army to meet the new uprising; in his absence
the Pannonians again made trouble, and he was compelled to

---

say, "The Homanadeis and the Homanadensian War," *JRS*, 7 (1917), 228–275.
Groag, "Sulpicius" (90), *RECA*, 2. Reihe, IV (1931), 829–831. T. R. S. Broughton,
"Some Notes on the War with the Homonadeis," *AJP*, 54 (1933), 134–144. Ronald
Syme, "Galatia and Pamphylia under Augustus," *Klio*, 27 (1934), 131–138; he
himself suggests 4–3 B.C. as the date, but leaves the question without a positive
decision. J. G. C. Anderson, *CAH*, X (1934), 270–273, 877–878, 921.

[6] Dio liv. 34. 5–7. Velleius ii. 98. Tacitus *Ann.* vi. 10. Livy *epit.* 140. Florus ii. 27.
S. E. Stout, *The Governors of Moesia* (Princeton, 1911), 1. Hermann Dessau,
Geschichte der römischen Kaiserzeit, I (Berlin, 1924), 395. Syme, "Galatia and
Pamphylia under Augustus," 127–131. In *RECA*, see Groag, "Calpurnius" (99), III
(1899), 1397; Fluss, "Moesia," XV (1932), 2372.

[7] Dio liv. 28. 1–2.

[8] *Res gestae* 30. Dio liv. 31. 2–4; 33. 5; 34. 3. Velleius ii. 39. 3; 96. 2–3. Suetonius
Augustus 21; *Tiberius* 9. Frontinus ii. 1. 15. Livy *epit.* 141. Florus ii. 21, 24–25.
Eutropius vii. 9. Aurelius Victor *epit.* i. 7. Orosius vi. 21. 14, 23. Jordanes *Rom.* 243.

carry on war with both peoples at the same time. As a result of these campaigns, the Roman frontier was advanced to the banks of the Danube.[9]

In the West, in 13, war threatened with the Germans, and the legions were brought up from their camps in the interior to bases on the Rhine. In 12 the Sugambri and their allies, again under the leadership of Maelo, crossed the river; they were, however, defeated by Drusus, who was awaiting the attack, and who in turn crossed the Rhine and devastated the lands of the invaders. Later in the same year Drusus led an expedition for the subjugation of the tribes living on the coast of the North Sea; after some success in dealing with the Frisii, Ampsivarii, and Bructeri, he encountered difficulties in the country of the Chauci, and the expeditionary force was extricated only with the aid of the Frisii. In 11 Drusus again crossed the Rhine; in this campaign he subdued the Usipetes and proceeded through the territory of the Sugambri into that of the Cherusci, and reached the river Weser. On its return march the Roman army was all but destroyed at an unidentified place named Arbalo.[10]

At the end of 11 b.c. it was voted by the Senate that the temple of Janus should be closed, on the grounds that the wars con-

[9] *Res gestae* 30. Carl Patsch, *Beiträge zur Völkerkunde von Südosteuropa*, V (Wien, 1932), 100–101, is of opinion that the frontier was advanced to the Danube from Vienna to Budapest and Belgrade.

[10] For the campaigns of Drusus in Germany, see Dio liv. 32–33, 36; lv. 1. Strabo vii. 1. 3–4 (291). Suetonius *Claudius* i. 2–3. Velleius ii. 97. 2–3. Livy *epit.* 139–142. Florus ii. 30. Eutropius vii. 9. Aurelius Victor *epit.* i. 7. Orosius vi. 21. 15–17.

Alexander Riese, *Das rheinische Germanien in der antiken Litteratur* (Leipzig, 1892), 51–60. Hans Dragendorff, "Okkupation Germaniens durch die Römer," Römisch-germanische Kommission, *Bericht*, 1 (1904), 13–36; 3 (1906–1907), 151–167; 5 (1909), 73–88. Emil Ritterling, "Zur Geschichte des römischen Heeres in Gallien unter Augustus," *Bonner Jahrbücher*, 114/115 (1906), 159–188. Gerhard Kropatschek, "Der Drususfeldzug 11 vor Chr.," *Bonner Jahrbücher*, 120 (1911), 19–38. Franz Cramer, *Deutschland in römischer Zeit* (Berlin, 1912), 19–43. Friedrich Koepp, *Die Römer in Deutschland* (2. Aufl., Bielefeld, 1912), 13–45. Camille Jullian, *Histoire de la Gaule*, IV (Paris, [1913]), 94–152. Emil Sadée, "Rom und Deutschland vor 1900 Jahren," *Bonner Jahrbücher*, 124 (1917), 1–16. Ludwig Schmidt, *Geschichte der germanischen Frühzeit* (Bonn, 1925), 72–118. For additional references, see Friedrich Kauffmann, *Deutsche Altertumskunde*, I (München, 1913), 355. *CAH*, X (1934), 940–943. For the career of Nero Claudius Drusus, see Stein, "Claudius" (139), *RECA*, III (1899), 2703–19.

ducted by Calpurnius Piso, Tiberius, and Drusus had ceased. Nevertheless the gates were not shut, for disturbances broke out anew on the Danube and the Rhine.[11]

It would seem to have been in 10 B.C.—later, according to Dio, than the principal operations in Thrace—that the Bessi again rebelled, and were again put down by Piso.[12] At the beginning of 10 the Dacians crossed the Danube on the ice and plundered Pannonia, and the Delmatae rose in revolt. Tiberius, who was in Gaul, was again sent to the front, and the army of the Dacians was defeated and crushed.[13] Thereafter a Roman army, commanded by Tiberius, was led across the Danube and penetrated far into the enemy's country; the Dacians were thus compelled to submit to the orders of the Roman people.[14] Notwithstanding the earlier campaigns against the Pannonians and Dalmatians, they once more began a rebellion in 9 B.C., which Tiberius suppressed; but after his departure for Gaul they again gave trouble, in 8 B.C., and were dealt with by Sextus Appuleius.

On the Rhine, Drusus had not been opposed by the Sugambri in 11 B.C., because, it is said, they were then at war with the Chatti, who had refused to ally themselves with the Cherusci, Suebi, and Sugambri against the Romans. In 10, however, the Chatti joined the alliance, and Drusus carried on a campaign in which "the Germans, particularly the Chatti, were either harried or subjugated." In 9 he attacked the Marcomanni, and subsequently marched through the country of the Cherusci, crossed the Weser, and reached the Elbe, "pillaging everything on his way." On the return march to the Rhine, Drusus died, either of disease or of injuries received in a fall from his horse.[15]

In succession to Drusus, the command on the Rhine passed to Tiberius, and when in 8 B.C. he crossed the river, all the Ger-

---

[11] Dio liv. 36. 2.   [12] Dio liv. 34. 7.   [13] *Res gestae* 30. Dio liv. 36. 2–3.

[14] *Res gestae* 30. *Consolatio ad Liviam* 387–388. Strabo vii. 3. 12 (304), 13 (304), 13 (305). Suetonius *Augustus* 21. Eutropius vii. 9.

[15] Dio liv. 36. 3–4; lv. 1–2. See also note 10. For the campaign against the Marcomanni, see Florus ii. 30 (23). Orosius vi. 21. 15. See also Strabo vii. 1. 3 (290).

mans (except the Sugambri) made overtures of peace. Tiberius traversed every part of Germany without loss or hindrance, so that, to all appearance, the country had been reduced to the status of a tributary province. On the conclusion of the campaign, 40,000 of the Sugambri and Suebi were transferred to the left bank of the Rhine. Peace was finally restored in 7 B.C., when Tiberius suppressed "some disturbance in the province of Germany."[16]

The wars carried on by Drusus (13 to 9 B.C.) had the result that various German tribes abandoned their place of abode and moved beyond the reach of Roman invasion. Suetonius presents the official view when he says that Augustus "forced the Germans back to the farther side of the Albis (Elbe), with the exception of the Suebi and Sugambri, who submitted to him and were taken into Gaul and settled in lands near the Rhine."[17] Notably, and presumably in 8 B.C., the Marcomanni moved from the river Main into Bohemia.

In 7 B.C., presumably, L. Domitius Ahenobarbus, who was in command on the upper Danube, crossed the river and penetrated as far as the Albis (the Elbe, or quite likely the Saale) without encountering opposition. Dio says that on this expedition Ahenobarbus "intercepted the Hermunduri, a tribe which for some reason or other had left their own land and were wandering about in quest of another," and settled them in a part of the territory which had been vacated by the Marcomanni.[18]

XI

The Romans in Armenia, 6 B.C.–A.D. 4.—In Parthia, in or about 2 B.C., Phraates IV was murdered by his (illegitimate) son

---

[16] Velleius ii. 97. 4. Dio lv. 6. 1–3; 8. 3. Suetonius *Augustus* 21; *Tiberius* 9. Eutropius vii. 9. Orosius vi. 21. 24.

[17] Suetonius *Augustus* 21.

[18] Dio lv. 10a. 3. Tacitus *Ann.* iv. 44. Suetonius *Nero* 4.

The date of the expedition has been much discussed. It is placed at some time between 7 and 2 B.C. by Ronald Syme, *CAH*, X (1934), 365; in 7 B.C. by Haug, "Hermunduri," *RECA*, VIII (1912), 906, and by Richard Hennig, *Terrae incog-*

Phraataces, whose reign is memorable chiefly because he intervened in Armenia and was brought to book by Augustus. Phraataces was dethroned, A.D. 4 or 5, after a short reign, and was succeeded by Orodes III.[1]

In Armenia, Tigranes II, who had been established in his dominions by Tiberius in 20 B.C., was succeeded, before 6 B.C., by his son Tigranes III. The leanings of the new king were to the side of Parthia; consequently, since "Armenia was becoming estranged," Augustus resolved (6 B.C.) to send Tiberius to the East. Tiberius, however, declined the appointment and withdrew to Rhodes.[2] Augustus nevertheless gave support to a pretender, Artavasdes II, who subsequently (in or before 1 B.C.) was driven out by the Armenians, "not without a measure of discredit," as Tacitus says, "to our arms."[3] When thus the Armenians revolted and the Parthians joined them, Augustus sent Gaius Caesar to uphold the interests of Rome (1 B.C.).[4] Phraataces, on receiving news of the measures taken by the emperor, sent an embassy to court, but was told bluntly to withdraw from Armenia; some time later (presumably in A.D. 2) he had a meet-

nitae, I (Leiden, 1936), 266–268; in 3 B.C. by Johannes Klose, *Roms Klientel-Randstaaten am Rhein und an der Donau* (Breslau, 1934), following Eduard Norden, *Die germanische Urgeschichte in Tacitus Germania* (3. Abd., Leipzig, 1923); in A.D. 1 by Carl Patsch, *Beiträge zur Völkerkunde von Südosteuropa*, V (Wien, 1932), 110, following Ludwig Schmidt, *Geschichte der deutschen Stämme*, II (Berlin, 1913).

[1] Josephus *Antiq.* xviii. 2. 4 (39–44). Dio lv. 10a. 4. George Rawlinson, *The Sixth Great Oriental Monarchy* (London, 1872), 217–221. Alfred von Gutschmid, *Geschichte Irans* (Tübingen, 1888), 116–118. Warwick Wroth, *Catalogue of the Coins of Parthia* (London, 1903), xl–xlii. J. G. C. Anderson, *CAH*, X (1934), 275, 278.

[2] Dio lv. 9. 4. Velleius ii. 99. Suetonius *Tiberius* 10–13.

[3] Tacitus *Ann.* ii. 4.

[4] For Gaius Caesar and affairs in Armenia, see *Res gestae* 27. Dio lv. 10. 18–21; 10a. 4–9. Velleius ii. 100. 1, 101–102. Tacitus *Ann.* ii. 4; iii. 48. Florus ii. 32. Strabo xi. 14. 6 (529). Zonaras x. 36.

Theodor Mommsen, *Res gestae divi Augusti* (2. ed., Berolini, 1883), 109–118. Pascal Asdourian, *Die politischen Beziehungen zwischen Armenien und Rom* (Venedig, 1911), 67–76. Gardthausen, "Iulius" (134), *RECA*, X (1917), 425–428. Joseph Sandalgian, *Histoire documentaire de l'Arménie*, II (Rome, 1917), 496–502. Jacques de Morgan, *Histoire du peuple arménien* (Paris, 1919), 89–90. Anderson, *CAH*, X (1934), 273–277.

ing with Gaius on an island in the Euphrates and reached an agreement in regard to the matters of dispute. Meanwhile Tigranes III, who was in possession of Armenia, made a diplomatic submission to the emperor and was recognized as king. Shortly afterwards, however, Tigranes was killed (A.D. 2) "in a war with barbarians." Gaius filled the vacancy by appointing Ariobarzanes, son of Artabazus, king of Media, with the result that the Armenians were offended and took up arms. Gaius entered Armenia with an army (in A.D. 2), but though at first his campaign was attended with success, he was wounded, in A.D. 3, before Artagira, a fortress not far west of Artaxata, and died, in A.D. 4, on his way to Italy. Ariobarzanes was confirmed in the possession of Armenia by the Roman government, and on his death was succeeded by his son Artavasdes III.

The Danube and Rhine frontiers, 6 B.C.–A.D. 5.—Velleius Paterculus says that, after Tiberius retired to Rhodes (6 B.C.), "the Parthian, breaking away from his alliance with us, laid hold of Armenia, and Germany revolted when the eyes of its conqueror were no longer upon it."[5] Dio Cassius provides the information that Gaius Caesar was appointed to the command of the legions on the Danube, and goes on to say that, as a matter of fact, Gaius himself fought no war—not because no war broke out, but because he (as heir to Augustus) was learning to rule, and the undertakings which involved danger were assigned to others.[6] It is probable, therefore, that in and before 1 B.C. the legions on the Danube were actively engaged.[7]

Contemporaneously there was an outbreak on the part of the

---

[5] Velleius ii. 100. 1.

[6] Dio lv. 10. 17. Ritterling, "Legio," *RECA*, XII (1924), 1231: "Er scheint zuerst die Heere in den Donauländern, also das illyrische und besonders wohl das makedonische, besucht zu haben . . ."

[7] Orosius (vi. 22. 1) says that in 2 B.C. the temple of Janus was closed for the third time during the reign of Augustus, and goes on (22. 3, 5) to associate this with the supposed universal peace at the time of the birth of Christ. Regarding the statement of Orosius, Mommsen, *Res gestae*, 51, remarks: ". . . tota narratio evidenter interpolata est fraude tam pia quam absurda . . ." It is not known when the third closing took place.

Germans (1 B.C. or A.D. 1), and Domitius Ahenobarbus, who had been transferred to the Rhine (probably in 6 B.C.), met with a reverse in an encounter with the Cherusci; this, indeed, "caused the other barbarians likewise to conceive a contempt for the Romans," but "in view of the Parthian war which was impending no attention was paid to the Germans at this time."[8]

Again, seemingly in A.D. 2–3, the Dacians once more became troublesome, and Aelius Catus transferred fifty thousand Getae from the farther side of the lower Danube and settled them in Thrace—Strabo says that in his time they lived there and were called Moesi.[9] Also, about the same time, an unknown commander whose name ended in -cius (not M. Vinicius) crossed the Danube, defeated a body of Bastarnae, and came in contact with the Cotini (on the river Gran) and the Anartii (in northeastern Hungary). The fragmentary inscription from which the facts are derived provides no information in regard to the date of the expedition or the circumstances under which it was undertaken.[10]

On the Rhine, in A.D. 2, "an extensive war" (*immensum bellum*) broke out with the Germans, during the governorship of Marcus Vinicius,[11] who to all appearance achieved no outstanding success. In this year Tiberius was recalled from Rhodes, and in A.D. 4 was again sent to Gaul.[12] He at once took vigorous

---

[8] Dio lv. 10a. 3. Tacitus *Ann.* i. 63. For the date, "about 1 B.C.," see Syme, *CAH*, X (1934), 368. In A.D. 1, Fitzler & Seeck, "Iulius" (132), *RECA*, X (1917), 368. Hermann Dessau, *Geschichte der römischen Kaiserzeit*, I (Berlin, 1924), 426. Groag, in Ritterling, *Fasti des römischen Deutschland* (Wien, 1932), 8–9.

[9] Strabo vii. 3. 10 (303). The Aelius Catus mentioned by Strabo is identified with the Sextus Aelius Catus who was consul in A.D. 4, and his activities on the lower Danube are usually dated after A.D. 4; see Mommsen, *Res gestae*, 132; Ritterling, "Legio," *RECA*, XII (1924), 1238; Patsch, *Beiträge zur Völkerkunde von Südosteuropa*, V, 114. The date in the text is that proposed by Syme; for his argument, see "Lentulus and the Origin of Moesia," *JRS*, 24 (1934), 126–128.

[10] For the literature and discussion of the problem, see Ronald Syme, "M. Vinicius (cos. 19 B.C.)," *Classical Quarterly*, 27 (1933), 142–148, and *CAH*, X (1934), 366–367. See also Patsch, *Beiträge zur Völkerkunde von Südosteuropa*, V, 104–107.

[11] Velleius ii. 104. 2. Dio lv. 13. 1a. Gelzer, "Iulius" (154), *RECA*, X (1917), 488.

[12] *Res gestae* 26. Velleius ii. 104–107. Dio lv. 13. 1a–2; 28. 5. Suetonius *Tiberius* 16. Pliny *NH* ii. 67 (167). Gelzer, "Iulius" (154), *RECA*, X (1917), 488–489.

measures against the peoples beyond the Rhine, and in the initial campaign subdued the Canninefates, the Attuarii (Chattu-
arii), the Bructeri, and the Cherusci, and crossed the river
Weser. The army spent the winter on the headwaters of the river
Lippe. In A.D. 5 the Roman fleet set sail from the Rhine and
continued the voyage to the coast of Jutland. At the same time
Tiberius led the army from the winter quarters on the Lippe
into the country of the Chauci. After this people had submitted,
he marched through the territory of the Langobardi, and when
he had subdued them, proceeded to the Elbe, where the Charudes, Semnones, and other peoples entered into friendly relations. From the Elbe, Tiberius conducted his army back to its
winter quarters, and the fleet, which had joined him on its return
voyage, sailed to the Rhine.

XII

The war against Maroboduus, A.D. 6, *and its sequel.*—The most
notable result of the war carried on by Drusus against the peoples of Germany was the migration of the Marcomanni. After
the campaign of 9 B.C., and presumably in 8, the Marcomanni
moved from their settlements on the river Main and occupied
lands in Bohemia. The migration was inspired and directed by
Maroboduus, who as a youth had been brought up at Rome and
had been accorded the favor of Augustus, and who, on his return, had assumed the rulership of his people.

"No considerations of haste," says Velleius Paterculus,[1]
"should lead us to pass over this man Maroboduus without mention. A man of noble family, strong in body and courageous in
mind, a barbarian by birth but not in intelligence, he achieved
among his countrymen no mere chief's position gained as the
result of internal disorders or chance or liable to change and
dependent upon the caprice of his subjects, but, conceiving in
his mind the idea of a definite empire and royal powers, he

---

[1] Velleius ii. 108–109, tr. F. W. Shipley (Loeb Classical Library).

resolved to remove his own race far away from the Romans and to migrate to a place where, inasmuch as he had fled before the strength of more powerful arms, he might make his own all powerful." In these new dominions "races and individuals who revolted from us found in him a refuge, and in all respects, with but little concealment, he played the part of a rival to Rome. His army, which he had brought up to the number of seventy thousand foot and four thousand horse, he was steadily preparing, by exercising it in constant wars against his neighbors, for some greater task than that which he had in hand. He was also to be feared on this account, that, having Germany at the left and in front of his settlements, Pannonia on the right, and Noricum in the rear of them [i.e., to the south], he was dreaded by all as one who might at any moment descend upon all. Nor did he permit Italy to be free from concern over his growing power, since the summits of the Alps which mark her boundary were not more than two hundred miles distant from his boundary line." Tiberius asserted in the Senate that "not Philip himself had been so grave a menace to Athens, not Pyrrhus nor Antiochus to the Roman people," as was Maroboduus. Tacitus says that in this speech Tiberius "magnified the man's power, the ferocity of the peoples under his sway, and his proximity to Italy as a foe."[2]

Once established in his new domain, Maroboduus proceeded to bring under subjection the tribes northward to the Baltic and from the Elbe to the Vistula. Strabo mentions as having been "acquired" by Maroboduus the Lugii, the Zumi (Buri), the Butones (Gutones, Gothi), the Mugilones (Burgundiones), the Sibini (Ptolemy's Sidini, the Rugii of later times), and the Sem-

---

[2] Tacitus *Ann.* ii. 63.

On Maroboduus, see Ludwig Schmidt, *Geschichte der deutschen Stämme*, II. 2 (Berlin, 1913), 158–160, 166–171. Ronald Syme, "Maroboduus," *CAH*, X (1934), 364–369. Johannes Klose, *Roms Klientel-Randstaaten am Rhein und an der Donau* (Breslau, 1934), 67–73. In *RECA*, XIV (1930) : Franke, "Marcomanni," 1613–17; Stein, "Maroboduus," 1907–10.

nones.[3] On his expedition to the Elbe in A.D. 5, Tiberius had
come in contact with allies of Maroboduus; after his return the
Roman government reached the decision to destroy the Marcomannic kingdom. For the purpose of the conquest twelve legions were assembled, and the invasion was planned to be
carried out by two armies advancing simultaneously from the
Danube and the Rhine.[4] In A.D. 6 Tiberius marched against
Maroboduus from Carnuntum, while C. Sentius Saturninus
penetrated through the country of the Chatti. The two armies
had proceeded some distance on their respective routes when
Tiberius learned that the Pannonians, in his rear, had risen in
revolt, thus making his return imperative. Before turning back,
he made a treaty with Maroboduus, who asserted, at a later
time, that the armies had parted on equal terms.

The projected overthrow of Maroboduus was followed, in
time to save his kingdom from subjugation, by uprisings in
Pannonia and Dalmatia and by invasions of Dacians and Sarmatians. Before turning to these outbreaks, it will be desirable
to consider the movement of events in the Roman East.

Parthia, Armenia, and Asia Minor, A.D. 4–6.—In A.D. 4 or 5
the Parthians had expelled Phraataces and set up Orodes III as
his successor; in 6 or 7 Orodes was assassinated, and the Parthians then asked Augustus to send Vonones, one of the four
sons of Phraates IV, to occupy the throne. The reign of Vonones
began at some time between A.D. 6 and 8.[5]

---

[3] Strabo vii. 1. 3 (290). For the identification of the peoples mentioned by Strabo,
see Kaspar Zeuss, *Die Deutschen und die Nachbarstämme* (München, 1837).

For the extent of the kingdom of Maroboduus, see Camille Jullian, *Histoire de la
Gaule*, IV (Paris, [1913]), 126 note 3. Friedrich Kauffmann, *Deutsche Altertums-
kunde*, I (München, 1913), 332. For its importance, Oscar Almgren, "Zur Bedeu-
tung des Markomannenreichs in Böhmen für die Entwicklung der germanischen
Industrie in der frühen Kaiserzeit," *Mannus*, 5 (1913), 265–278. Haakon Shetelig,
Préhistoire de la Norvège (Oslo, 1926), 139–140. Josef Schránil, *Die Vorgeschichte
Böhmens und Mährens* (Berlin, 1928), 249–254.

[4] Velleius ii. 108–110. Tacitus *Ann.* ii. 46. Dio lv. 28. 5–7.

[5] *Res gestae* 33. Josephus *Antiq.* xviii. 2. 4 (43–46). Tacitus *Ann.* ii. 1–2. Suetonius *Tiberius* 16.

In Armenia, Artavasdes III, who had succeeded his father in A.D. 4, was murdered in or about A.D. 6, and his place was filled by Tigranes IV, who also owed his appointment to Augustus. After a brief experience of kingship, Tigranes returned to Rome, and the Armenians set up a woman to rule over them—Erato, widow of Tigranes III—but with no better success.[6]

In Asia Minor, in A.D. 6, the Isaurians rose in rebellion: "they began with marauding expeditions, but were led into all the horrors of war, until they were utterly subdued."[7]

In the kingdom of Bosporus the reign of Dynamis came to an end in A.D. 7/8; it is not unlikely that a struggle of some sort took place after her death, for a king of whom nothing is known issued coins in A.D. 8/9 and 9/10, and Aspurgus, who had been associated with Dynamis in the government, did not become ruler until 10/11.[8]

The Pannonian–Dalmatian war, A.D. 6–9—Under the date of A.D. 6, Dio states that many wars took place, including expeditions against the Germans by various leaders, more especially that of Tiberius against the Marcomanni.[9] It is of some moment to observe that the war against Maroboduus was not undertaken in response to a barbarian invasion; it was due solely to the judgment of the Roman government that "nothing remained to be conquered in Germany except the people of the Marcomanni";[10] in other words, the war was begun on the initiative of

[6] *Res gestae* 27. Tacitus *Ann.* ii. 4. J. G. C. Anderson, *CAH*, X (1934), 277–279.

[7] Dio lv. 28. 3. Ronald Syme, "Galatia and Pamphylia under Augustus," *Klio*, 27 (1934), 140, says the Isaurians "may have been the Homanadenses themselves, but were perhaps rather a kindred tribe of Cilician brigands beyond and to the south and south-east of the Homanadenses."

[8] J. G. C. Anderson, *CAH*, X (1934), 269, 1058. E. H. Minns, *Scythians and Greeks* (Cambridge, 1913), 595, 611. In *RECA*, see Rohden, "Aspurgos," II (1896), 1739–40; Brandis, "Bosporos" (3), III (1899), 781.

In A.D. 14/15 Aspurgus received the title of king from Tiberius, and took the names Tiberius Julius; he died in 37/38.

[9] Dio lv. 28. 1, 5. When the war against Maroboduus was abandoned, Sentius Saturninus remained in Germany; Groag remarks, "Sentius" (9), *RECA*, 2. Reihe, II (1923), 1525: "Er wird das Werk der Pazifizierung der germanischen Stämme, das seine Vorgänger begonnen hatten, fortgesetzt ... haben."

[10] Velleius ii. 108. 1.

the Romans, with the object of overthrowing a monarch who had risen to power in too close proximity to the borders of the empire. As has been pointed out, the Roman army did not actually come in contact with the Marcomanni, for Tiberius was compelled to return precipitately to the Danube on account of uprisings in Dalmatia and Pannonia. Here, too, it should be noticed that the hostilities were commenced by peoples already incorporated into the empire who saw in the absence of the legions an opportunity to regain their freedom. An important factor in the situation was that the revolting tribes had learned the language of the Romans and had come into possession of the secret of Roman discipline; like Maroboduus and Arminius, one or other of the Batos may have had a Roman education.

The rebellion,[11] which taxed the energies and resources of the Roman government, began in a mutiny of some Daesitiates (a tribe situated in the vicinity of Sarajevo) who had been brought together for military service and were urged on by a chief named Bato. The uprising then spread to the Pannonian Breuci (on the Save), who, under the leadership of another Bato, promptly marched against Sirmium. In the absence of M. Valerius Messalla Messalinus, governor of Illyricum, who had accompanied Tiberius, A. Caecina Severus and Rhoemetalces, king of Thrace, hastened westward, and defeated the Breuci on the Drave. Later, however, the Pannonians and Dalmatians united their forces and occupied a position which threatened Sirmium, and from this position Caecina was unable to dislodge them. Meanwhile Tiberius and Messalinus had reached Siscia

[11] Velleius ii. 110–115. Dio lv. 29–34; lvi. 11–16. Suetonius *Tiberius* 16, 20.

Otto Hirschfeld, "Zur Geschichte des pannonisch-dalmatischen Krieges," *Hermes*, 25 (1890), 351–362. Adolf Bauer, "Zum dalmatisch-pannonischen Krieg 6–9 n. Chr.," *AEM*, 17 (1894), 135–148. E. G. Hardy, "Legions in the Pannonian Rising," in his *Studies in Roman History*, I (2d ed., London, 1910), 162–179. Edmund Groag, "M. Plautius Silvanus," *JOAI*, 21–22 (1922–24), Beiblatt, 445–478. Reinhold Rau, "Zur Geschichte des pannonisch-dalmatischen Krieges der Jahre 6–9 n. Chr.," *Klio*, 19 (1924), 313–346. Carl Patsch, *Beiträge zur Völkerkunde von Südosteuropa*, V (Wien, 1932), 110–116. Syme, "Galatia and Pamphylia under Augustus," 139–143.

(on the upper Save), the defense of which was imperative for the security of Italy. Messalinus had proceeded southward from Bohemia by forced marches in advance of the main army and, after a reverse, had defeated the Pannonian Bato in the face of heavy odds.

Tiberius, then, was in possession of Siscia, and Caecina Severus of Sirmium, the two points necessary for the control of Pannonia, when (in A.D. 6) Moesia was invaded by Dacians and Sarmatians[12]—in correspondence with the disturbances in the East. On a comparable occasion (13 B.C.) it had been possible for Calpurnius Piso to bring an army from Asia Minor to the Balkans; this time, however, no transfer of troops could be made, because of the Isaurian war. Hence Caecina was forced to withdraw from Sirmium, with the legions under his command, to drive the Dacian and Sarmatian invaders from his own province. As a result of this new complexity the Dalmatians were left free to overrun the country and to spread the revolt; conversely, Tiberius was left without the means necessary for taking the offensive.

In A.D. 7 Tiberius received reinforcements from Italy—the first of them under the command of Velleius Paterculus—and as the invasions from beyond the Danube were not renewed and the Isaurians had been overcome, Caecina Severus, accompanied by M. Plautius Silvanus with two legions from Asia Minor, again marched westward. On the way to Siscia, Caecina was attacked by the two Batos and suffered a serious reverse, though eventually he succeeded in joining Tiberius. In A.D. 8 the Romans were aided significantly by dissensions among the Danubian allies, and the Pannonians laid down their arms at the river Bathinus (probably the Bosna). Bato of the Daesitiates put to death the Pannonian Bato, undoubtedly on a charge of treachery, and retreated into the mountainous region of southeastern Dalmatia. In A.D. 9 three armies coöperated in putting

---

[12] Dio lv. 30. 4.

an end to the rebellion. The final operations conducted by Tiberius were directed against the Daesitiates and the Pirustae. At the end of the year C. Vibius Postumus, who had been appointed governor of Dalmatia (Illyricum), was left "to complete the subjugation of the remaining districts";[13] Velleius adds that the achievements of Postumus were shared by Lucius Apronius.

The defeat of Varus, A.D. 9.—The peoples south of the Danube and the Drave had scarcely been "pacified" when the German tribes, which had been reduced to submission by Tiberius in 8 B.C. and again in A.D. 5, rose in rebellion, under the leadership of Arminius,[14] a chieftain of the Cherusci. This time, also, the uprising took place within territory occupied by Roman troops, and it is worthy of comment that Arminius had served in the Roman army and had been granted Roman citizenship. The outbreak took the form of an attack upon the three legions, commanded by P. Quinctilius Varus, which had been stationed during the summer of A.D. 9 among the Cherusci. Varus lost his life, his army was annihilated, and his head was cut off and taken to Maroboduus. The Germans seized all the Roman forts east of the Rhine, with the exception of Aliso, from which, however, the garrison was withdrawn in the following year. In the emergency created by the destruction of Varus and his legions, Tiberius once again assumed command on the Rhine (A.D. 10).

For the time being Maroboduus remained in possession of his kingdom.

XIII

Parthia and Armenia, A.D. 10–18.—Vonones, who had been sent to Parthia by Augustus and who had become king not later than

[13] Dio lvi. 15. 3. Velleius ii. 116. Compare the statement of Florus ii. 25.

[14] On Arminius and Varus, see Velleius ii. 117–120. Suetonius *Augustus* 23; *Tiberius* 17–18. Dio. lvi. 18–23; 25. 2. Florus ii. 30 (29–39). Strabo vii. 1. 4 (291). Tacitus *Ann*. i. 3, 55, 61–62. Orosius vi. 21. 26–27.

The defeat of Varus has given rise to a literature of extraordinary proportions; for surveys of this literature, see Victor Gardthausen, "Chronologische Uebersicht der neueren Literatur seit 1820 [über die Varusschlacht]," in his *Augustus und seine Zeit*, II (Leipzig, 1904), 808–815. Erich Wilisch, "Der Kampf um das

A.D. 8, proved unacceptable to some of the Parthian nobility, and about 10 (9/10 or 10/11) the dissatisfied element called in Artabanus, king of Media Atropatene. When, however, the new claimant appeared with an army, the majority of the Parthians stood by Vonones, and Artabanus was defeated. Nevertheless, on the occasion of a second attempt by the Median king, Vonones was overcome and barely succeeded in making his escape to Seleucia. Here he continued to rule until the autumn of 11, and although he may have lost control of the city for some months (11–12), issued coins at Seleucia as late as the end of A.D. 12. Thereafter, at what time is uncertain, he fled to Armenia.[1]

The Armenians had soon tired of Erato as a ruler, but when they had expelled her from the country (seemingly in 11), anarchy ensued, and "the drifting, disintegrated people, ownerless rather than emancipated, welcomed the fugitive Vonones to the throne."[2] Vonones may have taken refuge in Armenia in 11 or 12, but the country seems to have been without a king at the death of Augustus, and when Vonones sent envoys to Rome to obtain the recognition of his claim to the kingship, it was Tiberius who refused his request. Artabanus also was opposed to the pretentions of Vonones, and threatened war when his

---

Schlachtfeld im Teutoburger Walde," *NJKA*, 23 (1909), 322–353. Friedrich Koepp, "Zur Literatur über die Varusschlacht," in Ludwig Bäte, and others, *Hermann der Cherusker und sein Denkmal* (Detmold, 1925), 180–196. Walther Judeich, "Die Überlieferung der Varusschlacht," *RMP*, N.F. 80 (1931), 299–309. Walther Kolbe, "Forschungen über die Varusschlacht," *Klio*, 25 (1932), 141–168. Alfred Franke, "Teutoburgiensis saltus," *RECA*, 2. Reihe, V (1934), 1166–71.

[1] Tacitus *Ann.* ii. 2–3. Josephus *Antiq.* xviii. 2. 4 (46–50). Cauer, "Artabanos" (7), *RECA*, II (1896), 1293–96. J. G. C. Anderson, *CAH*, X (1934), 278. R. H. McDowell, *Coins from Seleucia on the Tigris* (Ann Arbor, Mich., 1935), 223–224, 237.

[2] Tacitus *Ann.* ii. 3–4. Josephus *Antiq.* xviii. 2. 4 (50–52).

Authorities are agreed that a significant change of rulers took place in Armenia in or about A.D. 11. Pascal Asdourian, *Die politischen Beziehungen zwischen Armenien und Rom* (Venedig, 1911), 77–81. Joseph Sandalgian, *Histoire documentaire de l'Arménie*, II (Rome, 1917), 503–507. Jacques de Morgan, *Histoire du peuple arménien* (Paris, 1919), 91.

dispossessed rival appeared to have gained a footing in the northern kingdom. Since, in the event of war in Armenia, Rome would be drawn into the conflict, Q. Caecilius Metellus Creticus Silanus, governor of Syria, forced Vonones to withdraw into Roman territory (A.D. 16), and Armenia was again reduced to a state of anarchy.

In A.D. 17 Tiberius directed the attention of the Senate to the disturbed condition of affairs which was evident in Cappadocia, Commagene, Cilicia, Syria, and Judaea, as well as in Armenia. Thereafter he removed Creticus Silanus from office and sent Germanicus to restore order. In 18 Germanicus entered Armenia, and at Artaxata bestowed the crown upon Zeno (Artaxias), son of Polemo of Pontus.[3] In 19 Germanicus died in Syria; shortly afterwards a struggle for the possession of the province arose between Cn. Calpurnius Piso and Cn. Sentius Saturninus, in which the former was defeated and was sent to Rome.[4]

The Danube and Rhine frontiers, A.D. 10–20.—In A.D. 12 the Dacians took Aegissus, in the Dobrudja, which was under the protection of Rhoemetalces, king of Thrace; the city was recaptured by the Thracians with the assistance of a Roman force commanded by Publius Vitellius.[5] In 14, after the death of Augustus, disturbances broke out in Thrace, the nature of which is obscured by the accusations made (about 19) against Rhescuporis, who had come into possession of the northern part of the kingdom after the death of his brother Rhoemetalces. According to Tacitus, "the moment that Rhescuporis heard of the change

[3] Tacitus *Ann.* ii. 43, 56–58, 64. Strabo xii. 3. 29 (556). Anderson, *CAH*, X (1934), 744–747.

[4] Tacitus *Ann.* ii. 75–81.

[5] Ovid *ex Ponto* i. 8. 11–24; iv. 7. 19–28.

Orosius (vi. 22. 2) says that in the extreme old age of Augustus there was an outbreak of the Dacians (*Dacorum commotio*). Ronald Syme, "Lentulus and the Origin of Moesia," *JRS*, 24 (1934), 119, dates this *commotio* in A.D. 10; more usually, however, it is placed in 11 or 12, see, for the problems involved, G. F. Hertzberg, *Die Geschichte Griechenlands unter der Herrschaft der Römer*, I (Halle, 1866), 525 note 10.

of sovereigns, he began to throw predatory bands across the border, to demolish fortresses, and to sow the seeds of war"— activities which were directed against his nephew Cotys, who had inherited the more prosperous part of his father's dominions.[6] In the winter of 15–16 the Dacians again invaded the Dobrudja, and took Troesmis. The city was recovered by the joint forces of Rhescuporis and L. Pomponius Flaccus, of whom Ovid says that, besides recovering Troesmis, he made safe the banks of the Ister (Danube), held the Moesi to peace, and cowed the Getae with the sword.[7]

On the Rhine, Tiberius had been satisfied during the year A.D. 10 merely to keep watch on the situation; it may therefore have been in response to some new activity on the part of the Germans that in A.D. 11, accompanied by Germanicus, he crossed the river and harried the country.[8] During A.D. 12 he was still occupied with the "German war," so that it was not until the beginning of 13 that he celebrated the triumph awarded him for his victories over the Pannonians and Dalmatians. In 13 the command on the Rhine devolved upon Germanicus, who was sent by Augustus "to put an end to such traces of war as still remained."[9] Tiberius was assigned to Illyricum, and he had

---

[6] Tacitus *Ann.* ii. 64–67; iii. 38. Velleius ii. 129. 1.

The division of the Thracian kingdom by Augustus after the death of Rhoemetalces led to friction between Rhescuporis and Cotys, and amicable relations between uncle and nephew were not promoted by the wife of the latter, daughter of the Polemo of Pontus who had been given the kingdom of Bosporus by Agrippa and sister of the Zeno who was made king of Armenia by Germanicus; evidently it was the misfortune of Rhescuporis to have incurred the hostility of an ambitious family which had the ear of the imperial court. Later on, Rhescuporis was accused of having brought together (in 18 or 19) forces of infantry and cavalry, on the pretext that war threatened with the Bastarnae and Scythians; but the fictitious element in the case should in all probability be attributed to his accusers. On the other hand, Rhescuporis may very well have endeavored to turn to his own advantage outbreaks which occurred in 14 and 18.

[7] Ovid *ex Ponto* iv. 9. 75–80. S. E. Stout, *The Governors of Moesia* (Princeton, 1911), 4.

[8] Dio lvi. 24. 6; 25. 2–3; 26. 2. Velleius ii. 121. Suetonius *Tiberius* 18–19. Gelzer, "Iulius" (154), *RECA*, X (1917), 494–495.

[9] Velleius ii. 123.

already set out for the province when he was recalled to the deathbed of Augustus, and the control of the empire.[10]

The death of Augustus in August, A.D. 14, was followed by mutinies in the armies on the Danube and the Rhine, which, Tacitus remarks, could be traced only to the change of emperors.[11] Drusus, son of Tiberius, was successful in dealing with the situation on the Danube. Germanicus was less fortunate on the Rhine; when, however, he had, with difficulty, restored discipline, he led 12,000 legionary soldiers across the river and attacked the Marsi, possibly without provocation. Since, in devastating the country, he destroyed the altar of Tamfana, the Bructeri, Tubantes, and Usipetes fell upon the Roman army on its return march.[12]

In A.D. 15 Germanicus learned that dissension had arisen between Arminius and his father-in-law, Segestes, the leaders of the Cherusci, and seized the opportunity to make war on the Germans.[13] In campaigns which were carried on from the camps

[10] Velleius ii. 123. Suetonius *Augustus* 97; *Tiberius* 21. Dio lvi. 30. 5. Tacitus *Ann.* i. 5.

On the reign of Tiberius, see Victor Duruy, *De Tiberio imperatore* (Lutetiae, 1853). Adolf Stahr, *Tiberius: Leben, Regierung, Charakter* (Berlin, 1863; 2. Aufl., 1885). Ludwig Freytag, *Tiberius und Tacitus* (Berlin, 1870). E. S. Beesly, *Cataline, Clodius, and Tiberius* (London, 1878), 85–148. J. C. Tarver, *Tiberius, the tyrant* (New York, 1902). Andreas Spengel, "Zur Geschichte des Kaisers Tiberius," *SAWM* (1903), 1–63. Arno Lang, *Beiträge zur Geschichte des Kaisers Tiberius* (Jena, 1911). Gelzer, "Iulius (Tiberius)," *RECA*, X (1917), 478–536. C. A. Holtzhausser, *An Epigraphic Commentary on Suetonius' Life of Tiberius* (Philadelphia, 1918). T. S. Jerome, "Tacitus on Tiberius," in his *Aspects of the Study of Roman History* (New York, 1923), 319–380. Olive Kuntz, *Tiberius Caesar and the Roman Constitution* (Seattle, 1924. Univ. of Washington Publications in the Social Sciences, II. 1). G. P. Baker, *Tiberius Caesar* (New York, 1929). F. B. Marsh, *The Reign of Tiberius* (London, 1931). Ernst Kornemann, "Kaiser Tiberius," in his *Staaten, Völker, Männer* (Leipzig, 1934. Das Erbe der Alten, Heft 24), 78–95. Emanuele Ciaceri, *Tiberio, successore di Augusto* (Milano, 1934).

[11] For the mutinies, see Tacitus *Ann.* i. 16–52. Velleius ii. 125. Suetonius *Tiberius* 25.

[12] Tacitus *Ann.* i. 49–51.

[13] For the campaigns of Germanicus in A.D. 15 and 16, see Tacitus *Ann.* i. 55–72; ii. 5–26. Dio lvii. 18. 1. Strabo vii. 1. 4 (291–292).

Julius von Pflugk-Harttung, "Ueber den Feldzug des Germanicus im Jahre 16," *RMP*, N.F. 41 (1886), 73–84. Friedrich Knoke, *Die Kriegszüge des Germanicus in Deutschland* (Berlin, 1887; 2. Aufl., 1922). Wilhelm Liebenam, "Bemerkungen zur

at Mogontiacum (Mainz) and Vetera (Xanten), the Chatti were
subdued, the Marsi were defeated, and Segestes, who had been
hemmed in by Arminius, was rescued. These activities stirred
the Cherusci and neighboring tribes to rally to the support of
Arminius. Germanicus met the new situation by sending his
army in three divisions to the river Ems. The troops devastated
the country between the Ems and the Lippe, but the battle which
ensued was indecisive, and on the return march to the Rhine the
Roman army suffered great hardships.

Germanicus prepared for the campaign of A.D. 16 by building a large number of ships. While the fleet was being assembled
at the island of the Batavi, an attack was made on the Chatti,
and Germanicus led six legions to the relief of a fort on the
Lippe. After these preliminary operations, Germanicus sailed
with eight legions and auxiliaries to the mouth of the Ems. From
this point he conducted the army to the vicinity of the Weser,
where Arminius was encountered and (perhaps) defeated in
two battles. On the return voyage to the Rhine the fleet suffered
shipwreck and was in great part destroyed, and the disaster inspired the Germans to a renewal of the hostilities. C. Silius Caecina Largus was sent, therefore, to make a new attack upon the
Chatti, while Germanicus himself once again proceeded against
the Marsi.

At the conclusion of the campaign of A.D. 16 Germanicus was
invited by Tiberius to return to Rome and celebrate the triumph
which had been awarded him. Thereafter he was sent to the East,
to settle difficulties in the provinces and in Armenia.

End of the kingdom of Maroboduus.—According to Tacitus,
when Germanicus was recalled, Tiberius remarked that, "since
the vengeance of Rome has been satisfied, the Cherusci and the

---

Tradition über Germanicus," *Jahrbücher für classische Philologie*, 143 (1891), 793–
816. Otto Dahm, *Die Feldzüge des Germanicus in Deutschland* (Trier, 1902). Gerhard Kessler, *Die Tradition über Germanicus* (Berlin, 1905), 17–65. Albert Wilms,
Der Hauptfeldzug des Germanikus im Jahre 15 n. Chr. (Hamburg, 1909). Kroll,
"Iulius" (138), *RECA*, X (1917), 444–451.

other insurgent tribes may be left to their internal feuds."[14] The expression has all the appearance of a retrospective interpretation, but the Roman armies had scarcely been withdrawn from Germany when hostilities broke out between Arminius and Maroboduus. In A.D. 17 the Semnones and Langobardi deserted the king of the Marcomanni and joined the Cherusci; conversely, Inguiomerus, uncle of Arminius, went over to the side of Maroboduus. The armies of the two leaders fought an indecisive battle, possibly in the region of the river Saale, after which Maroboduus withdrew to Bohemia. He then applied to Tiberius for support, but no assistance was given, though the emperor sent his son Drusus to the Pannonian frontier.[15]

In A.D. 18 or 19 Catualda, a young man who had been exiled by Maroboduus and who had found shelter among the Goths, invaded the territory of the Marcomanni with a strong force and, having won over the nobles to join him, seized the palace and an adjacent fortress, and by this means came into possession of the long-accumulated treasures of the Marcomannic king. Maroboduus, deserted by his people, took refuge in Noricum and placed himself under the protection of Drusus; he was assigned an abode at Ravenna by Tiberius, and there spent the remaining eighteen years of his life.[16]

After the expulsion of Maroboduus, Arminius, in A.D. 19, attempted to set up a kingdom among the Cherusci in succession to that of the Marcomanni. He was, however, "assailed by armed force, and while fighting with varied fortunes, fell by the treachery of his kinsmen."[17] About A.D. 20 Catualda was in turn driven across the Danube by Vibilius, king of the Hermunduri, and was sent by Tiberius to Forum Iulii (Fréjus), in Gallia Narbonensis. His followers, with those of Maroboduus, were sent back across

[14] Tacitus *Ann.* ii. 26.

[15] Tacitus *Ann.* ii. 44–46.

[16] Tacitus *Ann.* ii. 62–63. Velleius ii. 129. 3. Suetonius *Tiberius* 37. 4. Stein, "Maroboduus," *RECA*, XIV (1930), 1909–10.

[17] Tacitus *Ann.* ii. 88. Rohden, "Arminius," *RECA*, II (1896), 1199.

the Danube and were settled between the rivers Marus (March) and Cusus (Waag) under a king named Vannius, of the tribe of the Quadi; Tacitus says that Drusus made Vannius king of the Suebi (Marcomanni and Quadi).[18] In May, A.D. 20, Drusus was accorded an ovation.

XIV

Disturbances in Thrace and in Gaul, A.D. 21–28.—In the earlier years of the reign of Tiberius, various disturbances which occurred within the territory under Roman control are ascribed by Tacitus to rigorous measures in local government.

In A.D. 21 the Coelaletae, Odrysae, and Dii took up arms and besieged Rhoemetalces of Thrace in Philippopolis. The uprising was put down by Publius Vellaeus; "neither battle nor engagement," Tacitus remarks, "is a term applicable to an affair in which half-armed men and fugitives were butchered with no effusion of Roman blood."[1] In A.D. 25 C. Poppaeus Sabinus, governor of Moesia, inflicted a crushing defeat upon some tribes in the mountains of Thrace who had refused "to supply our armies with their bravest men";[2] the victor was rewarded with the honors of a triumph.

In A.D. 21 an uprising in Gaul, in which the Treveri and Aedui were conspicuous, and which was led by Julius Florus and Julius Sacrovir, is said to have resulted from oppressive taxation, the burden of heavy debts, and the grinding rates of interest. After much trouble the insurrection was suppressed by C. Silius Caecina Largus.[3] In A.D. 28 the Frisii rose in revolt in conse-

---

[18] Tacitus *Ann.* ii. 63; xii. 29. Ludwig Schmidt, "Das regnum Vannianum," *Hermes,* 48 (1913), 292–295. Anton Gnirs, *Die römischen Schutzbezirke an der oberen Donau* (Augsburg, 1929). Ernst Schwarz, "Wo lag das Swebenreich des Vannius?" *Forschungen und Fortschritte,* 9 (1933), 35. Johannes Klose, *Roms Klientel-Randstaaten am Rhein und an der Donau* (Breslau, 1934), 95–96.

[1] Tacitus *Ann.* iii. 38–39.

[2] Tacitus *Ann.* iv. 46–51; see also vi. 39 and xiii. 45.

The award of the triumphal ornaments took place in 26; the rising had commenced, most probably, in 25. S. E. Stout, *The Governors of Moesia* (Princeton, 1911), 6. Gelzer, "Iulius" (154), *RECA,* X (1917), 510–511.

[3] Tacitus *Ann.* iii. 40–47; iv. 18. Franz Cumont, "Comment la Belgique fut romanisée," *Annales de la Société royale d'archéologie de Bruxelles,* 28 (1919), 94.

quence of the administration of the tribute by Olennius, a centurion; they defeated Lucius Apronius, who was in command of the legions in Lower Germany, and gained their independence.[4]

No disturbances in the East with which the Romans were directly concerned can be pointed out as offering a background for the uprisings between A.D. 21 and 28. It may be remarked, however, that during the greater part of the reign of Artabanus III civil war raged throughout Parthia, and the situation in which the Parthian monarch found himself was so critical that he was forced to come to terms with bandits who had seized Nisibis (about A.D. 20) and plundered the province of which the son-in-law of Artabanus was governor. The bandit-state continued to exist in virtual independence for fifteen years.[5]

XV

Parthia, Armenia, and Rome, A.D. 34–37.—In A.D. 34 Artabanus III of Parthia dispatched his son Arsaces to seize the throne of Armenia, which had become vacant upon the death of Artaxias, and when this had been accomplished, even made an attempt upon Cappadocia.[1] Contemporaneously a conspiracy was formed against Artabanus by Sinnaces and Abdus, men of conspicuous wealth, and emissaries were sent to Tiberius requesting that one of the Parthian princes at Rome be permitted to head a revolution. In response, Tiberius sent Phraates and then Tiridates, who was "of the same stock as Artabanus," to claim

---

[4] Tacitus *Ann.* iv. 72–74; xi. 19.

[5] Tacitus *Ann.* vi. 31. Josephus *Antiq.* xviii. 9. Alfred von Gutschmid, *Geschichte Irans* (Tübingen, 1888), 120. Cauer, "Artabanos" (7), *RECA*, II (1896), 1294. Adolf Büchler, "Anilai and Asinai," *Jewish Encyclopedia*, I (1901), 604.

The procedure by which Anilai and Asinai rose to power is described in detail by Josephus, *Antiq.* xviii. 9. 1. When they had collected a band of ruffians, "they sent to such as fed cattle, and ordered them to pay so much tribute out of them as might be sufficient for their maintenance, proposing also that they would be their friends, if they would submit to them, and that they would defend them from all their other enemies on every side, but that they would kill all the cattle of those that refused to obey them."

[1] For events in Armenia and Parthia, see Dio lviii. 26. Tacitus *Ann.* vi. 31–37, 41–44. Josephus *Antiq.* xviii. 4. 4–5 (96–105). Petrus Patricius fr. 2 *(FHG*, ed. Müller, IV, 184). J. G. C. Anderson, *CAH*, X (1934), 747–750.

the Parthian throne, and entrusted the conduct of affairs in the East to Lucius Vitellius. In 35, at the instigation of the Roman government, Mithridates, brother of Pharasmanes, king of Iberia, invaded Armenia and took Artaxata. His victory was facilitated by the murder of Arsaces. Artabanus at once sent an army under Orodes, another of his sons, against the Iberians. Pharasmanes, on his side, made an alliance with the Albanians and, furthermore, "suddenly poured the Sarmatians into Armenia by the Caspian route."[2] With this support the Iberians defeated Orodes (A.D. 36), whereupon Artabanus brought "the whole strength of his kingdom" into the war. At this juncture Vitellius threatened an invasion of Mesopotamia, and Artabanus was forced to withdraw from Armenia. Within the Parthian dominions, in the same year (36), Sinnaces and his father, Abdageses, succeeded in their designs; they seated Tiridates III on the throne and drove Artabanus from his dominions. The latter retreated to the borders of Scythia and enlisted the Dahae and Sacas in his cause; before the end of the year he returned, Tiridates fled to Syria, and in 37 Vitellius made peace.

In A.D. 36 Aretas IV, king of the Nabataeans, inflicted a defeat upon Herod Antipas, tetrarch of Galilee and Peraea. Tiberius, therefore, ordered Lucius Vitellius, governor of Syria, to march against Petra with two legions; while on his way southward Vitellius received news of the death of Tiberius, and turned back.[3]

In 36 Vitellius found it necessary to send troops against the Cietae, in the Taurus Mountains.[4]

The Danube and Rhine frontiers, A.D. 34–37.—Suetonius says that Tiberius, in the last years of his reign, "suffered Armenia

---

[2] Tacitus *Ann.* vi. 33. 3.

[3] Josephus *Antiq.* xviii. 5. 3 (120–125). Emil Schürer, *Geschichte des jüdischen Volkes im Zeitalter Jesu Christi*, I (3.–4. Aufl., Leipzig, 1901), 445–447. Otto, "Herodes" (24), *RECA*, Supptbd. II (1913), 179–180. Albert Kammerer, *Pétra et la Nabatène* (Paris, 1929), 246–247.

[4] Tacitus *Ann.* vi. 41.

to be overrun by the Parthians, Moesia to be laid waste by the Dacians and Sarmatians, and the Gallic provinces by the Germans;[5] and this statement epitomizes in a sentence the uniform experience of the Roman people.

Hinc movet Euphrates, illinc Germania bellum.[6]

Observations and Comments

The correspondence of events, East and West.—The details which have been presented up to this point include all wars and invasions which are known to have occurred on the eastern and northern borders of the Roman empire during a period of one hundred years.

To avoid misunderstanding, it should be noted that the war contemplated by Caesar against Burebista (44 B.C.) and that initiated by Augustus against Maroboduus (A.D. 6) were not undertaken to suppress barbarian invaders, but were determined upon by the Romans because they regarded the Dacian and Marcomannic kingdoms as political powers which constituted a menace to their own security. So, too, the uprisings of the Pannonians in A.D. 6–9 and of the Germans under Arminius in A.D. 9 were not incursions or invasions, since the territory in which they occurred was at the time in Roman possession (§ XII); and in this group must also be reckoned the disturbances in Thrace and Gaul between A.D. 21 and 25 and the rising of the Frisii in A.D. 28 (§ XIV).

With these stipulations, it may now be said that all the wars carried on by the Romans on the Danube and the Rhine during the period under consideration began with aggressions on the part of the barbarian peoples; indeed, from Caesar's adventure into Gaul (58 B.C.) until the death of Tiberius (A.D. 37) there was, so far as the record goes, no occasion on which a Roman commander made war on border tribes without immediate provocation. This statement, of course, does not imply that the armies

---

[5] Suetonius *Tiberius* 41.   [6] Virgil *Georg.* i. 509.

of the empire remained on the defensive when war actually broke out. The situation, indeed, is fully described in the statements of Augustus, on the one hand, that he never made war without just and due cause, and, on the other, that he "extended the boundaries of all the provinces which were bordered by races not yet subject to our power." The procedure of following provocation with conquest accounts for the fact that the names of tribes concerned in border disturbances, especially in the region of the Danube, disappear as time goes on and give place to others, and it is of some importance to note that risings of peoples such as the Iapodes are not heard of after the campaigns of Octavian in 35–33 B.C., and that the Pannonians are not mentioned as enemies after A.D. 9.

The incursions of the barbarian peoples appear in history as sporadic and meaningless violations of the Roman peace. There is, however, another side to the picture, for it now becomes evident that the barbarian attacks which have been described in the foregoing pages took place only in response to antecedent disturbances in the Roman East. When, indeed, the wars on the eastern and northern frontiers of the empire are examined side by side, the observation is inescapable that wars in the Roman East and barbarian outbreaks on the Danube and the Rhine constitute a sequence which has all the precision of a formal pattern many times repeated. So, in dealing with the history of the frontier wars under Caesar, Augustus, and Tiberius, the "events" to be considered are not various happenings in three or four separate regions which may appropriately be dealt with in different chapters, but a number of happenings in which certain occurrences uniformly made their appearance in succession to an initial disturbance; and within the period specified there may be distinguished possibly as many as twenty occasions on which wars, interventions, or other disturbances in the Roman East were linked with uprisings and incursions in the regions of the lower Danube and the Rhine.

In dealing with the events of a hundred years, it is not to be expected that the evidence discoverable in the classical sources will be of the same character throughout, or that it will always be found equally detailed. Consequently it will not awaken surprise if sometimes the accessible information leaves much to be desired, especially when evidence is called for concerning the repetition many times in succession of certain specific occurrences in widely separated regions. The surprise comes, indeed, when it is found that in every instance of disturbance there are definite indications at most of the different points, if not all, required by the established pattern. And, further, with the exception of rebellions in territory held by Roman troops, the occurrences which fall within this pattern exhaust the list of the known disturbances on the eastern and northern frontiers of the Roman empire during the period under consideration. Thus there were no outbreaks in Europe which were not in correspondence with wars in the Roman East, and there were no wars in the Roman East which were not accompanied by disturbances in Europe. Consequently, as a result of inquiry into the background of the recurrent uprisings and invasions of the barbarian peoples, it appears that (between 63 B.C. and A.D. 37) these outbreaks occurred in direct response to wars in the Roman East, either in the kingdom of Bosporus, in Armenia, or in northern Syria.

The Black Sea as a link between East and West.—It has been shown that, in the times of Caesar, Augustus, and Tiberius, the barbarian uprisings and invasions in Europe occurred in response to disturbances on the northeastern and eastern frontiers of the Roman empire. How, then, is this relationship of events to be accounted for?

In approaching the question, it may be pointed out that on more than one occasion outbreaks on the Danube followed conflicts in the kingdom of Bosporus, and it is not difficult to imagine ways in which disturbances in the region of the Maeotis might have spread through contiguous areas as far as Moesia. Strabo, indeed, speaks[1] of Scythians from the Crimea and the vicinity of the Borysthenes (Dnieper) who, after crossing the Tyras and the Danube, had forced themselves upon the inhabitants of Thrace. On the theory that wars beget wars, it might also be supposed that hostilities in southern Russia had given rise to waves of disturbance which in the end broke upon the Roman defenses of the Rhine. The conception that the barbarian invasions of Roman territory were the final outcome of conflicts which had been transmitted from people to people derives a measure of support from the reference, in the life of Marcus Aurelius, to the "tribes who had been driven on by the more distant barbarians and had retreated before them." The description suggests, in fact, that the territory of tribe after tribe, in unbroken succession from some undetermined starting point, had been subject to attack until finally the Bastarnae, Pannonians, and Germans crossed the Roman frontier.

There is difficulty, however, in fitting this picture to the known circumstances of the wars in the Bosporan kingdom from 17 to 8 B.C., for the hostile actions of the Bosporans were directed, not against the peoples of southern Russia, but against Polemo of Pontus, the agent of the Roman government. Thus, while the civil war in Bosporus was certainly related to the uprisings on the Danube and the Rhine, it can scarcely be regarded as the center of disturbance where "the more distant barbarians" were set in motion. The difficulty becomes even clearer when it is observed that other initiatory disturbances in the Roman East occurred in Armenia, and consequently in a region separated from the scene of the barbarian outbreaks by the Black Sea. It follows, therefore, that the attacks of the barbarian tribes on the European frontiers of the empire are not to be accounted for in terms of impulses communicated by one tribe to another in unbroken succession from an original point of disturbance.

---

[1] Strabo vii. 4. 5 (311).

It follows, too, that an explanation of the phenomena, to be acceptable, must do full justice to the fact that the corresponding disturbances in the Roman East and in Europe involved the inhabitants of regions separated by the Euxine, the Thracian Bosporus, and the Hellespont. In this unexpected form, the problem might well have proved embarrassing had it not been for the wealth of information which has been preserved concerning the empire of Mithridates the Great.

The empire of Mithridates[2] consisted, first, of the kingdom of Pontus, on the southeastern coast of the Pontus Euxinus (Black Sea); second, of Colchis, the territory just below the Caucasus which comprised the drainage basin of the river Phasis (Rion); third, of the kingdom of Bosporus, which embraced the Crimea, the Taman peninsula, and the eastern shores of the Maeotis up to the mouth of the river Tanais (Don). Beyond these territorial possessions the power of Mithridates was extended through alliance with the kingdom of Armenia, where Tigranes was his son-in-law; with the Greek cities on the western coast of the Black Sea from Olbia to Apollonia in Thrace; with the tribes of Southern Russia, especially the Bastarnae, on the eastern frontage of the Carpathians; and with the peoples of the Danube, seemingly as far westward as the Scordisci, at the junction of the Danube and the Save. Dio, indeed, draws attention to the extent of the influence of Mithridates in the Balkans by saying that at his instigation the Thracians on one occasion "overran Epirus and the rest of the country as far as Dodona, going even to the point of plundering the temple of Zeus."[3]

The unity of this highly diversified empire was based upon the commerce of the Black Sea.[4] Polybius (who died the year before Mithridates became king of Pontus) had spoken of "all

---

[2] For the literature, see § I notes 1 and 2.

[3] Dio xxxi. 101. 2.

[4] See Ludwig Preller, "Ueber die Bedeutung des schwarzen Meeres für den Handel und Verkehr der alten Welt," in his *Ausgewählte Aufsätze* (Berlin, 1864), 441–467. Théodore Reinach, *Mithridate Eupator, roi de Pont* (Paris, 1890), 232–233.

those many products furnished by the Pontus [Euxinus] which men in general require in their daily life;"[5] but his statement conveys little suggestion of the varied interests represented in the countries over which Mithridates ruled. In the kingdom of Pontus, Sinope, the capital, which was "the most noteworthy of the cities in that part of the world;"[6] maintained communication by sea, westward, with Thrace and by way of the Thracian Bosporus with Rhodes, Delos, and Attica, and even with Egypt; eastward, with the ports of Amisus, Trapezus, and Phasis; northward, with Panticapaeum and Phanagoria, on the Straits of Kerch, and with Olbia, at the mouth of the Hypanis (Bug). By land, Sinope was connected over an ancient and frequented route with Tarsus, in Cilicia, and by another road with Comana Pontica, "a notable emporium for the people of Armenia."[7] Comana, which was also linked with Amisus and Trapezus, received commodities which had been conveyed along the great trade route through Armenia, Media, and Parthia from Central Asia.[8] Phasis, in Colchis, was an alternative outlet for the eastern trade, which here followed the course of the river Cyrus (Kura) up to its source, then crossed the mountains by a wagon road to the valley of the Phasis (Rion), and continued downstream to the Black Sea. Colchis was in itself highly productive; the country round about contained mines of gold, silver, iron,

---

[5] Polybius iv. 38. 3.

[6] Strabo xii. 3. 11 (545). D. M. Robinson, "Ancient Sinope," *AJP*, 27 (1906), 125–153, 245–279. Walter Leaf, "The Commerce of Sinope," *JHS*, 36 (1916), 1–15. Ruge, "Sinope," *RECA*, 2. Reihe, III (1927), 252–255.

[7] Strabo xii. 3. 36 (559). Sir W. M. Ramsay, *The Historical Geography of Asia Minor* (London, 1890. Royal Geographical Society, Supplementary Papers, IV), 27, 58, 262–263. Robinson, "Ancient Sinope," 137–138. See also J. A. R. Munro, "Roads in Pontus, Royal and Roman," *JHS*, 21 (1901), 52–66.

[8] On the roads leading eastward from Pontus and Colchis, see W. E. D. Allen, "The March-lands of Georgia," *Geographical Journal*, 74 (1929), 135–156, especially "The two trunk roads to Asia," 135–136.

In his description of Trebizond, H. F. B. Lynch, *Armenia*, I (London, 1901), 32, says: "Strings of Bactrian camels may be seen in the streets, about to start on the long stages which separate the seaport from Erzerum and Tabriz. The various peoples of Asia and of Europe still meet in the bazars."

and copper, and produced "everything that pertains to ship-building"; moreover, the inhabitants carried on a linen indus-try which was famous far and wide.[9]

The kingdom of Bosporus was of importance, chiefly, because it was the main source of food supplies for the cities of northern Asia Minor and of the Aegean, as well as for Roman troops in the event of war in Armenia. The capital and principal port of the kingdom was Panticapaeum, on the Crimean side of the straits; Phanagoria, on the eastern side, was the center to which commodities were "brought down from the Maeotis and the bar-barian country that lies above it." Tanais, on the Don, which "next to Panticapaeum, was the greatest emporium of the bar-barians," was a market for the Asiatic and the European no-mads—the dividing line was the river Don—"where slaves, furs, and such other things as barbarians possess" were exchanged for "clothing, wine, and the other things that belong to civilized life."[10]

Tanais carried on trade with the "European" no less than with the "Asiatic" barbarians. The city was destroyed, however, by Polemo of Pontus, and it may have been after this occurrence that the Roman government (in or about 14 B.C.) established relations with the Sarmatians on both sides of the Don. Augus-tus[11] does not give the names of these Sarmatian peoples, but those to the west were, almost certainly, the Roxolani,[12] who oc-cupied or spread over the plains between the Don or the Donets and the Dnieper. In the time of Mithridates, as both earlier and later, trade with the peoples between the Dnieper and the Car-

<hr>

[9] For Colchis, see Titus von Margwelaschwili, *Colchis, Iberien und Albanien um die Wende des 1. Jahrhunderts v. Chr.* (Halle a. S., 1914).

On the route through Colchis, see Strabo xi. 2. 17–18 (498–499); 3. 4–5 (500–501); 7. 3 (509). Pliny *NH* vi. 52.

[10] See Strabo vii. 4. 4–5 (309–310); xi. 2. 3 (493), 10 (495). E. H. Minns, *Scythians and Greeks* (Cambridge, 1913), 563–569. Herrmann, "Tanais," *RECA*, 2. Reihe, IV (1932), 2166–69.

[11] *Res gestae* 31

[12] Strabo vii. 3. 17 (306).

pathians was carried on through the "great emporium" of Olbia.[13] This center was of such importance to the peoples of the plains and waterways that, when it was destroyed by Burebista, the "Scythian" tribes helped to repair the damage he had done, because they missed the convenience of the city for trade; the information comes from Dio of Prusa, who visited Olbia about A.D. 95, and the statement of Jordanes (xxxii) that the Scythians had allowed the Greeks to build Olbia and the other coast towns "to afford them means of trade" may have reference to the same event. West of Olbia, in the direction of the Carpathians, were situated the Bastarnae, who were allies of Mithridates and provided his best troops.[14] The different tribes of the Bastarnae (Peucini, Atmoni, and Sidoni) stretched from the mouth of the Danube, along the eastern frontage of the Carpathians, up to the sources of the Vistula. Presumably they controlled the Carpathian passes, such as the Jablonica, over which trade from the Euxine had long been carried on with the peoples of northern Hungary and present-day Czechoslovakia.[15] Pontus and Bosporus were also in communication with Dacia, and even with peoples in Illyricum.

It is evident, then, that the barbarians of Southern Russia and Eastern Europe carried on trade with the Greek cities on the Black Sea, and that this trade was an integral part of a highly complex system of commerce which, in the first century B.C., was dominated by the kingdom of Pontus. As a measure of the importance of the commerce between the opposite coasts of the

---

[13] Strabo vii. 3. 17 (306). Minns, *Scythians and Greeks*, 450–489. M. I. Rostovtzeff, *Iranians & Greeks in South Russia* (Oxford, 1922), 63–65, 162–163.

[14] Appian *Mithr.* 15, 69, 71. Justin xxxviii. 3. See also Strabo vii. 2. 4 (294); 3. 2 (296); 3. 13 (305); 3. 17 (306). Tacitus *Germania* 46. Ihm, "Bastarnae," *RECA*, III (1899), 110–113. Erich Sehmsdorf, *Die Germanen in den Balkanländern* (Leipzig, 1899). Ludwig Schmidt, *Geschichte der deutschen Stämme*, I (Berlin, 1910), 459–466. Minns, *Scythians and Greeks*, 124–125.

[15] See especially Vasile Pârvan, *Dacia* (Cambridge, 1928), 40, 64, 79. It is probable, therefore, that the Bastarnae had relations of long standing with the Anartii, in northern Hungary, who are mentioned with them in the inscription of the Roman general *-cius*.

Euxine, it may be pointed out that when Mithridates, in 65 B.C., retreated to his northern dominions, Pompey did not follow in pursuit, but dispatched a fleet to blockade the ports of the Bosporan kingdom.[16] The pressure thus exerted had significant results: in 63 the merchants of Phanagoria rose in revolt, and this uprising was quickly followed by the final collapse of Mithridates' power; in 63 and the following years Olbia "became a prey to the indiscriminate attacks of the surrounding tribes";[17] from 64[18] to 59 the Romans were busily engaged in defending the country south of the lower Danube from invaders, especially the Bastarnae; between 63 and 59 the Boii and Taurisci were overcome and dispersed by the Dacians under Burebista; while, contemporaneously, the German tribes from the Vistula[19] to the Rhine were involved in wars.

The inhabitants of the lands comprised in the empire of Mithridates were united, not sundered, by the Black Sea—even though its waters were not traversable by migrating barbarians. On the other hand, the wars in the Roman East, which, in Cicero's opinion, had the effect of disturbing the money market at Rome,[20] by interrupting the trade between the northern and

---

[16] Plutarch (*Pompey* 36) says that Pompey "stationed ships to keep guard against the merchants sailing to Bosporus, and death was the penalty for such as were caught." On the effects of the blockade, see Reinach, *Mithridate Eupator*, 402, 404.

[17] Minns, *Scythians and Greeks*, 464.

[18] Carl Patsch, *Beiträge zur Völkerkunde von Südosteuropa*, V (Wien, 1932), 38–41.

[19] For the archaeological evidence relating to these disturbances, see Karl Schumacher, "Gallische und germanische Stämme und Kulturen im Ober- und Mittel-Rheingebiet zur späteren La-Tènezeit," *Praehistorische Zeitschrift*, 6 (1914), 230–292, see 281; "Germanisches Spätlatènegrab von Muschenheim," *Germania*, 4 (1920), 75–77. Gustav Kossinna, "Wandalen in der Wetterau," *Mannus*, 11–12 (1919–20), 405–408; "Die Wandalen in Nordjütland," *Mannus*, 21 (1929), 233–255—these events "gegen Mitte des 1. Jahrhunderts v. Chr.," 255. Walther Schulz, "Geschichte der Bevölkerung Mitteldeutschlands von der jüngeren Steinzeit bis zum Untergang des Thüringer Reiches," *Mannus*, 5. Ergbd. 1927), 19–25.

[20] As quoted by G. H. Stevenson in *The Legacy of Rome*, ed. by Cyril Bailey (Oxford, 1924), 145: "The credit of the Roman money-market is intimately bound up with the prosperity of Asia; a disaster cannot occur there without shaking our credit to its foundations."

southern coasts of the Black Sea, created the conditions which gave rise to the descents of barbarian tribes on the Danube and Rhine frontiers.

The activities of the barbarians.—In turning to consider the activities of the barbarians which were affected by the wars in the Roman East and the consequent interruptions of trade, a distinction must be made between the interests of the peoples situated in the mountainous country south of the Danube and the ways of life of the German and other northerly tribes.

First, then, it should be understood that the Danube and the Save constituted a highway which connected the Black Sea with the head of the Adriatic.[21] From northern Italy, as Strabo says (iv. 207, v. 214), merchandise was conveyed on wagons to the headwaters of the Save, and was then carried down in boats to the Pannonians and the Scordisci. All the peoples on the Danube made use of boats, and not only did they follow the main stream down to the Black Sea, but they also utilized its tributaries to penetrate far into the lands to the north and south. Thus the Theiss and its tributaries were open ways into the heart of Transylvania, as were the Bosna and the Drin into Illyricum. Still more important, however, was the connection maintained up the Morava, through the territory of the Dardani, over the divide to the valley of the Axius or Vardar, and so down to Thessalonica and the Aegean Sea. From Nish, on the Morava, another route led eastwards to Sofia, then through the country of the Bessi and the valley of the Maritsa to Adrianople, and across country to Byzantium.

Now, if consideration be given to the positions, relative to these routes, of the peoples who, in and after the time of Burebista, participated in attacks upon the provinces of Macedonia and Illyricum, it will be found that the Bessi, Dentheletae, Dardani, Iapodes, and others were situated on or in proximity to passes, while the Scordisci and Pannonians occupied the region

---

[21] Brandis, "Danuvius," *RECA*, IV (1901), 2126–27.

where the Morava, from the south, the Theiss, from the north, and the Save and Drave, from the west, joined the Danube.

In the Alpine regions, the Iapodes made descents upon Aquileia, Tergeste, and Pola. The Norici, Raeti, and Vindelici "used to overrun, from time to time, the neighboring parts, not only of Italy, but also of the country of the Helvetii, the Sequani, the Boii, and the Germans."[22] The Salassi controlled access to the Great and the Little St. Bernard passes, and collected tolls from all who crossed the mountains from Italy to Gaul.[23] Strabo says (iv. 205) they even robbed Caesar of money, for when he refused their demands, they loosed the rocks of the mountainside upon his legions, "under the pretext that they were engaged in building roads"; they also exacted from Decimus Brutus the toll of a drachma (about fifteen cents) a head for his men, at the time of his retreat from Mutina; then, too, they "affronted" Valerius Messalla Corvinus, when he was getting ready to attack them, by making him pay on the spot for firewood. The peoples in the Alps exacted tolls from merchants and other travelers, and it may be inferred that those in the Balkans followed the same practice. Hence the caravans[24] which at certain times in the year traversed the mountain crossings in the Alps and the routes south of the Danube were a source of revenue to the inhabitants of the various districts. On the other hand, these peoples are mentioned as giving trouble and as descending from their passes to make raids upon the settled population of the lowlands only when wars occurred in the Roman East.

On the Danube-Save route the Romans met with prolonged resistance on the part of the Pannonian tribes, situated on the Save and its tributaries and between the Save and the Drave. Strabo emphasizes the degree to which the rivers in this region were utilized for traffic, but, unfortunately, says nothing of the manner in which the traffic was controlled by the peoples who held the river banks. There is, however, little reason to suppose that

---

[22] Strabo iv. 6. 8 (206).　　　[23] Caesar BG iii. 1.　　　[24] Strabo iv. 6. 6 (204).

the situation in Illyricum differed greatly from that in Gaul. In the latter country "tolls were exacted on the goods which were transported on the great water-ways, and it was from the farm ing of these dues that the nobles derived a large part of their wealth."[25] Hence Bato the Breucian and Pinnes may have been leaders whose wealth and prestige had suffered from the Roman conquest of Pannonia. On the rivers, as on the passes, uprisings and raids followed any interruption of the seasonal traffic.

The northern barbarians, too, were interested in trade and trade routes.[26] In the economy of German life, horses, cattle, slaves, furs, and amber were important articles of use and barter.[27] Caesar says of the tribes beyond the Rhine that they depended chiefly upon their cattle for food, and upon the skins of wild animals, more particularly the reindeer, for wearing apparel.[28] According to Tacitus, the Germans, both men and

---

[25] T. R. Holmes, *Caesar's Conquest of Gaul* (2d ed., Oxford, 1911), 16.

Concerning tolls on the Euphrates, Strabo remarks, xvi. 1. 27 (748) : "The Scenitae are peaceful, and moderate towards travelers in the exaction of tribute, and on this account merchants avoid the land along the river and risk a journey through the desert, . . . for the chieftains who live along the river on both sides . . . are each invested with their own particular domains and exact a tribute of no moderate amount."

[26] Modern authorities are interested almost exclusively in the trade of the Roman merchants with the northern peoples. See, for example, Walther Stein, "Handel," *RGA*, II (1914), 382–390, and the literature, 390; and now Olwen Brogan, "Trade between the Roman Empire and the Free Germans," *JRS*, 26 (1936), 195–222. It is not surprising, therefore, that, as Karl Schumacher says, *Siedelungs- und Kulturgeschichte der Rheinlände*, II (Mainz, 1923), 287, "im freien Germanien sind die Handelsverhältnisse noch wenig klargestellt."

For trade among the Germans, see Wilhelm Wackernagel, "Gewerbe, Handel und Schiffahrt der Germanen," in his *Kleinere Schriften*, I (Leipzig, 1872), 35–85. Ludwig Schmidt, *Geschichte der deutschen Stämme*, I (Berlin, 1910), 44. Stein, "Handel," *RGA*, II (1914), 375. Much, "Germani," *RECA*, Supptbd. III (1918), 569–571.

[27] Wackernagel, 67–75.

[28] For the use of skins and furs by the northern peoples, see Caesar *BG* iv. 1; vi. 21. Tacitus *Germania* 17, 46. Jordanes iii. 21; in v. 37 he says that the Hunuguri in his time were known to the Romans from the fact that they traded in marten skins. Ovid *Trist.* iii. 10. 19; *ex Ponto* iv. 8. 83; 10. 2. Seneca *Ep.* xc. 16. See also Virgil *Georg.* iii. 383. Justin ii. 2. Ammianus Marcellinus xxxi. 2. 5.

Karl Müllenhoff, *Deutsche Altertumskunde*, IV (Neue Abd., Berlin, 1920), 296. L. Fougerat, *La pelleterie et le vêtement de fourrure dans l'antiquité* (Paris, [1914]), 193–214, with illustrations. Otto Schrader, *Reallexikon der indogermanischen Altertumskunde*, II (2. Aufl., Berlin, 1929), 156–159: Pelzkleider.

women, wore the skins of wild animals, though the nearer tribes obtained other clothing from traders, and the women went in for trailing linen garments striped with purple. Jordanes describes the Suiones in Scandinavia as "a people famed for the dark beauty of their furs, who, though they live in poverty, are most richly clad." Ovid says that the "skin-clad" Getae wore furs to keep out the cold. Seneca remarks that the Scythians of Southern Russia garbed themselves in skins of the fox and the marten, which were soft to the touch and impervious to the winds. Tacitus contributes the further information that the Germans trimmed or decorated the skins they wore with the fur of "creatures native to the outer ocean and its unknown seas," and these products of the far north must have been obtained from the Finns or the Lapps.[29]

From the Rhine to the Don, in fact, the use of furs was an outstanding characteristic of barbarian life, and the trade which brought to the Germans the products of the remotest north implied a far-reaching system of routes and markets, even though "the tribes of the interior practiced barter in the simpler and older fashion."[30] Caesar[31] gives particulars concerning one such route which began at the frontiers of the Helvetii, followed the course of the upper Danube to the territories of the Daci and Anartii, and then turned "to the left," presumably to the basin of the Vistula; at the end of sixty days the traveler came to a country which contained wild animals not seen elsewhere, and of these Caesar attempts to describe the reindeer, the elk, and the aurochs or wild ox. The part of this route which lay between the territory of the Helvetii and Bohemia was held by the Boii until they were dispossessed and dispersed by Burebista.[32]

---

[29] Much, "Germani," 570. See also Hans Schall, *Vom Tauschhandel zum Welthandel* (Leipzig, 1931), 191–192.

[30] Tacitus *Germania* 5.   [31] Caesar *BG* vi. 25. Much, "Germani," 569–570.

[32] Joseph Déchelette, *Manuel d'archéologie préhistorique, celtique et gallo-romaine*, II. 3 (Paris, 1914), says of the route along the upper Danube which was held by the Boii: "Il est évident, d'après la composition de ces monnaies, que des relations commerciales régulières reliaient Stradonitz (Bohême) avec la Gaule orientale, à travers l'Helvétie et la Vindélicie. Entre Bibracte et l'oppidum boïen

It is significant, indeed, that long stretches of the northern routes were controlled by aggregations of tribes. Thus the people known as the Bastarnae consisted of a number of tribes spread out from the mouth of the Danube to the upper waters of the Vistula. Across the Carpathians, the Bastarnae had dealings with the Anartii, also an aggregation of tribes,[33] and at the Vistula they were in contact with the Lugii, whose name may signify companions or partners bound by oath.[34] West of the Lugii, whose territory extended to the Oder, were the Suebi—not one tribe only[35]—who occupied the country between the Oder and the Elbe and held possession of the eastern bank of the Elbe as far north as the Cimbric peninsula. The great tribal organizations of the north were not simply kindred-groups; and when Ptolemy,[36] at a later time, spoke of the Langobardi, Angli, and Semnones as Suebi, and of the Buri, Diduni, and Omani as Lugii, he was not attempting to classify these peoples with reference to their blood relationships, but to indicate their status on important routes of trade. It is less difficult, therefore, to envisage the process by which, among the northern barbarians, commodities were passed on from one tribe to another in continuous succession until they reached their destination, as the "first fruits" of the Hyperboreans[37] were handed on from one Scythian people to another until, by way of Sinope, they reached the temple of Apollo at Delos, or as the "sapphire-colored skins"

---

une route de caravanes, jalonnée de comptoirs et de marchés, permettait aux industriels établis au cœur du territoire celtique d'échanger au loin leurs produits. Non seulement le numéraire helvète est abondant à Stradonitz, mais les monnaies de la Gaule qui y circulent sont aussi celles que le commerce apportait à l'ancienne Helvétie" (983–984).

"La grande voie commerciale qui reliait la Gaule centrale au *Boïohemum*, à travers le territoire des Helvètes et des Vindéliciens, suivait le Doubs, le haut Rhin et le haut Danube" (985).

[33] Tomaschek, "Anartes," *RECA*, I (1894), 2063–64.

[34] Rudolf Much, in *Der ostdeutsche Volksboden*, hrsg. von Wilhelm Volz (Breslau, 1926), 108.

[35] Tacitus *Germania* 38.

[36] Ptolemy ii. 10.

[37] Pausanias i. 31. 2. See also Herodotus iv. 33.

from Scandinavia were sent through innumerable tribes until they reached the frontier posts of the Romans.[38]

Now, when wars occurred in the Roman East, disturbances broke out on the northern routes, all the way from the Black Sea to the Elbe and the Rhine, and these disturbances took effect in a distinctive manner. Thus, on such occasions, the Bastarnae, whose established interests and activities lay toward the north and the Vistula, made raids on the Getae, in Wallachia, or across the Danube into the Dobrudja. In other words, they turned away from the route with which they were immediately concerned and attacked peoples with whom ordinarily they had no trade relations. Similarly, in Caesar's time, the Suebi attacked the Usipetes and Tencteri and the Ubii, and carried their incursions as far as the Rhine.

Raids, when they occurred, were sudden and unexpected. Such, indeed, was the dread of these sudden attacks that, as Caesar reports, the German tribes endeavored to gain security by maintaining a wilderness upon their borders.[39] For the tribes south of the Danube the river was a protection against invaders, but not in winter, when the ice made a bridge for the Sarmatians to pass over.[40] On the other hand, according to Tacitus,[41] the Suiones did not customarily go armed, since the ocean forbade sudden inroads on the part of their enemies. In the actual event of an incursion, the people who were the victims of attack moved away. Strabo says (iv. 196) that, in the time before Caesar's conquest, the Gauls would make off, households and all, whenever attacked by others stronger than themselves; in his own day the Germans who were driven out by the Suebi sought refuge on the western side of the Rhine (iv. 194); so, too, when the

---

[38] Jordanes *Getica* iii. 21. See also Strabo xvi. 4. 19 (778), where, in his description of Arabia, he says: "Those who live close to one another receive in continuous succession the loads of aromatics [from the Sabaeans] and deliver them to their next neighbors, as far as Syria and Mesopotamia."

[39] Caesar *BG* iv. 3; vi. 23. Tacitus *Germania* 40 mentions tribes who were "protected by forests and rivers."

[40] Ovid *Trist.* iii. 10.   [41] Tacitus *Germania* 44.

Romans invaded the country, the German tribes would either yield and then later revolt again, or else quit their settlements. "It is a common characteristic of all the peoples in this part of the world," he remarks in speaking of the region between the Rhine and the Elbe, "that they migrate with ease . . . [for] they live in small huts that are merely temporary structures, and subsist for the most part off their herds, as the nomads do, so that, in imitation of the nomads, they load their household belongings on their wagons and with their beasts turn whithersoever they think best."[42] In the region of the lower Danube, the Getae also moved when they were attacked, and on these occasions they crossed the river into the territory of the Triballi, who admitted them under compulsion. Strabo says further that the Scythians, Bastarnae, and Sarmatians on the farther side of the Danube often prevailed over the Getae to the degree that they actually crossed over to attack those whom they had previously driven out (vii. 305). It is evident, however, that, when the invaders withdrew, the Getae returned to their former habitat, for Strabo remarks that their migrations both ways across the Danube were continuous.

The feature which stands out with reference to all the northern peoples is that they migrated with ease. When, however, the Roman frontier was advanced to the Rhine, and later to the Danube, this ease of movement was strikingly curtailed. The line of demarcation set up and protected by the Romans introduced a new element into the situation which the barbarians were slow to comprehend and which they found it difficult to accept. "Origi-

---

[42] Strabo vii. 1. 3 (291). For his description of the true nomads, see vii. 3. 17 (307). For the controversial literature on the supposed nomadism of the Germans, see Alfons Dopsch, *Wirtschaftliche und soziale Grundlagen der europäischen Kulturentwicklung*, I (2. Aufl., Wien, 1923), 57–59. Concerning the wagons of the northern peoples, see P. R. von Bieńkowski, "Über skythische Wagen," *Wiener Studien*, 24 (1902), 394–397. Hugo Mötefindt, "Der Wagen im nordischen Kulturkreise zur vor- und frühgeschichtlichen Zeit," *Festschrift Eduard Hahn* (Stuttgart, 1917), 209–240; "Die Entstehung des Wagens und des Wagenrades," *Mannus*, 10 (1918), 31–63. Jörg Lechler, "Neues über Pferd und Wagen in der Steinzeit und Bronzezeit," *Mannus*, 25 (1933), 123–136.

nally," says Tacitus, "there was the same poverty and the same freedom on either bank of the river."[43] The Usipetes and Tencteri exercised the old freedom and crossed the Rhine, only to be massacred by Julius Caesar. The Salassi and the Pannonians were crushed by the armies of Augustus, and the survivors sold into slavery, because they failed to respect the Roman conquest of their respective dominions. Yet it may be observed that the Ubii, who as fugitives were permitted by Agrippa to remain on the left bank of the Rhine, became the defenders, as Tacitus says, of the bank itself; that the wandering Hermunduri, who were allotted a place of abode by Domitius Ahenobarbus, became the most trustworthy of all the peoples who were not actually within the Roman dominions; and that the Getae, when settled in Thrace by Aelius Catus, continued to cultivate the soil in peace.

If the movements of the Getae and the Ubii be compared with the more obtrusive activities of the Bastarnae and the Suebi, it will be noticed that the Romans had to deal with two distinct classes of "invaders." First, they had to deal with tribes who had been set in motion by the more distant barbarians, and who in their flight crossed the border; and, second, with the "more distant" barbarians themselves, who had been turned from their ordinary ways of life by some unusual occurrence, and who crossed the frontier knowingly, in search of plunder. It is not clear that the Romans ever came to discriminate the first of these classes from the second. They observed the barbarians from a distance and from behind the protection of an armed frontier, and saw in the incursions only the spasmodic activities of tribes who appeared to be actuated by an unalterable disposition to maraud and war. In answer to persistent uprisings the Romans inflicted punishment upon the disturbers of their peace, and even dispossessed them of their territory. Nevertheless, though the successive advances of the frontier were attended by the "paci-

---

[43] Tacitus *Germania* 28.

fication" of tribes who had proved troublesome, these advances were followed, not by a cessation of disturbances, but by the appearance of new raiders and invaders; consequently, as Strabo remarks (iv. 194), though the foremost were always put down, peoples in other places in their turn took up the war.

To the barbarians the action of the Romans in pushing forward their lines of demarcation was no less unintelligible than were their own outbreaks to the imperial government. The barrier maintained by the legions deprived them, in a manner at once sudden and incomprehensible, of an immemorial freedom of movement. Hence the immediate factor in the border wars was not the martial spirit of any particular tribe or tribes, but the mutually unintelligible conduct of men responsive to different modes of existence; and, in contemplating the relations of barbarians and Romans, it is never possible to escape from the contrast of tribal groups, on the one hand, who would "load their household belongings on their wagons and with their cattle turn whithersoever they thought best," and, on the other, of military leaders who, like Augustus, would assert, "I extended the boundaries of all the provinces which were bordered by races not yet subject to our empire." But, above and in addition to the contrast of peoples who moved with ease and those who drove forward their lines of territorial possession, it is now to be understood that the unrest of the barbarians which gave occasion for the successive acquisitions of barbarian territory by the Romans was the response of men set in a particular mold of existence to situations created by the Roman government in the process of extending its authority over the more distant regions of Bosporus, Syria, and Armenia.

Chapter II

GAIUS · CLAUDIUS · NERO

Rome and Parthia

I

THE PARTHIAN INVASION of Armenia in A.D. 34 was the beginning of a period of disturbance on the eastern frontier which continued down to 63. Tiberius had sought, at one and the same time, to keep the empire from war and to prevent the Parthians from gaining control of Armenia. Hence he had induced Mithridates the Iberian to seize the Armenian throne. After the death of Tiberius, however, the emperor Gaius,[1] known as Caligula, summoned Mithridates to Rome and imprisoned him, and permitted the government of Armenia to fall into the hands of the Parthians (38).[2]

Armenia and Bosporus, A.D. 38.—In 38 Artabanus III of Parthia was forced to take refuge with Izates II of Adiabene, and the Parthian throne was occupied by Cinnamus (of whom nothing else is known). Later, however, Artabanus was restored, and in gratitude to Izates gave him the city of Nisibis.[3]

[1] Vaglieri, "Caligula," *DER*, II (1900), 31–37. Hugo Willrich, "Caligula," *Klio*, 3 (1903), 85–118, 288–317, 397–470. R. U. Linnert, *Beiträge zur Geschichte Caligulas* (Nürnberg, 1909). Gelzer, "Iulius" (133), *RECA*, X (1917), 381–423. R. R. Rosborough, *An Epigraphic Commentary on Suetonius' Life of Gaius Caligula* (Philadelphia, 1920). T. S. Jerome, "The Historical Tradition about Gaius," in his *Aspects of the Study of Roman History* (New York, 1923), 381–421. M. P. Charlesworth, "The Tradition about Caligula," *CHJ*, 4 (1933), 105–119. J. P. V. Balsdon, "Notes concerning the Principate of Gaius," *JRS*, 24 (1934), 13–24; *The Emperor Gaius* (Oxford, 1934).

[2] Tacitus *Ann.* xi. 8. Dio lx. 8. 1. Seneca *de tranquill.* xi. 12. Willrich, "Der Orient unter Gaius," *Klio*, 3 (1903), 297–304. Geyer, "Mithridates" (33), *RECA*, XV (1932), 2214–15. J. G. C. Anderson, *CAH*, X (1934), 750–751.

[3] Josephus *Antiq.* xx. 3. 1–3 (54–68). Cauer, "Artabanos" (7), *RECA*, II (1896), 1295–96. Weissbach, "Kinnamos" (3), *RECA*, XI (1921), 483.

Gaius also intervened in Bosporus. When Aspurgus died, in 37 or 38, his wife, Gepaepyris, came into control of the kingdom either in her own right or as regent for Mithridates III. In 38 or 39 Gaius gave the kingdom to Polemo II of Pontus, and in resentment at this action Mithridates issued coins with his name in full, thus symbolizing a revolt against the domination of Rome.[4]

Events on the Rhine, A.D. 39–40.—In 39, German tribes made incursions into Gaul; they were driven back by Ser. Sulpicius Galba. In the autumn, Gaius arrived in Gaul and led an army, said to have numbered 200,000 men, across the Rhine, but no important engagement would appear to have taken place. In 40 the emperor concentrated troops in the vicinity of Boulogne for an invasion of Britain; he actually put to sea—in the month of March—but at once returned and gave up the attempt.[5] It may be noted that, on his arrival in Gaul, Gaius put to death Cn. Cornelius Lentulus Gaetulicus, governor of Upper Germany.

II

Parthia, Armenia, and Bosporus, A.D. 41–43.—In or about A.D. 40 Artabanus III of Parthia died and was succeeded by his son Vardanes. At once war broke out between Vardanes and his

---

[4] Dio lix. 12. 2; lx. 8. 2. For the history of this Mithridates, see E. H. Minns, *Scythians and Greeks* (Cambridge, 1913), 595–598, 601–603, 611. In *RECA*, see Brandis, "Bosporos" (3), III (1899), 782–783; Stein, "Gepaepyris," VII (1910), 1227–28; Kahrstedt, "Kotys" (10), XI (1922), 1554; Geyer, "Mithridates" (16), XV (1932), 2206–07.

Coins of Gepaepyris occur in 37/38 and 38/39; coins of Mithridates with his name in full, 39/40 to 41/42. Minns, 611. Polemo never established his claim to the kingdom. Minns, 604.

[5] Suetonius *Caligula* 43–48, 51; *Galba* 6. 2–3. Dio lix. 21–22; 25. 1–3. Eutropius vii. 12. 2. Aurelius Victor *de Caes.* iii. 11. Orosius vii. 5. 5. Tacitus *Agricola* 13.

In addition to the literature cited in note 1, see Alexander Riese, "Der Feldzug des Caligulas an den Rhein," *NHJ*, 6 (1896), 152–162. Willrich, "Gaius und der Westen," *Klio*, 3 (1903), 304–317. Georg Teuber, *Beiträge zur Geschichte der Eroberung Britanniens durch die Römer* (Breslau, 1909), 1–15, 82–86. Emil Ritterling, "Zur Germanenkrieg d. J. 39–41 n. Chr.," *RGK*, 6 (1913), 1–4. Camille Jullian, *Histoire de la Gaule,* IV (Paris, [1913]), 161–164. Ludwig Schmidt, *Geschichte der deutschen Stämme,* II. 2 (Berlin, 1915), 352–353. Johannes Janssen, "Ad expeditionem Gai principio in Germaniam," *Mnemosyne,* n.s., 48 (1920), 205–206. Ritterling, "Legio," *RECA*, XII (1924), 1244–48. Münzer, "Sulpicius" (63), *RECA*, 2. Reihe, IV (1931), 776–777.

brother Gotarzes.[1] In 41 Gotarzes ousted Vardanes. In 42 Vardanes regained the throne. Gotarzes thereupon withdrew to the
eastern provinces and raised an army from among the Dahae
and Hyrcanians. Vardanes marched against him, and the opposing forces met on the Bactrian border. Before a battle was
fought, however, the brothers "came to a sudden agreement,"
by which Vardanes retained the crown and Gotarzes remained
as viceroy in Hyrcania.

While the claimants to the Parthian throne were thus engaged,
the kingdom of Armenia again experienced a change of rulers,
for the emperor Claudius (41–54)[2] reversed the decisions of
Gaius respecting the kingdoms in the East. In 41 he sent Mithridates the Iberian back to Armenia; Demonax, the Parthian governor, was routed, and the reconquest of the country was carried
out (presumably in 42) by Roman troops, who stormed the fortified places while Iberian cavalry scoured the plains.[3]

On his reurn from Eastern Persia, Vardanes took possession
of Seleucia (42), which had been in revolt for seven years.[4] He
then occupied himself with Armenia; "he was eager," Tacitus

---

[1] Tacitus *Ann.* xi. 8–9. Josephus *Antiq.* xx. 3. 4 (69).

For the conflict between Vardanes and Gotarzes, see Alfred von Gutschmid, *Geschichte Irans* (Tübingen, 1888), 123–128; "Gotarzes," in his *Kleine Schriften*,
hrsg. von Franz Rühl, III (Leipzig, 1892), 43–124. Warwick Wroth, *Catalogue of the
Coins of Parthia* (London, 1903), xlv–xlviii. Eugen Täubler, *Die Parthernachrichten
bei Josephus* (Berlin, 1904), 19–20. Stein, "Gotarzes," *RECA*, VII (1912), 1674–83.
Kiessling, "Hyrkania," *RECA*, IX (1914), 506–507. Ernst Herzfeld, "Sakastan," in
his *Archaeologische Mitteilungen aus Iran*, IV (Berlin, 1932), 58–66. Sir J. C.
Coyajee, "The House of Gotarzes, a Chapter of Parthian History in the Shahnameh,"
JASB, n.s., 28 (1933), 207–224. J. G. C. Anderson, *CAH*, X (1934), 754–755. R. H.
McDowell, *Coins from Seleucia on the Tigris* (Ann Arbor, Mich., 1935), 225–228.

[2] Hermann Lehmann, *Claudius und seine Zeit* (Gotha, 1858). Adalbert Ziegler,
Die politische Seite der Regierung des Kaisers Claudius I (Linz, 1879–1882).
Gaheis, "Claudius" (256), *RECA*, III (1899), 2778–2839. Ferrero, "Claudius,"
DER, II (1900), 290–303. A. P. Ball, *The Satire of Seneca on the Apotheosis of
Claudius* (New York, 1902). Karl Vivell, *Chronologisch-kritische Untersuchungen
zur Geschichte des Kaisers Claudius* (Freiburg i. B., 1911). Hugo Willenbücher,
Der Kaiser Claudius, eine historische Studie (Mainz, 1914). Arnaldo Momigliano,
L'opera dell'imperatore Claudio (Firenze, [1932]); *Claudius, the Emperor and
his Achievement*, tr. by W. D. Hogarth (Oxford, 1934).

[3] Tacitus *Ann.* xi. 8–9. Dio lx. 8. 1.

[4] Tacitus *Ann.* xi. 9.

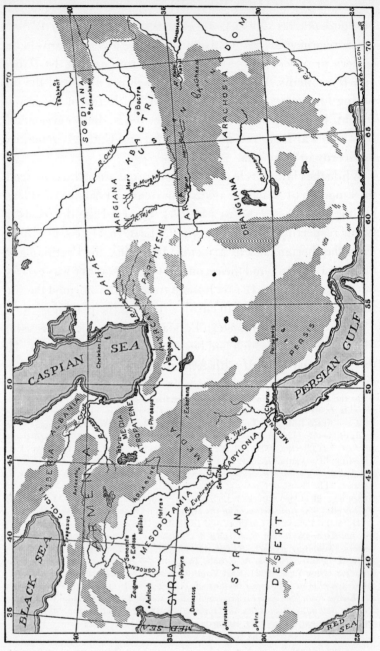

4. PARTHIA.

says, "to recover Armenia, but was stopped by Vibius Marsus, governor of Syria, who threatened war."[5]

Further, in his effort to reach a settlement of eastern affairs, Claudius recognized Mithridates III as king of Bosporus, in 41, and compensated Polemo by a grant of territory in Cilicia.[6]

The Rhine and Britain, A.D. 41–43.—In 41, outbreaks in Germany necessitated campaigns against the Chatti and the Chauci, and these were conducted respectively by Ser. Sulpicius Galba and P. Gabinius Secundus.[7]

In 43 the disturbed state of affairs in Britain which followed the death of Cunobelinus (Cymbeline) induced Claudius to send Aulus Plautius to subjugate the island. Claudius himself joined the expedition for a short time. The opposition to the Roman advance was led by Caratacus and Togodumnus.[8]

III

Parthia and Bosporus, A.D. 43–49.—Gotarzes did not long remain content with his relegation to Hyrcania, but "repented of having relinquished the throne," and in A.D. 43 again collected an army. On this occasion he was defeated by Vardanes at the river Erindes, possibly the Charindas on the western border of Hyrcania. The victor continued his campaign by reducing the tribes as far as the river Sindes, presumably the modern Tejend; there, however, his success ended, for the Parthian levies refused to go farther, and "after erecting monuments in which he recorded his greatness, . . . he returned covered with glory."[1] Nevertheless, Gotarzes was again in possession of Seleucia in

---

[5] Tacitus *Ann.* xi. 10. Josephus *Antiq.* xx. 3. 4 (69–73).

[6] Dio lx. 8. 2. In 41, E. H. Minns, *Scythians and Greeks* (Cambridge, 1913), 596; Anderson, *CAH,* X (1934), 752. In 42, Brandis, "Bosporos" (3), *RECA,* III (1899), 782; Carl Patsch, *Beiträge zur Völkerkunde von Südosteuropa,* V (Wien, 1932), 139.

[7] Dio lx. 8. 7. Suetonius *Claudius* 24. 3. Tacitus *Hist.* i. 49. Plutarch *Galba* 3.

[8] Dio lx. 19–23, 30. 1–2. Suetonius *Claudius* 17; 24. 3; *Vespasian* 4. 1–2. Tacitus *Agricola* 13; *Hist.* iii. 44. Eutropius vii. 13. Orosius vii. 5. 5. See also R. G. Collingwood, *CAH,* X (1934), 790–802; for the literature, see 988–989.

[1] Tacitus *Ann.* xi. 10.

the summer of 44 and as late as the beginning of 45, though in the latter year Vardanes once more recovered the city.[2]

In Bosporus, notwithstanding the friendly attitude of Claudius, Mithridates III[3] is reported to have continued his hostility to the Roman government and even to have made preparations for war. To allay suspicion, it is said, he sent his brother Cotys as an envoy to the emperor. While at Rome, however, Cotys revealed the designs of Mithridates. Claudius thereupon appointed him king and, in 45 or 46,[4] sent him to Bosporus with an escort of Roman troops commanded by A. Didius Gallus, governor of Moesia. When Mithridates had been ejected, Gallus withdrew, leaving only a guard under C. Julius Aquila.

Mithridates did not submit passively to his ejection, but proceeded to rouse the neighboring tribes and to enlist deserters. At the outset he defeated the king of the Dandaridae (Dandarii) and took possession of his dominions east of the Maeotis, and this initial success gained him the support of Zorsines, king of the Siraci. Cotys and his protector, Julius Aquila, fearing an immediate invasion of Bosporan territory, thereupon made an alliance with Eunones, king of the Aorsi. With his assistance they defeated Mithridates, in 48, and forced Zorsines to capitulate, "to the great glory of the Roman army, which all men knew to have come after a bloodless victory within three days' march of the river Tanais."[5] Mithridates took refuge with Eunones, who gave him up, and the defeated king was conducted to Rome, in 49, by Junius Cilo,[6] procurator of Bithynia and Pontus.

---

[2] R. H. McDowell, *Coins from Seleucia on the Tigris* (Ann Arbor, Mich., 1935), 227.

[3] Dio lx. 28. 7; 32. 4a (Petrus Patricius). Tacitus *Ann.* xii. 15–21. See also § 1 note 4.

[4] In 44 or 45, J. G. C. Anderson, *CAH*, X (1934), 753. In 46, Brandis, "Bosporos" (3), *RECA*, III (1899), 783; S. E. Stout, *The Governors of Moesia* (Princeton, 1911), 9; Groag, "Didius" (6), *RECA*, V (1905), 411; Carl Patsch, *Beiträge zur Völkerkunde von Südosteuropa*, V (Wien, 1932), 139.

[5] Tacitus *Ann.* xii. 17.

[6] Tacitus *Ann.* xii. 21. See also M. I. Rostovtseff, "Pontus, Bithynia and the Bosporus," *ABSA*, 22 (1916–18), 15–17. C. T. Seltman, "The Administration of Bithynia under Claudius and Nero," *Numismatic Chronicle*, 5th ser., 8 (1928), 101–103.

Northern Europe and Britain, A.D. 47.—In or about A.D. 45
Rhoemetalces III of Thrace was murdered by his wife, and in
46 Claudius annexed the kingdom in the face of obstinate resistance.[7] It is of interest to note that the trade of Byzantium
was so adversely affected by the wars in Bosporus and Thrace
that the Roman government subsequently remitted the tribute
of the city for a period of five years.[8]

It would seem also to have been in close association with the
war in Bosporus (46–48) that the Jazyges moved from southern Russia into the valley of the Theiss, from which they drove
the Dacians.[9] The Roxolani may have taken possession of the
territory which the Jazyges had left vacant.[10]

In 47 the Cherusci, who "had lost all their nobles in civil
wars," sent envoys to Rome with the request that Italicus, nephew
of Arminius, be given them as king. Claudius made Italicus a
present of money and provided him with an escort; "never before," he said, "had a native of Rome, no hostage but a citizen,
gone to mount a foreign throne." Italicus was well received by
the Cherusci, but shortly "some who had found their fortune in
party feuds" fled to the tribes on the border and collected a large
force in opposition to his rule. In the conflict which ensued the
king was victorious. Subsequently, however, he was deposed,
and recovered his throne only with the aid of the Langobardi.

---

[7] Arthur Stein, *Römische Reichsbeamte der Provinz Thracia* (Sarajevo, 1920),
1–3. Lenk, "Thrake," *RECA*, 2. Reihe, VI (1936), 452.

[8] Tacitus *Ann.* xii. 62–63.

[9] Pliny iv. 80. See especially Patsch, *Beiträge zur Völkerkunde von Südosteuropa,*
V, 141–142. E. H. Minns, *Scythians and Greeks* (Cambridge, 1913), 124, thinks
that it may have been as a result of this invasion that the Carpi crossed the Carpathians (from west to east) and established themselves in Bessarabia.

The date at which the Jazyges moved is uncertain; it is known, however, that
they were recent arrivals in the region of the upper Theiss in the year A.D. 50.
See Karl Müllenhoff, *Deutsche Altertumskunde,* III (Berlin, 1892), 35, 39, 53.
Arnold Heeren, *De chorographia a Valerio Flacco adhibita* (Gottingae, 1899), 71–
73. Ulrich Kahrstedt, "Die Karpodaken," *Praehistorische Zeitschrift,* 4 (1912), 84.
In *RECA,* Brandis, "Dacia," IV (1901), 1952–53; Vulić, "Iazyges," IX (1914), 1189–
91; Treidler, "Jazyges," Supptbd. VI (1935), 126–127.

[10] Minns, *Scythians and Greeks,* 121. Kretschmer, "Sarmatae," *RECA,* 2. Reihe, I
(1920), 2545.

"And still," says Tacitus, "in prosperity or adversity, Italicus did mischief to the interests of the Cheruscan nation."[11]

In 47 the Chauci, under the leadership of Gannascus (who had long served in the Roman army), made raids on the sea-coast of Gaul and incursions into Lower Germany.[12] Cn. Domitius Corbulo destroyed their ships and restored order. He also extended Roman authority over the Frisii, who had been "hostile and disloyal" since their revolt in A.D. 28. Later, Corbulo contrived the death of Gannascus, an action which aroused the hostility of all the Chauci, but when he proceeded against them he was recalled peremptorily by Claudius.

In 47 P. Ostorius Scapula[13] succeeded Aulus Plautius in Britain. The new governor was at once called upon to put down a rebellion of the Iceni (in Norfolk and Suffolk). He then, presumably in 48, proceeded to devastate the territory of the Degeangli, in Flintshire, but was recalled by uprisings of the Brigantes, in Yorkshire, and of the Silures, in Monmouth and Glamorgan. The Silures were led by Caratacus, and for a time successfully maintained the war against the Romans. In 50 or 51, however, Ostorius defeated Caratacus, and the latter was given up to the Romans in 51 by Cartimandua, queen of the Brigantes. Tacitus says that when Caratacus (familiarly, Caractacus) was taken to Italy as a prisoner, "all were eager to see the great man, who for so many years had defied the power of Rome."[14]

IV

Rome and Parthia, A.D. 49–50.—In Parthia, Vardanes was murdered in A.D. 45 or 46, and after a time of confusion Gotarzes

---

[11] Tacitus *Ann*. xi. 16–17. Johannes Klose, *Roms Klientel-Randstaaten am Rhein und an der Donau* (Breslau, 1934), 52.

[12] Tacitus *Ann*. xi. 18–20. Dio lx. 30. 4–6. Klose, 43.

[13] Tacitus *Ann*. xii. 31–38; *Hist*. iii. 45; *Agricola* 14. For the date, see Donald Atkinson, "The Governors of Britain from Claudius to Diocletian," *JRS*, 12 (1922), 60, 62. On the campaigns of Ostorius, see esp. R. G. Collingwood, "The Fosse," *JRS*, 14 (1924), 252–256.

[14] Tacitus *Ann*. xii. 36. See also Dio lx. 33. 3c (Zonaras xi. 10).

succeeded him.[1] At once, however, a group of conspirators sent a delegation to Claudius with the request that Meherdates, son of Vonones I, be sent to occupy the throne (47). After long deliberation Claudius gave his consent, and in 49 Meherdates was escorted to Zeugma, on the Euphrates, by C. Cassius Longinus, governor of Syria. Notwithstanding the support of Abgar V, king of Osroëne, Izates II, king of Adiabene, and Carenes, Parthian governor of Mesopotamia, he was defeated by Gotarzes, in 50, and imprisoned.[2]

Northern Europe and Britain, A.D. 50–51—In 50 "an immense host" of the Lugii, from the headwaters of the Vistula and the Oder, advanced against the kingdom of Vannius.[3] The opportunity presented by this invasion was grasped by Vangio and Sido, nephews of Vannius, and Vibilius, king of the Hermunduri,[4] who joined with the Lugii in the attack upon the kingdom of the Marcomanni and Quadi. To supplement his own army, which consisted primarily of infantry, Vannius employed horsemen of the Jazyges, who had recently appeared west of the Carpathians. Notwithstanding this support, he was unable to withstand the combined forces of the Hermunduri and Lugii and withdrew his men into forts and fortresses. The Jazyges, however, dispersed themselves throughout the country and precipitated a battle in which Vannius was defeated. Meanwhile Claudius had sent legions and auxiliaries to the Danube against the possibility that the victor in the struggle might, in the elation of success, disturb also the peace of the empire. When, there-

---

[1] Tacitus *Ann.* xi. 10. Josephus *Antiq.* xx. 3. 4 (73).

[2] Tacitus *Ann.* xii. 10–14. Alfred von Gutschmid, *Geschichte Irans* (Tübingen, 1888), 127. Stein, "Gotarzes," *RECA,* VII (1912), 1679.

[3] Tacitus *Ann.* xii. 29–30. Tacitus (29) speaks of "the opulent realm which Vannius had enriched during thirty years of plunder and tribute." Franke, "Marcomanni," *RECA,* XIV (1930), 1617. Johannes Klose, *Roms Klientel-Randstaaten* (Breslau, 1934), 97–99.

[4] The Hermunduri were "loyal" to Rome and enjoyed special privileges of trade with Augusta Vindelicorum. Tacitus *Germania* 41. Under Vibilius they reached the highest point of their prosperity. Haug, "Hermunduri," *RECA,* VIII (1912), 907. See also Klose, 60–66.

fore, Vannius was overthrown, he took refuge with the Romans, who assigned to him, with his followers, a settlement in Pannonia. The Marcomannic kingdom was divided between Vangio and Sido, and these kings were described, at a later time, as having long been loyal to the Roman government.

Farther west, in 50, the Chatti invaded the region of the Wetterau and the lower Main; they were defeated by P. Pomponius Secundus, commander in Upper Germany, and, "fearing to be hemmed in on the one side by the Romans, on the other by the Cherusci, with whom they were perpetually at war," they made peace and sent hostages to Rome.[5]

In Britain, after the capture of Caratacus, the war against the Romans was carried on with renewed vigor (51), more especially by the Silures, and Ostorius Scapula died (52), "worn out by the burden of his anxieties." Shortly after his death the Silures inflicted a defeat upon the legion commanded by T. Manlius Valens. A. Didius Gallus, the new governor (52–57 or 58), pursued a policy of extreme caution, and after a time peace was restored.[6]

V

Parthia and Armenia, A.D. 51–54.—In A.D. 51 Gotarzes died or lost his life in an uprising, and was succeeded by Vologeses I after a short interval in which the throne was occupied by Vonones II.[1]

In 51 Pharasmanes, king of Iberia, sent his son Radamistus with a large army to attack Mithridates, the Iberian.[2] The invasion caught the Armenian king off his guard, and he was forced to take refuge with the Roman garrison in the fortress of Gorneae. After a time he was induced to leave this protection, and

---

[5] Tacitus *Ann.* xii. 27–28. Otto Dahm, "Der Raubzug der Chatten nach Obergermanien im Jahre 50 n. Chr.," *Bonner Jahrbücher*, 101 (1897), 128–135. Ludwig Schmidt, *Geschichte der deutschen Stämme*, II. 2 (Berlin, 1915), 353–354.

[6] Tacitus *Ann.* xii. 38–40; xiv. 29; *Agricola* 14.

[1] Tacitus *Ann.* xii. 14. Josephus *Antiq.* xx. 3. 4 (74).

[2] Tacitus *Ann.* xii. 44–51. In 52 there was an uprising of the Cietae, in the Taurus Mountains, *Ann.* xii. 55, as there had also been in 36, *Ann.* vi. 41.

was murdered by his nephew. Vologeses seized the opportunity afforded by the death of Mithridates and, in 51 or 52, invaded Armenia with the object of placing his brother Tiridates on the throne. On his approach Radamistus fled, and the cities of Artaxata and Tigranocerta surrendered; but for some reason Vologeses abandoned his plans and withdrew to Parthia. Radamistus then returned, only, however, to be driven out by the Armenians, and in 53 or 54 Tiridates with a Parthian army took possession of the country.[3] It is noteworthy that in the face of these occurrences the Roman government took no steps to protect its interests in Armenia.

Corbulo on the Euphrates frontier, A.D. 54–63.—In 54 Nero succeeded Claudius as emperor, and before the end of the year sent Cn. Domitius Corbulo to reëstablish Roman prestige in the East.[4] In 55 Corbulo arrived in Cappadocia and set about his

---

[3] Tacitus *Ann.* xiii. 6.

[4] For Parthian and Armenian affairs in the time of Nero, and especially the Armenian war, see Tacitus *Ann.* xiii. 6–9, 34–41; xiv. 23–26; xv. 1–8, 24–31. Dio lxii. 19–26.

Emil Egli, "Feldzüge in Armenien von 41–63 n. Chr.; ein Beitrag zur Kritik des Tacitus," in Max Büdinger, ed., *Untersuchungen zur römischen Kaisergeschichte,* I (Leipzig, 1868), 265–363. Hermann Schiller, *Geschichte des römischen Kaiserreichs unter der Regierung des Nero* (Berlin, 1872). George Rawlinson, *The Sixth Great Oriental Monarchy* (New York, [1873]), 262–286. Wilhelm Laufenberg, *Quaestiones chronologicae de rebus parthicis armeniisque a Tacito . . . enarratis* (Bonnae, 1875). Alfred von Gutschmid, *Geschichte Irans* (Tübingen, 1888), 129–133. Henry Furneaux, "The Roman Relations with Parthia and Armenia from the Time of Augustus to the Death of Nero," in his *The Annals of Tacitus,* II (Oxford, 1891), 96–126. B. W. Henderson, "The Chronology of the Wars in Armenia, A.D. 51–63," *Classical Review,* 15 (1901), 159–165, 204–213, 266–274; see also *Journal of Philology,* 28 (1903), 99–121, 271–286; *The Life and Principate of the Emperor Nero* (London, 1903). Edouard Maynial, "Recherches sur la date des salutations impériales de l'empereur Néron," *Revue archéologique,* 3. sér., 39 (1901), 167–177; 4. sér., 4 (1904), 172–178. H. S. Jones, "La chronologie des salutations impériales de Néron," *Revue archéologique,* 4. sér., 3 (1904), 263–272; 7 (1906), 142–144. D. T. Schoonover, *A Study of Cn. Domitius Corbulo as Found in the 'Annals' of Tacitus* (Chicago, 1909). C. F. Lehmann-Haupt, *Armenien einst und jetzt,* I (Berlin, 1910), 383–406, 501–523. Antonio Abbruzzese, "Le relazioni politiche fra l'impero romano e l'Armenia da Claudio a Traiano," *Bessarione,* 3. ser., 8 (1911), 408–428. Pascal Asdourian, *Die politischen Beziehungen zwischen Armenien und Rom von 190 v. Chr. bis 428 n. Chr.* (Venedig, 1911), 85–98, 178–180. Henri de la Ville de Mirmont, "Cn. Domitius Corbulo," *Revue historique,* 118 (1915), 1–53. Joseph Sandalgian, *Histoire documentaire de l'Arménie,* II (Rome, 1917), 514–536. In *RECA,* Supptbd.

preparations for war. He established his base of operations at Trapezus (Trebizond), in Pontus, but the Roman army also occupied Chersonesus, in the Crimea, in 54 or 55, and in 56 or 57 occupied and rebuilt Tyras, at the mouth of the Dniester.[5]

While the Romans were making ready to eject the Parthians from Armenia, Vologeses was occupied with disturbances in his own dominions. In 55 a claimant to the Parthian crown, in the person of Vardanes, son of Vologeses, appeared in Hyrcania,[6] and "a great band" of Dahae and Sacas invaded Parthyene[7] (the old province of Parthia). Vologeses, who was engaged in war with Izates of Adiabene, was compelled to relinquish his campaign in order to defend his eastern possessions. Vardanes held his ground, however, until the middle of 58; thereafter the Hyrcanians asserted their independence and set up a state which en-

III (1918) : Hohl, "Domitius (Nero)," 349–394; Stein, "Domitius (Corbulo)," 394–410. David Magie, "Roman Policy in Armenia and Transcaucasia and its Significance," *Annual Report of the American Historical Association,* 1919, I (Washington, 1923), 295–304. Adolf Günther, *Beiträge zur Geschichte der Kriege zwischen Römern und Parthern* (Berlin, 1922), 75–101. Werner Schur, *Die Orientpolitik des Kaisers Nero* (Leipzig, 1923. *Klio,* XV. Beiheft) ; "Untersuchungen zur Geschichte der Kriege Corbulos," *Klio,* 19 (1925), 75–96; "Zur neronischen Orientpolitik," *Klio,* 20 (1925), 215–222; "Die orientalische Frage im römischen Reiche," *NJWJ,* 2 (1926), 270–282. Ritterling, "Legio," *RECA,* XII (1924), 1254–57. W. E. Gwatkin, *Cappadocia as a Roman Procuratorial Province* (Columbia, Mo., 1930. Univ. of Missouri Studies, V, 4), 41–54. Arnaldo Momigliano, "Corbulone e la politica romana verso i Parti," *Atti del II Congresso nazionale di studi romani,* I (Roma, 1931), 368–375. Mason Hammond, "Corbulo and Nero's Eastern Policy," *HSCP,* 45 (1934), 81–104. J. G. C. Anderson, *CAH,* X (1934), 758–773, 880. Geyer, "Tigranes" (6), *RECA,* 2. Reihe, VI (1936), 980–981.

[5] For Trapezus, see Tacitus *Ann.* xiii. 39.

For Chersonesus, see Brandis, "Chersonesos" (20), *RECA,* III (1899), 2269. M. I. Rostowzew, "Römische Besatzungen in der Krim und das Kastell Charax," *Klio,* 2 (1902), 80–83. Bogdan Filow, *Die Legionen der Provinz Moesia* (Leipzig, 1906. *Klio,* VI. Beiheft), 14 note 5. E. H. Minns, *Scythians and Greeks* (Cambridge, 1913), 522–523, points out that in the coinage of Chersonesus every year from A.D. 46 to 54 is represented, and that then there is a gap until the beginning of the reign of Vespasian.

For Tyras, Minns, *Scythians and Greeks,* 447.

[6] Tacitus *Ann.* xiii. 7. The pretender may have been "son of Vardanes," without personal designation. See Gutschmid, *Geschichte Irans,* 130. Schur, *Die Orientpolitik des Kaisers Nero,* 73. Ernst Herzfeld, "Sakastan," in his *Archaeologische Mitteilungen aus Iran,* IV (Berlin, 1932), 102–104. Anderson, *CAH,* X (1934), 879.

[7] Josephus *Antiq.* xx. 4. 2 (91).

dured for at least a century.[8] They at once sent an embassy to Nero, soliciting an alliance with the Romans, and in 59 Corbulo expedited the embassy on its return journey.

The active phase of the Armenian war did not begin until 58. The account of the war given by Tacitus leaves some uncertainty in regard to the precise dating of the different campaigns; nevertheless, as the narrative is divided into four parts, the order of events is unmistakable.

The first episode[9] tells how Corbulo advanced into Armenia (late in 57), how he distributed his forces to cope with the guerrilla tactics of Tiridates, and, finally, how he marched to Artaxata, which he took and destroyed (in 58); the narrative closes with a statement concerning the enthusiasm with which news of Corbulo's success was received at Rome.

The second episode[10] tells how Corbulo marched south to Tigranocerta (59) and received the surrender of the city, how (60) he opposed Tiridates, who had renewed the war, and how he installed Tigranes on the Armenian throne and retired to Syria to assume the duties of governor.

In the narrative of Tacitus, the third episode[11] provides a contrast to the victories of Corbulo, for it recounts the humiliation, first, of Tigranes, and, second, of L. Caesennius Paetus, the officer sent out to take over the command when Corbulo was appointed governor of Syria. Tigranes, once he had become king, invaded the Parthian province of Adiabene; Vologeses, therefore, returned from the Hyrcanian war and proceeded against him (61), and Tigranes was forced to retire into Tigranocerta, where he was besieged. Corbulo effected an understanding with Vologeses, and peace was restored.

[8] Concerning the new Hyrcanian state, Kiessling, "Hyrkania," *RECA*, IX (1914), 508, says: "Der neue Staat (Tacitus *Ann.* xiii. 37) reicht sicher bis an den Persischen Golf hinunter, Karmanien gehört neuerlich dazu, wie aus Tacitus xiv. 25 zu entnehmen ist." Schur, *Die Orientpolitik*, 80, remarks of the kingdom that "Es hatte die grossen Verbindungswege zwischen dem iranischen Osten und Westen fest in der Hand."

[9] Tacitus *Ann.* xiii. 34–41.   [10] Tacitus *Ann.* xiv. 23–26.   [11] Tacitus *Ann.* xv. 1–18.

In 61 Paetus arrived to take command on the Armenian front, and at once announced that "he would soon impose on the conquered tribute and laws and Roman administration, instead of the empty shadow of a king."[12] In 62 he led an army into Armenia, but was forced by Vologeses to make an ignominious capitulation at Rhandeia. After this disaster Corbulo reached an agreement with Vologeses in accordance with which Romans and Parthians alike withdrew from Armenia. The narrative for the year 62 ends by directing attention to the trophies which had been erected on the Capitoline Hill in anticipation of victory.

The fourth episode[13] tells how Nero decided to continue the war and appointed Corbulo to supreme military command in the East; how Corbulo (in 63) made his preparations and entered Armenia with a powerful army; and, finally, how Tiridates yielded and laid down his crown before the statue of Nero. At the conclusion of the war a settlement was arrived at by which Tiridates was to be invested with the kingdom of Armenia at Rome.[14]

In 62/63 Cotys, king of Bosporus, was deposed, and the kingdom was placed under Roman administration.[15]

The lower Danube, Northern Europe, and the Rhine, A.D. 58–63.—In 58 (presumably) Tiberius Plautius Silvanus Aelianus, governor of Moesia, gave refuge in his province to more than one hundred thousand people from beyond the Danube. The information is derived from an inscription set up in honor of Plautius Silvanus, which also says that he checked at the outset an uprising of the Sarmatians, that he brought to submission a number of kings hitherto unknown to the Romans, that he rendered services to the Bastarnae, the Roxolani, and the Dacians, peoples who apparently had suffered from enemies not designated, and that he aided Chersonesus (in the Crimea) when the

---

[12] Tacitus *Ann.* xv. 6.   [13] Tacitus *Ann.* xv. 24–31.

[14] Tacitus *Ann.* xvi. 23. Suetonius *Nero* 13. Dio lxiii. 1–7. The actual investiture by Nero did not take place until 66.

[15] Minns, *Scythians and Greeks,* 599, 611.

city was attacked by the Scythians. The inscription does not provide information in regard to the dates of these various occurrences, but it is evident that they spread over a number of years. There is reason to believe that the movement of the trans-Danubians may be assigned to A.D. 58, and that the other events fell between this date and 63.[16]

In 58 "a great battle" was fought between the Hermunduri and the Chatti.[17] In the same year the Frisii,[18] under their leaders Verritus and Malorix, moved into the Roman military territory—unoccupied lands reserved for the use of the legions—on the eastern bank of the lower Rhine; after prolonged negotiations they were forced to withdraw by L. Dubius Avitus. Also in 58 the Ampsivarii were driven from their home on the river Ems by the Chauci; they, too, sought refuge in the unoccupied territory, and Boiocalus, their leader, appealed to Dubius Avitus for permission to remain. While the subject was under discussion, Boiocalus took offense, and in exasperation endeavored to stir the Bructeri, Tencteri, and other tribes to war. The tribes were intimidated, however, by the armies which Dubius Avitus and T. Curtilius Mancia led across the Rhine. The Ampsivarii thereupon retreated to the Usipetes and Tubantes. "Driven out of these countries, they sought refuge with the Chatti and then with

---

[16] Since the events recorded are not dated in the inscription, the time at which they took place has been the subject of prolonged controversy. See Wilhelm Liebenam, *Die Legaten in den römischen Provinzen von Augustus bis Diocletian* (Leipzig, 1888), 269–272. Alfred von Domaszewski, "Die Dislocation des römischen Heeres im Jahre 66 n. Chr.," *RMP*, N.F. 47 (1892), 207–218. Bogdan Filow, *Die Legionen der Provinz Moesia* (Leipzig, 1906. *Klio*, VI. Beiheft), 6–23. S. E. Stout, *The Governors of Moesia* (Princeton, 1911), 12–16. Ritterling, "Legio," *RECA*, XII (1925), 1574, 1650. Vasile Pârvan, *Getica* (Bucureşti, 1926), 103, 733; *Dacia* (Cambridge, 1928), 180–181. Hermann Dessau, "Zur Reihenfolge der Statthalter Moesiens," *JOAI*, 23 (1926), Beiblatt, 345–358; *Geschichte der römischen Kaiserzeit*, II. 1 (Berlin, 1926), 211 note 3. Carl Patsch, *Beiträge zur Völkerkunde von Südosteuropa*, V (Wien, 1932), 164–166. Philippe Fabia, "Sur une page perdue ... des Annales de Tacite," *REA*, 34 (1932), 139–158. Fluss, "Moesia," *RECA*, XV (1932), 2377. Léon Halkin, "Tiberius Plautius Aelianus, légat de Mésie sous Néron," *Antiquité classique*, 3 (1934), 121–161.

[17] Tacitus *Ann.* xiii. 57.

[18] Tacitus *Ann.* xiii. 54. Ihm, "Frisii," *RECA*, VII (1910), 106.

the Cherusci, and after long wanderings, as destitute outcasts, received now as friends and now as foes, their entire youth were slain in a strange land, and all who could not fight were appropriated as booty."[19]

Uprisings also took place in Britain. D. Veranius Nepos, successor of Didius Gallus, attempted to put down an uprising of the Silures, but was prevented by death from carrying on the war.[20] C. Suetonius Paulinus,[21] who succeeded to the governorship in 58 or 59, was forced to spend two years in "reducing the tribes and strengthening the garrisons." He then attacked the island of Mona (Anglesey), "which had a powerful population and was a refuge for fugitives." While Suetonius was engaged in this campaign, Boudicca (more generally known as Boadicea), widow of Prasutagus, king of the Iceni, led a revolt on the east coast of Britain.[22] The Trinovantes joined the Iceni, and together they destroyed Camulodunum (Colchester). Q. Petilius Cerialis, commander of the Ninth Legion, hastened from Lindum (Lincoln), but was defeated, and he himself barely escaped. On receiving news of the rebellion, Suetonius marched southward; he was, however, unable to defend Londinium and Verulamium (St. Albans), and these cities were sacked by the Britons. In the final battle, the place of which is unknown, Boudicca was utterly defeated, and shortly afterwards took poison (61).

VI

The Roman expedition to the Caspian Gates, A.D. 67–68.—In A.D. 64/65 the kingdom of Pontus, including Colchis, was in-

[19] Tacitus *Ann.* xiii. 55–56.

[20] Tacitus *Ann.* xiv. 29; *Agricola* 14.

[21] Tacitus *Ann.* xiv. 29–39; *Agricola* 14–16. Dio lxii. 1–12. Suetonius *Nero* 18 says that Nero "even thought of withdrawing the army from Britain."

[22] See, in *RECA*, Henze, "Boudicca," III (1899), 797; Hübner, "Britanni," III (1899), 871; Haverfield, "Iceni," IX (1914), 821; Hohl, "Domitius" (29), Supptbd. III (1918), 373; Macdonald, "Londinium," XIII (1927), 1397; Miltner, "Suetonius" (3), 2. Reihe, IV (1931), 592. See especially R. E. M. Wheeler, "London in A.D. 60," in Royal Commission on Historical Monuments, *Roman London* (London, 1928), 27–32.

corporated into the Roman empire.[1] In 67 (possibly even in 66)
Nero began to send troops forward to Iberia, either in preparation for an expedition against the Albanians (Tacitus), or to
gain possession of "the Gates which led through Iberia into the
country of the Sarmatians" (Pliny). In 68, the detachments
were recalled to serve against C. Julius Vindex in Gaul.[2]

Events in Europe, A.D. 67–68.—In the winter of A.D. 67–68
the Roxolani wiped out two Roman cohorts on the lower Danube, and as no attention was paid to the incident, they again
invaded Moesia in the winter of 68–69, with a force of nine
thousand horsemen. While returning homeward weighted down
with booty, they were attacked by the Moesian troops, and, as
rain had set in and the horses of the Roxolani were continually
sinking deep in the melting snow, they "were cut down as if their
hands were tied."[3]

While Nero was still in Greece (67), the inhabitants of Britain and of Gaul "were becoming more vexed and inflamed than
ever."[4] In Gaul, C. Julius Vindex, governor of Gallia Lugdunen-
sis, raised a revolt against Nero (early in 68). Thereafter Ser.

---

[1] Polemo II "gave up" his kingdom. Suetonius *Nero* 18. *SHA* "Aurelianus" xxi.
11. Eutropius vii. 14. Aurelius Victor *de Caes.* v. 2; *epit.* v. 4. Franz Cumont,
"L'annexion du Pont Polémoniaque et de la Petite Arménie," in *Anatolian Studies
Presented to Sir William Mitchell Ramsay* (Manchester, 1923), 109–119.

[2] Tacitus *Hist.* i. 6. Suetonius *Nero* 19. Dio lxiii. 8. 1. Pliny *NH* vi. 40.
Tacitus states that the expedition was directed against the Albani. Mommsen,
The Provinces of the Roman Empire, II (London, 1909), 62 note 1, says, however,
that the expedition "cannot possibly have been directed against the Albani . . .
only the Alani can be meant." See also Ritterling, "Legio," *RECA,* XII (1924),1259–
60. J. G. C. Anderson, *CAH,* X (1934), 777, 883–884. Mommsen's conjecture is carried further by Rostovtzeff, *Iranians & Greeks in South Russia* (Oxford, 1922), 117,
who speaks of "Nero's project for attacking the Alans in the very seat of their
power, the steppes of Northern Caucasus," and goes on to say that "it seems to have
been Nero's intention to concentrate his forces in the kingdom of Bosporus, which
was to be made a Roman province for the purpose, and thence to open an offensive
against the Sarmatian armies." At this point it is to be noticed merely that Roman
troops were sent to Transcaucasia with the intent of war.

[3] Tacitus *Hist.* i. 79; iii. 24. The Roxolani, Tacitus says, wore coats of mail formed
of plates of iron or very tough hide; for this type of armor, see Berthold Laufer,
Chinese Clay Figures, I (Chicago, 1914. Field Museum of Natural History, Anthro-
pological Series, XIII. 2), 220–222.

[4] Dio lxii. 22. 1a (Zonaras xi. 13).

Sulpicius Galba was proclaimed emperor in Spain (April), and Nero ended his career (June). Of the claimants to the principate in the "year of the four emperors," Galba lost his life in January, M. Salvius Otho in April, and Aulus Vitellius in December, 69.

VII

The Roman East, A.D. 69.—In the summer of A.D. 69, T. Flavius Vespasianus[1] was proclaimed emperor in Egypt and Syria.[2] In Pontus, Anicetus, "once a very powerful personage" and formerly commander of the fleet for Polemo II of Pontus, led an uprising against Vespasian in the name of Vitellius, and with a force "which was far from negligible" seized Trapezus (Trebizond). He was defeated later on by Virdius Geminus and betrayed into the hands of the Roman commander.[3]

The Danube and the Rhine, A.D. 69–70.—Late in 69 (November) the Dacians "stormed the winter quarters of the auxiliary infantry and cavalry, and occupied both banks of the Danube"; they were repulsed by C. Licinius Mucianus, governor of Syria, who was on his way through Moesia to support the cause of Vespasian in Italy.[4] In the winter of 69–70 the Sarmatians crossed

---

[1] B. W. Henderson, *Civil War and Rebellion in the Roman Empire, A.D. 69–70* (London, 1908). E. G. Hardy, "Plutarch, Tacitus, and Suetonius on Galba and Otho," in his *Studies in Roman History,* 1st series (2d ed., London, 1910), 294–333; "The Four Emperors' Year," in his *Studies,* 2d series (London, 1909), 130–268. In *RECA,* see Nagl, "Salvius" (21), 2. Reihe, I (1920), 2035–55; Münzer, "Sulpicius" (63), IV (1931), 772–808.

E. A. Freeman, "The Flavian Caesars" [1863], in his *Historical Essays,* 2d series (London, 1873), 307–339. H. C. Newton, *The Epigraphical Evidence for the Reigns of Vespasian and Titus* (Ithaca, N. Y., 1901). Weynand, "Flavius" (206) (207), *RECA,* VI (1909), 2623–95, 2695–2729. Wilhelm Weber, *Josephus und Vespasian* (Stuttgart, 1921). H. M. T. Skerrett, *C. Suetonii Tranquilli . . . divus Vespasianus* (Philadelphia, Pa., 1924). A. W. Braithwaite, *C. Suetonii Tranquilli divus Vespasianus* (Oxford, 1927). Henderson, *Five Roman Emperors: Vespasian, Titus, Domitian, Nerva, Trajan, A.D. 69–117* (Cambridge, 1927). Christine Longford, *Vespasian and Some of His Contemporaries* (Dublin, 1928).

[2] Tacitus *Hist.* ii. 82 says that, as a measure of precaution, Vespasian sent envoys to Parthia and Armenia, so that "when the legions were engaged in the civil war, the country in their rear might not be exposed to attack." Vologeses responded by offering Vespasian 40,000 Parthian cavalry. Tacitus *Hist.* iv. 51. Suetonius *Vespasianus* 6. 4.

[3] Tacitus *Hist.* iii. 47–48.   [4] Tacitus *Hist.* iii. 46.

the Danube, defeated and killed Fonteius Agrippa, governor of
Moesia, and laid waste the province; the invaders were eventually driven out (70) by Rubrius Gallus.[5]

On the upper Danube, in 69, the supporters of Vespasian en-
rolled in their support the leaders of the Jazyges, and Sido and
Italicus, kings of the Suebi.[6]

"At the same time there was trouble in Germany; indeed,"
Tacitus continues, "the Roman cause almost suffered disaster
because of the negligence of the generals, the mutinous spirit of
the legions, the assaults from without the empire, and the treachery of our allies."[7] In 69 Julius Civilis, a Batavian who had long
served in the Roman army, led an uprising which at the beginning was in the interest of Vespasian. He gained the support
of the Canninefates and Frisii, the Bructeri, and the Tencteri;
finally "all Germany," including the Chatti, Usipetes, and Mat-
tiaci, joined him. Legionary soldiers, in addition to German
auxiliaries, deserted the Roman standards. Civilis was defeated
only after eight legions had been sent into Gaul; he retreated to
the island of the Batavi, where he finally surrendered, in 70, to
Q. Petilius Cerialis.

In Britain hostilities broke out in 69 among the Brigantes between opposing parties led by Venutius, "who hated the name of
Rome," and Cartimandua, who had delivered Caratacus to the
emperor Claudius; Roman troops were drawn into the war when
the queen appealed to Vettius Bolanus for aid.[8]

Parthia and China

Between A.D. 34 and 63 disturbances and wars in Armenia and
Bosporus were followed by barbarian outbreaks in Europe.

---

[5] Tacitus *Hist.* iii. 46. Josephus *BJ* vii. 4. 3 (89–95).

[6] Tacitus *Hist.* iii. 5, 21. Martin Bang, *Die Germanen im römischen Dienst* (Berlin, 1906), 58–59.

[7] Tacitus *Hist.* iii. 46; iv. 12–37, 54–79, 85–86; v. 14–26. Josephus *BJ* vii. 4. 2
(75–88). Dio lxvi. 3. 3. See, more particularly, Camille Jullian, *Histoire de la Gaule*,
IV (Paris, [1913]), 199–222. Stein, "Iulius" (186), *RECA*, X (1917), 550–567.

[8] Tacitus *Hist.* iii. 44–45.

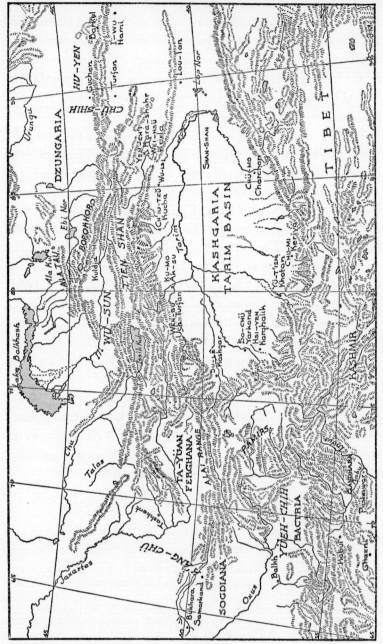

5. The "Western Regions" of the Chinese.

Also, as has been pointed out, the disturbances in Armenia during the period were coincident with civil wars in Parthia which involved Hyrcania and the eastern provinces of the empire as well as Mesopotamia. But between 6 B.C. and A.D. 18 the disturbances in Armenia which led Augustus to interfere in the affairs of the kingdom had likewise been accompanied by civil wars east of the Euphrates, so that during these two periods disorders in Armenia which were followed by barbarian uprisings in Europe were contemporaneous with unrest and strife in the Parthian dominions. Now, when the comparison of events is extended to Central Asia, it becomes evident in turn that the two periods under discussion were also times of disturbance in Chinese Turkistan. Consequently, in order to gain some realization of the conditions under which various outbreaks took place in Europe, it will be necessary to carry the investigation eastward to include events recorded by the historians of China.

The history of the kingdoms in the Tarim basin (Chinese Turkistan) is closely bound up with the history of political affairs in China, and more particularly with the changes of governmental policy in regard to the peoples on the borders of the empire. In the present publication, which is an initial contribution to a study of the barbarian invasions, it has, however, seemed desirable to restrict the statement given to the actual occurrences on the frontier, though later, in dealing with the events of the third century, a detailed discussion of the conditions which ultimately led to the downfall of the Han dynasty will be imperative.

I

Events in Kashgaria, Bactria, and Parthia, 60–57 B.C.—Any historical narrative must of necessity begin *in medias res,* but in dealing with occurrences in Central Asia which belong to the period here taken for investigation (58 B.C.–A.D. 107) a point of departure which is not entirely arbitrary may be found in the circumstance that in 60 B.C. the Han government, after a long-

continued struggle with the Mongolian Hsiung-nu, succeeded
in establishing a durable control over both the northern and
southern routes in the Tarim basin. In 60 B.C., Hsien-hsien-
ch'an, the Jih-chu prince of the Hsiung-nu, and head of the Hu-
yen tribe at Barkul, abandoned his allegiance to the *shan-yü*
or great khan of the Hsiung-nu (frequently spoken of as the
Huns) and placed himself in the hands of Chêng Chi, commander of the Chinese troops in the "Western Regions"; thereafter he was accorded a position of honor at the court of Hsüan
Ti (73–48 B.C.). Prior to 60 B.C. the Chinese had been in control
of the southern route in the Tarim basin; the Hsiung-nu, on the
other hand, had exercised authority over the oasis-kingdoms
south of the T'ien Shan, and the Jih-chu prince had maintained
a body of officials for the collection of tribute from them. The
defection of Hsien-hsien-ch'an permitted the Chinese to take the
place of the Hsiung-nu on the northern route, and in 59 Chêng
Chi was appointed the first "protector general" of the Western
Regions, with jurisdiction over the kingdoms as far west as the
Wu-sun, on the river Ili, and the K'ang-chü, on the Jaxartes.[1]

The change of control on the northern route in the Tarim was
followed by significant events beyond the Pamirs, in Russian
Turkistan, Afghanistan, and northern India.

---

[1] J. A. M. de Moyriac de Mailla, *Histoire générale de la Chine*, III (Paris, 1777),
140–141. Alexander Wylie, "Notes on the Western Regions," *JAI*, 10 (1881), 22–23.
E. H. Parker, "The Turko-Scythian Tribes," *China Review*, 20 (1893), 124–125.
J. J. M. de Groot, *Die Hunnen der vorchristlichen Zeit* (Berlin, 1921), 205–207;
Die Westlande Chinas in der vorchristlichen Zeit, hrsg. von Otto Franke (Berlin,
1926), 50. Léon Wieger, *Textes historiques: histoire politique de la Chine depuis
l'origine jusqu'en 1912* (2e éd., Hsien hsien, 1922), 522–523. See also Sir Aurel
Stein, *Serindia* (Oxford, 1921), 1236–37. Walter Fuchs, "Das Turfangebiet," *Ost-
asiatische Zeitschrift*, 13 (1926), 126.

Concerning the title "protector general," Edouard Chavannes, "Les pays d'Occident d'après le Heou Han chou," *T'oung pao*, 2. sér., 8 (1907), 154 note 1, says:
"Pour reconnaître les mérites de Tcheng Ki, le gouvernement Chinois le chargea
de protéger, non plus seulement la route du Sud, à l'Ouest de Chan-chan (au Sud
du Lop nor), mais encore la route du Nord à l'Ouest de Kiu-che (Tourfan) ; il
eut donc à protéger simultanément les deux routes et c'est pourquoi on l'appela
(le Protecteur) général." See also Stein, "The Seat of the Protector General,"
Innermost Asia (Oxford, 1928), 790–797.

The northern route[2] ran from Kan-su, by way of Turfan, to Kashgar; from the latter point it passed westward across the Ts'ung-ling Mountains[3] to Ta-yüan (Ferghana), through which it continued to the country of the K'ang-chü, situated between the Jaxartes (Syr Darya) and the Oxus (Amu Darya). The southern route[4] in the Tarim ran, from the same starting point, by way of Yarkand, across the Pamirs to the territory of the Yüeh-chih. Each of the two routes continued through Balkh and Merv to the dominions of Parthia.

In (chronological) succession to the changes which took place during 60–59 B.C. in the Tarim basin, events of importance occurred in western India, for in 58 the Sacas were defeated

---

[2] According to the *Hou Han Shu*, "La route du Nord est celle qui, partant de la cour royale antérieure de Kiu-che (Tourfan), longe les montagnes du Nord, suit le Fleuve et, allant vers l'Ouest, débouche à Sou-le (Kachgar); plus à l'Ouest, la route franchit les Ts'ong-ling (Pamirs) et débouche à Ta-yüan (Ura-tepe), dans le K'ang-kiu (Samarkand) et chez les Yen-ts'ai (Alains)." Chavannes, *T'oung pao*, 8 (1907), 170. See also Wylie, *JAI*, 10 (1881), 21. Chavannes, "Les pays d'Occident d'après le Wei lio," *T'oung pao*, 6 (1905), 531 note 1. Groot, *Westlande*, 47–48.

On the routes in the Tarim, see M. S. Bell, "The Great Central Asian Trade Route from Peking to Kashgaria," *PRGS*, n.s., 12 (1890), 57–93. Fernand Grenard, "Routes du Turkestan," in J. L. Dutreuil de Rhins, *Mission scientifique dans la Haute Asie*, III (Paris, 1898), 212–223. Chavannes, *T'oung pao*, 6 (1905), 529–535. Albert Herrmann, *Die alten Seidenstrassen zwischen China und Syrien*, I (Berlin, 1910), 77–116; "Die Seidenstrassen vom alten China nach dem römischen Reich," *MGGW*, 58 (1915), 472–500. Stein, *Serindia*, 407, 417–419; "Innermost Asia; its Geography as a Factor in History," *Geographical Journal*, 65 (1925), 377–403, 473–501; *On Ancient Central-Asian Tracks* (London, 1933). Owen Lattimore, "Caravan Routes of Inner Asia," *Geographical Journal*, 72 (1928), 497–531.

[3] See "The Ts'ung-ling Mountains," Sven Hedin, *Southern Tibet*, VIII (Stockholm, 1922), 3–88; Ts'ung-ling was the name given by the Chinese in the first century B.C. to the mountain passages that led to the countries west of the Tarim basin.

For description of routes from Kashgar westward, see Hugo Toepfer, "Der Weg von Osch nach Kaschgar," *Geographische Zeitschrift*, 7 (1901), 323–333, 377–383. Hedin, *Through Asia*, I (New York, 1899), 126–142; *Central Asia and Tibet*, I (London, 1903), 14–39; *Southern Tibet*, IX (Stockholm, 1922), 1–85. Stein, *Innermost Asia*, 847–851. See also Herrmann, *Historical and Commercial Atlas of China* (Cambridge, Mass., Harvard-Yenching Institute, 1935), 17, 27.

[4] Of the two great routes, "celle qui va parallèlement aux montagnes du Sud en passant au Nord de ces montagnes et qui suit le Fleuve pour se diriger vers l'Ouest et arriver à So-kiu (Yarkand), est la route du Sud; cette route du Sud franchit à l'Ouest les Ts'ong-ling (Pamirs) et débouche dans les royaumes des Ta Yue-tche (Indo-scythes) et de Ngan-si (Parthes)." Chavannes, *T'oung pao*, 8 (1907), 169–170. See also Wylie, *JAI*, 10 (1881), 21, 39. Groot, *Westlande*, 47–48, 92.

by the Indian king Vikramaditya of Ujjain, and the victory
was commemorated by the establishment of the Vikrama era
(58 B.C.).[5]

Again, in Parthia, as has already been pointed out (ch. I,
§ II), Phraates III was murdered, in or about 58, by his sons
Mithridates and Orodes. Thereafter war broke out between the
two brothers, and Mithridates was forced to seek refuge in
Syria, where he enlisted the interest of Gabinius. His invasion of
Parthia in 56 was at first successful, but in 54 he was defeated
and put to death. It was also in 54 that M. Licinius Crassus made
his first incursion into Parthian territory.

Events in Kashgaria, Bactria, and Parthia, 56–6 B.C.—For
half a century after the establishment of Chinese control over
Kashgaria, order was maintained on the routes to the West. On
one occasion only was there an outbreak such as to interfere with
the peaceful movement of the caravans. In 42 B.C. the Ch'iang,[6]
who inhabited the Tsaidam depression and the vicinity of Kuku
Nor, made a descent upon the route in Kan-su and penetrated
into the valley of the river Wei. The incursion created alarm at
the Han court, but by the end of the same year the invaders had
been driven back.

No available information concerning events in the region between the Oxus and the Indus points to any special disturbance
in or about 42. Farther west, however, at the end of 41 the Parthians, under the leadership of Pacorus and Labienus, invaded
Syria, and the wars which followed from this occurrence continued until 30. It should perhaps be pointed out that the earlier

---

[5] E. J. Rapson, *CHI*, I (1922), 571, see also 167–168.

W. W. Tarn, *The Greeks in Bactria & India* (Cambridge, 1938), 329–330, 334–335, is of opinion that in 58 the Saca king Maues was defeated on the river Jhelum, and that in the same year his governor at Kapisa was expelled in consequence of a Greek rising led by Amyntas.

[6] The Ch'iang had also made attacks in 62–60 B.C.; for the two occurrences, see Mailla, *Histoire générale de la Chine*, III, 135–140, 167–168. Wylie, "History of the Western Keang," *REO*, 1 (1882), 436–437. Wieger, *Textes historiques*, I, 514–522, 549–550. Groot, *Westlande*, 197–199, 201–220. See also Chavannes, *T'oung pao*, 6 (1905), 526 note 8. Stein, *Serindia*, 1130–31.

Parthian war (54–50) had been precipitated by the action of Crassus in crossing the Euphrates.

The invasion of Mesopotamia from Syria in 27 B.C. by Tiridates II suggests a continuation of the events of 31 (see ch. I, § VII). There may, however, have been disturbances in the Parthian East which afforded Tiridates the opportunity for his momentarily successful attempt to gain the throne. Horace, alluding to the situation in 27–25, pictures Maecenas as "fearing what the Seres may be plotting, and Bactra once ruled by Cyrus, and the discordant tribes on the banks of Tanais."[7] It seems, indeed, to have been between 30 and 25 that the Pahlavas (Parthians) overthrew Hermaeus, the last of the Yavana rulers (the successors of Alexander), whose kingdom was situated in the upper Kabul valley.[8]

Events in Kashgaria, Parthia, and Armenia, 6 B.C.–A.D. 33.— In or about 6 B.C. conditions in Kashgaria underwent a change, and the disturbances which had their beginning at that time continued until A.D. 16.

Nothing is recorded concerning the earlier phases of the outbreaks beyond the fact that between 6 B.C. and A.D. 5 the thirty-six kingdoms of the Western Regions were split up into fifty-five.[9] It may, however, be suggested as a possibility that the condition of unrest in the Tarim reflected the interest and activity of Wang Mang, who was in control of the government, in promoting trade with the countries of southeast Asia and the Indian Ocean.[10]

In or about A.D. 2 the Han government established a "new

---

[7] Horace *Carm.* iii. 29. 26–28. "Tanais" here means the Jaxartes, see the edition of Hermann Schütz (3. Aufl., Berlin, 1889), 252.

[8] E. J. Rapson, *CHI*, I (1922), 560–561, 701, but various dates have been given for the event.

For the career of Hermaeus, see now Tarn, *The Greeks in Bactria & India*, 339–343, 349–350, 473. By way of addendum to his account, it is of interest to note that, in 25 B.C., after the disappearance of Hermaeus, the Chinese government resumed relations with Chi-pin.

[9] Chavannes, *T'oung pao*, 8 (1907), 155.

[10] For Wang Mang's activities in the south, see Paul Pelliot, *T'oung pao*, 13 (1912), 459–461. Albert Herrmann, "Ein alter Seeverkehr zwischen Abessinien und Süd-China bis zum Beginn unserer Zeitrechnung," *ZGEB*, 1913, 553–561.

route of the north" in order to shorten the distance between the
Yü-mên-kuan, the "Jade Gate," and Ulterior Chü-shih, the modern Guchen or Ku-ch'êng-tzŭ. The establishment of the new route
excited the hostility of the king of Ulterior Chü-shih, and after
some dispute he moved away with his people and joined the
Hsiung-nu.[11]

In A.D. 9 Wang Mang, who had been in control of the central
government since 1 B.C., usurped the throne of China, and serious difficulties at once arose with the Hsiung-nu and the kingdoms of the Western Regions. In 10 the people of Ulterior Chü-
shih again revolted, and in the same year the Hsiung-nu gained
possession of Anterior Chü-shih, the modern Turfan.[12] After this
occurrence, as the whole of Kashgaria was in revolt, some even
of the Chinese officials in the Tarim deserted to the Mongolian
tribes. In 16 "the Hsiung-nu made a grand attack on the northern border of China, while the Western Regions were broken up
and scattered like loose tiles."[13] At the same time Yen-ch'i (Kara-
shahr) revolted, and in the fighting which ensued the "protector
general" lost his life. His successor attacked Yen-ch'i with
the assistance of levies from So-chü (Yarkand) and Ch'iu-tzŭ
(Kucha), but was defeated by the combined forces of Yen-ch'i,
Ku-mo (Ak-su), and other kingdoms. The consequence of these
disturbances was that communications between China and the
Tarim basin were completely cut off.

The series of outbreaks in the western territories of China
from 6 B.C. to A.D. 16 constitutes the background for the long
succession of disturbances in Parthia and Armenia which began
when Augustus ordered Tiberius to Armenia in 6 B.C. In A.D. 17

[11] Wylie, *JAI*, 11 (1882), 109–110. Chavannes, *T'oung pao*, 6 (1905), 533 note 1,
see also 528, 556. Groot, *Westlande*, 177–178. See also Stein, *Serindia*, 418–419,
705–710; *Innermost Asia*, 571–572.

[12] Wylie, *JAI*, 11 (1882), 110–111. Parker, *China Review*, 21 (1895), 130–131.
Chavannes, *T'oung pao*, 8 (1907), 155. Groot, *Hunnen*, 270–272; *Westlande*, 179–
180.

[13] Wylie, *JAI*, 11 (1882), 112. See also Mailla, *Histoire générale de la Chine*,
III, 242. Wieger, *Textes historiques*, I, 617. Groot, *Westlande*, 181–182.

Tiberius directed attention in the Senate to serious commotions in the East, yet a settlement of Armenian affairs was achieved without difficulty by Germanicus in A.D. 18, a circumstance which may be set down to the stabilization of conditions in Kashgaria under the auspices of the Hsiung-nu.

The termination of Chinese control and the renewal of Hsiung-nu domination in the Western Regions was followed by the rise of Gondopharnes,[14] the patron of St. Thomas (the apostle of India) and the central personage, in Christian legend, of the "three wise men of the East." Gondopharnes ruled over an empire in northwest India, and his exploits appear to have included the conquest of Parthian territories in eastern Iran. It is probable that the "surrounding nations" with which Artabanus III waged war at some time between A.D. 18 and 33 were in the Parthian East.

A review of events from 60 B.C. to A.D. 33 shows that the major disturbances in Parthia from 58 to 54 B.C. and from 3 B.C. to A.D. 11 (to 18 in Armenia) followed upon important changes in Kashgaria, first, when the Chinese took the place of the Hsiung-nu on the northern route in the Tarim, and, second, when uprisings of the kingdoms in the Western Regions permitted the Hsiung-nu to regain their former position of dominance. Wars in the Tarim basin, then, were followed by disturbances in Parthia and Armenia, and eventually by barbarian outbreaks in Europe.

It should not be overlooked, however, that various wars occurred on the Euphrates frontier while the kingdoms of Kashgaria were at peace, for Parthia and Rome were in conflict from 54 to 50 and from 41 to 30 B.C. In the first of these instances, hostilities were begun by Licinius Crassus; in the second, the Parthian invasion of Syria was instigated by the Roman refugee Labienus, and the continuation of the war was the response in-

---

[14] Rapson, *CHI*, I (1922), 576–580. Louis de la Vallée-Poussin, *L'Inde aux temps des Mauryas* (Paris, 1930), 272–280. Ernst Herzfeld, *Archaeological History of Iran* (London, British Academy, 1935), 61–66.

spired by the ambitions of Antony. Hence it becomes evident
that the disturbances in which Parthia was involved arose either
from wars in Kashgaria or from hostilities initiated by Rome.

II

Events in Kashgaria, Bactria, Parthia, and Armenia, A.D. 33–
51.—The end of Wang Mang's usurpation came in A.D. 23, when
he was killed in a military revolt.[1] In 23–24 the Tibetan Ch'iang
again renewed their attacks on the route in Kan-su.[2]

In A.D. 25 Liu Hsiu succeeded in placing himself upon the
throne as the first emperor (Kuang-wu Ti) of the Later Han
dynasty, with his capital at Lo-yang in Ho-nan. The disorders
which attended the overthrow of Wang Mang had, however, permitted various leaders[3] to set themselves up independently in the
border provinces, and when Liu Hsiu assumed the imperial dignity, Kung-sun Shu, governor of Ssŭ-ch'uan, proclaimed himself emperor of Ch'êng, Wei Hsiao established himself in
Shen-hsi and Kan-su, and Lu Fang, aided by the Hsiung-nu,
seized territory in northern Shan-hsi. It was not until 32 that
Kuang-wu Ti was in a position to proceed vigorously against
these contestants for power. In that year, however, he took the
field in person against Wei Hsiao, who died shortly after sus-
taining a defeat. In 33 the emperor sent Wu Han against Lu
Fang and his allies, the Hsiung-nu; the Chinese general was defeated in the first encounter, but in 34 gained the advantage,
and Lu Fang fled. In 35 Kung-sun Shu sent an army into the
valley of the Wei Ho; after the defeat of this invasion, Wu Han

---

[1] For an appreciative estimate of the work of Wang Mang, see Hu Shih, "Wang
Mang, the Socialist Emperor of Nineteen Centuries Ago," *JNCB*, 59 (1928), 218–
230. Edouard Chavannes, *Les documents chinois découverts par Aurel Stein dans
les sables du Turkestan oriental* (Oxford, 1913), vii, thinks that "Wang Mang
paraît avoir maintenu le prestige des armes chinoises dans l'Ouest jusqu'à la fin
de son règne, et c'est pendant l'époque troublée du début de la seconde dynastie
Han que le pouvoir de la Chine subit une éclipse momentanée."

[2] Alexander Wylie, "History of the Western Keang," *REO*, 1 (1882), 437–438.

[3] Carl Arendt, "Synchronistische Regententabellen zur Geschichte der chinesischen Dynastien," *MSOS*, 3 (1900), 71–72.

advanced into Ssŭ-ch'uan and fought a battle under the walls of the capital, Ch'êng-tu (36) ; Kung-sun Shu died of a wound received in the battle, and Ch'êng-tu was sacked.

While these events were in progress, the Ch'iang invaded the western borders of Shen-hsi (34), and campaigns in 35 and 36 were required in order to bring them into subjection.[4]

It is not essential to continue here the account of Kuang-wu Ti's efforts to restore order in China. It is, however, of importance to point out that the founder of the Later Han dynasty consistently refused to be drawn into war for the recovery of Chinese control in the Western Regions, since his decision left Kashgaria open to the ambitions of Hsien of Yarkand.

When, in the reign of Wang Mang, the kingdoms of the Tarim threw off their allegiance and accepted the domination of the Hsiung-nu, Yen, king of So-chü (Yarkand), maintained relations with China, in opposition to the Hsiung-nu, and this policy was followed by his son K'ang (18–33). In 33 Hsien,[5] brother of K'ang, became king of So-chü, and at once extended his dominions by the conquest of Hsi-yeh (Karghalik) and Chü-mi (near Keriya). Moreover, in the course of the next few years all the kingdoms east of the Pamirs, as they were suffering under the heavy tribute exacted by the Hsiung-nu, accepted his leadership. In 38 Hsien, in concert with An, king of Shan-shan (Lop),[6]

[4] Wylie, REO, 1 (1882), 439. Léon Wieger, Textes historiques (2ᵉ éd., Hsien hsien, 1922), 659–660.

[5] Chavannes, "Les pays d'Occident d'après le Heou Han chou," T'oung pao, 8 (1907), 155, 157, 196–197. Wieger, Textes historiques, I, 659–660.

For the history of Yarkand, see Carl Ritter, Die Erdkunde von Asien, V (Berlin, 1837), 389–408. E. H. Parker, "Yarkand," AQR, 3d ser., 21 (1906), 22–35. Chavannes, T'oung pao, 8 (1907), 196–204. Sir Aurel Stein, Ancient Khotan (Oxford, 1907), 86–88; Serindia (Oxford, 1921), 82–84.

[6] Chavannes, T'oung pao, 8 (1907), 197. Wieger, Textes historiques, I, 660.

For the history of Shan-shan, see Sir George Macartney, "Notices from Chinese Sources on the Ancient Kingdom of Lau-lan or Shen-shen," Geographical Journal, 21 (1903), 260–265. Chavannes, "Les pays d'Occident d'après le Wei lio," T'oung pao, 6 (1905), 531–533 note. Karl Himly, "Einleitung," in August Conrady, Die chinesischen Handschriften und sonstigen Kleinfunde Sven Hedins in Lou-lan (Stockholm, 1920), 1–16. Stein, "Historical Notices of Lop, Shan-shan, and Lou-lan," Serindia, 318–345. Albert Herrmann, Lou-lan; China, Indien und Rom im Lichte der Ausgrabungen am Lobnor (Leipzig, 1931).

sent an embassy to Kuang-wu Ti with tribute and presents, but the effort to enlist the support of the emperor against the Hsiung-nu led to no satisfactory result. In 41 Hsien again approached the court with the request that he be appointed "protector general of the Western Regions"; the dignity was first granted and then revoked,[7] with the result that the king of So-chü declared his independence by assuming the title, and claimed recognition in Kashgaria as *shan-yü* or great khan. In addition, he at once embarked on a career of conquest by attacking Ch'iu-tzŭ (Kucha)[8] and other kingdoms on the northern route.

The continued aggressions of Hsien had the result that in 45 eighteen kingdoms, among them Shan-shan (Lop) and Chü-shih (Turfan), sent envoys to Kuang-wu Ti asking that a "protector general" be appointed as a defense against the growing power of So-chü. The request was denied, and the immediate consequence was that Hsien redoubled his exertions to subdue the kingdoms of the Western Regions.[9] In 46 he attacked An, king of Shan-shan, and drove him into the mountains, and in the winter of the same year defeated and killed the king of Ch'iu-tzŭ (Kucha) and annexed his kingdom. Consequently, and presumably in 47, Shan-shan and Turfan submitted to the Hsiung-nu.

At this point the king of Kuei Sai (supposedly the Saca ruler of a principality on the upper Oxus) killed the representative of Hsien; the latter in requital attacked and overthrew the king,

---

[7] For the circumstances, see Chavannes, *T'oung pao*, 8 (1907), 197–198. Wieger, *Textes historiques*, I, 661–663.

[8] For the history of Kucha, see Parker, "The Ancient City and State of Kutchar," *AQR*, 3d ser., 32 (1911), 141–166. Sylvain Lévi, "Le 'Tokharian B', langue de Koutcha," *Journal asiatique*, 11. sér., 2 (1913), 311–380. Heinrich Lüders, "Zur Geschichte und Geographie Ostturkestans," *SAWB*, 1922, 246–247. Paul Pelliot, "Note sur les anciens noms de Kučā, d'Aqsu et d'Uč-Turfan," *T'oung pao*, 22 (1923), 126–132. Stein, *Innermost Asia* (Oxford, 1928), 803–807.

[9] Chavannes, *T'oung pao*, 8 (1907), 198–200. Wieger, *Textes historiques*, I, 663–664.
The king of Shan-shan appealed to the emperor, but "The Son of Heaven" replied: "Maintenant il est impossible de faire sortir des commissaires et de grandes armées; si vous, les divers royaumes, vous avez une puissance qui ne vous satisfait pas, allez où il vous plaira, que ce soit à l'Est ou à l'Ouest, au Sud ou au Nord." Chavannes, 200.

and appointed in his place a certain Ssŭ-chien, a native of the country.[10] Thereafter Hsien installed his son Tsê-lo as king of Ch'iu-tzŭ and, for his protection, established Ssŭ-chien in a near-by kingdom.

The assault upon the envoy of So-chü (Yarkand) by the king of Kuei Sai may have some relation to the warfare then in progress in the Pamirs and Hindu Kush. South of the Oxus, within the years 40 and 50, Kujula Kadphises[11] (known to the Chinese as Ch'iu-chiu-ch'io), the *hsi-hou*[12] of Kuei-shuang, consolidated the five principalities of the Yüeh-chih, and declared himself king; he was the founder of the Kushan dynasty.

Some time after Hsien's annexation of Ch'iu-tzŭ (Kucha), and presumably in 50, the people of the kingdom rebelled and called in the Hsiung-nu, and in the uprising both Tsê-lo and Ssŭ-chien lost their lives.[13] The kingdom of Kucha, which thus passed from the control of Yarkand, was the focus of important routes

---

[10] Chavannes, *T'oung pao*, 8 (1907), 200 and note 1. The kingdom has not been identified, and its position is not known. Chavannes expresses himself with reserve: "on peut donc se demander si le pays ... n'aurait pas été une principauté du haut Oxus gouvernée par un prince de race Saka et soumise au roi de Yarkand." He adds, "mais je ne trouve aucun moyen de confirmer ou d'infirmer cette hypothèse." Wieger, *Textes historiques*, I, 695, states that Hsien subdued "des petits royaumes de Kotan, de Sogdiane, et des Säi (Saces) du bas Oxus." See also Joseph de Guignes, *Histoire générale des Huns*, I. 2 (Paris, 1756), 113.

[11] The extensive literature on the Kushan kings consists primarily in studies of the literary, numismatic, and epigraphical evidence bearing upon the dates of Kujula Kadphises and Kanishka. Although different opinions are held in regard to these dates, the balance appears weighted in favor of the view that Kadphises I had taken Kabul before A.D. 50, that Wima Kadphises had conquered northwest India before 64, and that Kanishka began his reign in 78. For the literature, see Louis de la Vallée-Poussin, *L'Inde aux temps des Mauryas* (Paris, 1930), 301–374.

[12] Chavannes, *T'oung pao*, 8 (1907), 189–192. See also Hirth, "Nachworte zur Inschrift des Tonjukuk," in Wilhelm Radloff, *Die alttürkischen Inschriften der Mongolei*, 2. Reihe (St. Pétersbourg, 1899), 45–50; W. W. Tarn, "Seleucid-Parthian Studies," *PBA*, 1930, 108; and Berthold Laufer, *The Language of the Yüe-chi or Indo-Scythians* (Chicago, 1917), 6–7.

[13] "Au bout d'un certain nombre d'années." Chavannes, *T'oung pao*, 8 (1907), 200. The specific dates for events between 46 and 55 are not given in the sources. It is known definitely that Hsien took Kucha in 46 and that he annexed Khotan at the end of the period A.D. 25–55. Within these dates fall his expedition to the Oxus, his loss of Kucha "some years later," followed by his invasion of Ta-yüan and his restoration of Yen-liu.

which converged upon it from different directions.[14] It commanded passes which gave access to the regions north of the T'ien Shan and to the country of the Wu-sun; it was the northern terminus of a practicable route across the Taklamakan from Khotan and Yarkand; more especially, it was the halfway station, between Turfan and Kashgar, on the great northern route in the Tarim. The loss of this possession deprived Hsien, at one and the same time, of his hold upon the northern route and of the revenue he derived from tolls levied upon the traffic to and from the West. Nevertheless, the king of Yarkand did not dispute the possession of Ch'iu-tzŭ with the Hsiung-nu; on the other hand, he shifted the point at which he sought to control the trade and, for this purpose, placed a king devoted to his interests over Ta-yüan (Ferghana). In or about 50, then, Hsien led an army across the mountains into Ferghana. The reason assigned for this expedition was that Yen-liu, king of Ta-yüan, had "diminished the tribute and taxes" due to So-chü. Hsien deposed Yen-liu, and appointed Ch'iao-sai-t'i, king of Chü-mi (near Keriya), in his place. When, however, the invading army retired from Ferghana, the K'ang-chü (Sogdiana) made war on the new king, so that "more than a year" after his installation Ch'iao-sai-t'i was driven out and returned to Yarkand. Hsien thereafter restored Yen-liu (in 51?).

The wars of Hsien from 33 to 51 (as recorded in the Chinese annals) are paralleled by disturbances in Parthia (as set forth in the narrative of Tacitus). Thus, his first efforts in Kashgaria (33) were followed by the Parthian invasion of Armenia in 34. Again, his attempts to extend his dominions in the Tarim, which were continuous from 41 to 51, were followed by the conflict between Gotarzes and Vardanes which disrupted Parthia from 41 to 46, and by the opposition to Gotarzes which continued from 46 until his death in 51. Hsien's invasion of Ta-yüan (50) and the war carried on against him by the K'ang-chü were followed

---

[14] Stein, *Innermost Asia*, 805–806.

by the Iberian and Parthian struggle for the possession of Armenia from 51 to 54, which in the end precipitated the intervention of Rome.

Events in Kashgaria, Bactria, Parthia, and Armenia, A.D. 54–63.—In or about 55 Hsien attacked Yü-t'ien (Khotan) and annexed it.[15] In 56 the Ch'iang again rose, and their attacks were not suppressed until 59.[16] In 60 the people of Yü-t'ien rebelled against Hsien and defeated him in two battles. The Hsiung-nu at once took advantage of this situation and, with an army collected from Ch'iu-tzŭ (Kucha) and other kingdoms, attacked So-chü, but were unable to take Hsien's capital. In 61 some of the leading men of So-chü entered into conspiracy with Kuang-tê, the new king of Yü-t'ien, and the latter advanced against So-chü with an army said to have numbered 300,000 men. Kuang-tê seized Hsien at a parley and subsequently put him to death. When news of these occurrences reached the Hsiung-nu, they again assembled an army from the kingdoms on the northern route; on this occasion they laid siege to Yü-t'ien, which they captured and subjected to the payment of an annual tribute.

Kujula Kadphises, when he had established his power north of the Hindu Kush, invaded An-hsi (Parthia), took Kao-fu (Kabul), and subdued P'u-ta (Ghazni?) and Chi-pin (Gandhara). These conquests were made at the expense of Gondopharnes.[17] In or about A.D. 60, Kujula Kadphises was succeeded

[15] At the end of the period A.D. 25–55. Chavannes, *T'oung pao*, 8 (1907), 171; for the events of A.D. 60–61, see 171–172, 201–204.

For the history of Khotan, see Abel Rémusat, *Histoire de la ville de Khotan* (Paris, 1820). Ritter, *Die Erdkunde von Asien*, V, 343–389. A. F. R. Hoernle, "Indo-Chinese Coins [from Khotan] in the British Collection of Central Asian Antiquities," *Indian Antiquary*, 28 (1899), 46–56. Chavannes, *T'oung pao*, 8 (1907), 171–174. Stein, "Historical Notices of Khotan," in his *Ancient Khotan*, 151–184. See also F. W. Thomas, "The Language of Ancient Khotan," *Asia Major*, 2 (1925), 251–271.

[16] Wylie, *REO*, 1 (1882), 441–442.

[17] V. A. Smith, *The Early History of India* (3d ed., Oxford, 1914), 230–235. E. J. Rapson, *CHI*, I (Cambridge, 1922), 562, 576–581, 583. La Vallée-Poussin, *L'Inde aux temps des Mauryas*, 270–280. Ernst Herzfeld, "Sakastan," in his *Archaeologische Mitteilungen aus Iran*, IV (Berlin, 1932), 79–80, 91–116. In *RECA*, Otto, "Hyndopherres," IX (1914), 183–191; Kiessling, "Hyrkania," IX (1914), 511; Herrmann, "Sakastane," 2. Reihe, I (1920), 1811.

by his son Wima Kadphises[18] (Yen-kao-chên), and the second
of the Kushan kings completed the work of his father by the conquest, supposedly before 64, of northwest India.[19] The result
of the successes of the Kushans was that they gained control of
the routes from India by way of Kabul, and from China by way
of Yarkand.[20]

While Kujula Kadphises was pushing forward his conquest
of the dominions of Gondopharnes, the latter, in 55 (the year
in which Hsien attacked Khotan), supported a pretender[21] in
rebellion against Vologeses I and in the seizure of Hyrcania. The
success of this venture was of no long duration, for the Hyrcanians rose against the candidate of Gondopharnes, and he is
not heard of after June, 58.

In Armenia, the struggle between the Iberians and Parthians
came to an end in 54, when Tiridates, the nominee of Vologeses I,
gained possession of the country. Thereafter Nero sent Domitius Corbulo to the Euphrates frontier. Now, although Corbulo
took command in 55, he remained inactive until the end of 57,
and this inactivity has been the subject of prolonged speculation.
If, however, it be understood that there is evidence of friendly
relations between Kadphises and Rome, that Kadphises was at
war with Gondopharnes, and that the unnamed pretender was
holding Hyrcania in the interest of Gondopharnes, it will be
recognized that when Vologeses I was endeavoring to eject the
pretender from Hyrcania, he was, in reality, coöperating with

[18] Rapson, *CHI*, I, 583–585, 703. Some difficulty has arisen from the statement in
the *Hou Han Shu* that Wima Kadphises "à son tour" conquered India, see Chavannes, *T'oung pao*, 8 (1907), 192.

[19] Kadphises I and II maintained their capital at Balkh; Kadphises II appointed
a governor over his possessions in India. Chavannes, *T'oung pao*, 8 (1907), 188
note, 192, 193.

[20] "The Yueh-chi conquests opened up the overland path of commerce between
the Roman empire and India. Kadphises I... imitated, after his conquest of Kābul,
the coinage either of Augustus in his latter years, or the similar coinage of Tiberius
(A.D. 14 to 38)." Vincent Smith, *The Early History of India*, 254. Alfred Foucher,
L'art gréco-bouddhique du Gandhâra, II. 2 (Paris, 1922), 514, 520–526. E. H.
Warmington, *The Commerce between the Roman Empire and India* (Cambridge,
1928), 296–302.

[21] The name of the pretender may have been Vardanes; see p. 96, note 6.

Kadphises against Gondopharnes. It follows, too, that war against Vologeses on the part of Rome would have relieved the pressure upon the candidate of Gondopharnes in Hyrcania. The continued success of Kadphises obviously contributed to the disappearance of the pretender in Hyrcania; on the other hand, the advance of Corbulo into Armenia, late in 57, would seem to indicate that the Hyrcanians had already gained the upper hand. Vologeses, however, did not turn westward (as was to be expected) to save the Armenian kingdom for Tiridates when it was invaded by Corbulo; he relinquished the attempt to recover Hyrcania only when Tigranes, the Roman appointee in Armenia, invaded Adiabene. Between 57 and 60 Corbulo carried out his program in Armenia with complete success, and then became governor of Syria. In 61 there was in the West, no less than in the kingdom of Yarkand, a notable reversal of fortune, for in that year Vologeses I defeated Tigranes, and in 62 he forced the capitulation of Paetus. Nevertheless, in 63 Corbulo had no difficulty in arranging terms of peace.

The sequence of events on the Euphrates frontier has been endowed by Tacitus with an interest which overshadows all other happenings of the time. Consequently, in the events of the years from 55 to 61, the actions of Hsien may seem negligible and of little importance. Yet even his death was an event of significance, for, just as in A.D. 18 disturbances in Armenia came to an end when the Hsiung-nu (in 16) regained control of Kashgaria, so in 63 wars in Armenia terminated abruptly when the overthrow of Hsien (in 61) permitted the Hsiung-nu again to become dominant in the Western Regions.

Observations and Comments

The close correspondence of occurrences in Kashgaria and Parthia during the time of Hsien of Yarkand is not a unique phenomenon; correspondences of the same type are to be observed in 60–58 B.C. and from 6 B.C. to A.D. 18. The special interest of the period from A.D. 33 to 63 is that for it only are there reasonably full accounts of events both in Chinese Turkistan and Iran. The information which is available for this period indicates that wars in Kashgaria led to outbreaks in Bactria, in the Parthian dominions, and on the Euphrates frontier.

When the regions directly affected by outbreaks of war in Kashgaria are considered with reference to the map of Asia, it at once becomes evident that the disturbances followed the course of the great "silk route," which ran from Sera Metropolis, in western China, to the city of Antioch, in the Roman province of Syria.[22] If, however, wars which involved the stations on the routes in the Tarim (the oasis-kingdoms of the Western Regions) invariably gave rise to conflicts west of the Pamirs at different points on the transcontinental route, it follows that these conflicts were coincident with interruptions of trade. The "silk route" was the principal means of communication between the Farther East and the Mediterranean West, and the wealth of the Parthian state was derived from the control and exploitation of the traffic which passed over it. The consequence of this dependence upon the carrying trade was that, from the Oxus to the Euphrates, peace was contingent upon the regularity of the caravans from Central Asia and, conversely, that disturbances which affected even the occupant of the Parthian throne followed any interruption of the traffic from the remoter Orient.

As a result of inquiry into the antecedents of the Parthian attack upon Armenia in A.D. 34, it now appears that, while barbarian outbreaks in Europe occurred in correspondence with disturbances on the Euphrates frontier, the disturbances and wars in Armenia and Parthia which were not initiated by Rome likewise occurred in correspondence with the efforts of the Han government, of the Hsiung-nu, or of Hsien of Yarkand to gain control over the routes in the Tarim basin.

---

[22] The fact that this route has been described by many authorities makes it unnecessary to enter into a discussion of its existence and use. For the literature, see General Bibliography, IV: "Communications East and West."

Chapter III

VESPASIAN · DOMITIAN · TRAJAN

W ITH THE COMING of the Flavian emperors, activities on the northern frontier of the Roman empire give evidence, to all appearance, of a new policy and a re-awakened energy. Thus, territory between the upper Rhine and the upper Danube was occupied by Vespasian and walled off by Domitian, and the wars carried on by the latter against Dece-balus ended with the annexation of Dacia by the emperor Tra-jan. On the northern frontier there were many wars between A.D. 70 and 107. Unfortunately, however, the historical accounts of the barbarian invasions during these years are meager and in-definite, so that the evidence for more than one conflict is to be found only in inscriptions and coins. In regard to the period, in-deed, it is proper to recall the well-known statement of Orosius (vii. 34. 5) that he "should now set forth at length the mighty battles of Diurpaneus, king of the Dacians, with the Roman general Fuscus, and the mighty losses of the Romans, if Cor-nelius Tacitus, who composed the histories of these times with the greatest care, had not said that Sallustius Crispus and very many other historians had approved of passing over in silence the number of our losses, and that he for his own part had chosen the same course before all others." So, again, when information is sought concerning the history of Parthia, the same difficulty presents itself; the Roman historians make only incidental ref-erences to affairs beyond the Euphrates, and the Parthian coins, though they have been subjected to painstaking scrutiny by nu-

mismatists, yield little beyond a name list of kings. Consequently it is a relief to find that the Chinese records for the
period are relatively full and precise, and that, in particular,
they give ample details in regard to the career, in the "Western
Regions," of the great administrator Pan Ch'ao, which lasted for
thirty years.

When, however, it comes to the point of comparing the events
in the histories of Rome, Parthia, and China, a difficulty of quite
another sort presents itself. From A.D. 73 to 102, Pan Ch'ao
was actively engaged in upholding Chinese authority in Kashgaria; on the other hand, within the same period representatives
of the Han government were employed on two occasions (72–
77, 89–91) in the endeavor to destroy the organization of the
Hsiung-nu in Mongolia. Now, when the events of the period are
examined closely, it becomes evident that not only were hostilities in the Tarim basin (as in the time of Hsien) followed by
disturbances in Parthia, but hostilities in Mongolia were likewise followed by disturbances among the northern peoples of
Eurasia as far west as the Vistula and the upper Danube. The
Han government, in fact, sent its officials to regain a position
of dominance in the West, and the conflicts which ensued affected not only the peoples north and south of the T'ien Shan,
but also those north and south of the Caspian and the Black
Sea. Thus a single command of the emperor of China set in motion disturbances which by two entirely distinct geographical
courses eventually reached the northern frontier of the Roman
empire. The new difficulty, then, which arises is that the events
of the period, though they had their beginning in decisions
reached in China and their end (for this inquiry) in a single
chronological series of occurrences in Central Europe, must of
necessity be described under two separate heads. With the intent of emphasizing the essential unity of the disturbances which
spread outward from China (southwestward through Persia,
northwestward through Russia), and which came to a focus in

Central Europe, it would seem desirable to place in the foreground a statement of the terminal occurrences on the Roman frontier, events which are associated more particularly with the reigns of Domitian and Trajan.

Wars in Europe, A.D. 70–107

Vespasian and Domitian on the Rhine and Danube, A.D. 70–84.—After the restoration of peace on the Rhine, in A.D. 70, Vespasian engaged the legions in rebuilding the forts which had been destroyed in the disorders of the preceding years. It may have been in continuation of the same policy that in 74 he entrusted to Cn. Pinarius Cornelius Clemens, legate of Upper Germany, the occupation of the valley of the Neckar and the region of the Black Forest, the area between the upper reaches of the Rhine and Danube which came to be known as the *agri decumates*.[1] The campaign of Cornelius Clemens, which is known from inscriptions, stands out conspicuously because the literary sources make no reference to barbarian outbreaks at or about this particular time. Yet within the years 74–76 the coins of Vespasian record eight salutations for victories concerning which the histories of the period provide not even sufficient grounds for reasonable conjecture.[2] Hence it is of importance to note that, in addition to the governor of Germania Superior, an unnamed general received the honors of a triumph for successes against the Germans (*ob res in Germania prospere gestas*),[3] and that the

---

[1] See Karl Zangemeister, "Zur Geschichte der Neckar-Länder in römischer Zeit," *NHJ*, 3 (1893), 9–16. H. C. Newton, *The Epigraphical Evidence for the Reigns of Vespasian and Titus* (Ithaca, N. Y., 1901), 15–17. Ernst Fabricius, *Die Besitznahme Badens durch die Römer* (Heidelberg, 1905). Weynand, "Flavius" (206), *RECA*, VI (1909), 2661–63. B. W. Henderson, *Five Roman Emperors* (Cambridge, 1927), 89–94. Emil Ritterling, *Fasti des römischen Deutschland* (Wien, 1932), 22–23.

[2] For the coins of 74–76, see Harold Mattingly and E. A. Sydenham, *The Roman Imperial Coinage*, II (London, 1926), 12–13; Mattingly, *Coins of the Roman Empire in the British Museum*, II (London, 1930), xxiv–xxv. See also Edouard Maynial, "Les salutations impériales de Vespasien," *MEFR*, 22 (1902), 347–359. Weynand, *RECA*, VI (1909), 2658–59, 2664, 2667, 2668–69.

[3] *CIL*, VI, 37,088. Edmund Groag in Ritterling, *Fasti des römischen Deutschland*, 23, points out that there is no good reason to identify him with Cornelius Clemens.

brothers Cn. Domitius Tullus and Cn. Domitius Lucanus were decorated for services rendered (in succession) *adversus Germanos,* presumably in the years 74 and 75.[4] Further, at some time in the years 75–78 an army under the command of Q. Julius Cordinus Rutilius Gallicus is known to have carried on war against the Bructeri,[5] on the river Ems; the antecedents of the campaign are not known, but it achieved the success of captur-

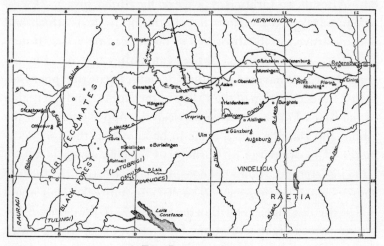

6. THE RAETIAN *limes.*

ing Veleda, the German prophetess who had been the inspiration of the uprising led by Julius Civilis.[6]

For the decade between 71 and 81 no information is available in narrative form concerning affairs on the lower Danube; there is, however, reason to believe that in 76 Domitian, younger son of Vespasian, conducted an expedition against Sarmatians (presumably the Roxolani) who had invaded Moesia.[7]

[4] See Kappelmacher, "Domitius" (65 and 84), *RECA*, V (1905), 1428–30, 1433–35, who places the services of the brothers later than 73, and who thinks that the war in which they were successively engaged may have ended in 75.

[5] Statius *Silv.* i. 4. 89–90. "In the years 75–78," Ronald Syme, *CAH*, XI (1936), 158; "at the latest in 77," Groag, "Rutilius" (19), *RECA*, 2. Reihe, I (1914), 1259. The date 78 is derived from a military diploma of that year, see Ritterling, *Fasti des römischen Deutschland*, 58.

[6] Tacitus *Hist.* iv. 61, 65; v. 22; *Germania* 8.   [7] Maynial, *MEFR*, 22 (1902), 357.

In 82 there would appear to have been disturbances both on the lower Danube and on the Rhine, though the evidence is unsatisfactory.[8] In 83 Domitian[9] (who had succeeded his brother Titus in 81) made war on the Chatti,[10] and thereafter began the systematic fortification of territory beyond the Rhine.[11]

The Romans in Britain, A.D. 71–84.—The strife between Venutius and Cartimandua in 69 had, as Tacitus says, left the Romans with a war on their hands. When, therefore, Petilius Cerialis had ended the rebellion of Julius Civilis, in Gaul, he

---

[8] Some disturbance on the lower Danube is inferred by Ritterling from movements of troops in 83, *WDZ, Korrespondenzblatt*, 25 (1906), 28; see also Syme, *JRS*, 18 (1928), 44. Julius Asbach argues that the beginning of the war with the Chatti was in 82, *Bonner Jahrbücher*, 81 (1886), 29; see also Henderson, *Five Roman Emperors*, 99.

[9] Albert Imhof, *T. Flavius Domitianus: ein Beitrag zur Geschichte der römischen Kaiserzeit* (Halle, 1857). Franz Pichlmayr, *T. Flavius Domitianus: ein Beitrag zur römischen Kaisergeschichte* (Amberg, 1889). Stéphane Gsell, *Essai sur le règne de l'empereur Domitien* (Paris, 1894). Weynand, "Flavius" (77), *RECA*, VI (1909), 2541–96. Giuseppe Corradi, "Domitianus," *DER*, II (1913–14), 1960–2046. R. F. Gephart, *C. Suetonii Tranquilli vita Domitiani* (Philadelphia, Pa., 1922). Henderson, *Five Roman Emperors*, 11–24. Paul Couissin, "Les triomphes de Domitien," *Revue archéologique*, 5. sér., 28 (1928), 65–94.

[10] Suetonius *Domitianus* 6. Frontinus *Strateg.* i. 1. 8; 3. 10; ii. 3. 23; 11. 7. Dio lxvii. 3. 5; 4. 1. Zonaras xi. 19. Eutropius vii. 23. 4. Julius Asbach, "Die Kaiser Domitian und Traian am Rhein," *WDZ*, 3 (1884), 1–26; "Die Kriege der Flavischen Kaiser an der Nordgrenze des Reiches," *Bonner Jahrbücher*, 81 (1886), 26–48. K. H. Zwanziger, *Der Chattenkrieg des Kaisers Domitian* (Würzburg, 1885). Hermann Vieze, *Domitians Chattenkrieg im Lichte der Ergebnisse der Limesforschung* (Berlin, 1902). Weynand, "Flavius" (77), *RECA*, VI (1909), 2555–59. Ludwig Schmidt, *Geschichte der deutschen Stämme*, II. 2 (Berlin, 1915), 355–357. Ronald Syme, "Rhine and Danube legions under Domitian," *JRS*, 18 (1928), 41–55. See also Georg Wolff, *Die südliche Wetterau in vor- und frühgeschichtlicher Zeit* (Frankfurt a. M., 1913), 18.

Suetonius says that Domitian made war on the Chatti "of his own volition," and this is taken to mean that he began the war without provocation. On the other hand, the statement may be taken equally well in the sense that, after an incursion of the Chatti (in 82), Domitian set himself deliberately to punish the German tribes.

[11] On the Roman frontier system in Germany, see Theodor Mommsen, "Der Begriff des Limes" [1894], in his *Gesammelte Schriften*, V (Berlin, 1908), 456–464. H. F. Pelham, *Essays*, ed. by Francis Haverfield (Oxford, 1911), 164–178: "The Roman Frontier System"; 179–211: "The Roman Frontier in Southern Germany." Ernst Kornemann, "Die neueste Limesforschung (1900–1906) im Lichte der römisch-kaiserlichen Grenzpolitik," *Klio*, 7 (1907), 73–121; see also 9 (1909), 500–502. Fabricius, "Limes," *RECA*, XIII (1926), 572–604.

For the archaeological investigations on the frontier, see *Limesblatt: Mittei-*

7. Britain.

was sent by Vespasian to Britain; there, in the term of his governorship (71–74), he reduced the Brigantes to subjection and extended the province to include York. Between 74 and 77 or 78, the next governor, Sex. Julius Frontinus, dealt similarly with the Silures, in Wales.

The successor of Frontinus, Cn. Julius Agricola,[12] first of all completed the conquest of Wales and then advanced into northern England (79–80). During his fourth and fifth seasons (81–82) he occupied the Scotch Lowlands up to the isthmus between the Firth of Forth and the Firth of Clyde. In 83 he extended his operations to Perth. In 84 Agricola again marched northward; on this occasion, however, the tribes had assembled, under a

lungen der Streckenkommissare bei der Reichslimeskommission, 1892–1903 (Trier, 1903). *Der obergermanisch-raetische Limes des Römerreiches,* im Auftrage der Reichs-Limeskommission, hrsg. von Oscar von Sarwey, Felix Hettner, Ernst Fabricius, 1 ff. (Heidelberg, &c., 1894 ff.). Römisch-germanische Kommission, 1 ff. *Bericht* (Frankfurt a. M., 1905 ff.). *Römisch-germanisches Korrespondenzblatt* (Trier, 1908–1916). *Germania: Korrespondenzblatt der Römisch-germanischen Kommission* (Frankfurt a. M., 1917 ff.). See also *Saalburg Jahrbuch: Bericht des Saalburgmuseums,* beginning in 1910. Contributions of importance are also to be found in the *Bonner Jahrbücher,* which began publication in 1842, and the *Westdeutsche Zeitschrift für Geschichte und Kunst,* published between 1882 and 1913.

For the *limes* in Austria, see Akademie der Wissenschaften in Wien, *Der römische Limes in Österreich* (Wien, 1900 ff.). Wilhelm Kubitschek, *Heimatkunde von Nieder-Oesterreich.* Heft 8. *Die Römerzeit* (Wien, [1921]). Eduard Nowotny, "Vom Donau-Limes," *AWW, Anzeiger,* 62 (1925), 89–142.

[12] Information in regard to the campaigns of Agricola is available only in the *Agricola* of Tacitus. The campaigns occupied the years 77 to 83 or 78 to 84, see R. K. McElderry, "The Date of Agricola's Governorship of Britain," *JRS,* 10 (1920), 68–78. J. G. C. Anderson, "When Did Agricola Become Governor of Britain?" *Classical Review,* 34 (1920), 158–161; "The Chronology of Agricola's Career," in *Cornelii Taciti de vita Agricolae,* ed. by H. Furneaux (2d ed., rev. by J. G. C. Anderson, Oxford [1922]), 166–173. Donald Atkinson, "The Governors of Britain from Claudius to Diocletian," *JRS,* 12 (1922), 60, 63–64.

For recent surveys of the archaeological evidence bearing upon the Roman advance in Britain, see Francis Haverfield, *The Roman Occupation of Britain,* rev. by George Macdonald (Oxford, 1924). R. E. M. Wheeler, "The Roman Occupation," in his *Prehistoric & Roman Wales* (Oxford, 1925), 217–274. R. G. Collingwood, *The Archaeology of Roman Britain* (London, [1930]); *Roman Britain* (new ed., Oxford, 1934). Sir George Macdonald, *Roman Britain, 1914–1928* (London, [1931]); *The Roman Wall in Scotland* (2d ed., Oxford, 1934). T. D. Kendrick & C. F. C. Hawkes, *Archaeology in England and Wales, 1914–1931* (London, [1932]), 209–302.

leader named Calgacus, at Mons Graupius (unidentified) to oppose his advance, and were defeated only after a severe struggle. In 85 he was recalled by Domitian.

Domitian's Dacian war, A.D. 85–86.—Late in 85 or early in 86 the Romans became involved in war with the Dacians.[13]

After the civil war of A.D. 68–69 and the frontier disturbances which accompanied it, the Dacians appear to have been reunited into a single kingdom under the leadership of Duras or Diurpaneus; at the beginning of the war with Rome in the reign of Domitian, Diurpaneus abdicated in favor of Decebalus, whose fame stands on a parity with that of Burebista. Dio, in speaking of Decebalus, says "he was shrewd in his understanding of warfare and shrewd also in the waging of war; he judged well when to attack and chose the right moment to retreat; he was an expert in ambuscades and a master in pitched battles; and he knew not only how to follow up a victory well, but also how to manage well a defeat. Hence he showed himself a worthy antagonist of the Romans for a long time."[14]

---

[13] Dio lxvii. 6. 1–6; 7. 1–4; 10. 1–3; lxviii. 9. 3. Suetonius *Dom*. 6. Tacitus *Agricola* 41. Jordanes *Getica* xiii. 76–78. Eutropius vii. 23. Orosius vii. 10. 4.

For the campaigns of Domitian on the Danube and the topography of Dacia, see Julius Jung, *Roemer und Romanen in den Donaulaendern* (2. Aufl., Innsbruck, 1887), 10–15; *Zur Geschichte der Pässe Siebenbürgens* (Innsbruck, 1892). Gsell, *Essai sur le règne de l'empereur Domitien*, 202–232. Victoria Vaschide, *Histoire de la conquête romaine de la Dacie* (Paris, 1903), 27–30. Carl Patsch, "Zum Dakerkriege des Cornelius Fuscus," *JOAI*, 7 (1904), 70–72. Bogdan Filow, *Die Legionen der Provinz Moesia von Augustus bis auf Diokletian* (Leipzig, 1906. *Klio*, VI. Beiheft), 36–47. Ernst Köstlin, *Die Donaukriege Domitians* (Tübingen, 1910). Schmidt, *Geschichte der deutschen Stämme*, II, 173–174. James Berry, "Transylvania and its Relations to Ancient Dacia and Modern Rumania," *Geographical Journal*, 53 (1919), 129–152. Henderson, *Five Roman Emperors*, 155–168. Ronald Syme, "Rhine and Danube Legions under Domitian," *JRS*, 18 (1928), 41–55. In *RECA*, see Stein, "Cornelius" (158), IV (1901), 1341; Brandis, "Dacia," IV (1901), 1965–67; Weynand, "Flavius" (77), VI (1909), 2561–64; Ritterling, "Legio," XII (1924), 1277–78; Franke, "Marcomanni," XIV (1930), 1618; Fluss, "Moesia," XV (1932), 2378–79.

The statements made in regard to the outbreak of the war are enigmatical: Dio says merely that the Romans "became involved" in it; Suetonius remarks that the war was justified "by the destruction of a legion and its commander" (but says nothing of the circumstances preceding the defeat); Jordanes says that the Dacians broke the truce "through fear of the avarice" of Domitian.

[14] Dio lxvii. 6. 1, tr. Earnest Cary (Loeb Classical Library).

In 85 the Dacians invaded Moesia, and in opposing them Oppius Sabinus, governor of the province, was killed. Consequently, in January, 86, Domitian proceeded to Moesia and, though the Dacians made overtures, sent against them a large army under the command of Cornelius Fuscus, prefect of the praetorian guard. The Roman army advanced toward Transylvania (in all probability along the river Aluta), but near the Red Tower pass Fuscus was defeated and killed, and his shattered forces were compelled to make a disastrous retreat.

Also in 85 some occurrence in the West gave occasion for the issue of a noteworthy series of coins bearing the legend *Germania capta,* but the literary sources make no reference to a campaign.[15]

It may well have been in 85 that Chariomerus, king of the Cherusci, appealed to Domitian for aid, presumably against the Chatti; the emperor sent him money in lieu of troops.[16] Somewhat earlier (in or about 83) the Chatti had driven Chariomerus from his kingdom, "on account of his friendship for the Romans," but he had gathered a following and made good his return.

Domitian's wars on the Danube and the Rhine, A.D. 88–89.— The order of events in 88 and 89 is not altogether clear,[17] but appears to be as follows.

Late in 88 or at the beginning of 89 war again broke out with the Dacians. On this occasion Tettius Julianus crossed the Danube at Viminacium and marched to Tapae, near the Iron Gate pass, where he defeated the army of Decebalus.

Also late in 88 the Chatti invaded the territory which the Romans had recently annexed in the region of the river Main; they

---

[15] Gsell, *Essai sur le règne de l'empereur Domitien,* 196–197. Ernst Babelon, "Quelques monnaies de l'empereur Domitien (*Germania capta*)," *Revue numismatique,* 4. sér., 21 (1917–1918), 25–44. Joseph Vogt, *Die alexandrinischen Münzen* (Stuttgart, 1924), 50. Mattingly, *Coins of the Roman Empire,* II, xcii–iii.

[16] Dio lxvii. 5. 1. The date is uncertain, but see Schmidt, *Geschichte der deutschen Stämme,* II, 134.

[17] See Gsell, "Chronologie des expéditions de Domitien pendant l'année 89," *MEFR,* 9 (1889), 3–16. Weynand, "Flavius" (77), *RECA,* VI (1909), 2566–71. Syme, *JRS,* 18 (1928), 44–45.

destroyed blockhouses and other military property, and the troops in occupation may have suffered severe losses.[18] Later, and seemingly on the 1st of January, 89, L. Antonius Saturninus, governor of Upper Germany, induced the two legions stationed at Mogontiacum (Mainz) to renounce their allegiance to Domitian; the rebellion was, however, soon suppressed by L. Appius Maximus Norbanus, governor of Lower Germany. Suetonius attributes this success to the fortunate circumstance that at the critical moment the forces of the barbarians were unable to cross the Rhine in support of Saturninus, for the ice on the river suddenly broke up on the day of battle.[19] Thereafter a Roman army, in all likelihood commanded by Norbanus, carried on a campaign against the Chatti.

Next, after the suppression of the disturbance in Upper Germany, and still in the first half of the year 89, Domitian led an army in person against the Marcomanni and Quadi. The reason assigned by Dio for the campaign is that the Marcomanni and Quadi had failed to render assistance against the Dacians. The emperor was defeated by the Suebic tribes, who were assisted by the Jazyges.[20]

Further, as a consequence of the reverse sustained by the emperor peace was arranged with the Dacians. Decebalus, through his representative, Diegis, delivered up the captives and arms he had taken, while Domitian gave "large sums of money to Decebalus on the spot as well as artisans of every trade pertaining to both peace and war, and promised to keep on giving large sums in the future."[21] After the peace, however, Domitian sent an expedition, under the command of C. Velius Rufus, through

---

[18] With this invasion Syme, *JRS*, 18 (1928), 44 note 4, associates the statement of Tacitus, *Agricola* 41, that while Domitian was emperor armies were lost in Moesia, Dacia, *Germania*, and Pannonia.

[19] Suetonius *Dom.* 6, 7. Dio lxvii. 11. 1. Aurelius Victor *Epit.* xi. 10. See especially Emil Ritterling, "Zur römischen Legionsgeschichte am Rhein. II. Der Aufstand des Antonius Saturninus," *WDZ*, 12 (1893), 203–234. Syme, *CAH*, XI (1936), 172–175.

[20] Dio lxvii. 7. 1–2.

[21] Dio lxvii. 7. 2–4.

Dacian territory against the Marcomanni, Quadi, and Jazyges; but no details concerning the outcome have been preserved.[22]

War in Pannonia, A.D. 92.—At the end of 89 it was assumed by the Romans that peace had been restored in Central Europe; nevertheless within three years war again broke out.

In A.D. 91 or 92 the Lugii became involved in war with the Marcomanni and Quadi; they called upon Domitian for assistance, and he sent a hundred knights to help them. Thereupon the Marcomanni and Quadi, with the Marsigni and possibly the Semnones, in conjunction with the Jazyges, invaded Pannonia, where in 92 they annihilated a Roman legion. Domitian hurried to the front and spent the months from May, 92, to January, 93, in driving the invaders back.[23] At some time in the course of these disturbances Masyus, king of the Semnones, accompanied by the priestess Ganna, made the journey to Rome, where he was honored by Domitian.[24]

War in Pannonia, A.D. 97.—In 97, toward the close of the reign of the emperor Nerva, Roman troops gained a victory in Pannonia over the Marcomanni and Quadi. Little is known of this war beyond the fact that news of the victory was opportunely received by the emperor Nerva on the day that he formally adopted Trajan as his son and heir.[25] There is some evidence that the war was still going on in 98.[26]

[22] Theodor Mommsen, "Inschrift aus Baalbek," *SAWB*, 1903, 823–824. Ritterling, "Zu den Germanenkriegen Domitians an Rhein und Donau," *JOAI*, 7 (1904), Beiblatt, 23–38. Alfred von Domaszewski, "Die Inschrift des Velius Rufus," *Philologus*, 66 (1907), 164–170. The date of the expedition is not a matter of certainty.

[23] Suetonius *Dom.* 6. Dio lxvii. 5. 2. Tacitus *Agricola* 41; *Hist.* i. 2. Eutropius vii. 23. Statius *Silv.* iii. 3. 169–170. Martial viii. 15. 1; ix. 101. 7.

Mommsen, "Zur Lebensgeschichte des jüngeren Plinius" [1869], in his *Gesammelte Schriften,* IV (Berlin, 1906), 366–468, especially 447–452: "Der suebisch-sarmatische Krieg Domitians und der suebische Krieg Nervas." Gsell, *Essai sur le règne de l'empereur Domitien,* 225–229. Syme, *JRS*, 18 (1928), 41–55. In *RECA*, see Weynand, "Flavius" (77), VI (1909), 2575; Vulić, "Iazyges," IX (1914), 1190; Ritterling, "Legio," XII (1924), 1278, 1789–90; Schönfeld, "Lugii," XIII (1927), 1716; Franke, "Marcomanni," XIV (1930), 1617–18.

[24] Dio lxvii. 5. 3.

[25] Pliny *Paneg.* 8. 2. Mommsen, *Gesammelte Schriften,* IV, 449.

[26] *Année épigraphique,* 1923, no. 28. Syme, *JRS*, 18 (1928), 45.

Contemporaneously, the Chauci attacked and drove out the Angrivarii, who thereupon made alliance with the Chamavi and attacked the Bructeri. Tacitus says that, in the battle between the tribes, "more than sixty thousand men fell, not before the arms and spears of Rome, but—what was even a greater triumph for us—merely to delight our eyes. Long may it last, I pray, and persist among the nations, this—if not love for us—at least hatred for each other: since now that the destinies of the Empire have passed their zenith, Fortune can guarantee us nothing better than discord among our foes."[27] The Bructeri were defeated, and their king evidently took refuge with the Romans, for in or about 96 he was reinstated by Vestricius Spurinna, governor of Lower Germany.[28]

Trajan's wars against Decebalus, A.D. 101–106.—The experience of Tiberius in Germany in the years A.D. 4 and 5 led Augustus to decide that war should be undertaken against Maroboduus, king of the Marcomanni. The experience of Trajan[29] in Pannonia led him to make war on Decebalus, king of the Dacians. Dio gives as reasons for the war that Trajan "was grieved at the amount of money the Dacians were receiving annually" (in accordance with the settlement effected by Domitian), and

---

[27] Tacitus *Germania* 33. If, however, significance is to be attached to the statement of Orosius (vii. 12. 2; see also Eutropius vii. 2) that Trajan, on becoming emperor, restored Germany beyond the Rhine *in pristinum statum*, the emotional utterance of Tacitus may have had a more explicit background than is apparent at first sight.

[28] Pliny *Epist.* ii. 7. Though doubts have been freely expressed concerning the date of Spurinna's expedition, no other date has been confidently proposed. See Syme, *JRS*, 18 (1928), 43 note 1. Ritterling, *Fasti des römischen Deutschland,* 61–63.

[29] For the reign of Trajan, see Johannes Dierauer, "Beiträge zu einer kritischen Geschichte Trajans," in Max Büdinger, ed., *Untersuchungen zur römischen Kaisergeschichte,* I (Leipzig, 1868), 1–219. Camille de la Berge, *Essai sur le règne de Trajan* (Paris, 1877). R. H. Lacey, *The Equestrian Officials of Trajan and Hadrian: Their Careers, with Some Notes on Hadrian's Reforms* (Princeton, 1917). Walter Otto, *Zur Lebensgeschichte des jüngeren Plinius* (München, 1919. *SAWM,* 1919, 10. Abh.). Roberto Paribeni, *Optimus princeps: saggio sulla storia e sui tempi dell' imperatore Traiano* (Messina, [1926–1927]). Henderson, *Five Roman Emperors,* 177–211. P. L. Strack, *Untersuchungen zur römischen Reichsprägung des zweiten Jahrhunderts. I. Die Reichsprägung zur Zeit des Traian* (Stuttgart, 1931).

that "he observed that their power and their pride were increasing"[30]—under a king who was inexorably hostile to Rome.

In 101 Trajan crossed the Danube[31] at Lederata (below Belgrade) and marched to Tapae, where he fought an indecisive battle with Decebalus, and returned to winter quarters at Drobetae. In the course of the winter the Dacians crossed the Danube, below Oescus, and the Roxolani overran the Dobrudja. In 102 the emperor advanced from Drobetae eastward to Burridava on the river Aluta, and up this stream toward the Red Tower pass. Decebalus asked for peace, but, while negotiations were under way, Roman troops seized near-by strongholds of the Dacians, and Decebalus broke off the discussion of terms. Trajan then forced his way through the Red Tower pass, and Decebalus surrendered Sarmizegethusa, his capital. In the peace concluded Decebalus agreed to surrender Roman artisans and deserters, to give up his weapons and engines of war, and to destroy his fortifications; and a Roman garrison was stationed at Sarmizegethusa.

---

[30] Dio lxviii. 6. 1–2.

[31] Dio lxviii. 6. 8–14.

On the Dacian wars, see A. D. Xénopol, "Les guerres daciques de l'empereur Trajan," *Revue historique*, 31 (1886), 291–312. Conrad Cichorius, *Die Reliefs der Traianssäule* (Berlin, 1896–1900). Eugen Petersen, *Trajans dakische Kriege, nach dem Säulenrelief erzählt* (Leipzig, 1899–1903). Victoria Vaschide, *Histoire de la conquête romaine de la Dacie* (Paris, 1903). Franz Studniczka, *Tropaeum Traiani: ein Beitrag zur Kunstgeschichte der Kaiserzeit* (Leipzig, 1904. *AAWL*, XXII, 4). Alfred von Domaszewski, "Die Dakerkriege Traians auf den Reliefs der Säule," *Philologus*, 65 (1906), 321–344. Filow, "Die Legionen der Provinz Moesia," 47–61. Paul Schwartz, "Der erste Dakerkrieg Trajans," in *Festschrift zur Einweihung des neuen Gymnasial-Gebäudes beim kön. Pädagogium in Putbus* (Putbus, 1908), 45–78. H. S. Jones, "The Historical Interpretation of the Reliefs of Trajan's Column," *PBSR*, 5 (1910), 433–459. G. A. T. Davies, "Trajan's First Dacian War," *JRS*, 7 (1917), 74–97; "Topography and the Trajan Column," *JRS*, 10 (1920), 1–28. W. W. Hyde, "Trajan's Danube Road and Bridge," *Classical Weekly*, 18 (1924), 59–64. Jérôme Carcopino, "Les richesses des Daces et le redressement de l'empire romain sous Trajan," *Dacia*, 1 (1924), 28–34. Ritterling, "Legio," *RECA*, XII (1924), 1280–82. Roberto Paribeni, "L'ordinamento della conquista di Traiano," *Dacia*, 2 (1925), 1–21. Karl Lehmann-Hartleben, *Die Trajanssäule* (Berlin, 1926). Carl Uhlig, "Die Wälle in Bessarabien, besonders die sogenannten Traianswälle," *Praehistorische Zeitschrift*, 19 (1928), 185–250. I. A. Richmond, "Trajan's Army on Trajan's Column," *PBSR*, 13 (1935), 1–40.

In 105 it became known to the Roman government that Decebalus was "sending envoys to his neighbors,"[32] that he was en-
croaching upon the territory of the Jazyges, and that he was
receiving Roman deserters. Finally he imprisoned Longinus,
commander of the Roman garrison, and demanded from Trajan
the restoration of the trans-Danubian territory which the Romans had occupied. The demand was not complied with; in 106
Trajan crossed the Danube by the stone bridge he had built at
Drobetae and again entered Sarmizegethusa. Decebalus ended
his life, and in 107 Dacia was incorporated into the empire.

Further, it may be mentioned that in A.D. 106 or 108 the Romans were forced to withdraw the garrisons which Agricola had
established in Scotland.[33]

War in Pannonia, A.D. 107.—In 107 P. Aelius Hadrianus, as
legate in Lower Pannonia, "held the Sarmatians (Jazyges) in
check."[34]

China, Parthia, and the Roman East

I

Events in the Roman East, A.D. 72–77.—In A.D. 72, on the pretext that Antiochus IV and his sons had entered into alliance

---

[32] Dio lxviii. 10. 3; for the war, see lxviii. 10–14.

It has been suggested that these "neighbors" were the Parthians. The argument
in favor of this interpretation is based upon the story of Callidromus, given by
Pliny *Epist.* x. 74. Callidromus had been slave to Laberius Maximus, governor of
Moesia during Trajan's first Dacian war; he was taken prisoner by Susagus, a
Dacian leader, in Moesia, and was sent as a present to Pacorus, king of Parthia;
finally he succeeded in escaping to Nicomedia, and was sent by Pliny, who was
governor of Bithynia, to Trajan. In the opinion of R. P. Longden, *CAH,* XI (1936),
239, "that Decebalus and Pacorus had been in correspondence was a fact which
was probably known or guessed in Rome long before Pliny went to Bithynia."

[33] Sir George Macdonald, *JRS,* 25 (1935), 188. The article on "The Dating-value
of Samian Ware" is a reply to the argument of T. D. Pryce and Eric Birley, "The
First Roman Occupation of Scotland," *JRS,* 25 (1935), 59–80, that the evacuation
had taken place before the death of Domitian (96). It should not be overlooked
that the occurrence contemporaneously of disturbances in Wales is indicated by
"half a dozen coin hoards dating from *ca.* A.D. 100," Wheeler, *Prehistoric and Roman
Wales,* 230.

[34] *SHA* "de vita Hadriani" iii. 9.

with Parthia, L. Caesennius Paetus, governor of Syria (70–72), suddenly invaded Commagene and after a brief struggle annexed it. Antiochus was sent as a prisoner to Rome; his sons took refuge with the Parthians.[1]

In 73 (presumably) the world south of the Caucasus Mountains was thrown into confusion when the Alani invaded Media and Armenia. "Masses of them," says Josephus, "fell upon the Medes, who suspected nothing, and plundered a populous country, filled with all manner of livestock, none venturing to oppose them." Pacorus, king of Media, was driven into the mountains, being forced to abandon all his possessions. "Pursuing their raids with perfect ease and unresisted, the Alani advanced as far as Armenia, laying everything waste." Tiridates, king of Armenia, was defeated, and narrowly escaped capture. The invaders "made havoc of the country, and, carrying off masses of the population and booty of all kinds from both kingdoms, returned once more to their own land."[2] Josephus remarks that at this time the Alani inhabited the banks of the river Don (Tanais) and the Sea of Azov (Maeotis).

After this onslaught Vologeses I of Parthia proposed to Vespasian a joint military undertaking against the invaders, and asked for Roman auxiliaries with one of the emperor's sons as their leader; Domitian was eager to go, but the plan came to nothing.[3] On the other hand, Vespasian did not remain inactive, for in 75 he sent a military force to Iberia, to aid Mithridates in strengthening the defenses of his kingdom against attacks from beyond the Caucasus.[4] In connection with this undertaking it is not improbable that the Romans entered Armenia; Statius, indeed, indicates that at some point in his career Rutilius Gallicus

[1] Josephus BJ vii. 7. 1–3 (219–243).

[2] Josephus BJ vii. 7. 4 (244–251). For discussion of the invasion, see p. 162, below.

[3] Suetonius Dom. 2. 2. Dio lxvi. 15. 3.

[4] H. C. Newton, The Epigraphical Evidence for the Reigns of Vespasian and Titus (Ithaca, N. Y., 1901), 19–20.

had conducted an army into Armenia, and the reference has been assigned to A.D. 75.[5]

Again, in 76–77, for reasons which are not known, Vologeses of Parthia invaded Syria; but he was defeated and driven back by M. Ulpius Traianus, governor of Syria,[6] whose son, later the emperor Trajan, appears to have taken part in the campaign.[7]

In the light of the close correspondence between events in the Roman East and Central Europe from 60 B.C. to A.D. 70, the disturbances in Armenia and Syria from 72 to 76–77 may be taken as confirmatory of the scanty evidence provided by inscriptions and coins that serious uprisings of German tribes took place between 74 and 77–78, and that on one occasion at least Moesia was invaded by Sarmatians. On the other hand, the outbreaks in the Roman East which have just been mentioned occurred in unmistakable correspondence with new developments in the "Western Regions" of the Chinese, in which Pan Ch'ao played a leading part.

Kashgaria and Parthia, A.D. 73–78.—While Vespasian was engaged in rectifying the frontiers of the Roman empire on the Rhine and on the Euphrates, Ming Ti (58–75) was endeavoring

---

[5] Statius *Sylvae* i. 4. 79–80. For the date, see Mommsen, *Provinces of the Roman Empire*, II (London, 1909), 64 note 1.

Further, there is some reason to believe that about 75 the Romans placed an Iberian named Sanatruces on the Armenian throne. See Kévork Aslan, *Etudes historiques sur le peuple arménien* (Paris, 1909), 119–120. Pascal Asdourian, *Die politischen Beziehungen zwischen Armenien und Rom* (Venedig, 1911), 100–103.

[6] Weynand, "Flavius" (206), *RECA*, VI (1909), 2668. G. A. Harrer, *Studies in the History of the Roman Province of Syria* (Princeton, 1915), 12–13. B. W. Henderson, *Five Roman Emperors* (Cambridge, 1927), 63. Waldemar Wruck, *Die syrische Provinzialprägung von Augustus bis Traian* (Stuttgart, 1931), 119–124. Ronald Syme, *CAH*, XI (1936), 143, thinks that the incident was restricted to "a threat of hostilities [which] was countered or averted in some way or other by M. Ulpius Traianus."

The invasion has commonly been accounted for on the supposition that it was due to the resentment of Vologeses at Vespasian's refusal to aid him against the Alani. Vespasian did, however, coöperate by sending troops to Iberia. If, on the other hand, the Romans had set up a new king in Armenia (see note 5), this action would have been in contravention of the agreement with Parthia effected by Corbulo in 63, and would thus have afforded a reason for indignation.

[7] Pliny *Paneg.* 14.

to recover the position of dominance in Mongolia and Kashgaria which China had held before the usurpation of Wang Mang.[8] His decision was forced by inroads of the Hsiung-nu into Kan-su.

In A.D. 61, as has already been pointed out, Hsien of Yarkand was overthrown by Kuang-tê, king of Khotan. The Hsiung-nu at once attacked Kuang-tê and subjected him to the payment of tribute, and thereafter exercised control over the kingdoms of the Western Regions. In 72 Ming Ti set himself to curb the power of the Hsiung-nu. In 73 an army under Tou Ku occupied I-wu (Hami),[9] and in 74 the Chinese regained possession of Turfan and Guchen. After his success over the Hsiung-nu in 73, Tou Ku dispatched his subordinate, Pan Ch'ao, "en mission dans les pays d'Occident."[10] Before the end of 73 Pan Ch'ao had induced Kuang, king of Shan-shan (Lop), and Kuang-tê, king of Yü-t'ien (Khotan), to recognize the authority of Ming Ti, and thus succeeded in reëstablishing Chinese influence upon the southern route in the Tarim basin. Contemporaneously, however, Chien, king of Ch'iu-tzŭ (Kucha), acting in the interest of the Hsiungnu, had seized Su-lê (Kashgar) and had put the king to death. Undeterred by this move of his opponents, Pan Ch'ao presented

---

[8] "Depuis l'époque où les pays d'Occident avaient rompu (avec la Chine), il s'était écoulé soixante-cinq ans (9–73) lorsqu'ils reprirent les relations." Edouard Chavannes, "Les pays d'Occident d'après le Heou Han chou," *T'oung pao*, 8 (1907), 156–157.

[9] C. C. Imbault-Huart, "Le pays de 'Hami ou Khamil; description, histoire, d'après les auteurs chinois," *Bulletin de géographie historique et descriptive*, 1892, 121–195. Sir Aurel Stein, "The Historical rôle of Hami," *Serindia* (Oxford, 1921), 1147–51; "Historical Relations between Barkul and Hami," *Innermost Asia* (Oxford, 1928), 539–545.

Concerning the route to Hami, see Karl Futterer, "Geographische Skizze der Wüste Gobi zwischen Hami und Su-tschôu," *Petermanns Mitteilungen*, Ergänzungsheft 139 (1902). Stein, *Serindia*, 732, 1093, 1141–42. See also M. S. Bell, "The Great Central Asian Trade Route from Peking to Kashgaria," *PRGS*, n.s., 12 (1890), 57–93.

[10] A translation of the biography of Pan Ch'ao is given by Edouard Chavannes, "Trois généraux chinois," *T'oung pao*, 7 (1906), 216–245. Reference may also be made to the biographical study of Pan Ch'ao's sister by Nancy Lee Swann, *Pan Chao: foremost woman scholar of China* (New York, [1932]).

For the details given in the text, see Chavannes, *T'oung pao*, 7 (1906), 218–223; 8 (1907), 172, 204–205. Léon Wieger, *Textes historiques*, I (2e éd., Hsien hsien, 1922), 696–704.

himself before Kashgar in 74, and succeeded, without recourse to war, both in ousting Chien and in gaining possession of the city. On the other hand, in 75, Yen-ch'i (Kara-shahr) and Ch'iu-tzŭ attacked and killed the "protector general" who had been appointed in 74, and Ch'iu-tzŭ joined with Ku-mo (Ak-su) in an attack upon Pan Ch'ao, who in consequence was forced to remain on the defensive for more than a year. In 75 Ming Ti died, and his successor, Chang Ti (76–87), recalled the Chinese troops from the Western Regions; hence, in 77, when he was looking for support which would enable him to hold Kashgar, Pan Ch'ao received notice of his recall. Nevertheless, on his homeward way, he was persuaded by Kuang-tê, king of Yü-t'ien, to disregard the orders of the emperor and to continue to uphold Chinese interests at Kashgar.[11]

The military activities of China from 72 to 77 constitute the background for the disturbances in Armenia and Parthia from 73 to 77.

The effects of the policy of the Han government were not restricted, however, to the territories bordering upon the Euphrates. At this point attention may again be directed to the fact that the ascendancy of China in the Tarim basin which was achieved in 60–59 B.C. was followed in western India by changes which mark the starting point of the Malva or Vikrama era, 58 B.C. And the reason for referring back to this epoch is that the advance into Kashgaria in the reign of Ming Ti was likewise followed in western India by the commencement of the Saca era, A.D. 78. Authorities are not in agreement in regard to the events which gave significance to the year 78, but it seems probable that, in the Kushan empire, Wima Kadphises was succeeded by Kanishka,[12] and the accession of this notable personage may rep-

---

[11] Chavannes, *T'oung pao*, 7 (1906), 223. Wieger, *Textes historiques*, I, 704.

For the history of Su-lê (Kashgar), see E. H. Parker, "Kashgar," *AQR*, 3d ser., 20 (1905), 328–337. Sir Aurel Stein, "Kāshgar during the Han epoch," in his *Ancient Khotan* (Oxford, 1907), 52–57.

[12] E. J. Rapson, *CHI*, I (1922), 583, says that "the chronology of this period has been one of the most perplexing problems in the whole of Indian history"; this

resent a change of dynasty,[13] if not a revolution; in any event, the new monarch made Peshawar his capital, instead of Balkh, which had been favored by the earlier Kushans. Kanishka is famous as one of the great patrons of Buddhism; in the Chinese annals he is spoken of only as "king of the Yüeh-chih." In Parthia also the events of 60–59 B.C. were followed by notable changes, for, in 58 B.C., Phraates III was murdered, and thereafter civil war ensued between his sons Mithridates III and Orodes II. Similarly, in A.D. 78 a rebellion against Vologeses I was led by Pacorus II.[14]

II

Kashgaria, Parthia, and the Roman East, A.D. 78–91.—In 78 Pan Ch'ao appears to have established friendly relations with the Wu-sun, in the Ili valley, the K'ang-chü, between the Jaxartes and the Oxus, and the Yüeh-chih, that is, the Kushan kingdom in Afghanistan and Northwest India. In the same year the K'ang-chü supported him when, with levies from Su-lê (Kashgar), Yü-t'ien (Khotan), and other kingdoms, he carried on a successful campaign against Ku-mo (Ak-su) and Wên-su (Uch

---

remark is fully borne out by the discussion on the date of Kanishka, by James Kennedy, J. F. Fleet, F. W. Thomas, and others, which appeared in the *Journal of the Royal Asiatic Society* during the year 1913. For a survey of the extensive literature, see Louis de la Vallée-Poussin, *L'Inde aux temps des Mauryas* (Paris, 1930), 343–374. Maurice Winternitz, *A History of Indian Literature*, tr. by Mrs. S. Ketkar and Miss H. Kohn, II (Calcutta, 1933), 611–614. See also R. D. Banerji, "The Scythian Period of Indian History," *Indian Antiquary*, 37 (1908), 25–75. V. A. Smith, *The Early History of India* (3d ed., Oxford, 1914), 255–258, 278. Wecker, "Indoskythia," *RECA*, IX (1916), 1376–77. Alfred Foucher, *L'art gréco-bouddhique du Gandhâra*, II. 2 (Paris, 1922), 505–511. Rapson, *CHI*, I, viii-x, 582–583. Hemchandra Raychaudhuri, *Political History of Ancient India* (2d ed., Calcutta, 1927), 294–301. H. H. Dodwell, ed., *The Cambridge Shorter History of India* (Cambridge, 1934), 76–82.

[13] Vincent Smith, *The Early History of India*, 256–257.

For the possibility that Ujjain was recaptured by the Sacas in A.D. 78, see W. W. Tarn, *The Greeks in Bactria & India* (Cambridge, 1938), 335, 501.

[14] R. H. McDowell, *Coins from Seleucia on the Tigris* (Ann Arbor, 1935), 119–120, 229–230. Warwick Wroth, *Catalogue of the Coins of Parthia* (London, 1903), lix, attributes certain coins of 77/78 and 78/79 to Vologeses II. Jacques de Morgan, *Numismatique de la Perse antique* (Paris, 1927), 159–160.

Turfan).¹ At this point Pan Ch'ao requested of the Han government reinforcements to enable him to proceed against Ch'iu-tzŭ
(Kucha) and Yen-ch'i (Kara-shahr), but between 78 and 80
(when he received support) Ch'iu-tzŭ gained possession of So-
chü (Yarkand), and at the same time Su-lê (Kashgar) rose
against his authority. When, therefore, a force under the command of Hsü Kan arrived from China in 80, he employed it
to recover possession of Su-lê. In 83 Ch'iu-tzŭ again attacked
Su-lê. In 84 additional troops reached Pan Ch'ao from China,
and he led them, together with levies from Su-lê and Yü-t'ien
(Khotan), against So-chü (Yarkand). On the other hand, the
king of So-chü persuaded Chung, king of Su-lê, to take his part,
and in this course Chung received support from the K'ang-chü
(Sogdiana). To cope with the situation, Pan Ch'ao dispatched
an envoy "d'apporter des présents considérables en étoffes de
soie"² to the king of the Yüeh-chih (Kanishka), requesting him
to persuade his ally, the king of the K'ang-chü, to withdraw his
support from the king of Su-lê. The negotiations were successful, the K'ang-chü, accompanied by Chung, retired from the
Tarim basin, and Pan Ch'ao (after a prolonged absence) again
became master of Kashgar. Between 85 and 87 Pan Ch'ao received assistance a second time from the Yüeh-chih, when troops
were sent to join in an attack upon the Chü-shih of Turfan.³ In
86 Chung, the deposed king of Su-lê, with the aid of the K'ang-
chü made an attempt to regain his kingdom, but was captured
by Pan Ch'ao and put to death. Thereafter, in 87, with troops
drawn from Yü-t'ien (Khotan) and other kingdoms, Pan Ch'ao
at length succeeded in capturing So-chü (Yarkand), notwith-

¹ For Pan Ch'ao's activities from 78 to 90, see Edouard Chavannes, "Trois
généraux chinois," T'oung pao, 7 (1906), 224–233. Léon Wieger, Textes historiques,
I (2ᵉ éd., Hsien hsien, 1922), 704–706, 716.

² Chavannes, T'oung pao, 7 (1906), 230. See also Edouard Specht, "Les Indo-
Scythes et l'époque du règne de Kanichka," Journal asiatique, 9. sér., 10 (1897),
184–185. Ludwig Bachhofer, "Die Ära Kanishkas," Ostasiatische Zeitschrift, 14
(1927), 40–43.

³ Chavannes, T'oung pao, 7 (1906), 232. Walter Fuchs, "Das Turfangebiet,"
Ostasiatische Zeitschrift, 13 (1926), 129; for the date, see 155 note 35.

standing the aid rendered by Ch'iu-tzŭ and other kingdoms on the northern route.

The occurrences of the years 84 to 87 would seem to indicate that the difficulties of his position in Kashgaria forced Pan Ch'ao into some measure of dependence upon the ruler of the Kushan empire. It is not surprising, therefore, to find that in 87 the king of An-hsi (usually Parthia, here almost certainly Hyrcania) sent an embassy to the Han court,[4] for it may be presumed that the linkage of the Chinese in the Tarim with the Kushans would have entailed a reduction of the traffic on the silk route through Hyrcania and Parthia. At the same moment, however, the king of the Yüeh-chih (Kanishka) sent an embassy to propose a formal alliance with China, and to ask for the hand of a Chinese princess in marriage.[5] In these circumstances Pan Ch'ao seems to have allowed the Parthian mission to proceed through Kashgaria, but, for reasons which are not known, he arrested and sent back the envoy of Kanishka, and thus provoked war. In 90 the king of the Yüeh-chih sent an army, under the command of the "viceroy" Hsieh, across the Ts'ungling to coöperate with Ch'iu-tzŭ against the Chinese. The Kushan expeditionary force was, however, dispersed by Pan Ch'ao, and Ch'iu-tzŭ, after an opposition which had been continuous since 73, submitted. Thereafter, it is said, the Yüeh-chih sent tribute to the Han court.[6]

The various incidents in Pan Ch'ao's struggle to maintain his position in the Tarim basin are reflected, though the information is meager, in the affairs of Parthia and the Roman East, for the hostilities in Kashgaria from 78 to 90, into which were drawn both the K'ang-chü and the Yüeh-chih (Kushans), were paralleled by strife in Mesopotamia.

[4] Chavannes, "Les pays d'Occident d'après le Heou Han chou," *T'oung pao*, 8 (1907), 177.

[5] The date is given as 88 by Chavannes, *T'oung pao*, 7 (1906), 232, but is corrected by him to 87, *T'oung pao*, 8 (1907), 177 note 5.

[6] Chavannes, *T'oung pao*, 8 (1907), 193–194.

First, in 78 Pacorus rebelled against Vologeses I; the latter may have held his ground until 80, but early in that year his reign had certainly come to an end. Pacorus, however, was not left in undisputed possession of the kingdom, for another claimant, Artabanus IV, held Seleucia in the later months of 80/81 and during 81/82. He evidently was driven out in 82, but may possibly have maintained a footing in northern Mesopotamia down to 88/89.[7] He is mentioned in Roman history as having aided and abetted a certain Terentius Maximus who, in the reign of Titus (79–81), gave himself out for Nero and obtained a following of some proportions in the region of the Euphrates.[8] The return of Nero at the head of a Parthian army appears as a recurrent theme in the Revelation of St. John.[9] Correspondingly, in Europe, there were disturbances in 82 on the lower Danube and the Rhine, and in the latter region Domitian in person carried on war against the Chatti in 83, and created a new frontier beyond the Rhine.

Second, in 83 Pan Ch'ao was again attacked at Kashgar, and in 84 was so hard pressed that he appealed for aid to the king of the Yüeh-chih (Kushans). The Roman sources, unfortunately, provide no information whatever concerning events in Parthia or the Roman East between 80–81 and 88–89; on the other hand, Moses of Chorene gives space to the statement that an army sent by Domitian suffered defeat in Armenia, and this occurrence, though undated, may with much hesitation be assigned to 84 or 85.[10] In Europe, the Dacians invaded Moesia in

[7] Jacques de Morgan, *Numismatique de la Perse antique* (Paris, 1927), 159–160.

[8] Dio lxvi. 19. 3bc (Zonaras xi. 18). Stein, "Terentius" (59), *RECA*, 2. Reihe, V (1934), 666.

[9] Rev. ix. 13–21; xvi. 12; xvii. 12–17.

[10] For the account, see Victor Langlois, *Collection des historiens ... d'Arménie*, II (Paris, 1869), 108. R. P. Longden, "Notes on the Parthian Campaigns of Trajan," *JRS*, 21 (1931), 24, remarks that "without better authority we cannot use the statement in Moses Chorenensis that Ardaches of Armenia had defeated Domitian's troops." Nevertheless the statement cannot be wholly ignored, especially in view of the all but complete silence of Roman historians concerning affairs in the East during Domitian's reign.

85, and in the same year Domitian won some notable success over the Germans (*Germania capta*).

Third, the friendly relations of Pan Ch'ao and the king of the Yüeh-chih were rudely broken in 87, and in 90 the latter actually sent an army across the Pamirs to attack the Chinese viceroy. These disturbances may be represented in Parthia by the "consecutive period of seven years, 86/87 to 92/93 inclusive, for which no issues of silver are known."[11] Further, in 88–89 (twenty years after Nero's death), another pseudo-Nero made his appearance in the Roman East, and was vigorously supported by the Parthians; indeed, on his account "the armies of Parthia were all but set in motion" against Rome.[12] Also, in or about 88 C. Vettulenus Civica Cerialis, while governor of Asia, was put to death for plotting revolution.[13] In or about 92 the Roman poets Statius, Martial, and Silius Italicus were still speaking expectantly of war in the East which would bring new laurels to Domitian.[14] In Europe, war with the Dacians was renewed late in 88, and about the same time an invasion of Roman territory by the Chatti was closely associated with the rebellion of Antonius Saturninus in Upper Germany.

III

Kashgaria and Parthia, A.D. 91–102.—In 91 Pan Ch'ao[1] received the submission of Ch'iu-tzŭ (Kucha), Ku-mo (Ak-su), and Wên-su (Uch Turfan), on the northern route, and was appointed

---

[11] R. H. McDowell, *Coins from Seleucia on the Tigris* (Ann Arbor, 1935), 230.

[12] Tacitus *Hist.* i. 2; ii. 8. Suetonius *Nero* 57. Stéphane Gsell, *Essai sur le règne de l'empereur Domitien* (Paris, 1894), 154, 233. Giuseppe Corradi, "Domitianus," *DER*, II (1913), 1991. Ronald Syme, *CAH*, XI (1936), 144–145. There is epigraphical evidence for a concentration of auxiliary troops in Syria in November, 88. *Année épigraphique*, 1927, no. 44.

[13] *PIR*, III, no. 352.

[14] Statius *Silv.* iii. 2. 136–137; see also iv. 1. 40–42; iv. 3. 153–154. Martial viii. 65; ix. 35. 3. Silius Italicus iii. 612–617.

[1] For Pan Ch'ao's activities from 91 to 102, see Edouard Chavannes, "Trois généraux chinois," *T'oung pao*, 7 (1906), 233–243. Léon Wieger, *Textes historiques*, I (2ᵉ éd., Hsien hsien, 1922), 720–722.

by Ho Ti (89–105) to the office of "protector general." He took
up his residence at Ch'iu-tzŭ, and in 94 completed the conquest
of the kingdoms in the Tarim basin by reducing Yen-ch'i (Kara-
shahr) to submission.[2]

The outcome of Pan Ch'ao's long-sustained efforts may be
judged from the statement in the *Hou Han Shu* that, "since the
time they had been compelled to submit by force of arms or had
been won over by gifts, all the kingdoms of the Western Regions
came to offer the rare products of their lands and to deliver up
as hostages those who were dear to them . . . Dispatch bearers
and post runners came and went uninterruptedly in every season
and month. Merchants and foreigners engaged in trade knocked
daily at the gates of the Barrier."[3] Among these foreigners may
well have been the agents of that Maes Titianus whose information concerning "the great silk route" was utilized by the geographer Ptolemy.

In 97 Pan Ch'ao sent Kan Ying on a tour of investigation to
the West.[4] The mission reached T'iao-chih, which has been identified as Mesopotamia, and brought back the information, first,

[2] Mailla, *Histoire générale de la Chine*, III (Paris, 1777), 397, made the statement that "Poussant ensuite de conquête en conquête jusqu'à la mer du nord (Mer
Caspienne), il soumit plus de cinquante royaumes, dont il prit les héritiers pré-
somptifs, qu'il envoya à la cour." Ferdinand von Richthofen, *China*, I (Berlin,
1877), 469, Alfred von Gutschmid, *Geschichte Irans* (Tübingen, 1888), 139, and
others have repeated the assertion that Pan Ch'ao made an expedition to the Caspian Sea in 94. Chavannes, *T'oung pao*, 7 (1906), 210, regards this as an "exploit
imaginaire," and W. Barthold, *Nachrichten über den Aral-See*, übersetzt von H. von
Foth (Leipzig, 1910), 15 note 3, points out that the statement originally made by
Mailla was an inference based upon a mistaken identification.

[3] *Hou Han Shu* cxviii; see also Chavannes, *T'oung pao*, 8 (1907), 216.

E. H. Parker, "Contributions to Topography," *China Review*, 16 (1888), 301,
notes that "A letter from Pan Ku to his brother, Pan Ch'ao, says: 'I now send 300
pieces of white silk, which I want you to trade for Bactrian horses, storax, and
rugs.'"

[4] Chavannes, *T'oung pao*, 8 (1907), 177–178, 184–185. Wieger, *Textes historiques*,
I, 720–722. Friedrich Hirth, *China and the Roman Orient* (Leipzig, 1885); "Syrisch-chinesische Beziehungen im Anfang unserer Zeitrechnung," in Roman Oberhummer & Heinrich Zimmerer, *Durch Syrien und Kleinasien* (Berlin, 1899), 436–
449. Richard Hennig, "Der Chinese Kan-ying an Euphrat," in his *Terrae incognitae*,
I (Leiden, 1936), 329–335.

that the Roman empire (Ta Ch'in) carried on trade with Parthia
(An-hsi) and India (T'ien-chu) by sea, and that in this commerce the profit was "ten for one"; second, that the king of Ta
Ch'in was constantly desirous of establishing communication
with the Han government, but was unable to do so because of
the obstacles interposed by the Parthians, who wished to monopolize the trade in Chinese silk with the Roman empire. Shortly
after the return of the mission to Kashgar, in 100, the "protector
general" applied to the Han court to be relieved of his duties
in the Tarim.[5]

The victory over the Yüeh-chih in 90 left Pan Ch'ao master
of the Western Regions and ushered in a period of unity and
peace in the Tarim. It may be taken as a reflection of this situation that in Parthia the mint at Seleucia issued coins of Pacorus
in 93/94 and down to 97. The prosperity in Mesopotamia was
not, however, of long duration, for after the spring of 97 the
mint was "entirely inactive" until 105/106, when Pacorus appears to have been driven from Seleucia and the city to have
come into the possession of Vologeses II.

Some light is thrown upon affairs in Parthia about 97 by the
experiences of Kan Ying. On his journey to the West, the Chinese traveler was, in fact, prevented by the authorities in Iran
from following the direct route across northern Mesopotamia to
Syria, and instead was conducted to a city at the head of the
Persian Gulf, from which, he was told, traffic was carried on by
sea with the Roman empire (Ta Ch'in). The situation thus described is intelligible if it is understood that after the spring of
97 the effective rule of Pacorus was limited to northern Mesopotamia, and that the eastern and southern parts of the country
were in possession of a king—Vologeses II or Osroes—who was
carrying on war against him. Consequently, though goods from
China and Kashgaria continued to pass through eastern and
central Persia, the direct route to Syria across northern Meso-

[5] For his memorial, see Chavannes, *T'oung pao*, 7 (1906), 238–239.

potamia was blocked by the opponents of Pacorus, even at the cost of carrying on trade with Syria by the sea route round Arabia. This procedure may have been followed from 97 to 105.

IV

Kashgaria and Parthia, A.D. 102–107.— In A.D. 102 Pan Ch'ao returned to China, where he died within the year at the age of seventy. His successor as "protector general," Jên Shang, at once encountered difficulties—of which he had been warned.[1] In 102 the Tibetan Ch'iang rebelled and were with difficulty put down. In 105 the Northern Hsiung-nu took Posterior Chü-shih (Guchen).[2] The kingdoms on the northern route in the Tarim also rose in revolt, and in 106 attacked Jên Shang at Su-lê (Kashgar) ;[3] a force under the command of Liang Ch'in was sent to his assistance. In 107 the Ch'iang rose, under a leader named Tien-ling, and seized the passes in Kan-su, so that, as stated in the biography of Pan Yung, "les contrées d'Occident furent de nouveau séparées de nous."[4] Hence, since communication with the West was cut off, and the written orders sent out could not be delivered, the Han government, in 107, abolished the post of "protector general" and recalled its officials from the Western Regions.[5] In this situation the Northern Hsiung-nu reasserted control over the kingdoms in the Tarim, and even demanded from them the entire amount of tribute which was in arrears.[6]

In A.D. 102 Pan Ch'ao retired, after thirty years of service,

---

[1] For Pan Ch'ao's advice to his successor, see Edouard Chavannes, "Trois généraux chinois," *T'oung pao*, 7 (1906), 244. Léon Wieger, *Textes historiques*, I (2ᵉ éd., Hsien hsien, 1922), 723.

[2] Sylvain Lévi, "Le 'Tokharien'," *Journal asiatique*, 222 (1933), 16.

[3] Chavannes, *T'oung pao*, 7 (1906), 255–257; 8 (1907), 160 and note 2.

[4] Chavannes, *T'oung pao*, 7 (1906), 247.

See also Alexander Wylie, "History of the Western Keang," *REO*, 1 (1882), 442–451. Wieger, *Textes historiques*, I, 705–706, 723–725. On Tien-ling, and the campaigns carried on against him, see Wylie, 451–457. Wieger, I, 730–731. Chavannes, *T'oung pao*, 7 (1906), 257–259, 261–262; 8 (1907), 233–234.

[5] Chavannes, *T'oung pao*, 7 (1906), 257; 8 (1907), 160. Wieger, *Textes historiques*, I, 729.

[6] Chavannes, *T'oung pao*, 7 (1906), 247; 8 (1907), 160.

and in the years 105 to 107 the Chinese were forced to relinquish their hold upon the routes and kingdoms of the Tarim basin.

In Parthia, in 105/106 or 106/107, the opponents of Pacorus gained possession of Seleucia;[7] there may even have been a concerted attack upon him by Vologeses II, from the east, and by Osroes from the south. The three-sided conflict was still in progress when Trajan invaded Mesopotamia.

In the Roman East, in 105–106, A. Cornelius Palma, governor of Syria, took Petra and annexed Arabia.[8]

In Central Europe, in 106 and 107, Trajan overcame Decebalus and annexed Dacia. Also, in 106 or 108 the Romans were forced to evacuate Scotland.

Observations and Comments

The happenings in Kashgaria and Parthia from A.D. 73 to 107 suggest comparison with events in the same regions in the time of Hsien of Yarkand, A.D. 33 to 61. In each group of occurrences, wars in the Tarim basin were followed by civil wars and other disturbances in Parthia, which on different occasions affected the eastern provinces of the Roman empire. Now, while in both groups disturbances in the Roman East were followed by outbreaks on the lower Danube and the Rhine, a further examination of occurrences in Europe shows that there were barbarian invasions in the times of Vespasian, Domitian, and Trajan which were not uniformly of this type. Outbreaks on the lower Danube and the Rhine did occur, as formerly, in corre-

---

[7] W. W. Wroth, *Catalogue of the Coins of Parthia* (London, 1903), lvii–lviii, 204, places the beginning of the reign of Osroes in 106/107, and the end of the reign of Pacorus II in 109/110; he assigns with hesitation certain coins of 111/112 and 112/113 to Vologeses II. R. H. McDowell, *Coins from Seleucia on the Tigris* (Ann Arbor, 1935), 193, 230–231, thinks that Vologeses II "appears to have been responsible for the issue of bronze in Seleucia from 105/106 through 108/109" (there was no issue in 106/107). Osroes occupied Seleucia in 109/110.

[8] Dio lxviii. 14. 5. Festus *Brev.* xiv. 3. Eutropius viii. 3. Ammianus Marcellinus xiv. 8. 13. Albert Kammerer, *Pétra et la Nabatène* (Paris, 1929), 260. P. L. Strack, *Die Reichsprägung zur Zeit des Traian* (Stuttgart, 1931), 194–197. Hölscher, "Petra," *RECA*, XIX (1937), 1177.

spondence with disturbances in the Roman East; but the invasions of Pannonia by the Marcomanni, Quadi, and Jazyges appear to be a new phenomenon. If, however, these invasions actually represent a separate type of disturbance, it follows that they must have had independent antecedents. When, in the light of this observation, the whole situation is resurveyed, the fact appears that, while Pan Ch'ao was occupied in Kashgaria, Chinese forces were also engaged in carrying on war against the Hsiung-nu in Mongolia. Hence, before a judgment may be reached concerning the background of events in Europe from 70 to 107, it will be necessary to inquire into the relations of the Chinese with the peoples of Mongolia, beginning with 60 B.C.

China, Mongolia, and Europe

I

China and Mongolia, 63–36 B.C.—The third war of the Romans against Mithridates the Great had its complement in the war against the Hsiung-nu which was carried on by the Han government during the reign of Hsüan Ti (73–49 B.C.).[1] Notably, the

---

[1] The source of information is the *Ch'ien Han Shu* (*Annals of the Early Han Dynasty*). The parts of this history which deal with the northern tribes have been translated as follows: Alexander Wylie, "History of the Heung-noo in their Relations with China," *JAI*, 3 (1874), 401–452; 5 (1876), 41–80. E. H. Parker, "The Turko-Scythian Tribes," *China Review*, 20 (1893), 1–24, 109–125; 21 (1895), 100–119, 129–137. J. J. M. de Groot, *Die Hunnen der vorchristlichen Zeit* (Berlin, 1921). See also Joseph de Guignes, *Histoire générale des Huns, des Turcs, des Mogols, et des autres Tartares occidentaux* (Paris, 1756–1758). Iakinth Bichurin, *Denkwürdigkeiten über die Mongolei*, übersetzt von K. F. von der Borg (Berlin, 1832). Parker, *A Thousand Years of the Tartars* (London [Shanghai], 1895; reprinted, London, 1924). The *Histoire générale de la Chine* (Paris, 1777–1785), by J. A. M. de Moyriac de Mailla, is a rendering into French of the monumental *T'ung Chien Kang Mu* (*Mirror of History*), which was compiled at the end of the twelfth century by Chu Hsi; this work has also been utilized by Léon Wieger, *Textes historiques: histoire politique de la Chine depuis l'origine jusqu'en 1912* (2e éd., Hsien-hsien, 1922–1923).

For occurrences from 66 to 58 B.C., see Parker, *China Review*, 20 (1893), 123–124. Groot, *Hunnen*, 202–203; *Westlande*, 201–216. Wieger, *Textes historiques*, I, 512–522. See also Edouard Biot, "Mémoire sur les colonies militaires et agricoles des Chinois," *Journal asiatique*, 4. sér., 15 (1850), 344–346. Alexander Wylie, "History of the Western Keang," *REO*, 1 (1882), 436.

year in which Pompey defeated Mithridates (66) saw the capture of Turfan (Anterior Chü-shih) by Chêng Chi; thereafter Mithridates retreated to Bosporus, but in the East the Hsiung-nu pursued the war with renewed vigor. Thus, in 64, Chêng Chi was forced to abandon Turfan, and in the year of Mithridates' death (63) the Han court was faced with a situation of the utmost gravity (63–61) when the Tibetan Ch'iang invaded Kan-su, in the neighborhood of Lan-chou, and the Hsiung-nu sent a hundred thousand horsemen to attack the northern borders of the empire. The peril of these aggressions lay in the fact that, should the Ch'iang and Hsiung-nu effect a juncture, the Chinese would be unable to maintain communications with the Western Regions. The immediate danger was averted; and the alarm at court was definitely relieved when, in 60, the *shan-yü* or great khan of the Hsiung-nu died, for his successor had been the recipient of favors from the Han court and, on coming into power, proceeded to put to death all those who had held important positions under his predecessor. It was to escape this fate that Hsien-hsien-ch'an, as has already been mentioned, sought Hsüan Ti's protection, with the result that Turfan was again occupied by the Chinese. But not all the Hsiung-nu malcontents fled, and after a time of strife the new *shan-yü* was overthrown (58). In succession to this struggle the Hsiung-nu tribes were divided into no less than five khanates.

It may be pointed out here—without presumption of a relation between the occurrences in Mongolia and in Europe—that in 61 or 60 B.C. the Boii were driven from their homeland north of the Danube, and that the disturbances of the period affected other peoples on the upper Danube, as well as the Helvetii, near Lake Constance, and the Allobroges, in Gaul. In 59 some, at least, of the Boii joined the Helvetii and participated in the great migration of 58, which was turned back by Julius Caesar. Contemporaneously, the German tribes from the Vistula to the Rhine were involved in wars.

8. MONGOLIA.

After the death of the *shan-yü* in 58, a struggle over the succession, in which five leaders participated, continued for some years.[2] By 53, however, the rivals had been reduced to the brothers Hu-han-hsieh Khan and Chih-chih Khan. In that year Chih-chih inflicted a severe defeat upon Hu-han-hsieh, whereupon the latter moved southward to the great bend of the Huang Ho and entered into negotiations with the Han government. In 51 he submitted himself as a vassal, and was charged with the obligation of defending the frontier.

Chih-chih, who had remained in possession of the khan's headquarters (presumably on the Orkhon), became alarmed at the favors bestowed upon his brother by the Han government, and in 49 moved to the "right" or western land of the Hsiung-nu. There he sought an alliance with the Wu-sun; the khan to whom he applied was, however, unwilling to take the part of the adventurer and sent a force of 8000 horsemen against him. Chih-chih defeated the Wu-sun troops, but did not follow up his advantage; instead, he turned northward against the Hu-chieh, the Chien-k'un, and the Ting-ling. He overcame these peoples in succession, and afterwards sent expeditions on several occasions against the Wu-sun.

Up to this time Chih-chih had not broken off communication with the Chinese government. In 45, however, he requested that his son, who had been in attendance at court since 53, be returned to him. Yüan Ti gave his consent, and the young prince was sent back with an escort. At this juncture Chih-chih committed the offense of putting to death, with his entire retinue, the dignitary who had accompanied his son homeward. There-

---

[2] For occurrences from 58 to 36 B.C., see Wylie, *JAI*, 5 (1876), 41–50; "Notes on the Western Regions," *JAI*, 10 (1881), 42, 49–65. Parker, *China Review*, 20 (1893), 124–125; 21 (1895), 100–106. Groot, *Hunnen*, 209–238. De Guignes, *Histoire générale des Huns*, I. 2, 85–95. Bichurin, *Denkwürdigkeiten*, 187–190. Mailla, *Histoire générale de la Chine*, III, 142–146, 150–155, 162–163, 172–177. Wieger, *Textes historiques*, I, 522–526, 544–549. See also Friedrich Hirth, "Ueber Wolga-Hunnen und Hiung-nu," *SAWM*, 1899, II, 245–278. Kiessling, "Hunni," *RECA*, VIII (1913), 2583–2600. Josef Marquart, "Über das Volkstum der Komanen," *AGWG*, N.F., 13 (1914), I, 65–68.

after, knowing that he had thus rendered himself obnoxious to China, and fearing that he would be attacked by Hu-han-hsieh, he became anxious to move still farther away. Now, just then, the king of the K'ang-chü was suffering from attacks by the Wu-sun, so when he heard that Chih-chih "was hard put to it by his enemies,"[3] he took steps to enlist the services of the Hsiung-nu leader. Chih-chih embraced the opportunity so precipitately (in 43) that he set out in the depth of winter; as a consequence he lost many of his people on the road and arrived in the land of the K'ang-chü with a bare remnant of 3000 men. The king nevertheless treated him with honor, and provided him with troops to carry on war against the Wu-sun. Chih-chih devastated their territory as far as the capital, so that their western border lay desolate and without inhabitants for more than 1000 *li*.[4] Elated by his success against the Wu-sun, Chih-chih treated the K'ang-chü king without ceremony, put many persons to death, insulted Chinese envoys, demanded tribute from the Ho-su[5] and Ta-yüan, and built for himself a city on the river Tu-lei.[6]

In 36 B.C., Kan Yen-shou, "protector general" of the Western Regions, and Ch'ên T'ang, the deputy protector, acting on their own initiative and without the knowledge of the Han govern-

---

[3] Parker, *China Review*, 21 (1895), 106.

[4] For the translation, see Groot, *Hunnen*, 229, as against the statement of Hirth, "Ueber Wolga-Hunnen und Hiung-nu," 271, and Kiessling, "Hunni," 2587, that Chih-chih was allotted "ein unbewohntes Gebiet im Westen" by the K'ang-chü. As Phelps Hodges, *Britmis* (London, 1931), 258, says, the *li* "is more a measure of time and distance combined than any definite linear measure." H. B. Morse, *The Trade and Administration of the Chinese Empire* (London, 1908), 173–174, says that "in practice it is one-hundredth of the distance a laden porter will cover in a day of ten hours marching." Ordinarily, it may be assumed that 10 *li* equal 3 miles, see Eric Teichmann, *Travels of a Consular Officer in North-West China* (Cambridge, 1921), 32.

[5] Hirth, "Hunnenforschungen," *Keleti szemle*, 2 (1901), 85, says: "Einem chinesischen Scholiasten des 7. Jahrhunderts verdanken wir die Mittheilung, dass dieser Name [Ho-su] mit An-ts'ai identisch ist, also sich ebenfalls auf die Alanen bezieht"; see also his "Ueber Wolga-Hunnen und Hiung-nu," 272, and Groot, *Hunnen*, 229.

[6] Identified by Groot, *Hunnen*, 232, with the river Talas; by Albert Herrmann, *Die alten Seidenstrassen zwischen China und Syrien* (Berlin, 1910), 91, with the river Chu.

ment, led an expedition against Chih-chih from Kashgaria. The project had been conceived by Ch'ên T'ang, who urged upon his superior officer that the Hsiung-nu leader was threatening the Wu-sun and Ta-yüan and was scheming to bring them under subjection to the K'ang-chü. Should he succeed in gaining possession of the two kingdoms, argued the deputy protector, and should he attack I-li on the north, conquer An-hsi (Parthia) on the west, and overcome the Yüeh-chih (Bactria) and Wu-i-shan-li (Herat) on the south, he would create great trouble in the Western Regions. Since this statement has contributed largely to Chih-chih's fame, it is of interest to note that the biographer of the deputy protector prefaced his narrative with the remark that Ch'ên T'ang was possessed of a fertile imagination.[7] The expedition from the Tarim was a complete success; the Chinese gained the support of fifteen princes from among the Wu-sun and K'ang-chü, took Chih-chih's stronghold, and decapitated him.

The departure of Chih-chih westward, in 49 B.C., and his conquest of the Hu-chieh, the Chien-k'un, and the Ting-ling stand in close chronological relationship with the events which led to the downfall of Pharnaces, king of Bosporus. In 48 Pharnaces, with the aid of Spadines, king of the Aorsi, and Abeacus, king of the Siraci, made himself master of the eastern coast of the Maeotis. It is by no means improbable that Pharnaces turned to his own advantage some disturbance which had affected the peo-

---

[7] Wylie *JAI*, 10 (1881), 51–59. Groot, *Hunnen*, 230–238.

Apart from the possibilities contemplated by Ch'ên T'ang, there is no ground for the view taken by Hirth, Kiessling, and Groot "dass Tsit-ki [Chih-chih] zur Zeit der mächtigste Potentat Mittelasiens war" (Groot, *Hunnen*, 229). There is no suggestion in the sources that, after his arrival in K'ang-chü territory, Chih-chih made war on any other people than the Wu-sun, and he carried on this war with the aid of K'ang-chü troops. The numerical strength of his "hervorbrechenden" Hsiung-nu may be judged from the following facts: (1) the Wu-sun sent 8000 men against him, and Chih-chih considered that "the Wu-sun troops were numerous"; (2) he had 3000 men when he came to the K'ang-chü; (3) after the capture of his stronghold, the Chinese executed 1518 persons (including Chih-chih's son), carried off 145, and distributed "more than 1000" among the local lords who had assisted them. Kiessling's article on the "Hunni" in *RECA* is dominated throughout by the view, derived from Hirth, that this was "the first great western drive of the Huns."

ples of the region between the Volga and the Don. On the other
hand, since Chih-chih merely sent ambassadors to Ta-yüan (Ferghana) and the Yen-ts'ai, shortly after 43 B.C., this occurrence
can scarcely be connected with the Scythian attacks which led
Asander, king of Bosporus, to fortify the isthmus of Perekop;
the latter occurrence cannot be closely dated, but it falls in the
earlier years of Asander's reign (47–17 B.C.).

II

China and Mongolia, A.D. 2–16.—From 51 B.C. to A.D. 9, the relations of the Han government with the tribes in Mongolia were
uniformly peaceful. When, however, Wang Mang usurped the
throne (A.D. 9), one of his first acts was to lower the rank accorded to the *shan-yü* or great khan of the Hsiung-nu, with the
result that the Hsiung-nu remained hostile during his reign
(9–23) and made frequent raids across the border.[1] After an
abortive attempt, in 11, to assemble levies from all parts of
China on the northern frontier,[2] Wang Mang succeeded, in 16,
in putting an army into the field; nevertheless little was accomplished, because of the cautious procedure of the generals in
command, even though the emperor, in 19, was still sending forward reinforcements.

　　In the Western Regions[3] disturbances had broken out some-

---

[1] E. H. Parker, "The Turko-Scythian tribes," *China Review,* 21 (1895), 129–137.
J. J. M. de Groot, *Die Hunnen der vorchristlichen Zeit* (Berlin, 1921), 264–288.
Léon Wieger, *Textes historiques,* I (2ᵉ éd., Hsien-hsien, 1922), 617–618.

[2] In his *Histoire générale des Huns,* I. 2 (Paris, 1756), 106, De Guignes states
that in the year A.D. 11 Wang Mang "leva une armée de trois cens mille hommes
qu'il fit partir dans le même tems par dix routes différentes. Ces troupes pénétrerent
jusques dans le centre de la Tartarie, & s'avancerent jusques dans le pays de Tim-
lim [Ting-ling], que nous avons dit être situé au Nord des Ou-sun à l'Orient des
sources du Jaïck. Tout l'Empire des Huns fut soumis, mais on ignore les détails de
cette fameuse expédition." De Guignes, however, converted a project into an accomplished fact, see Parker, *China Review,* 21 (1895), 132–134.

[3] Alexander Wylie, "Notes on the Western Regions," *JAI,* 11 (1882), 109–112.
Parker, *China Review,* 21 (1895), 130–131. Edouard Chavannes, "Les pays d'Occident d'après le Wei lio," *T'oung pao,* 6 (1905), 533 note 1. J. J. M. de Groot, *Die
Westlande Chinas in der vorchristlichen Zeit* (Berlin, 1926), 177–182. See especially Sir Aurel Stein, *Innermost Asia,* II (Oxford, 1928), 571–572.

what earlier than on the northern frontier of China. In or about A.D. 2 the Han government opened a "new route of the north" in order to shorten the distance between the Yü-mên-kuan, the "Jade Gate," and Ulterior Chü-shih (Guchen, Ku-ch'êng-tzŭ). Ku-kou, the king of Ulterior Chü-shih, took the view, however, that the new road was designed to curtail his freedom, and so moved away with his people and joined the Hsiung-nu.

After a time confidence was restored, but in A.D. 10 Hsü Chih-li, then king of Ulterior Chü-shih, fearing exactions by the "protector general," determined to go over to the Hsiung-nu; before his plans could be put in execution, however, his intentions were discovered by the deputy protector, and he was seized and beheaded. On the other hand, his brother led off all the flocks and herds of the kingdom. Later in the same year the Hsiung-nu made an attack on Anterior Chü-shih (Turfan), in which the Chinese commander was killed.

In A.D. 14 a treaty was again entered into by Wang Mang and the Hsiung-nu, but again, as is said, the emperor played false with the *shan-yü,* and hostilities were resumed. In 16, as has already been mentioned, the Hsiung-nu made a grand attack upon the northern frontier, "while the Western Regions were broken up and scattered like loose tiles." The first of the kingdoms to revolt was Yen-ch'i (Kara-shahr), and in the rising the "protector general" lost his life. A Chinese force was dispatched to the Tarim, but the attempt to regain Yen-ch'i met with disaster, and the Chinese officials were forced to defend themselves in Ch'iu-tzŭ (Kucha).

Central Europe, A.D. 4–18.—The information available concerning occurrences in Central Europe during the years just before and after A.D. 2 is both scant and obscure. Thus the inscription in honor of the general whose name ended in *-cius* (see ch. I, § XI) is undated as well as incomplete. Nevertheless it states that he crossed the Danube, evidently between Vienna and Budapest, overcame the Quadi (?) and Bastarnae, and came in

contact with the Cotini and Anartii. The year of this event is not
known, and various dates between 19 B.C. and A.D. 6 have been
suggested for it; nevertheless the preponderance of opinion
points to the time of the expedition as between 6 B.C. and A.D. 4.
Now, the arguments for one date or another are based, in the
last resort, on "reasons of policy and strategy";[4] in this situation
it must be insisted upon that there is no record of the Romans'
having proceeded against barbarian tribes at any time without
immediate provocation. The question, then, is not so much "at
what date a legate of Augustus is likely to have crossed the Danube between Vienna and Budapest" as at what date it is likely that
an outbreak occurred of the peoples between the river March
and the upper Theiss. In the light of other outbreaks to be mentioned, the answer to this question would be about A.D. 3–4. The
Marcomanni do not come into consideration, for the reason that,
up to his defeat by Arminius, Maroboduus was quite able to defend and to maintain order in his original kingdom.

No outbreak in Central Europe is mentioned by Roman historians which matches the disturbances at Guchen in A.D. 10,
unless, indeed, the expedition of Cn. Cornelius Lentulus (see
ch. I, § IX) is, as quite commonly, to be placed about A.D. 11.
On the other hand, it is certain that Pannonia was set off from
Illyricum as a province between the years A.D. 10 and 14, and
this administrative action, taken while war was in progress on
the Rhine and while the lower Danube was threatened by the
Dacians, indicates that need had arisen for a separate military
command on the river between Vienna and Budapest. The name
of no legate in the new province between 10 and 14 is given by
modern authorities, yet there is reason to believe that the officer
in command during 12 and 13 was L. Aelius Lamia.[5] Velleius

---

[4] Ronald Syme, "M. Vinicius (cos. 19 B.C.)," *Classical Quarterly*, 27 (1933), 146.

[5] For his career, see Velleius ii. 116. 3. See also Maria Marchetti in *Bullettino
della Commissione archeologica comunale di Roma*, 40 (1912), 133–138; Edmund
Groag in Ritterling, *Fasti des römischen Deutschland* (Wien, 1932), 11; S. J. de
Laet in *Antiquité classique*, 6 (1937), 137–138.

Paterculus says of Lamia that he rendered most distinguished services (*splendidissimis functus ministeriis*) in Germany, Illyricum, and Africa, and since, in all probability, he was in Germany in 10 and 11 and in Africa in 15 and 16, his term in Illyricum or Pannonia would have been in the intervening years (12 and 13). Unfortunately Velleius gives no indication in regard to the activities of Lamia further than to say that he was not awarded the honors of a triumph. The provision made for the defense of the Danube suggests strongly that disturbances among the peoples to the north had given rise to apprehension.

Definite information, fortunately, is forthcoming in regard to occurrences in Europe which parallel events in the region of the T'ien Shan in A.D. 16, for it is well known (see ch. I, § XIII) that in 18 a host from the Vistula (which included Goths), under the leadership of Catualda, invaded the kingdom of the Marcomanni, and that Maroboduus, with his defeated followers, was forced to take refuge with the Roman army in Pannonia. The fact that Tiberius had sent his son Drusus to take command on the frontier shows that the disturbances beyond the Danube had been judged a matter of serious concern by the government at Rome. The fact also throws some light on the situation in A.D. 12–14.

III

China and Mongolia, A.D. 25–52.—The death of Wang Mang was followed by struggles between various claimants for the throne. Thus, when Liu Hsiu, in A.D. 25, became emperor as Kuang-wu Ti, a competitor, Lu Fang, declared himself emperor in northern Shan-hsi and received the support of the Hsiung-nu. In 33 Kuang-wu Ti sent Wu Han against these allies, and in 34 the usurper was driven out. In 39 Wu Han, with the aid of many generals, again attacked the Hsiung-nu, but on this occasion he was forced to retire, and various tribes of the Hsiung-nu established themselves inside the Wall. In 40 Lu Fang returned and submitted to the Han government; in reality the Hsiung-nu sent him back in hope of obtaining a reward—which they did not receive. The emperor conferred upon the returned wanderer the title of King of Tai, and presented him with 20,000 pieces of silk. Nevertheless the adventurer again deserted to the Hsiung-nu in 42, but this move was speedily followed by his death. In 44 and 45 the Hsiung-nu made new incursions; in the latter year they acted in concert with the Wu-huan and the Hsien-pi, and the generals sent against them had little success.

In A.D. 46, Hsien of Yarkand attacked the kingdoms of Shan-shan and Ch'iu-tzŭ (Kucha); as a consequence Shan-shan and Turfan sought the protection of the Hsiung-nu (47).

In A.D. 46 the great khan of the Hsiung-nu died, and a struggle ensued over the selection of his successor.[1] At the instigation of the Han government the Wu-huan struck at the embroiled tribes and drove them north of the desert (Gobi). In 48 eight tribes of the Hsiung-nu who favored an alliance with China conferred upon Pi,[2] grandson of Hu-han-hsieh Khan, the title borne by his grandfather, and the government accepted their offer to settle on the border (in the vicinity of Wu-yüan) and defend it against raids. As a consequence of this agreement the tribes of the Hsiung-nu were divided into a "southern" group allied to China and an independent "northern" organization. In 49 the Southern Hsiung-nu attacked the northern tribes and inflicted such a defeat upon their former associates that the latter abandoned 1000 li of territory and moved away to lands west of the river Ongin. The Hsien-pi also attacked the Northern Hsiung-nu.[3] This disruption of the Hsiung-nu in 48 and 49 was an event

---

[1] For events from A.D. 46 to 52, see E. H. Parker, "The History of the Wu-wan or Wu-hwan Tunguses of the First Century," *China Review*, 20 (1893), 81, 85, 93; "The Turko-Scythian Tribes," *China Review*, 21 (1895), 255–261. Joseph de Guignes, *Histoire générale des Huns*, I. 2 (Paris, 1756), 113–115. J. A. M. de Moyriac de Mailla, *Histoire générale de la Chine*, III (Paris, 1777), 336–338, 341–345. Léon Wieger, *Textes historiques*, I (2ᵉéd., Hsien hsien, 1922), 663, 667–668.

[2] Pi is said to have prepared the way for his submission by sending to the emperor a map of the Hsiung-nu dominions. Parker, *China Review*, 21 (1895), 255.

[3] They were induced to do so by the Han government, see Parker, *China Review*, 20 (1893), 93. Wieger, *Textes historiques*, I, 668.

of the first importance, for the separation of the two branches became permanent.

The immediate effect of the division among the Hsiung-nu was that the northern tribes were cut off from intercourse and trade with China. The evidence for this deprivation is that in 51 the northern khan opened negotiations through the prefect at Wu-wei, in Kan-su, and when this official refused to receive his envoy, applied directly to the Han court. After a prolonged discussion[4] permission was given, in 52, for the resumption of trade between the Northern Hsiung-nu and the empire.

In Mongolia, the disruption of the Hsiung-nu led (in 49) to war between the two divisions, and conditions on the northern frontier of China remained unsettled until 52. In the Western Regions, the loss of Ch'iu-tzŭ (Kucha) by Hsien of So-chü (Yarkand) was followed by his attack on Ta-yüan (Ferghana), and this in turn provoked the K'ang-chü to hostilities, about 50. The events of A.D. 46–50 in Mongolia and Kashgaria were followed by disturbances farther west. Notably, in or about 50, the Yen-ts'ai changed their name to A-lan,[5] and contemporaneously the Alani are mentioned for the first time by western writers. The Aorsi, it may also be said, are referred to for the last time in 49, at the conclusion of the Mithridatic war. In 50 the Lugii and other tribes from the headwaters of the Vistula and Oder

---

[4] For the discussion, see Parker, *China Review*, 21 (1895), 259–260.

[5] Edouard Chavannes, "Les pays d'Occident d'après le Heou Han chou," *T'oung pao*, 8 (1907), 195 and note 2; "Les pays d'Occident d'après le Wei lio," *T'oung pao*, 6 (1905), 558 note 5, 559 note 1. See also Abel Rémusat, *Nouveaux mélanges asiatiques*, I (Paris, 1829), 239–240. Friedrich Hirth, "Ueber Wolga-Hunnen und Hiung-nu," *SAWM*, 1899, II, 249–251.

The statement concerning the change of name from Yen-ts'ai to A-lan has reference to the period A.D. 25–55, see Chavannes, *T'oung pao*, 8 (1907), 168, and see also 150, but the actual date is not given. The occurrence is brought into relation with the appearance of the Alani in Europe by Alfred von Gutschmid, *Geschichte Irans* Tübingen, 1888), 69–70, and by Josef Marquart, *Ērānšahr* (Berlin, 1901), 156, and "Untersuchungen zur Geschichte von Eran," *Philologus*, Supptbd. 10 (1905), 83, see also 82–87, 240–241.

Strabo (i. 2. 34) remarks that "change of name is frequent and noticeable among all nations." See also Ferdinand von Richthofen, *China*, I (Berlin, 1877), 51.

attacked the kingdom of Vannius (Marcomanni and Quadi).
The Hermunduri joined in the conflict on the side of the Lugii,
and Vannius, though he had been aided by the Jazyges, was
overthrown. No invasion of Pannonia followed these struggles,
but the emperor Claudius, in anticipation of such an event, had
sent additional troops to the Danube. Also in 50 the Chatti invaded the region of the Wetterau and the lower Main.

The wars of A.D. 49–50 would seem also to have affected the
peoples south of the Caucasus, for Pharasmanes, king of Iberia,
excused the attack upon his brother Mithridates (the Iberian),
king of Armenia, in 51, on the ground that the latter had refused
him assistance in a recent war with the Albanians.[6]

IV

China and Mongolia, A.D. 72–77.—After the fall of Hsien of
Yarkand (A.D. 61), the Northern Hsiung-nu became dominant
in the Western Regions. In 62 they extended their activities to
the great bend of the Huang Ho, where, however, they were opposed by the Southern Hsiung-nu. In 64 the northern *shan-yü*
opened negotiations for a renewal of trade, and the application
was approved by the Han government; but when, in 65, a mission was sent to the northern khan, the Southern Hsiung-nu took
offense and rose in revolt. Notwithstanding the efforts of the
Chinese commanders on the frontier, the Hsiung-nu, both Northern and Southern, continued for several years to burn cities and
settlements and to kill or carry off great numbers of people.[1]

In 72 the Northern Hsiung-nu invaded Tun-huang and the
other prefectures in Kan-su; in consequence of this aggression,
Ming Ti, at the earnest solicitation of Kêng Ping, determined to
reoccupy the Western Regions. Late in 72 an army was sent for-

---

[6] Tacitus *Ann*. xii. 45.

[1] For these occurrences, see E. H. Parker, "The Turko-Scythian Tribes," *China
Review*, 21 (1895), 261–262. J. A. M. de Moyriac de Mailla, *Histoire générale de
la Chine*, III (Paris, 1777), 356–357, 362. Léon Wieger, *Textes historiques*, I
(2ᵉ éd., Hsien hsien. 1922), 695.

ward to the Nan Shan, in order to take the field in the early
spring, and in 73 four armies marched against the Hsiung-nu
by different routes.[2] One of these forces, under the command of
Tou Ku and Pan Ch'ao, put to flight the Hu-yen tribe, the most
southerly group of the Northern Hsiung-nu, and occupied I-wu
(Hami). In 74 Tou Ku and Kêng Ping advanced to Barkul,
where the Hu-yen were again defeated. The Han generals then
divided their forces, and while Kêng Ping attacked Ulterior
Chü-shih (Guchen), Tou Ku proceeded against Anterior Chü-
shih (Turfan); the operations were entirely successful, and Ulterior Chü-shih was placed under the command of Kêng Kung.
(At the same time, as has been mentioned earlier, Pan Ch'ao
occupied Kashgar.) In 75, however, the *shan-yü* of the Northern Hsiung-nu sent 20,000 men against Kêng Kung, who before
long was hard put to it to defend himself at Guchen. Concurrently Yen-ch'i (Kara-shahr) and Ch'iu-tzŭ (Kucha), in alliance with the Hsiung-nu, attacked and killed the newly appointed
"protector general." It became necessary, therefore, for the commander on the Kan-su road to send support to the beleaguered
detachments in the T'ien Shan (76). The relieving force proceeded to Ch'iu-tzŭ, and later defeated the Northern Hsiung-nu
and the Chü-shih near Turfan. Kêng Kung was rescued, but at
the end of the campaign Guchen and Turfan were abandoned,
and in 77 Hami also was evacuated. In 77 the Ch'iang rose in
revolt; they submitted to Kêng Kung in the following year.

The war against the Northern Hsiung-nu from A.D. 72 to 77
was followed by serious disturbances south of the Caucasus
Mountains, for at some time between 72 and 75 the Alani in-

---

[2] For events from 72 to 77, see Parker, *China Review*, 21 (1895), 262–263.
Edouard Chavannes, "Les pays d'Occident d'après le Heou Han chou," *T'oung pao*,
8 (1907), 156–158, 211–212, 221–232. Mailla, *Histoire générale de la Chine*, III,
362–376. Wieger, *Textes historiques*, I, 695–696, 700–704. See also Chavannes, *Dix
inscriptions chinoises de l'Asie centrale* (Paris, 1902), 19–20. Sir Aurel Stein,
Serindia (Oxford, 1921), 732, 1147–51; *Innermost Asia* (Oxford, 1928), 540–541,
572–573. Walter Fuchs, "Das Turfangebiet," *Ostasiatische Zeitschrift*, 13 (1926),
127–130.

vaded Media and Armenia,[3] with results which have already
been described.

The account of the invasion given by Josephus has provoked controversy over the route by which the Alani reached Media and Armenia.
Stated briefly, the situation described by Josephus is that the Alani
made use of an unnamed pass, associated with the name of Alexander,
which gave access to Media (Atropatene, modern Azerbaijan), and
which in 73 was under control of Hyrcania (modern Astarabad). Now,
in the first place, it is to be noted that Alexander's name was connected
with the Caucasus Mountains, as well as with the "Caspian Gates" near
Rhagae, for Ptolemy (v. 8, 15) places the "columns of Alexander" north
of the Caucasus, and, indeed, north of the "Albanian Gates,"[4] the pass
of Derbent. Next, it is certain that, just as the Dariel pass led down to
(modern) Tiflis and Armenia, the pass of Derbent led to (modern)
Baku and Atropatene. Herodotus (iv. 12) says, indeed, that when the
Scythians pursued the Cimmerians southward, the latter fled by way of
the coast, and the Scythians followed, keeping the Caucasus on their
right, until they came into Media. Since, then, there was a pass associated with the name of Alexander by which the Alani could have reached
Media directly, it is obvious that the crux of the problem is whether it
was possible for the Hyrcanians to have been in control of this pass
about the year 73.

To appreciate the situation on the borders of the Caspian Sea, it is
necessary to recall Strabo's statement (xi. 506) concerning the upper
Aorsi, namely, that they ruled over most of the Caspian coast and were
thus able to import Indian and Babylonian merchandise; this information, which may be accepted as having reference to the century after
50 B.C., shows that the Aorsi made use of the Derbent route. As an ad-

---

[3] Josephus *BJ* vii. 7. 4 (244–251). The event is recorded by Josephus in the
fourth year of Vespasian's reign (72–73), but it was not until 75 that Vologeses
of Parthia became intent upon driving out the invaders. The date is given as 72
by Alfred von Gutschmid, *Geschichte Irans* (Tübingen, 1888), 133, and R. P.
Longden, "Notes on the Parthian Campaigns of Trajan," *JRS*, 21 (1931), 23–24;
as 72 or 73 by Eugen Täubler, "Zur Geschichte der Alanen," *Klio*, 9 (1909), 18–27,
and Joseph Markwart [Marquart], "Iberer und Hyrkanier," *Caucasica*, 8 (1931),
78; as 73, after July 1, by Georges Goyau, *Chronologie de l'empire romain* (Paris,
1891), 154; as 73–74 by J. H. Schneiderwirth, *Die Parther* (Heiligenstadt, 1874),
142, and Joseph Sandalgian, *Histoire documentaire de l'Arménie*, II (Rome, 1917),
537; and as 75 in the chronological table appended to *CAH*, XI (1936).

[4] See A. R. Anderson, "Alexander at the Caspian Gates," *TAPA*, 59 (1928), 141
note 16, 153 note 39.

dendum to Strabo's statement, it may be pointed out that, according to Marquart,[5] the upper Aorsi had also held a great part of the eastern coast of the Caspian, including the island of Cheleken, and had dominated the conveyance of Indo-Bactrian merchandise across the inland sea. As is well known, the Aorsi disappeared in or about A.D. 50, but it is not usually mentioned in connection with this event (1) that shortly thereafter, in 58, the Hyrcanians asserted their independence of Parthia, and (2) that independent Hyrcania extended northward to the mouth of the Oxus and included the island of Talca, the modern Cheleken (Ptolemy vi. 9). It is, therefore, reasonable to suppose that, when the organization of the Aorsi was broken up, the control of the commerce across the southern part of the Caspian came into the hands of the Hyrcanians. But at this point the subject takes on a broader aspect. In 58 the Hyrcanians had sent an embassy to Rome for the purpose of forming an alliance against Parthia (Tacitus *Ann.* xiv. 25). Nero, indeed, was definitely interested in promoting the Oxo-Caspian trade route,[6] and after the conclusion of the Armenian war (63) and the crowning of Tiridates at Rome in 66, he sent troops to Iberia in preparation, as Tacitus says (*Hist.* i. 6), for a campaign against the Albanians. Since it is clear that the Hyrcanians, in succeeding to the place of the Aorsi, must either have had or desired to have a footing on the Albanian coast, and since they are known to have desired an alliance with Rome, it would seem probable that the objective of Nero's campaign was to join hands with them by bringing under Roman domination the last link in an eastern trade route which would be entirely free from the exactions of the Parthians. Nero's preparations in the Caucasus came to nothing, and Vespasian adopted a new eastern policy, but the next item of information which has been preserved in relation to the Hyrcanians is that at the time to which Josephus refers they were in control of the pass of Derbent. The considerations which have been presented warrant the conclusion that the narrative of Josephus is to be accepted as it stands.

[5] Josef Marquart, "Über das Volkstum der Komanen," *AGWG*, N.F. 13 (1914), 108.

[6] The much-debated question whether trade was ever actually brought down the river Oxus to the Caspian Sea does not enter into the discussion. In formulating an eastern policy Nero, Seneca, and Burrus had before them the statements of Strabo (ii. 73 and xi. 509) and Pliny (vi. 52) that Indian wares reached the Black Sea by way of the Oxus, the Caspian, Albania (the river Cyrus), and the river Phasis. Further, they may be assumed to have consulted the Hyrcanian envoys on the possibilities of trade, and they had every opportunity to obtain information from Roman traders in Colchis, Iberia, and Armenia.

In succession to the hostilities on the borders of China and the disturbances which affected the Alani on the Don, uprisings took place in Central Europe. It is true that the literary sources make no reference to incursions at this juncture either on the Danube or on the Rhine, but other evidence leaves no doubt concerning the outbreak of war. In particular, it is known that in 74 Cn. Pinarius Cornelius Clemens[7] carried on a campaign from Strasbourg eastward to the upper Neckar (in Württemberg). The war certainly extended beyond the area in which Cornelius Clemens is known to have been active, for the distribution of the forts which were built in central Bavaria between 77 and 80, a number of them under the direction of C. Saturius, procurator of Raetia, indicates that the region north of Augsburg and west of Regensburg had been subject to invasion. It is noteworthy that the defensive works in this region were set up on the borders of the Hermunduri, and in the absence of any literary account of events between 74 and 76 it should be recalled that the Hermunduri had been involved in the complex occurrences of A.D. 18–20 and 50, and that later on they participated in the great invasion of 167, when they broke through the line of forts to which reference has just been made.[8]

V

China and Mongolia, A.D. 84–87.—In A.D. 84 the Northern Hsiung-nu "again expressed a desire for trade with both offi-

---

[7] See above, p. 123.

[8] Under Vespasian and Titus a line of forts was constructed which ran south of the Danube from Boiodurum (near Passau), through Künzing, Straubing, and Eining, as far at least as Ulm. Later another line of forts, the Raetian limes, was built north of the Danube from a point opposite Eining to the western border of Raetia, where it joined the defensive system of Upper Germany near Lorch (east of Stuttgart). See Fabricius, "Limes," *RECA*, XIII (1926), 605–608. The Raetian limes does not appear to have been originally laid out step by step from east to west; on the other hand, the advanced posts were evidently reached, through supporting positions, from stations on the Danube, by following up prehistoric routes which ran northward from the river into the territory occupied (from the beginning of the first century A.D.) by the Hermunduri. Compare the usual map of the limes, as in *CAH*, XI (1936), 158, with the map of prehistoric roads given

cials and people," and Chang Ti acceded to their request. When, however, princes and chiefs came with more than 10,000 cattle and sheep to trade with the Han merchants, the khan of the Southern Hsiung-nu sent a force to attack them. In the early spring of 85 a concerted movement was made against the northern tribes: "the southern horde attacked them in front [south], and the Ting-ling attacked them in the rear [north]; the Hsien-pi attacked them on the left [east], and the Turkistan tribes encroached upon their right [west], so that they were no longer able to maintain their position, and withdrew far to the north."[1]

by F. Winkelman, "Die vorrömischen und römischen Strassen in Bayern zwischen Donau und Limes," Römisch-germanische Kommission, 11. *Bericht* (Frankfurt a. M., 1920), map 1. As is well known (Tacitus *Germania* 41), the Hermunduri, about the middle of the first century, were permitted to cross the Danube without supervision and to enter Augusta Vindelicorum (Augsburg) for purposes of trade. On the other hand, the forts erected by Vespasian south of the Danube give the appearance of having been designed to control the approaches to Augsburg, and it is of interest to observe that the three forts nearest the city, Günzburg (107), Aislingen (108), and Burghöfe (122), would seem to have been burnt in the time of Domitian. Olwen Brogan, "The Roman Limes in Germany," *Archaeological Journal*, 92 (1935), 6 note 1. The inference to be drawn is that the Hermunduri, once allies of Rome, had crossed the Danube with hostile intent both in the time of Vespasian (74–76) and of Domitian (most probably in 92). Thus the evidence available points to an invasion of the Hermunduri in 74–76, while the fuller information in the literary sources for A.D. 50 and 167 suggests strongly that the disturbances under Vespasian must have extended to the Marcomanni. Further, it is difficult to ignore the fact that incursions of the Marcomanni into Pannonia (89, 92, 97) took place only after the construction of the Raetian forts north of the Danube.

An additional point may be brought up. In the prologue to his *Argonautica* (i. 5–12) Valerius Flaccus invokes Vespasian. In the sixth book (162, 231–238) he gives a description of the arms and tactics of the Sarmatians, evidently the Jazyges, which is "surprising in its novelty," since it is the first in classical literature. Ronald Syme, "The *Argonautica* of Valerius Flaccus," *Classical Quarterly*, 23 (1929), 129–137. Syme is of opinion that the familiarity with the Sarmatians was due to their wars with Rome in 89 and 92, and infers consequently that the sixth book of the *Argonautica* was not reached until 89 or 92, though it is usually supposed that Valerius died, at latest, in 90. On this interpretation the invocation to Vespasian must be explained away (Syme, 135–136). The simpler explanation, however, is that a war in which the Jazyges took part occurred in or about 75.

[1] For occurrences from 84 to 92, see E. H. Parker, "The Turko-Scythian Tribes," *China Review*, 21 (1895), 263–267, 291. Edouard Chavannes, "Les pays d'Occident d'après le Heou Han chou," *T'oung pao*, 8 (1907), 158, 212, 224. Joseph de Guignes, *Histoire générale des Huns*, I. 2 (Paris, 1756), 132. J. A. M. de Moyriac de Mailla, *Histoire générale de la Chine*, III (Paris, 1777), 388, 391–397. Léon Wieger, *Textes historiques*, I (2ᵉ éd., Hsien hsien, 1922), 705–706, 713–715, 717–718.

In 86 the southern khan followed up the assault and defeated a band of the Northern Hsiung-nu in the Cho-hsieh Hills (possibly the Khara-narin-ula). It seems probable that the war on the northern tribes was instigated by the Chinese, for the government paid a bounty for heads of the defeated tribesmen. Certainly it was by order of Chang Ti that the Hsien-pi and Wu-huan attacked the Northern Hsiung-nu in 87, and on this occasion the northern *shan-yü* was captured and beheaded. In consequence of the reverses sustained, many bands of the northerners presented themselves at the frontier and submitted to the Chinese authorities; the remainder, "in dread of the Ting-ling and the Hsien-pi, fled far away" to the west side of the river An-hou (presumably one of the rivers immediately west of the Ongin). Contemporaneously (between 85 and 87) Pan Ch'ao, with the aid of the Yüeh-chih, attacked the Chü-shih at Turfan.

In 89[2] the emperor Domitian suffered defeat at the hands of the Marcomanni and Quadi. Dio attributes the outbreak of hostilities to Domitian, who, he says, wished to requite the Marcomanni and Quadi for their failure to render assistance against the Dacians. On the other hand, whatever the views and intentions of Domitian may have been, the Suebic tribes were in Pannonia when they put his army to rout.

VI

China and Mongolia, A.D. 89–91.—After the death of the northern *shan-yü*, a conflict arose over the choice of his successor; hence, in 88, when this new factor in the situation was brought to the attention of the Han government, the decision was reached to send an army to coöperate with the Southern Hsiung-nu. In 89, therefore, Tou Hsien and Kêng Ping attacked the Northern Hsiung-nu and inflicted upon them a great defeat (presumably

[2] It is possible that the Alani may have invaded Armenia in or about 88. See Julius Klaproth, "Histoire de la Géorgie," *Journal asiatique*, 2. sér., 13 (1834), 49–55. M. F. Brosset, *Histoire de la Géorgie*, I (S.-Pétersbourg, 1849), 66 and note 3. See also J. A. Saint-Martin, *Mémoires historiques et géographiques sur l'Arménie*, I (Paris, 1818), 300.

in the neighborhood of the modern Ta-t'ung-fu); the northern khan fled, and more than 200,000 men were either killed or made prisoners. Tou Hsien erected a monument to commemorate the victory.[1] In 90 the Han general directed an attack upon I-wu (Hami), and the occupation of this position was followed by the submission of the Chü-shih (Turfan and Guchen). Contemporaneously (90) the Southern Hsiung-nu, accompanied by Chinese troops, again defeated the northern khan and captured his headquarters, west of the river An-hou; and though the khan himself escaped, "his jade seal, and also his queen, sons, and daughters were taken." In 91 Kêng K'uei advanced from the Etsin Gol for a distance of 5000 *li* into Hsiung-nu territory and defeated the northern tribes at some place on the road between Uliassutai and Kobdo. Thereafter the Northern Hsiung-nu fled, "no one knew whither," and "l'empire des Huns fut entièrement détruit."[2] Contemporaneously (91) Pan Ch'ao received the submission of Ch'iu-tzŭ (Kucha) and other kingdoms on the northern route in the Tarim basin.

Later, in 93, the Hsien-pi took advantage of the overthrow of the Northern Hsiung-nu and established themselves in territory of which the northern tribes had been dispossessed.[3]

As a result of the successes of Tou Hsien and Kêng K'uei from 89 to 91, the northern tribes[4] were completely disorganized and

[1] H. A. Giles, *A Chinese Biographical Dictionary* (London, 1898), no. 1956. Edouard Chavannes, *Dix inscriptions chinoises de l'Asie centrale* (Paris, 1902), 25 note 3.

[2] Joseph de Guignes, *Histoire générale des Huns*, I. 2 (Paris, 1756), 132.

[3] E. H. Parker, "The History of the Wu-wan or Wu-hwan Tunguses of the first century," *China Review*, 20 (1893), 93. Mailla, *Histoire générale de la Chine*, III (Paris, 1777), 397. Léon Wieger, *Textes historiques*, I (2ᵉéd., Hsien hsien, 1922), 719. The Hsien-pi had gained strength in A.D. 50, at the time of the wars between the northern and southern tribes. Parker, 85.

[4] De Guignes, *Histoire générale des Huns*, I. 2, 123, 278–279. Julius Klaproth, *Tableaux historiques de l'Asie* (Paris, 1826), 109–110. Léon Cahun, *Introduction à l'histoire de l'Asie* (Paris, 1896), 96–98. Friedrich Hirth, "Ueber Wolga-Hunnen und Hiung-nu," *SAWM*, 1899, II, 268–269. Kiessling, "Hunni," *RECA*, VIII (1913), 2600. E. H. Minns, *Scythians and Greeks* (Cambridge, 1913), 122. René Grousset, *Histoire de l'Asie*, II (3ᵉ éd., Paris, 1922), 191. Otto Franke, *Geschichte des chinesischen Reiches*, I (Berlin, 1930), 399.

dispersed. Some of the tribes found refuge in the mountains north of Kucha, in the Ili valley, in the vicinity of Lake Balkhash, and in the territory of the K'ang-chü; while others made their way into the region of the Irtish and the Ob.

The dispersion of the Northern Hsiung-nu was followed by movements of peoples and wars throughout Europe.

In the Bosporan kingdom, Rhescuporis I, in the later years of his reign, was engaged in war with barbarians, and his copper coins represent him triumphing over Scythians.[5] Further, the last dated coin of Rhescuporis was issued in 91/92, whereas the first coin of his successor, Sauromates I, was not struck until 93/94, and this gap suggests that there may have been serious difficulties in the kingdom in 92.

In Central Europe, in 92, as has been mentioned earlier, the Marcomanni, Quadi, and Jazyges invaded Pannonia, where they annihilated a Roman legion, and the emperor was engaged for the greater part of the year in driving them back.

VII

China and Mongolia, A.D. 95–97.—In A.D. 94–95 conflicts arose between different groups of the Hsiung-nu in the region of the great bend of the Huang Ho, and 200,000 of the Northern Hsiung-nu, who some years earlier had surrendered to the Han government, and who were involved in these conflicts, revolted; the Chinese officials raised a large army, including levies from the Wu-huan, Hsien-pi, and Southern Hsiung-nu, and defeated the northern tribesmen, who moved away from the frontier.[1]

In 96 Cho-ti, king of Ulterior Chü-shih (Guchen), was threatened with removal by the Han official resident in his kingdom.

---

[5] There are no literary sources for the reign of Rhescuporis I. For the numismatic evidence, see P. O. Burachov, *General Catalogue of Coins Belonging to the Greek Colonies* [in Russian] (Odessa, 1884), 252–253. Warwick Wroth, *Catalogue of Greek Coins; Pontus ... and the Kingdom of Bosporus* (London, 1889), 54–56. Minns, *Scythians and Greeks*, 599, 600, 611.

[1] E. H. Parker, "The Turko-Scythian Tribes," *China Review*, 21 (1895), 293–294.

Convinced that Wei-pei-ta, king of Anterior Chü-shih, had betrayed him to the Chinese, Cho-ti attacked Turfan and was so
far successful that he captured the wife and children of the king.
In 97 the Han government sent Wang Lin from Liang-chou on
a punitive expedition against Ulterior Chü-shih, with an army
which included 20,000 men recruited from the Tibetan Ch'iang
and other peoples on the borders of Kan-su. The advance of this
force drove Cho-ti to take refuge in the territory of the Northern
Hsiung-nu (presumably in the T'ien Shan north of Kucha); he
was, however, pursued and eventually decapitated.[2]

In 97 the Marcomanni and Quadi invaded Pannonia, and the
war appears to have extended into 98.

VIII

China and Mongolia, A.D. 105–107.—In 104 the khan of the
Northern Hsiung-nu sent an envoy to the Han court with tribute
offerings and proposals of friendship, and in 105 sent an envoy
to Tun-huang; but nothing came of these efforts. In 105, after
the death of Ho Ti, and while the government was in the hands
of the empress Têng, the Northern Hsiung-nu took possession of
Guchen, and by 107 had once again become dominant on the
northern route in the Tarim.

In 107 Hadrian, then governor of Lower Pannonia, was called
upon to defend his province against inroads of the Jazyges.

The details which have now been presented in regard to the
activities of the Han government from A.D. 72 to 107, a period
within which falls the career of Pan Ch'ao in Kashgaria, have
been introduced in order to throw light upon occurrences in
Europe in the reigns of Vespasian, Domitian, and Trajan. If
the statement of events set down at the beginning of this chapter
be now reëxamined, it will be seen that the hostilities on the
northern borders of the Roman empire occurred in correspond-

---

[2] Edouard Chavannes, "Les pays d'Occident d'aprés le Heou Han chou," *T'oung
pao*, 8 (1907), 212. Walter Fuchs, "Das Turfangebiet," *Ostasiatische Zeitschrift*, 13
(1926), 130. Sir Aurel Stein, *Innermost Asia* (Oxford, 1928), 573.

ence either with wars in the Roman East or with wars in Central
Asia. The point of interest and importance with respect to these
correspondences, however, is that, whereas the disturbances in
the Roman East were followed, as on earlier occasions, by outbreaks on the Lower Danube and the Rhine, the disturbances in
Central Asia were followed, with similar uniformity, by uprisings beyond the upper Danube and by invasions of Pannonia.
Thus, on the one hand, barbarian uprisings on the lower Danube
and the Rhine in 74–77, 82–83, 85–86, 88–89, and 105–106
came in succession to disturbances on the eastern frontier of
the empire, which in turn followed disturbances in Kashgaria,
while, on the other hand, outbreaks on the upper Danube in
74–76, 89, 92, 97–98, and 107 came in succession to disturbances in the eastern T'ien Shan, more particularly at Guchen
and Turfan. A comparison of the two series of dates will lead
to the observation that three times the uprisings on the lower
Danube, the upper Danube, and the Rhine were very nearly
coincident. During the period, Trajan's Dacian war of 101–102
was, to all appearance, the only conflict upon which the Romans
entered without immediate and direct provocation.

Observations and Comments

It is evident from the data which have been assembled that on
a number of occasions barbarian invasions affected the Roman
frontier on the upper Danube, a region which was not subject
to attack when uprisings in Europe followed wars in the Roman
East alone. It appears further that disturbances north of the
Danube and invasions of Pannonia took place at times which
exhibit a striking correspondence with wars in Mongolia. It follows, therefore, that attention must now be given to the question
whether outbreaks in Central Europe could by any possibility
have been connected with occurrences in the eastern T'ien Shan.

As for the disturbances in Parthia which occurred in correspondence with wars in Kashgaria, the regions affected, though

widely separated, were connected by the *iter longissimum*, the long road of the transcontinental silk route, and it is comprehensible that wars and consequent interruptions of trade on eastern stretches of the route should have been followed by interruptions and consequent disturbances farther west. As for the invasions of Pannonia, however, there is no evidence that Central Asia and Central Europe were linked together by a continuous trade route, and as a consequence the two groups of occurrences are not on an equal footing. But before the correspondence of events in Mongolia and Pannonia is ascribed to mere accidental coincidence, it will be necessary to examine, even laboriously, the relationships of peoples from Poland to Inner Mongolia.

The connections of peoples in Central Russia.—At the beginning of the first century of the present era, the geographer Strabo recorded certain particulars in regard to the inhabitants of the plains which lie north of the Black Sea. In this region he mentions (vii. 306) the Tyregetae and a group of Sarmatian tribes in which he includes the Jazyges and Roxolani. "Whether," he says, "any people dwell beyond the Roxolani, we do not know," and he ascribes (xi. 493) the lack of knowledge concerning the country beyond the mouth of the Don to the hostility of the nomads who "have blocked off whatever parts of the country are passable and whatever parts of the river happen to be navigable."

By the middle of the first century, however, the northern horizon of the classical world had been greatly extended, and definite evidence that peoples hitherto unknown had come within the purview of the Romans is contained in the summary statement which Pliny prefixed to his account of the Scythian peoples (*NH* iv. 80). In an enumeration of the barbarians beyond the Danube, Pliny speaks first of the Getae, who, he says, are called Daci by the Romans; then of the Sarmatae, called Sauromatae by the Greeks, adding parenthetically that to these belong the Hamaxobii or Aorsi; next he mentions degenerate Scythians

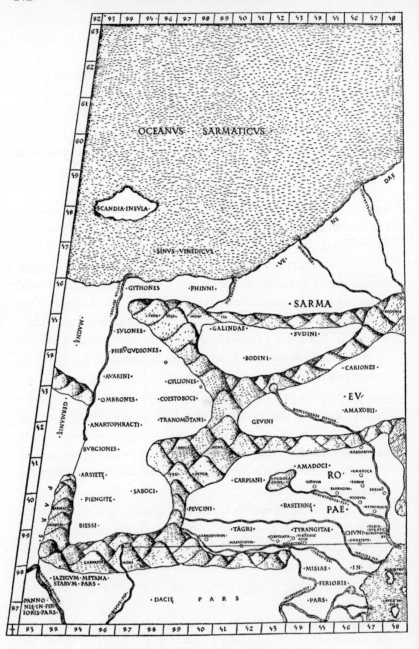

9. PTOLEMY'S MAP OF EUROPEAN SARMATIA.

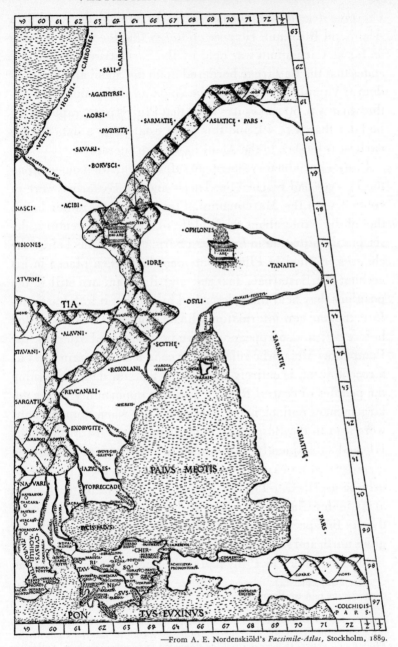

—From A. E. Nordenskiöld's *Facsimile-Atlas*, Stockholm, 1889.

9. PTOLEMY'S MAP OF EUROPEAN SARMATIA.

(*Scythae degeneres*), born of slaves, or Trogodytae;[1] and then Alani and Roxolani. He goes on to say that the upper Danube as far as Carnuntum was held by the Sarmatian Jazyges, and states that the Bastarnae bordered upon the Suebi and the kingdom of Vannius. The fact that the kingdom of Vannius was overthrown in A.D. 50 makes it evident that Pliny's paragraph cannot be later than A.D. 49, and this point establishes a date for the earliest reference to the Alani in western literature.

Pliny's introductory statement refers, then, to a moment when the Jazyges had reached the Theiss and the Bastarnae were in contact with the Marcomanni. Ptolemy, on the other hand, though he wrote about the middle of the second century, describes the situation in European Sarmatia as it was before the changes implied in Pliny's statement had taken place; in his account the Bastarnae, Jazyges, and Roxolani are still in the positions they held when described by Strabo. It follows, therefore, that the new information which he presents was assembled before 49; it also appears to have been obtained after 43, for Pomponius Mela, who refers to the conquest of Britain (43) as a recent event, is entirely ignorant of the new data concerning the peoples of central Russia. Now, the opportunity for an enlargement of outlook in this direction came when Roman troops were sent to the Bosporan kingdom in 45 to oust Mithridates III, and subsequently were forced to carry on war against the dispossessed monarch. The new information, then, may properly be ascribed to the intelligence department of the Roman army under Claudius, an emperor who is cited by Pliny as authority for specific details concerning the geography of the regions north and south of the Caucasus Mountains.

Ptolemy, much as Pliny had done, begins his account of the

---

[1] Here Pliny appears to introduce a literary allusion to the story of the *Scythae degeneres* as told by Herodotus iv. 3–4 and by Justin (Trogus Pompeius) ii. 5. Reference to the story, however, was contained in a source followed by Valerius Flaccus *Argonautica* vi. 86, and by Ammianus Marcellinus xxii. 8. 41, who, too, in the context, mentions the Trogodytae (near the mouth of the Danube). Hence Pliny would appear to have derived the statement from some "modern" authority.

peoples of European Sarmatia with a short general statement
(iii. 5. 19), in which he mentions only the Venedae, the Peucini
and Bastarnae, the Jazyges and Roxolani, and the Hamaxobii
and Alani Scythae. He then goes on to a more detailed description (20–25), and this on examination proves to embody lists
of the tribal names on various trade routes in the country between the Vistula and the Don.

First, Ptolemy gives the names of fourteen or more peoples
on a route which followed the eastern bank of the Vistula
southward from its mouth; the list begins with the Venedae and
Guthones and ends with the Piengitae and Biessi near the Carpathian Mountains. On the western bank a similar route left the
Vistula at the town of Ascaucalis (at the bend near Bromberg),
and finally reached Carnuntum on the Danube.

More striking, however, is the manner in which Ptolemy rep-
resents the Roxolani (to whom Strabo also had attached special
importance) as the center upon which converged a series of
routes from the west and north. Thus a route from the Venedae
is indicated as extending by way of the Galindae, Sudini, and
Stavani to the Alauni. Again, a route from the far north pro-
ceeds by way of the Acibi and Nasci, the Vibiones and Idrae,
and the Sturni to the Alauni. From the Alauni the line of connection then runs to the Hamaxobii, and from the latter to the
Roxolani. In greater detail, between the Alauni and Hamaxobii,
Ptolemy places the Cariones and Sargatii, and between the
Hamaxobii and Roxolani the Reucanali and Exobygitae. Further, from the north by way of the river Don, a route connects
the Ophlones, Tanaitae, and Osili with the Roxolani. Finally,
the Bodini, Gevini, and Carpiani are represented as in communication with the Bastarnae, while the Bastarnae themselves are
linked with the Roxolani by the Chuni.

The names which have just been enumerated exhaust those
given by Ptolemy in the region of central Russia west of the Don.
Since, however, the routes described all lead to the Roxolani,

it follows that the peoples who became known to the Romans between A.D. 45 and 49 were those, and probably those only, with whom the Roxolani maintained relations.

The connections of peoples between the river Don and the Caucasus Mountains.—Asiatic Sarmatia as described by Ptolemy included, in addition to the country between the Don and the Volga, the region from the lower course of the Don to the Caucasus Mountains. Within the latter area the eastern shores of the Maeotis or Sea of Azov were inhabited by tribes, spoken of collectively as Maeotae, who ordinarily were subject to the kingdom of Bosporus. In the interior, beyond the territorial jurisdiction of Bosporus, were many independent peoples, of whom the most significant were those situated on a route from the Don to the pass of Derbent.

According to the account given by Strabo, the Don-Derbent route, about 50 B.C., was in the hands of the Aorsi and Siraci, and in regard to the position of these peoples he goes into some detail. Thus, he says (xi. 491, 492) that in the region of the river Tanais (Don) there were, first, Scythian nomads and wagon dwellers, next, below them, Sarmatians, and, third, the Aorsi and Siraci, who extended southward as far as the Caucasus Mountains. At a later point in his description (xi. 506) he says that the Aorsi were more to the north than the Siraci, and that they lived along the Tanais; the Siraci, on the other hand, were situated on the river Achardeus (presumably the modern Yegorlyk). He remarks in the same connection that the two peoples were thought to be offshoots from the "upper" tribes of these names, and that the upper Aorsi might be said to rule over most of the Caspian coast. "Consequently," he continues, "they could import on camels Indian and Babylonian merchandise, which they received in their turn from the Armenians and the Medes"; he adds, too, that, "owing to their wealth, they could wear gold ornaments." This second and longer reference to the Aorsi and Siraci goes back evidently to an account of the war which Pharnaces carried on in 48–47 B.C. for the recovery of his father's dominions east of the Maeotis.

Tacitus likewise mentions the Aorsi and Siraci in his narrative of the war which Mithridates III (A.D. 47–48) waged against his brother Cotys and the Romans (*Ann.* xii. 15–21); but in this conflict the Aorsi and Siraci were on opposite sides, for when the latter gave their support to Mithridates, the former were promptly enlisted by his enemies. Now, the fact that Strabo and Tacitus both direct attention to the Aorsi has given this people or confederacy a relatively prominent place in ancient history; consequently it is of interest to note that all other geographers and historians, from Hecataeus to Ptolemy and Ammianus Marcellinus, mention the Iaxamatae[2] in their place on the Don, and that Ptolemy gives to the Iaxamatae and Siraceni the positions assigned by Strabo to the Aorsi and Siraci. The inference to be drawn from the information available is that the Iaxamatae constituted the unit of the Aorsi organization which was situated on the river Don; and it is not to be overlooked that the Aorsi became conspicuous only when the caravan leaders turned for the moment to the gainful pursuit of war.

Pliny does not refer to the Aorsi in his account (book vi) of the peoples north of the Caucasus;[3] on the other hand, in the sum-

[2] Herrmann, "Iaxamatae," *RECA*, IX (1914), 1179–80, cites ten authors, six Greek and four Latin, who mention the Iaxamatae, with varying orthography. He includes, however, the name "Mazamacae," from Pliny *NH* vi. 21, the identification of which with "Iaxamatae" is more than doubtful, especially since Detlefsen, in his text of Pliny's geographical books, reads it as "Mazacacae" or "Mazacasi."

[3] Pliny, in *NH* vi. 39, mentions a people under the name "Utidorsi," and Mayhoff, in the Teubner edition of the text, emends this to "Uti, Aorsi." Now Ptolemy, in his account of Scythia intra Imaum (vi. 14), has the name "Alanorsi," and Tomaschek, Herrmann, and others are of opinion that this in a similar manner should be altered to "Alani, Aorsi." An emendation purports to remove an erroneous reading due to the faulty transmission of a text, and thus to restore the words originally written by the author. The peculiarity in the instance under consideration is that the same error is supposed to have been made and uniformly retained by the copyists of two different works, the one in Latin, the other in Greek. It seems more reasonable to assume, with Marquart, "Untersuchungen zur Geschichte von Eran," *Philologus*, Supptbd. 10 (1905), 85–87, that the termination *-orsi* in the two names had some recognized significance.

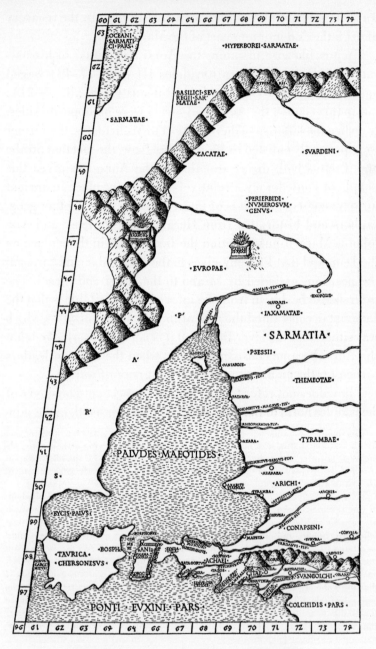

10. Ptolemy's map of Asiatic Sarmatia.

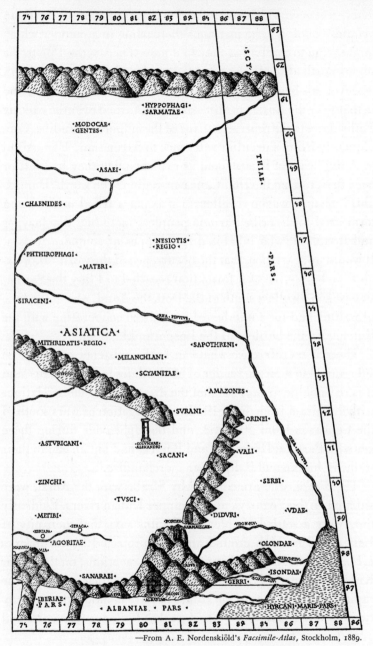

—From A. E. Nordenskiöld's *Facsimile-Atlas*, Stockholm, 1889.

10. PTOLEMY'S MAP OF ASIATIC SARMATIA.

mary statement which he prefixed to his account of the Scythian peoples (book iv), he mentions their name in a manner which might seem to imply that they had moved across the Don to the plains north of the Black Sea. As has already been pointed out, however, his brief survey was written not later than A.D. 49, and in that year the Aorsi, as allies of Rome, turned over the ex-king Mithridates to the representatives of the emperor Claudius. Consequently Pliny's peculiar reference to Sarmatian "Hamaxobii or Aorsi" cannot be accepted as evidence that they had left or been driven from the Don-Caucasus region. The word "Hamaxobii" means "wagon dwellers"; it is not a tribal name, but a term used to describe various peoples, including the Jazyges and Roxolani, who inhabited the steppes of southern Russia. It would appear, then, that the occurrence of the word "Hamaxobii" in his source of information recalled to Pliny the Sarmatian wagon dwellers south of the Don, the Aorsi, who at the time of writing had for a number of years been coöperating with the Romans on the borders of the Bosporan kingdom.

There is no reference whatever to the existence of the Aorsi subsequent to their surrender of Mithridates to the Romans, and it is reasonable to suppose that the disruption of their relations with the Siraci from 46 to 49, the prolongation of wars south of the Caucasus from 50 to 63, and the upheavals during those years in Parthia, Hyrcania, and Bactria had put an end to their traffic in Indian and Babylonian merchandise.

The Siraci, who are coupled by Strabo with the Aorsi, were situated on the Yegorlyk and the upper Kuban rivers. Evidently they were a settled people, for Tacitus says that their city of Uspe stood on high ground and was protected by earthworks (*Ann.* xii. 16), and Ptolemy (v. 8. 28) mentions, on the upper Kuban, the city of Seraca, which has been conjectured to be the capital and residence of the king. They are mentioned in inscriptions as late as A.D. 193.[4] The fact that Ptolemy (see v. 12 and

---

[4] E. H. Minns, *Scythians and Greeks* (Cambridge, 1913), 120.

vi. 9) refers to areas named Siracene in Armenia and Hyrcania, when taken in connection with Strabo's account of the trade carried on by the Aorsi with the Armenians and Medes, suggests the likelihood that the Siraci also had connections with peoples south of the Caucasus.

In A.D. 46 or 47 the Siraci took the side of Mithridates III against the Romans, and the base from which the deposed king maintained his opposition was adjacent to their territory. In his text Ptolemy states that the "Mithridatic region" was between the Hippici Mountains (the northern extension of the Central Caucasus) and the river Ra or Rha (Volga); on his map of Asiatic Sarmatia he places the "region" southeast of the Siraceni and on the frontage of the mountains toward the Volga. Consequently, though the Hippici Mountains are placed too far to the north (in keeping with the exaggerated extension which Ptolemy gives to the Maeotis), the relative positions of the Siraci, the Mithridatic-land, and the mountains remain in accord with the indications provided by Strabo, Pliny (*NH* vi. 17), and Tacitus.

In the course of the Mithridatic war the Romans acquired new information concerning the neighbors of the Siraci, and the fact that Ptolemy gives prominence to the Mithridatic region is clearly indicative of the time at which the information was obtained. Hence it is of interest to observe that, in addition to their connections with peoples to the north and south, the Siraci, up to A.D. 50, were similarly situated with reference to peoples on a highly important route to the east.[5] In his text, Ptolemy says of the Udae that they were near the Caspian Sea; on his map of Asiatic Sarmatia, however, he places them more definitely north of the river Udon (Kuma) and close to the mouth of the Ra (Volga). Now Pliny states (*NH* vi. 38) that the Udini (Udae) were situated on the right bank of the strait between the

---

[5] For archaeological evidence that the district of Stavropol (i.e., the territory of the Siraci) had connections with China in the first century A.D., see M. I. Rostovtzeff, *Iranians & Greeks in South Russia* (Oxford, 1922), 132.

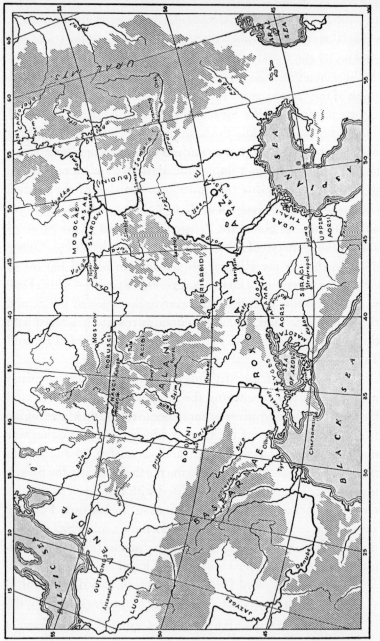

II. Sarmatia: Europe from the Vistula to the Volga.

Caspian Sea and the Northern Ocean and at its very entrance
(the Volga mouth). Hence it is apparent that Ptolemy and Pliny
followed the same source, namely, as Pliny intimates, M. Terentius Varro (a contemporary of Julius Caesar). In another
passage, however, Pliny (*NH* vi. 17), on the authority of Mithridates of Bosporus, corrects his statement concerning the Udini
and says that the region lying between the territory of the Sauromatae with whom Mithridates had taken refuge (the Siraci)
and the entrance of the Caspian (the Volga mouth) was in possession of the Thali. But the most significant aspect of Pliny's
information is his statement that the Sauromatae north of the
Caucasus held communication across the strait (the Volga) with
the Abzoae, on the eastern side, and that the Abzoae, like the
Sauromatae, consisted of numerous tribes with different names.
Thus the available evidence shows that up to A.D. 49 the Siraci
were situated next to the Thali, who in turn were in communication with the Abzoae beyond the Volga. Further, it should be
noted that Pliny's testimony is the only direct evidence in classical literature for the existence, between 50 B.C. and A.D. 50, of a
route from the Bosporan kingdom to Central Asia.[6]

The river Ra (Volga).—Ptolemy alone of all ancient geographers gives a description of the river Volga, with its tributary
the Kama, and the details he presents in his text and maps offer
a picture that is instantly recognizable (see maps 9 to 11). The
source of his information is unknown, but there can be no question that the data represent the firsthand observations of an explorer in the time of the emperor Claudius. Further, since the
field survey of the river could have been carried out only by a
traveler of intelligence, it follows that respect must also be ac-

---

[6] The existence of a route from the Bosporan kingdom to Central Asia is em-
phasized by Herrmann, Kiessling, and Kretschmer in *RECA*, see, for example, IX
(1914), 1178, 1181, 2245; 2. Reihe, I (1914), 4–5, 895–896, 1285, 2135; II (1921),
932–933, etc. They, however, are of the opinion that the route crossed the Volga at
Tsaritsin or Saratov and continued eastward by way of Orenburg to the Syr Darya;
but no evidence is cited in support of these statements.

corded to the data on the peoples in the region traversed, even though the names may have been incorrectly recorded.

It is one thing to observe and record positions on a journey; it is quite another to bring the data collected into relation with an existing body of knowledge and a long-established set of conventions. So, in the process of assimilating the new materials, Ptolemy was forced to make interpretations some of which, at least, now seem strange. Thus, a curious feature of his description of the region north of the Black Sea is the manner in which modern Russia is divided into three parts: European Sarmatia, Asiatic Sarmatia, and Scythia-within-Imaus (which includes the region between the Volga and the Altai Mountains). To comprehend this division, however, it is only necessary to recall that the Greeks at all times accepted the river Tanais (Don) as the line of demarcation between Europe and Asia, and that this convention led to no cartographical difficulties until the middle of the first century of the Christian era, when the northern parts of Sarmatia became known. Once, however, the course of the Volga had been described, a situation arose in which a revision or extension of the dividing line was called for, and Ptolemy met the difficulty by the simple expedient of continuing it due north from the source of the Don.

An examination of the details on Ptolemy's maps in relation to the new line of demarcation brings out certain points of interest. Thus, the source of the Volga is placed northeast, not, as it actually is, northwest, of the source of the Don, and to all appearance either the traveler or the cartographer is here responsible for a serious error. The traveler, however, recorded the position of a particular place which, according to Ptolemy, was three degrees north and six degrees east of the source of the Don, and consequently was at the confluence of the Oka and Volga, on the site of Nijni Novgorod. Hence the error in Ptolemy's description has reference only to his assumption that the observations recorded were intended to mark the source of the

Volga, and not, as in reality, an important center of trade. Similarly, the position which Ptolemy speaks of as the source of the
eastern Ra (the river Kama), when reckoned from the known
point of the Kama-Volga junction, proves to be the confluence
of the Chusovaya and Kama, in other words, the town of Perm.

The explorer's report from which Ptolemy's information was
derived was not likely to have been more detailed than the
description of the Black Sea coast which Flavius Arrianus prepared for the emperor Hadrian, and it certainly was less en-
lightening than Anthony Jenkinson's account (to be read in
Purchas) of his voyage in 1558 from Moscow to the Caspian by
way of the Oka and the Volga. So the meagerness of the information in the report, and especially the lack of frequent observations and notations of direction, left many problems for the
cartographer to solve as best he might. Thus, for example, Ptolemy has placed a list of names columnwise along the eastern
boundary of European Sarmatia—the names, from north to
south, being Careotae, Sali, Aorsi, Pagyritae, Savari, and Borusci. The boundary, however, was the line of demarcation
which Ptolemy himself had projected northward from the source
of the Don (about long. 39° E.), and certainly the arrangement of the names with reference to it was not the work of the
explorer. Hence the position, which is artificial, of the list of
names would appear to represent an effort on the part of the
cartographer to meet a difficulty occasioned by the inadequacy
of the information at his disposal. Actually, the names mentioned constitute a group in a longer list which (to reverse the
direction) begins with the Alauni, in the south, and continues
through the Sturni and Vibiones northward to the Nasci and
Acibi; the last of these names is placed by Ptolemy directly west
of the source of the Don and south of the Borusci. The significance of the details mentioned is that the Acibi and Borusci
stand in immediate relation to the upper course of the river Oka,
and that from this as a point of departure the route indicated

by the names would have continued, not due north, but either from Kaluga or Moscow, down the Oka, to the Volga. The inference that this route was actually followed by the explorer receives definite support from the fact that the most westerly position on the Volga for which he recorded the latitude and longitude was the site of Nijni Novgorod.

Below the mouth of the Oka the traveler noted the Modocae and Suardeni, on opposite banks of the Volga, and the Asaei, north of the great bend, at Kazan. He ascended the Kama as far as Perm, and later on continued his voyage down the Volga. It is of interest to observe that he gave particular attention to the country of the Budini (Phthirophagi, Materi, and Nesioti), situated within the arc formed by the river between its junction with the Kama and its junction with the Samara. The importance of this region appears in the fact that, though it lay on the eastern side of the Volga, it was included in Asiatic Sarmatia. Elsewhere the river was taken as the boundary between Asiatic Sarmatia and Scythia-within-Imaus, but here the division was indicated by a line drawn from the lower (Samara) bend to the "unknown land" in the north. The importance attached to the segment between this chord and the bow of the river appears also in the unusual circumstance that its position was fixed by observations for latitude and longitude at no fewer than three points, and this is the more noteworthy since the explorer recorded no other observations until he came to the mouth of the Volga and the Caspian Sea.

Between A.D. 45 and 49, the Romans for the first time came into possession of definite information concerning the Volga and its principal tributary. The information was obtained by a traveler who gained a footing with the Roxolani, and by their consent reached the Alani, situated presumably between the Don and the Desna and possibly about the latitude of Kursk. Next he came to the river Oka, then to the upper Volga, and subsequently to the Kama, which he ascended as far as Perm. Finally, after a stay in the land of the Budini, he navigated the Volga to its mouth.

The argument that the names which Ptolemy placed west of his Don-meridian represent the peoples encountered on the river Oka invites prolonged amplification, but one or two points only need be brought forward.

First, the region which may be defined by lines drawn at right angles from Moscow westward to the Baltic and from Moscow northward to the White Sea was entirely unknown to the explorer; this is clear from the absence of any observation for latitude and longitude within its extent, from the extraordinary attenuation of the area allotted to it, and from the fact that to it Ptolemy relegates the traditional names, such as Hippopodes, Hyperborei, and Hippophagi, which no Greek geographer, save Strabo, seems to have had the courage to discard.

Again, so far as they are identifiable, the peoples in Ptolemy's list of names belong to the Oka basin. The name of the Borusci, for example, appears to be preserved in that of Borovsk (a town situated between Moscow and the upper Oka). The name "Aorsi," which for several reasons is of interest, is believed to stand for the Finnish Erza, one of the two branches, Mokša and Erza, of the Mordvins; it seems to be established that in antiquity the Mordvins lived east of the Oka as far as the river Sura.[7]

Further, it is known that central Russia was linked by way of the Oka with the region of the Kama. Objects identical in form have been found in the provinces of Moscow, Nijni Novgorod, and Perm, and it appears that "the fixed population, the trappers, of Perm spread there from somewhere on the Oka."[8]

It must be admitted, however, that the argument encounters a difficulty of serious proportions when it is observed that the point which has been taken to represent the position of Nijni Novgorod is assigned the same latitude by Ptolemy as that here supposed to indicate the position of Perm (though the former is actually $1° 30'$ south of the latter). Since, then, the contention is that the peoples of central Russia were connected with those on the Kama by a route which followed the Oka to its conflu-

---

[7] Vivien de Saint-Martin, *Etudes de géographie ancienne*, II (Paris, 1852), 49. Karl Neumann, *Die Hellenen im Skythenlande*, I (Berlin, 1855), 213–215. John Abercromby, *The Pre- and Proto-historic Finns*, I (London, 1898), 7. Minns, *Scythians and Greeks*, 104.

[8] A. M. Tallgren, "Permian Studies," *ESA*, 3 (1928), 92.

ence with the Volga, it will be recognized that a consideration of this
difficulty becomes a matter of necessity.

In any discussion of Ptolemy's geography of Sarmatia, it should be
understood at the outset that the latitude he gives for places above the
Black Sea is generally three degrees farther north than it will be found
on modern maps.[9] So he reports the latitude of the entrance to the
Maeotis (Sea of Azov) as 48° 30′ N., whereas it is actually 45° 25′ N.,
and that of the Kama-Volga junction as 58° 30′ N., whereas it is really

TABLE 1

Place	Ptolemy's latitude	Modern latitude	Difference
Junction of Kama and Volga	58° 30′	55° 25′	3° 5′
Volga bend (Simbirsk)	56°	54° 25′	1° 35′
Volga bend (Tsaritsin)	56°	48° 45′	7° 15′
Don mouth (Rostov)	54° 30′	47° 15′	7° 15′
Entrance to Maeotis	48° 30′	45° 25′	3° 5′

55° 25′ N. On the other hand, it should be observed that the difference
between these points as given by Ptolemy is 10°, and this difference is
in precise accord with modern reckonings. It follows that where the
difference in the latitude given by Ptolemy is greater or less than 3°,
in comparison with present-day figures, some change or adjustment
has been made by the cartographer in the positions noted by the explorer. In the region of the Volga the comparisons shown in table 1 will
be found of interest.

It is evident from these figures that there is something radically wrong
in the latitudes given by Ptolemy (as compared with the actual latitudes) for the bends of the Volga at Simbirsk and Tsaritsin and for the
mouth of the Don. The nature of the deviation will become clearer if a
comparison is made of the difference between each position and that
next to it. (See table 2.)

[9] André Berthelot, *L'Asie ancienne centrale et sud-orientale d'après Ptolémée*
(Paris, 1930), 217, remarks, with reference to the Cimmerian Bosporus: "Ptolémée
la rejette de trois degrés vers le nord par une erreur qui a un caractère général
pour toutes les contrées que nous examinons ici, avec des modalités et des exceptions que nous signalerons."

The significance of these details is obvious: Ptolemy has increased the distance between the Kama junction and the bend at Simbirsk by 1° 30′, and that between the mouth of the Don and the entrance to the Maeotis by 4° 10′, and these adjustments compensate exactly for the distance (5° 40′) between the bend at Simbirsk and that at Tsaritsin. Evidently he had specific information, in terms of latitude and longitude, for the bend at Simbirsk, but had no data for the latitude and longitude of the bend at Tsaritsin, though he had correct information

TABLE 2

Place	Ptolemy's latitude	Modern latitude	Difference
Kama junction–Simbirsk	2° 30′	1°	+ 1° 30′
Simbirsk–Tsaritsin	None	5° 40′	— 5° 40′
Tsaritsin–Don mouth	1° 30′	1° 30′	None
Don mouth–entrance	6°	1° 50′	+ 4° 10′

in regard to the actual distance of Tsaritsin from the mouth of the Don. Consequently he took the bends at Simbirsk and Tsaritsin to be identical, and because he had positive data in regard to the position of the former and definite information concerning the marching distance of the latter from the mouth of the Don, he adjusted the positions of the mouth of the Don and of the bend at Simbirsk so as to bring the latter within 1° 30′ of the bend of the Don.

It will readily be understood that the modifications which Ptolemy made in the position of the bend of the Tanais (Don) must also have affected that of its source. For this point he gives the latitude as 58°; since, however, the actual latitude is 54°, it seems evident that he has advanced the source 1° to the north, over and above his usual excess of 3°. Further, when the relation of the Don source to the Don bend is considered, it becomes evident that before Ptolemy had effected his readjustments the difference between the source and the bend was 30′, whereas after the shifts had been made the difference was 2°; consequently this change indicates that he added 1° 30′ to the difference between the two points, in keeping with the 1° 30′ by which he increased the distance between the Kama junction and the bend of the Volga. That this was the operation by which the results already mentioned were obtained is shown by the fact that he reduced the difference between the Don source and the Kama junction from 1° 30′ to 30′.

In his effort to fit the bend of the Don to the Simbirsk bend of the Volga, Ptolemy found it necessary to add 1° 30′ to the distance between the Kama junction and the Volga bend, and similarly between the Don source and the Don bend. It has now to be pointed out that he applied the same procedure to the one position which was recorded on the upper Volga. Reasons have already been given for identifying Ptolemy's "western source" of the Ra with the Oka-Volga confluence, and his "eastern source" with the confluence of the Chusovaya and the Kama. In the *Geography* the latitude of the two sources is 61°. If, then, the regular excess of 3° be subtracted from 61°, the result (58°) should be the correct latitude of the positions under discussion. Actually the latitude of the eastern source (61° minus 3°) is the latitude of Perm (58°). On the other hand, the latitude of the western source (61° minus 3°) is 1° 30′ north of Nijni Novgorod, at the mouth of the Oka. So to have brought the western source up to the latitude of the eastern, Ptolemy must have advanced its position by 1° 30′, and that he did this is established by the fact that he gives the difference between the Oka junction and the Kama junction as 2° 30′, whereas correctly it is 1°.

The considerations which have been offered provide sufficiently demonstration that as a cartographer Ptolemy endeavored to bring the new information at his disposal into relation with the existing system of geographical knowledge. It is evident that he had before him precise data in regard to the Volga below the mouth of the Oka, the river Kama up to the mouth of the Chusovaya, and the bend of the Volga between the Kama and the Samara. It is clear that he had no record of latitude and longitude for the Volga bend at Tsaritsin, though he had information that a bend of the river matched a contrary bend of the river Don. Consequently, in the absence of fuller details, he set the Don bend opposite the only Volga bend for which observations were on record, namely, that at Simbirsk. Hence he found himself compelled to readjust certain positions given in the explorer's report, though he adhered strictly to the position of the Kama-Volga junction. In working out his revision, it is apparent that he felt free to make the Maeotis of great extent, since Herodotus had said (iv. 86) that it was "not much smaller" than the Euxine itself.

The minutiae which have been discussed have a direct bearing on the question of the connections of the northern peoples

about the middle of the first century after Christ. The results
arrived at show that Nijni Novgorod was even then an important
center of trade, and this fact indicates that, by way of the Oka,
the peoples of central Russia maintained communication with
those on the upper Volga and on the Kama. In the opposite
direction, there was ready access from the upper waters of the
Oka not only to the Don but to the Desna, the great tributary of
the Dnieper, and consequently to the land of the Alani, which,
following Ptolemy's hints, may be placed east of the Desna, on
its tributary the Seïm, and as far east as the upper Donets. The
existence of a route from central Russia, by the Oka and Volga
to the Kama, removes all improbability from Ptolemy's statements that there were Alauni northwest of the Roxolani, Asaei
(another name for the Alani) above the junction of the Kama
and Volga, and Alani Scythae in the vicinity of Perm.

From the Kama to the Jaxartes.—In the region which he designates *Scythia intra Imaum,* Scythia within the Imaus Mountains, Ptolemy includes the entire expanse from the Volga to
the Altai Mountains and the T'ien Shan. His description presents great difficulties, which arise not only from his own efforts
to reconcile new data with old beliefs, but also from the fact that
the information available to him was based only in part upon
firsthand observations.

The description of Scythia-within-Imaus records, first of all,
two groups of names in order from west to east: (1) to the north,
Alani Scythae, Suobeni, and Alanorsi; (2) below them, Setiani,
Massaei, Syebi, and (near the Imaus Mountains) Tectosaces.
In dependence upon this second group, there are given in order
from north to south: (1) below the Setiani, the Mologeni and
the Samnitae, the latter extending as far as the Rhymmici Mountains; (2) below the Massaei "and the Alani Mountains," the
Zaratae, Sasones, and Tybiacae, then, below the Zaratae, the
Tabieni, Iastae, and Machetegi, next, below these, the Norosbes
and Norossi, and finally, the Cachagae Scythae.

There is no reason to question that the names arranged in order from north to south represent in fact two southward routes from the Kama. The first of these may be envisaged as proceeding from the Setiani, on the river Vyatka (and the famous site of Ananyino), to the Samnitae, in the valley of the Samara. The second may be regarded as leading from the Massaei, presumably on the Chusovaya, by way of the rivers Ufa and Byelaya, first, to the Tybiacae, "east of the Rhymmici Mountains" (Obschii Syrt), second, to the Machetegi, "along the Norossus range" (the southern aspect of the Urals), then to the Norossi, and ultimately to the Cachagae Scythae. The details given, more especially in regard to the second of these routes, seem definitely to imply personal observation.

Ptolemy's account of the region between the Volga and the Urals contains, however, another set of names likewise representing a route to the Jaxartes. Intercalated between the peoples enumerated from west to east (Alani Scythae and the rest) and those given from north to south (below the Setiani and the Massaei) there appear ten names which are independent of the orderly arrangement just mentioned, and which certainly do not belong to the same report. Near the eastern source of the river Ra, Ptolemy says, are the Rhobosci, below whom are the Asmani and Paniardi and the Canodipsa region "along the river"; then come the Coraxi and Orgasi, and the Erymmi, who extend "as far as the sea"; after these, to the eastward, are the Asiotae, the Aorsi, and the Iaxartae. The characteristic which these names have in common is that they appear to have been incorrectly reported; they may have been set down from memory and confused with names familiar to the traveler (not improbably a native of the Bosporan kingdom). In any event, the names cannot be regarded as those by which certain tribes between the Kama and the Jaxartes were actually known.

Of the names in this list, that given as "Rhobosci" has long been subject to criticism, and is supposed to be an unwarranted duplicate of

"Borusci." The four names Asmani, Paniardi, Canodipsa, and Coraxi are variants of names found in the Don-Caucasus region.[10] The Orgasi are not elsewhere mentioned or suggested. The word "Erymmi" is an incorrect version of Pliny's Rumnici (*NH* vi. 50), which obviously is associated with the Rhymmici Mountains. Similarly, the word "Asiotae," which does not occur in any other author, is a faulty rendering of the name "Astacae" or "Astocae," which in Pliny's list comes next before the Rumnici. The final name, "Iaxartae" (in place of "Cachagae Scythae"), is simply a general designation derived, as Ptolemy says, from the name of the river. In the list, then, the actual names have been distorted or replaced by others, not, indeed, because Ptolemy borrowed names from the region of the Caucasus to fill blank places on his map, but to all appearance because the names of peoples on a particular route were supplied from memory by a traveler who was a native of the Caucasus or of Bosporus. It follows, in the circumstances, that the word "Aorsi" cannot be singled out as different in character from the rest; certainly the occurrence of the name in this grouping provides no historical proof for the presence of the Aorsi north of the Caspian Sea.

There is no reason to suppose that the character of the names in this list aroused suspicion in Ptolemy's mind or was recognized by him as matter for concern. On the other hand, there is definite evidence that to him the report of which he made use presented difficulties of a different kind. Thus, between the text of the *Geography* and the map of Scythia-within-Imaus there is a conflict in regard to the position of the river Rhymmus, for while in the text he says that the river joins the Ra (Volga), on the map he gives the name to an imaginary river which flows into the Caspian between the Volga and the Ural. As presented, the Rhymmus cannot be intended for the Uzen, since the latter is depicted as an affluent of the Daix (Ural). On the map, however, an unnamed river of the same proportions as the imaginary Rhymmus is exhibited in the position of the Samara, and from it, quite certainly, the name has been transferred. The insertion of the imaginary river and the transference of the name represent, in fact, the effort which Ptolemy made to come to terms with the statement in the report that the Erymmi extended "as far as the sea."

To appreciate the features of the Volga-Jaxartes region on Ptolemy's

[10] For discussions of these names, see Müller's edition of Ptolemy's *Geography* (1883), 429. Karl Müllenhoff, *Deutsche Altertumskunde*, III (Berlin, 1892), 95–100. Herrmann, "Samnitae," *RECA*, 2. Reihe, II (1920), 2134–38; "Die Herkunft der Ungaren," *Túran*, 1918, 356–357.

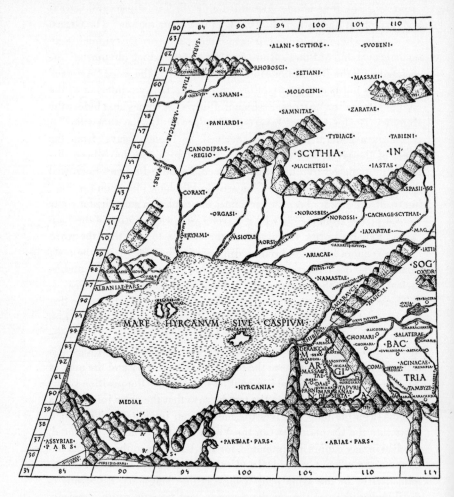

12. Ptolemy's map of Scythia within the Imaus Mountains.

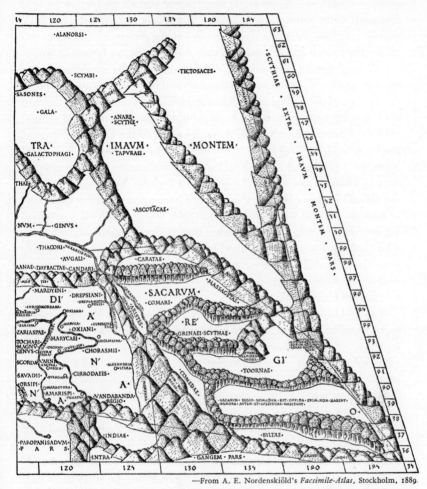

—From A. E. Nordenskiöld's *Facsimile-Atlas*, Stockholm, 1889.

12. PTOLEMY'S MAP OF SCYTHIA WITHIN THE IMAUS MOUNTAINS.

map, it should be observed, to begin with, that in succession to the Rhobosci he mentions, south of the river Kama, the Asmani and Paniardi, and then the Canodipsa region "along the river." After this he names the Coraxi and Orgasi, and then the Erymmi "as far as the sea"; on his map the three names are distributed from the junction of the Samara and Volga southward to the shores of the Caspian, and between the Volga and the (imaginary) Rhymmus. East of the Erymmi, Ptolemy says, are the Asiotae, next the Aorsi, and then the Iaxartae, and on his map the Erymmi, Asiotae, and Aorsi lie north of the Caspian between the Volga and the Ural rivers. Now this distribution would of necessity leave the Aorsi (west of the Ural) at a great distance from the people next in order on the list, the Iaxartae (east of the Aral Sea). To meet the difficulty thus indicated, Ptolemy fell back upon the old convention in accordance with which the river Jaxartes was represented as emptying into the Caspian. He, in fact, identified the lower course of the Emba with the Jaxartes, and represented its upper course as a tributary of the same river. By this arrangement he was able to bring the Iaxartae as far west as the upper Emba, and thus sufficiently near the Aorsi to fit the description given in his text.

It should be evident from what has just been said that Ptolemy made every possible endeavor to do justice to the information at his disposal, and especially to the statement in this particular report that the Erymmi extended "as far as the sea." Nevertheless, in following the report he overlooked the fact that "the river" mentioned in relation to the Canodipsa region was not the Volga but the Samara, in other words, the original Rhymmus. (As appears on his map of Scythia-within-Imaus, the "region" lay between the boundary of Asiatic Sarmatia and the Samara, and did not touch the Volga.) Now, if this oversight is repaired, it becomes apparent that the changes which Ptolemy introduced were unnecessary, for the Coraxi and Orgasi would be situated in the extensive valley of the Samara, and the Erymmi in the vicinity of the Rhymmici Mountains, from which their name was derived. If, then, the Erymmi are placed at Orenburg, the Asiotae, Aorsi, and Iaxartae, who lay to the east, would occupy the same relative positions as the Norosbes, Norossi, and Cachagae Scythae, on the old route from the southern Urals to the Jaxartes. The phrase "as far as the sea," in this interpretation, would have reference to the seasonal movement of the nomadic tribes to and from the mountainous country of the Erymmi. Further, when the Rhymmus is identified with the Samara, the rearrangement which follows indicates that the report which Ptolemy utilized, even though the names are incorrect, described an actual route from the Kama to the southeast.

The Caspian-Jaxartes region in the Chinese sources.—It has been pointed out, in speaking of the Don-Caucasus region, that Pliny put on record the fact that the Sarmatians west of the Volga held communication with a people, named the Abzoae, east of that river. Now, even a cursory examination of Ptolemy's description makes it evident that, though he gives many names between the Kama and the Jaxartes, he neither points out nor suggests any connection between the peoples on the opposite banks of the lower Ra. The inference to be drawn from the different statements of the two authors is that a change had taken place in the affiliations of the peoples north of the Caspian between the times represented by their accounts, and happily the circumstances attending this change are recorded by Chinese historians.

Shortly before 100 B.C. it became known to the Han government that northwest of the K'ang-chü, at a distance of 2000 *li* (about 700 miles), lay the country of the Yen-ts'ai. Ssŭ-ma Ch'ien, in his monumental *Shih Chi*, goes on to say that "it is a land of nomads, and its manners and customs are in the main the same as those of the K'ang-chü; it has fully 100,000 bowmen; the country lies near a great marsh which has no limit, for it is the Northern Sea."[11] Ssŭ-ma Ch'ien also gives particulars concerning the political and trade relations of China with Ta-yüan (Ferghana) and the Wu-sun (on the river Ili), and states further that intercourse was maintained with An-hsi (Parthia), Yen-ts'ai, and other distant countries.

---

[11] Friedrich Hirth, "The Story of Chang K'ién, China's Pioneer in Western Asia," *JAOS*, 37 (1916), 96. J. J. M. de Groot, *Die Westlande Chinas in der vorchristlichen Zeit* (Berlin, 1926), 15–16.

Hirth identified the "great sea" or "great marsh" with the Maeotis, but this view has not met with acceptance; in general, opinions differ only as between the Caspian and the Aral.

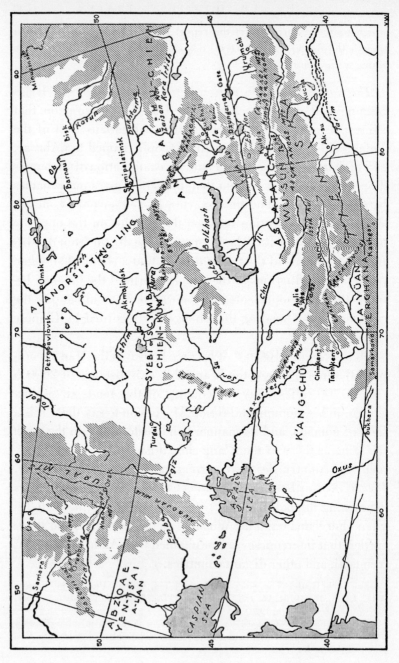

13. Scythia from the Ural Mountains to the T'ien Shan.

The *Ch'ien Han Shu,* the history of the Former or Early Han dynasty, for which Pan Ku and other relatives of Pan Ch'ao were responsible, gives much the same information.[12] It includes, however, an account of the activities of Chih-chih, in which it is said that while he was in the service of the K'ang-chü (43–36 B.C.) he sent ambassadors to Ho-su and Ta-yüan to demand the payment of an annual tribute. The significance of this statement lies in the fact that "Ho-su" was another name for "Yen-ts'ai."[13] Ta-yüan was situated on the route from Su-lê (Kashgar) which crossed the Pamirs and reached the Yen-ts'ai by way of the K'ang-chü.[14]

In the *Hou Han Shu,* the history of the Later Han dynasty, which was written by Fan Yeh, new information is provided concerning the peoples in the West. Thus, it is recorded that the kingdom of the Yen lay north of the Yen-ts'ai, that it was dependent upon the K'ang-chü and paid tribute in furs. The account then continues: "The kingdom of the Yen-ts'ai has changed its name into A-lan-liau; its capital is the city of Ti; it is dependent upon the K'ang-chü (*or,* they dwell on the land and in cities and depend upon the K'ang-chü)."[15]

The account of the Yen-ts'ai given by Fan Yeh relates specifically to the period A.D. 25–55.[16] The information which comes next in time is contained in the *Wei Lüeh,* and has reference to the years between A.D. 225 and 239. Though the date falls outside the period here under consideration, the description given by Yü Huan in this work contributes so much to an understanding of the situation in the steppes that it cannot be overlooked.

"The [new northern] route," he says, "turns to the northwest

[12] See Alexander Wylie, "Notes on the Western Regions," *JAI,* 10 (1884), 44.

[13] See above, p. 152, note 5.

[14] Edouard Chavannes, "Les pays d'Occident d'après le Heou Han chou," *T'oung pao,* 8 (1907), 170.

[15] Chavannes, *T'oung pao,* 8 (1907), 195–196, see also *T'oung pao,* 6 (1905), 558 note 5, 559 note 1.

[16] Chavannes, *T'oung pao,* 8 (1907), 150, 168.

and we have then the kingdoms of the Wu-sun and the K'ang-chü, which are the original kingdoms with no addition or diminution. Northern Wu-i is a separate kingdom north of the K'ang-chü. There is also the kingdom of Liu, there is also the kingdom of Yen, there is also the kingdom of Yen-ts'ai, called (by some authorities) A-lan; they all have the same customs as the K'ang-chü. To the west they border on Ta Ch'in [the Roman empire], to the southeast on the K'ang-chü. In these kingdoms there are many famous sables. The kingdoms raise and pasture cattle, following the river courses and grasslands. They are overlooking the great marsh, therefore at times they were under the control of the K'ang-chü, but now they do not depend upon them. (*Or,* The kingdoms raise and pasture cattle, following the river courses and the grasslands overlooking the great marsh. In former times they were under the control of the K'ang-chü, . . .)."[17]

The facts which have been presented make it evident that both European and Chinese authorities provide information concerning inhabitants of the country north of the Caspian Sea. In an inquiry which is concerned with the connections of peoples it becomes of importance, then, to consider whether it can be shown that the western and eastern sources refer, in any instance, to the same people. The evidence on both sides is simple and direct. On the one hand, Pliny states that certain peoples in Asiatic Sarmatia held communication "across the straits" (the Volga mouth) with the Abzoae, a people made up of many different tribes. On the other hand, Ssŭ-ma Ch'ien, Pan Ku, Fan Yeh, and Yü Huan all place north of the Caspian the Yen-ts'ai or Ho-su, an organization with 100,000 fighting men. To establish the identity of the peoples mentioned, it is necessary only to observe that, in the time of the Early Han, Ho-su was pronounced Hap-sŏ or Hap-

---

[17] See Chavannes, "Les pays d'Occident d'après le Wei-lio," *T'oung pao,* 6 (1905), 558–559. The alternative renderings have been suggested by Dr. P. A. Boodberg.

The account of the Yen-ts'ai given by Ma Tuan-lin is a late compilation, without independent authority; the translation by Abel Rémusat, *Nouveaux mélanges asiatiques,* I (Paris, 1829), 239–240, has been frequently cited.

suo,[18] for this, in accordance with Chinese usage, is a precise rendering of the word "Abzoae." Without question the Yen-ts'ai or Ho-su were the Abzoae, who were in communication across the Volga with the Thali and the Siraci, and through them with the Greek cities of the Taman peninsula.

Though the Yen-ts'ai and Abzoae have been mentioned in the same context by many authors of distinction, the identification just made has not hitherto been suggested. Indeed, for half a century or more, it has been accepted quite universally by historians that the Yen-ts'ai were the Aorsi, though the efforts to support that opinion have led only to long and inconclusive discussions. Since, however, the equation Yen-ts'ai = Aorsi is firmly established in the literature, some consideration must be given to the controversy.

The first fact to be noted is that in 1877 Baron von Richthofen,[19] in describing the trade routes from China to the West, spoke of a trading people (*Handelsvolk*), the Aorsi, who lived north of the Caspian and on the lower Volga, and remarked further that this people was known only from western sources.

Richthofen's statement in regard to the situation of the Aorsi is in accordance with a widely accepted interpretation of Strabo's account (xi. 506), which would place the "upper" Aorsi "more to the north" than those on the Don.[20] The interpretation gives rise to many difficulties. Notably it requires the judgment that Strabo's relatively long description of the trade carried on by the Aorsi with the Armenians and Medes is entirely erroneous. It involves the conclusion that knowledge existed of the peoples north of the Don, though Strabo says explicitly that information concerning this region was unobtainable (xi. 493). It necessitates speculation in regard to a habitat for the Aorsi "farther north" than the Don: the interior of Scythia,[21] the country north of the Caspian Sea,[22] or the region between the Ural and the Altai mountains.[23]

[18] For Hap-sǒ, see Groot, *Die Hunnen der vorchristlichen Zeit* (Berlin, 1921), 229; for Hap-suo, see Bernhard Karlgren, *Analytic Dictionary of Chinese and Sino-Japanese* (Paris, 1923), no. 823, also no. 75.

[19] Richthofen, *China*, I (Berlin, 1877), 463.

[20] See notes to the passage by H. L. Jones in the Loeb Classical Library edition of Strabo.

[21] Vivien de Saint-Martin, *Etudes de géographie ancienne*, II (Paris, 1852), 127.

[22] Alexander von Humboldt, *Asie centrale*, II (Paris, 1843), 179. Josef Marquart, "Untersuchungen zur Geschichte von Eran," *Philologus*, Supptbd. 10 (1905), 83–84.

[23] Eugène Cavaignac, *La paix romaine* (Paris, 1928), 238.

The difficulties disappear, however, when Strabo's account of the Aorsi is taken as a consistent statement.

The prestige of Richthofen's great work led two men independently in the year 1885 to correct his remark that the Aorsi were mentioned only by western writers. Thus Alfred von Gutschmid[24] asserted that since, as stated in the *Wei Lüeh,* the Yen-ts'ai extended westward to the borders of the Roman empire, "this compels us to conclude that they are the Aorsi"; in making this inference, however, Gutschmid overlooked the fact that the Aorsi had disappeared almost two hundred years before the time to which the passage in the *Wei Lüeh* refers.

Also in 1885 Friedrich Hirth identified the Yen-ts'ai with the Aorsi,[25] but on the ground that the old pronunciation of the Chinese word was An-ts'ai, and that the *An* represented a foreign *Ar*. Shortly thereafter he recognized that the old pronunciation would have been Am-ts'ai (not An-ts'ai), and in so doing remarked: "I am well aware of the difficulty presenting itself in the final *m,* which cannot be reasoned away ... Yet, the matter of fact seems to place this identification beyond doubt."[26] On the other hand, he referred to no historical data in support of his "matter of fact." In 1889 a new turn was given to the discussion by Wilhelm Tomaschek, who equated the Aorsi with the "Arzoae" mentioned, he says, by Pliny,[27] though the text of Pliny has "Abzoae," without variant readings. Tomaschek derived the form "Arzoae" from "Arsoae" in the Peutinger Table, but in giving preference to this source he did not direct attention to the number and variety of aberrant spellings to be found in it.[28] (The sole manuscript of the Peutinger Table is of the eleventh century; the original work may have been constructed toward the end of the fourth.) Hirth referred directly to Tomaschek's "Arzoae" when in 1889 he reaffirmed his position in regard to the identity of the Yen-ts'ai and introduced a new equation: "An-ts'ai = Arsai."[29] In 1905 Hirth's views received the endorsement of the great Sinologue, Edouard Chavannes.[30] Contemporaneously, however, the philological

---

[24] In the ninth edition of the *Encyclopaedia Britannica,* XVIII (1885), 594; the German translation (*Geschichte Irans*) was not published until 1888.

[25] Hirth, *China and the Roman Orient* (Shanghai, 1885), 139 note 1.

[26] Hirth, *JNCB,* 2d ser., 21 (1886), 215.

[27] Tomaschek, "Kritik der ältesten Nachrichten über den skythischen Norden," *SAWW,* 117 (1889), 37. See also his "Aorsoi," *RECA,* I (1894), 2659-60

[28] On the character of the names, see Konrad Müller, *Itineraria Romana* (Stuttgart, 1916), xxvii-xxix, xxxiv.

[29] Hirth, "Ueber Wolga-Hunnen und Hiung-nu," *SAWM,* 1899, I, 251, see also 249.

[30] Chavannes, *T'oung pao,* 6 (1905), 558-559.

arguments upon which the Yen-ts'ai had been identified with the Aorsi were effectively disposed of by Josef Marquart,[31] though it is of interest to note that Marquart nevertheless believed that in fact the two peoples were identical. In his next discussion of the point in question Hirth, while maintaining that "Abzoae," as given by Pliny, "may possibly be a mistake for Arzoae," definitely gave up the attempt to establish a connection between the names Am-ts'ai and Aorsi; "but," he went on, "why must we have a linguistic precedent for $m = r$ at all in face of so much circumstantial evidence?"[32] The evidence, however, is not adduced.

Notwithstanding Hirth's abandonment of his position, the identification of the Yen-ts'ai with the Aorsi, which he had sponsored, gained wide acceptance.[33] No new phase of the problem developed, indeed, until 1921, when J. J. M. de Groot, in his account of the exploits of Chih-chih, gave Hap-sŏ as the old pronunciation of Ho-su,[34] the alternative name for the Yen-ts'ai; yet he, too, thought that Hap-sŏ must represent the "Aorsi oder Arzoae." Then, in 1923, Bernhard Karlgren gave the pronunciation of the two syllables, prior to A.D. 500, as γâp-suo, and that of Yen-ts'ai as 'iam-ts'ai, from an earlier 'iam-ts'ad.[35] Finally, in a posthumous work published in 1926, Groot set down the old pronunciation of Yen-ts'ai as 'Am-ts'at or 'Am-sat.[36] This is the point at which the discussion now rests. It will be apparent that the entire controversy has turned upon the acceptance of the view, as expressed by Richthofen, that the Aorsi of Strabo and Tacitus were situated north of the Caspian. For this view there is no admissible evidence, and discussion ends when it is recognized that Pliny definitely placed the Abzoae east of the Volga, that the Chinese historians placed the Yen-ts'ai or Ho-su west of the Jaxartes, and that the Chinese *Hap-sŏ or *Hap-suo is an exact rendering of the word "Abzoae."

Pliny, then, records the fact that connections were maintained between the peoples west and east of the Volga-mouth, but his information is not of later date than A.D. 49. On the other hand, Ptolemy, whose information relating to the region north of the

[31] Marquart, *Philologus*, Supptbd. 10 (1905), 84–85, 240–241.

[32] Hirth, "Mr. Kingsmill and the Hiung-nu," *JAOS*, 30 (1909), 41–42.

[33] For example, E. H. Minns, *Scythians and Greeks* (Cambridge, 1913), 107, 120. Kiessling, "Hunni," *RECA*, VIII (1913), 2585.

[34] Groot, *Hunnen*, 229.

[35] See Karlgren, *Analytic Dictionary*, nos. 238, 1052, for the phonetic rendering.

[36] Groot, *Die Westlande Chinas*, 15–16.

Caspian is definitely earlier than the invasion of Armenia by
the Alani in or about A.D. 73, makes no reference to any connection between the peoples on the two sides of the lower Volga;
the routes he describes in the Volga-Ural region run from north
to south and southeast. Consequently it is to be inferred that
between 49 and 73 some important change had taken place in
the relations of the peoples east of the Volga. The nature of this
change is made clear in the passages quoted above from the
Chinese historians. Up to the middle of the first century, trade
was carried on between the kingdoms in the Tarim basin and
the Yen-ts'ai, north of the Caspian. But about the middle of the
century—certainly before A.D. 55—this east-west connection was
broken, and at one and the same time the Yen-ts'ai became dependent upon the Kang-chü and changed their name "against
that of" the Alani. In other words, in or about A.D. 50–55, the
Abzoae–Yen-ts'ai abandoned their old relations with the Sarmatians across the Volga and became a part of the confederacy
of the Alani. In the new alignment they were linked southeastward with the K'ang-chü, and through them with the Kushan
empire south of the Oxus. It is of immediate interest, therefore,
that a coin of the first Kushan sovereign, Kujula Kadphises,
should have been found on the Kama in modern times. Ammianus Marcellinus (xxxi. 2. 16) evidently had a basis for his
statement that the Alani stretched out as far as the river Ganges.
Nor, in the attempt to realize the actuality of the change, should
the detail, recorded by Yü Huan, be overlooked that in the early
part of the third century old men of the K'ang-chü still told of
their journeys—10,000 *li* in extent—beyond the kingdom of the
Yen-ts'ai to the kingdom of the Dwarfs, in other words, to the
country of the Lapps.[37] In the period to which the author of the
Wei Lüeh here refers, the Kama-Kushan alignment had ceased
to exist; "in former times," he says, "the Yen-ts'ai were under

---

[37] Chavannes, "Les pays d'Occident d'après le Wei lio," *T'oung pao*, 6 (1905),
561–562.

the control of the K'ang-chü; now they are no longer dependent upon them." So, too, in speaking of the Yen-ts'ai, he remarks not that they are named A-lan, but that some authorities spoke of them as A-lan. It is plain, therefore, that the adhesion of the Abzoae–Yen-ts'ai to the confederacy of the Alani implied no loss of identity and was no more permanent than their trade connection with the K'ang-chü and Northwest India. Indeed, after the revolutions which affected the entire continent of Asia at the end of the second and the beginning of the third century, the Abzoae ceased to be Alani, and in the Peutinger Table (of the fourth century) the names Abzoae, written Arzoae, and Alani appear independently in the Don-Caucasus region. It may be added that the name of the Yen-ts'ai or 'Am-ts'ai has not even now lost its place north of the Caspian, for the river Emba was known to Anthony Jenkinson (1557) as the Yem, and down to the middle of the nineteenth century appeared on maps as the Yem, Hyan, Djem, Iemm, or Iemba.

The different accounts of Pliny and Ptolemy are thus intelligible when viewed in the light of the detailed historical information contained in the Chinese sources.

From the Ural to the Altai Mountains.—In tracing the connections of peoples in the northern world, it is necessary at this point to return to the names given by Ptolemy from west to east in his account of Scythia-within-Imaus. To the north and adjoining the unknown land, he says, Scythia is inhabited by the peoples commonly called Alani Scythae, Suobeni, and Alanorsi, and the country below these by the Setiani, Massaei, and Syebi; near the Imaus Mountains, he adds, are the Tectosaces. Of these peoples, the Alanorsi, Syebi, and Tectosaces are unequivocally east of the Ural Mountains, and the Syebi are associated with mountains of the same name. Farther south, and also in order from west to east, he names the Aspisii or Aspasii, Galactophagi, Tapuri, and Anarei, whose position is determined by reference to the Aspasii, Tapuri, and Anarei mountains.

Now, it may be said at once that the coördinates which Ptolemy gives for the four mountain ranges just mentioned cannot be rectified, in terms of existing features, on any system which will give uniform results. Nevertheless, there are features in his representation which are in definite agreement with the steppe region as described by modern observers. Thus, the Aspasii Mountains are readily identifiable as the hilly country on the borders of Turgai and Akmolinsk which lies within long. 66° and 70° E. and lat. 47° and 50° N. The Tapuri Mountains are less easily accounted for, but in the eastern part of Scythia-within-Imaus the Anarei Mountains (as given on Ptolemy's map) may be recognized in the well-marked ranges of the Chingiz and Tarbagatai. Further, the Syebi Mountains, according to Ptolemy, cross the northwestern extremity of the Anarei Mountains in a direction from southwest to northeast, and it is of no little interest to observe that, as a matter of fact, the mountains of the Kirghiz Steppe meet the northwestern extension of the Chingiz "almost at right angles."[38] The junction of the two systems occurs not far north of Karkaralinsk. From Ptolemy's treatment, it would seem that the people named Syebi may be looked for on the upper tributaries of the Ishim and Nura rivers, and in the general vicinity of Akmolinsk; and a glance at the map will reveal the fact that they would thus be situated, as he says, "in the heart of the river country" (vi. 14. 8). There is reason, then, to believe that in the first century of the Christian era information was obtainable concerning the route across the steppes which was traversed, in A.D. 1254, by William of Rubruck on his return trip from Karakorum to the Volga.[39]

[38] See Eduard Suess, *The Face of the Earth*, tr. by H. B. C. Sollas, III (Oxford, 1908), 160–163. The relationship of the mountains was observed by Alexander von Humboldt, see the map in his *Asie centrale*, III (Paris, 1843). For recent information, see the map of "Central Asia," published by the Geographical Section, General Staff, War Office, London, 1931 (2d ed.).

[39] See W. W. Rockhill, *The Journey of William of Rubruck* (London, Hakluyt Society, 1900), 254–255. The distance covered was about 2600 miles, and occupied two months and ten days.

To judge from his map, it would appear that Ptolemy gives
an acceptable representation of the mountain ranges north of
Lake Balkhash—with the exception of the Tapuri Mountains.
It must be pointed out, however, that the mountains shown as
part of the Anarei range and here accepted as the Chingiz-Tarbagatai are not included in the Anarei Mountains as defined
(by latitude and longitude) in Ptolemy's text. This discrepancy
leads to the further observation that the people named Syebi
appear on the map and once in the text as Scymbi. Hence it
would seem that, from time to time, Ptolemy made additions to
his map without correcting the text fully to correspond.

The relation of the Chingiz-Tarbagatai to the Anarei Mountains was such that Ptolemy could regard the two as forming
one continuous range; on the other hand, a consideration of
the possibilities leads to the conclusion that the name Anarei,
as defined by latitude and longitude, stands for the mountains
(Talki, Borokhoro, and others) which lie on the northern side
of the Ili-Kunges valley. The Ascatancas would consequently
be the mountains on the south side of the same valley.

It must again be urged that Ptolemy's concern as a cartographer was to make use of and interpret the data reported by
travelers and explorers. In the instance under consideration his
business was to bring information reported from more northerly routes into relation with details provided by western merchants who had followed the great silk route from Parthia to
the Tarim basin. Now, a highly important artery of commerce
in ancient times led through Ferghana, the Chinese Ta-yüan,
and by way of Osh to Kashgar. Hence it is of interest to find
on Ptolemy's map a particularly good rendering of the Chatkal
and Ferghana ranges, which enclose Ferghana or Ta-yüan to
the north and come together at 42° N. and 72° E. It is a marked
peculiarity of Ptolemy's treatment, on the other hand, that he
identifies the Ferghana range with the Ascatancas Mountains,
though, as has been pointed out, these mountains border the Ili

valley to the south. Clearly, in his endeavor to systematize the information reported by a number of different travelers, Ptolemy was at the pronounced disadvantage of being left in ignorance even of highly significant features of the country which intervened between the routes followed and described.

Ptolemy certainly regarded the position and direction of the Ferghana Mountains as definitely established, and it may be presumed that his confidence in this information disposed him, in the absence of observations for positions in the T'ien Shan, to modify the direction of the Ili and Kunges rivers. Yet his reliance on the description of the route to the Ili valley was such that, when he altered the direction of this valley to the southeast, he altered the direction of the Kara Tau northwestward to exactly the same extent. Consequently, if the Tapuri and Ascatancas mountains be rotated counterclockwise through equal angles (with the apex of the Chatkal and Ferghana mountains as a center), they will be found to correspond respectively with the Kara Tau and the mountains south of the Ili-Kunges basin. When allowance is made for this effort on Ptolemy's part to harmonize incomplete data, it becomes evident that the Tapuri Mountains disappear from the region of the steppes and take their place parallel to the Jaxartes, and that the Anarei Mountains, since they necessarily retain their relation to the Ascatancas, cease to be continuous with the Chingiz-Tarbagatai and assume a position which leaves adequate space on the map for the Ala Tau and Ala Kul.

In the regions to which reference has just been made, Ptolemy was in possession of information regarding routes in Ferghana, in the Ili valley, and across the steppes from the southern Urals to the Tarbagatai Mountains. Moreover, he also knew of a route farther north, between the Urals and the Altai. As has been mentioned earlier, Ptolemy places, adjoining the "unknown land," the Alani Scythae, the Suobeni, and the Alanorsi. The Alani Scythae on his map are placed above Perm, and the Alanorsi

well to the east. Since in later times a well-known route led from
the northern Urals by way of Irbit, Tyumen, and Ishim to Omsk,
on the Irtish, and since Ptolemy gives, as a further indication
of the position held by the Alanorsi, that they were north of the
Anarei, it seems probable that the Alanorsi were situated on
the Irtish from Omsk southward toward Semipalatinsk.

The traveler whose report Ptolemy utilized had information
concerning a route from the northern Urals to the upper Irtish.
Here it will be recalled that in the fifth century B.C., Herodotus
had described a route to the upper Irtish which took its departure from Tanais, at the mouth of the Don. The details as given
by Herodotus are susceptible of different interpretations, and
the course followed may have been from the southern Urals to
the Tarbagatai Mountains; yet it seems more probable that it
continued through the land of the Budini to the Kama, reached
the Irtish at Omsk, and followed that river up to Semipalatinsk.
Whether the one alternative or the other be accepted, the point
aimed at is not in doubt. Herodotus says that the journey to the
land of the Argippaei was made both by Scythians and Greeks,
and that the Argippaei inhabited the foothills of great and inaccessible mountains, in other words, the Russian Altai.[40]

The actuality of the route farthest north, in the centuries before and after the Christian era, is directly substantiated, however, by the archaeological discovery of a common iron-age
culture at Perm, Tobolsk, and Barnaul (on the upper Ob), on
the river Katanda (a tributary of a tributary of the Ob), and
east of Semipalatinsk on the river Berel (a tributary of the
Bukhtarma, which flows into the Irtish).[41] Thus the Irtish was a

---

[40] On the route described by Herodotus, see Alexander von Humboldt, *Asie centrale*, I (Paris, 1843), 389–411. Wilhelm Tomaschek, "Kritik der ältesten Nachrichten über den skythischen Norden. II. Die Nachrichten Herodot's über den
skythischen Karawanenweg nach Innerasien," *SAWW*, 117 (1889), 1–70. Minns,
Scythians and Greeks, 106–114. André Berthelot, *L'Asie ancienne centrale et sud-
orientale d'après Ptolémée* (Paris, 1930), 34–51. G. F. Hudson, *Europe & China*
(London, [1931]), 27–52. Richard Hennig, *Terrae incognitae*, I (Leiden, 1936),
57–64.

[41] Minns, *Scythians and Greeks*, 248–253 and map.

thoroughfare connecting the upper Volga and the Kama with Central Asia, and the archaeological finds in the Altai are of burials in proximity to routes leading still farther east.

Evidence corroborative of Ptolemy's account of the peoples in western Siberia is also to be found in Chinese sources. When Chih-chih moved to the "right" or western land of the Hsiung-nu in 49 B.C., he first encountered and defeated I-li-mu Khan, a Hsiung-nu leader who similarly had moved westward in 56. He then sought an alliance with the Wu-sun, but his overtures were rejected, and in the conflict which ensued Chih-chih routed the Wu-sun troops. Nevertheless he did not follow up this success, but retired northward and attacked the Hu-chieh (Uigurs) ; after this people had submitted, he marched west and overthrew the Chien-k'un (Kirghiz) ; finally he again turned northward and reduced the Ting-ling.[42] These peoples he united under his personal leadership. The information is also provided that the Chien-k'un were situated at a distance of 7000 *li* (more than 2000 miles) from the *ordo* or headquarters of the Hsiung-nu *shan-yü* in Mongolia—presumably on the river Orkhon. From the indications in the sources, it has been inferred that the Hu-chieh (Uigurs) stretched westward from Kobdo to the Tarbagatai Mountains and as far as Semipalatinsk; that the Chien-k'un occupied the steppe region as the Kirghiz do to the present day; and that the Ting-ling were situated to the north and along the river Irtish.[43]

In the *Wei Lüeh*[44] a survey of the steppe peoples (in the third century) is given from the standpoint of the K'ang-chü, that is, from the south. So the Hu-tê (Hu-chieh)[45] were northwest of the Wu-sun and northeast of the K'ang-chü; the Chien-k'un were northwest of the K'ang-chü; the Ting-ling were north of the

[42] For the identifications given in the text, see Groot, *Hunnen*, 62, 79, 221, 227. Josef Marquart, "Ueber das Volkstum der Komanen," *AGWG*, N.F., 13 (1914), I, 65–68.

[43] Groot, *Hunnen*, 221.   [44] Chavannes, *T'oung pao*, 6 (1905), 558–561.

[45] Marquart, "Ueber das Volkstum der Komanen," 65–66.

K'ang-chü at a distance from the frontier of 3000 *li* (approximately 1000 miles—probably as far as Petropavlovsk and Omsk). The same source also says that to the north of the K'ang-chü was the independent kingdom of the Northern Wu-i and that to the northwest lay the kingdoms of the Liu, the Yen, and the Yen-ts'ai—then no longer dependent upon the K'ang-chü.

A point of special interest in relation to these accounts is that between the middle of the first century B.C. and the earlier half of the third century A.D. the Chinese authorities had knowledge of no greater number of peoples north of the Jaxartes than the Greek geographer Ptolemy. Further, as described from the east and from the west, the peoples mentioned appear in the same relative positions: thus, to the north, the Ting-ling match with the Alanorsi; below them, the Chien-k'un may be equated with the Syebi; farther south, the Chinese Yen-ts'ai, Yen, Liu, and Northern Wu-i match the Greek Abzoae, Aspasii, Galactophagi, and Tapuri; while to the east the Hu-chieh appear to stand in the place of Ptolemy's Anarei.

From the Irtish to the Huang Ho.—For the purpose of an inquiry into the connections of peoples from the Vistula to the Irtish, it has been necessary to scrutinize the statements in Ptolemy's description of Sarmatia and Scythia; on the other hand, for evidence concerning the connections of peoples from the Irtish to the Huang Ho it will be unnecessary to discuss his account of Scythia-beyond-Imaus and Serica, since more direct information is accessible in Chinese sources.

It may be said at once and with complete assurance that during the period here under consideration the region from Lake Balkhash to the great bend of the Huang Ho was under the dominance of the Hsiung-nu.[46] After the disruption of the tribes in A.D. 48, the Southern Hsiung-nu remained in Inner, while the Northern retained possession of Outer, Mongolia. The Hsiung-nu were

---

[46] See Albert Herrmann, *Historical and Commercial Atlas of China* (Cambridge, Mass., Harvard-Yenching Institute, 1935), 24, 26–27.

thus in contact with China along the line of the Wall in the modern provinces of Shan-hsi, Shen-hsi, and Kan-su. Again, they were in contact with the kingdoms in the Tarim basin through the Chü-shih at Guchen and Turfan,[47] and, indeed, exercised control over the kingdoms on the northern route in the Tarim up to 60 B.C., from A.D. 16 to 73, from 77 to 89, and after 107. Further, they were in contact, north of the T'ien Shan, with the Wu-sun, on the river Ili, and with the Ting-ling, on the Irtish.[48]

Evidence in regard to connections of the Mongolian tribes with peoples on the Irtish is not restricted, however, to the historical sources. At different places on tributaries of the Irtish and Ob, objects have been found which the possessors evidently had acquired in the course of trade with intermediaries who were in contact with the Chinese. Thus, among the articles disinterred on the banks of the river Katanda, west of the Altai divide, were a coat of silk lined with sable and adorned with gold plates, a garment of ermine dyed green and red, and pieces of Chinese silk.[49] More striking, however, is the evidence of Mongolian connections with peoples far to the west which was discovered in 1924 at Noin-ula, seventy miles north of Urga; for in graves which belong to the last years of the first century B.C. there were found not only a silk robe trimmed with fur and other materials of Chinese origin, but also textiles which had been

---

[47] On the different kingdoms of the Chü-shih north of the T'ien Shan, see Chavannes, *T'oung pao*, 6 (1905), 557; 8 (1907), 210–211. Groot, *Westlande*, 159, 161–162. On Guchen and Turfan in particular, see Sir Aurel Stein, *Innermost Asia*, II (Oxford, 1928), 549–586. Owen Lattimore, *High Tartary* (Boston, 1930), 146–148.

[48] For wars of the Hsiung-nu with the Wu-sun and with the Ting-ling, see Parker, *China Review*, 20 (1893), 122–123; 21 (1895), 104, 113, 263. Groot, *Hunnen*, 62, 199–200, 202, 220–221, 227, 253–254. Léon Wieger, *Textes historiques*, I (2° éd., Hsien hsien, 1922), 510–511, 545–548, 705.

[49] The discoveries were made by Wilhelm Radloff, see Minns, *Scythians and Greeks*, 248; A. A. Zakhárov, "Antiquities of Katanda (Altai)," *JAI*, 55 (1925), 37–57. For the objects found on the Berel steppe, see Zakhárov, "Materials on the Archaeology of Siberia," *ESA*, 3 (1928), 132–140. In general, for Chinese objects found in Siberia, see P. Reinecke, "Ueber einige Beziehungen der Alterthümer Chinas zu denen des skythisch-sibirischen Völkerkreises," *Zeitschrift für Ethnologie*, 29 (1897), 141–163.

manufactured at Olbia, on the Black Sea.[50] Furthermore, communication, which was neither momentary nor haphazard, between peoples on the Dnieper, the Kama, the Yenisei, and the Huang Ho is attested by the archaeological evidence that the areas indicated constitute four provinces of one homogeneous "Scythic" culture.[51] It is, therefore, scarcely a matter for surprise that Hsiung-nu "relics in northern Mongolia exhibit Hellenic, Iranian, and Mesopotamian designs, together with those of Chinese and local origin."[52] On the other hand, the most significant aspect of the evidence, taken as a whole, is that it puts beyond question the actuality of cultural connections between the Hsiung-nu in Mongolia and the peoples of western Siberia and northeastern Russia.

Notwithstanding the existence of a common culture which extended across northern Eurasia, the discovery of articles from the Black Sea in northern Mongolia, and even the likelihood that medicinal rhubarb came to Europe by way of the Volga,[53] it is not to be supposed that in the north there was a great trade route between China and Russia such as that by which Chinese silks were conveyed to Syria.

The bale of silk found in the Tarim and the silk coats trimmed with fur discovered in the Altai Mountains and Mongolia represent objectively the varying interests of the Chinese in rela-

---

[50] G. O. Boroffka, "Die Funde der Expedition Koslow in der Mongolei 1924/25," *Archäologischer Anzeiger, Beiblatt*, 1926, 341–368. W. P. Yetts, "Discoveries of the Koslov Expedition," *Burlington Magazine*, 48 (1926), 168–185. E. H. Minns, "Small Bronzes from Northern Asia," *Antiquaries Journal*, 10 (1930), 1–23; the objects may be dated 2 B.C., see p. 8. Joachim Werner, "Zur Stellung der Ordosbronzen," *ESA*, 9 (1934), 258–269.

[51] J. G. Andersson, "The Highway of Europe and Asia," *JRAS*, 1929, 422–425. See also "Der Weg über die Steppen," Museum of Far Eastern Antiquities, *Bulletin*, no. 1 (1929), 143–163. Andersson names the four provinces: Euxine, Ananino, Minusinsk, Sui-yüan.

[52] Yetts, *Burlington Magazine*, 48 (1926), 173.

[53] E. H. Warmington, *The Commerce between the Roman Empire and India* (Cambridge, 1928), 207–208. For objects of Chinese origin found in Kuban tombs, see Minns, *Scythians and Greeks*, 336, and Rostovtzeff, *Iranians and Greeks*, 132. For Chinese objects found in Germany, see Berthold Laufer, "Chinesische Altertümer in der römischen Epoche der Rheinlande," *Globus*, 88 (1905), 45–49.

tion to the western and northern peoples. The fabrics of Chinese manufacture interred in northern graves are accounted for in an obvious manner by the custom of making "presents" which the Han court observed in dealing with the Mongolian tribes. Thus, for example, a list of "presents" to the Hsiung-nu in the second century B.C. included wadded and lined silk gowns, embroidered robes, a girdle with yellow-gold girdle clasp, a yellow-gold buckle, pieces of silk, and different sorts of cloth.[54] Again, in 51 B.C., there were presented to Hu-han-hsieh, besides many other articles, seventy-seven sets of bedcovers, and in 49 B.C. a similar assortment, together with one hundred and ten suits of clothes.[55] Further, to illustrate the quantitative aspect of these transactions, it may be pointed out that "presents" to the *shan-yü*, in comparable circumstances, increased from 8000 pieces of embroidered silks and 6000 pounds of silk floss in 51 B.C. to 84,000 pieces of embroidered silks and 78,000 pounds of silk floss in 1 B.C.[56] On the other hand, after the civil wars which followed the usurpation of Wang Mang, the "presents" fell to no more than 10,000 pieces of embroidered silks and 10,000 pounds of silk floss.[57]

In actual practice, however, the giving of "presents" was not one-sided, but constituted a form of trade. It is said, for example, of Wu Ti (140–87 B.C.) that when foreigners came to court, "the emperor distributed treasures and silks as rewards and gifts and gave them back in richer measure all that they had brought to him in abundance."[58] The view of Chinese officialdom in the first century of our era is clearly indicated by the remark of Pan Piao, father of Pan Ch'ao, with reference to the Northern

---

[54] Parker, "The Turko-Scythian tribes," *China Review*, 20 (1893), 15. On the buckles, see, in the General Bibliography, the items on "The Art of the Peoples of Northern Eurasia"; see also Paul Pelliot, *T'oung pao*, 26 (1928), 139–143.

[55] Parker, *China Review*, 21 (1895), 103

[56] Compare the successive statements in Parker, *China Review*, 21 (1895), 103, 107, 111, 117.

[57] Parker, *China Review*, 21 (1895), 257.

[58] Groot, *Westlande*, 33. Wylie, *JAI*, 11 (1882), 113.

Hsiung-nu, that "we may well give them liberal presents—calculated on the value of what they offer us."[59]

The objects of trade most frequently mentioned as brought in by the Hsiung-nu were horses, cattle, sheep, and furs. Great numbers of horses were received from Mongolia by the Chinese, but since the Mongolian horse is in reality a pony,[60] the Han government was at all times desirous of procuring other breeds, in particular the "blood-sweating horses" of Ta-yüan (Ferghana).[61] The Wu-sun, Hu-chieh, and Chien-k'un also had "excellent" horses. On the other hand, the Hu-chieh and Chien-k'un

[59] Parker, *China Review*, 21 (1895), 259.

From the Chinese point of view, the government made "presents," but received "tribute." Parker, *China, her History, Diplomacy, and Commerce* (2d ed., London, 1917), 42, remarks that "the so-called 'tribute' of ancient times seems to have practically meant 'trade.'" Owen Lattimore, *Manchuria, Cradle of Conflict* (New York, 1932), 111, says: "An historical analysis of the real status of 'tributary' tribes would be of the greatest interest. Undoubtedly, many 'tributary' offerings were in fact a form of trade, the tribute being purchased by the appointed officials. In extreme instances, the nominal tribute to the suzerain power was actually a form of levy on the suzerain power; the 'presents' offered in exchange for the 'tribute' greatly exceeding the value of the 'tribute' itself . . ."

In his lecture "The Geographical Factor in Mongol History," *Geographical Journal*, 91 (1938), 12, Lattimore says further: "For every historical level of which we have any knowledge there is evidence that exchange of some kind, through trade or tribute, has been important in steppe-nomadic life." He continues (14) : "The Turks of the Orkhon were nomads by origin, but they developed a good deal of trade both with China and with the oases of Turkistan [as the Hsiung-nu had done earlier]. . . . The chieftains of the Orkhon Turks were converted gradually into potentates of a certain luxury, whose revenues were far from being restricted to the levy of a tribute in cattle and services from exclusively pastoral subjects." A comment made by W. W. Rockhill, *The Land of the Lamas* (New York, 1891), 141, though it applies to modern conditions, may be added: "It is curious to notice," he says, "how all the chieftains among the Mongols and Tibetans monopolize trade in their respective localities . . . A Mongol is afraid to trade a horse or a camel to any one if he knows his chief has one to sell, or, if he does venture to sell it, he most likely gives part of the price received to his chief, so that he may pardon him the liberty he has taken in infringing on what is almost a recognized right."

[60] See William Ridgeway, *The Origin and Influence of the Thoroughbred Horse* (Cambridge, 1905). Salim Beck, *The Mongolian Horse* (Tientsin, [1926]). These ponies are still one of the chief products of Outer Mongolia, see Sir Charles Bell, "The Struggle for Mongolia," *JCAS*, 24 (1937), 62.

[61] The subject is highly attractive, but does not here call for discussion. See Wylie, *JAI*, 10 (1881), 44–45. Hirth, *JAOS*, 37 (1917), 102–103, 109–113. Groot, *Westlande*, 35–42, 110–111. See especially W. W. Tarn, *Hellenistic Military and Naval Developments* (Cambridge, 1930), 77–83, 156–159. W. P. Yetts, "The Horse: a Factor in Early Chinese History," *ESA*, 9 (1934), 231–255.

could supply furs in great abundance as well as horses, and it is of particular interest to note that the distant Ting-ling and Yen-ts'ai are credited with "renowned" and highly esteemed sables.[62] Furs, indeed, were in demand by the Chinese, not merely for their own use, but because they constituted an important commodity in world trade, and an insight into the ways of commerce during the first century is provided by the information that dyed furs from China were shipped from Barbaricon, on the Indus, to Rome.[63]

China thus provided a market for the natural resources of Mongolia and of Siberia as far west as the Ural Mountains. As has been pointed out, however, access to the Chinese frontier from the north and northwest, either for persons or commodities, was in control of the Hsiung-nu, whose power extended from Lake Balkhash to the Huang Ho. Hence, in considering the problem presented by the correspondence of events in Mongolia and Europe, it is to be noted that, when the Han government decided to make war on the Hsiung-nu, the Chinese frontier was automatically closed to trade. In any such situation a stop was put to the exchange of commodities, and even the information[64] that trade was suspended would have affected the interests

---

[62] Chavannes, *T'oung pao*, 6 (1905), 559–560.

In his description of the "Land of Darkness," Marco Polo says: "Those people have vast quantities of valuable peltry; thus they have those costly Sables of which I spoke, and they have the Ermine, the Arculin, the Vair, the Black Fox, and many other valuable furs. They are all hunters by trade, and amass amazing quantities of those furs. And the people who are on their borders, where the Light is, purchase all those furs from them; for the people of the Land of Darkness carry the furs to the Light country for sale, and the merchants who purchase these make great gain thereby, I assure you. . . . One end of the country borders upon Great Rosia." (Yule, II, 484, and see also 486.)

[63] Pliny *NH* xxxiv. 145; xxxvii. 204. *Periplus of the Erythraean Sea* ii. 39. L. Fougerat, *La pelleterie et le vêtement de fourrure dans l'antiquité* (Paris, [1914]), 85–87. Warmington, *The Commerce between the Roman Empire and India*, 157–159, 362. Hudson, *Europe & China*, 93.

[64] The rapidity with which news might be supposed to travel may be judged from the fact, already mentioned, that William of Rubruck made the journey from Karakorum, in Mongolia, to the Volga in seventy days. In northern regions, during winter, as reported by Anthony Jenkinson, a man on a sled would travel four hundred miles in three days.

and well-being of tribes, all the way to the Urals, who were dependent upon the acceptance of their products by the Chinese. Under the conditions of life in ancient times, these interruptions of trade led to widespread disturbances and raids. On the other hand, and in the same automatic manner, the resumption of customary relations restored peace.

The situation on the borders of China accounts, then, for the extension of disturbances, in the event of war, as far west as the Ural Mountains. Now, in Europe, as has been shown, each break of relations between China and the Hsiung-nu in the eastern T'ien Shan was followed by outbreaks of peoples north of the upper Danube. Further, in spite of the meager information preserved in Roman sources concerning occurrences among the eastern Germanic tribes, it is known that four times at least, out of nine or ten, the outbreaks in Central Europe were preceded by uprisings in the region of the Vistula. Consequently it seems evident that the problem set by the observed correspondences of events in Mongolia and Europe now narrows down to the question of whether disturbances in the region of the Urals might possibly have been linked with outbreaks in Poland.

The Alani.—The difficulty of envisaging the way in which disturbances could have been communicated from the Urals to the Vistula arises from the total absence of historical data concerning events in the more northerly regions of Asia and Europe. Some insight into the situation north of the Black Sea may, however, be gained by acceptance and utilization of the scant geographical data which are available. As has been pointed out earlier in this discussion, the Romans, between A.D. 45 and 49, came into possession of new information concerning the inhabitants of central Russia. Thus both Pliny and Ptolemy mention the Alani, and refer to them in close connection with the Roxolani. Now a moment's consideration will suggest that, though the Alani thus come into view in the middle of the first century of the present era, the Roxolani had already been known for a century and a half; further, it will bring out the fact that the name "Roxolani" is a compound word in which the name "Alani" is the primary element,[65] and consequently will lead to the observation that the existence of a people named "Alani" must have antedated that of the "Roxolani." Evidently, then, though they were unknown to the Greeks, the Alani had occupied a central position in Russia at least as far back as 100 B.C.

The earliest information concerning the Alani, that contained in the writings of Pliny and Ptolemy, indicates that they were situated northwest of the Roxolani, northeast of the Bastarnae, and between the Dnieper, or rather the Desna, and the Donets or the upper Don. Ptolemy's description also makes it clear that the "Alauni" had as neighbors on the west the Stavani, who were in communication, through the Sudini and Galindae, with the Venedae, near the mouth of the Vistula;[66] and, further, that they had connections northward with the Borusci and the peoples on the river Oka. Again, Dionysius Periegetes, in his *Orbis descriptio* (305), written possibly in the reign of Domitian, mentions them in company with the major peoples of northern Europe— Germani, Sarmatae, Getae, Bastarnae, Daci, and Alani. Marcianus of Heraclea, whose *Periplus* is in the main an abridgment of Ptolemy, says (ii. 39) that "the Alanus mountain and the region next to it have long been inhabited by the Alani, a tribe of the Sarmatians, among whom also are the sources of the river Borysthenes which flows into the Euxine Sea."[67] The most extensive account of the Alani is, as is well known, that given by Ammianus Marcellinus, who, though he wrote in the fourth century, made use of much earlier authorities. Thus, in one passage

---

[65] The word "Roxolani" or "Roxalani" is taken to mean "Blond Alani" by Minns, *Scythians and Greeks*, 120; "White Alani" by Rostovtzeff, *Iranians & Greeks*, 115, 255. Jarl Charpentier, "Die ethnographische Stellung der Tocharer," *ZDMG*, 71 (1917), 360, thinks that the name meant "Alanen an der Wolga."

[66] P. J. Schafarik, *Slawische Alterthümer*, Deutsch von Mosig von Aehrenfeld, I (Leipzig, 1843), 545, gives the "Nachbarschaft der Alanen mit der Winden (Wanen)" as 100–1 B.C.

[67] *Periplus of the Outer Sea* ii. 39, tr. by W. H. Schoff (Philadelphia, 1927).

(xxii. 8. 31), he brings together Ixomatae, Maeotae, Jazyges, Roxolani, and Alani; in another (xxii. 8. 38), Aremphaei, Massagetae, Alani, and Sargetae; in a third (xxii. 8. 42), "European" Alani and Costobocae. The European Alani, he says, "plunder and hunt as far as the Maeotis and the Cimmerian Bosporus, and in the same way overrun Armenia and Media."

At the time the Romans acquired information concerning the people who are called "Alauni" by Ptolemy, they also learned of certain peoples named Asaei and Alani Scythae in the region of the Kama. It is now recognized that all these names are closely related, if not identical;[68] and the inference is permissible that the position of the Alani in the northeast was no less important than that which they held in central Russia. Indeed, they would appear to have held a place on the Kama similar to that of the Budini at an earlier time; and, like the Alani, the Budini possessed a second center of power to the southwest.[69]

---

[68] Marquart, "Ueber das Volkstum der Komanen," 182 note 1.

At a later time the Alani were known as Ās (Asaei) or Asi, and by the Russians as Yasy, see Emil Bretschneider, *Mediaeval Researches,* II (London, 1910), 84–85.

In his article "Samnitae," in *RECA*, 2. Reihe, II (1920), 2134–38, Herrmann elaborates the argument that the names of all the tribes which in Ptolemy's description occupy the northern parts of Scythia-within-Imaus, and including those mentioned above, really belong to Asiatic Sarmatia, more especially the region of the Caucasus. To satisfy this argument, he finds it necessary to show that, about the middle of the first century A.D., the Alani were situated north of the Caucasus. Herrmann says it is true that "in Pliny and Ptolemy the name does not occur in this region, and this," he continues, "appears all the more strange since they certainly possessed information from the same period concerning the tribes in the Caucasus." In this embarrassing situation he then asks, "But should there not occur in their writings some similar-sounding name in place of 'Alani'?" In answer, he refers to the name "Orineoi," as mentioned by Ptolemy, and "Orani," as given by Pliny. "Orineoi and Orani," he then says, "are two forms from which the name 'Alanoi' can be derived without any effort (*ohne jeden Zwang ableiten lässt*)." Therefore, he states, the Alani Scythae "must be placed, not, as Ptolemy maintains, to the north of Scythia-within-Imaus, but in Asiatic Sarmatia; and at the same time it becomes self-evident that the Ἀλανὰ ὄρη . . . corresponds to the Keraunian Mountains, i.e. the eastern Caucasus." The argument is not acceptable.

[69] See Minns, *Scythians and Greeks,* 103.

It may be pointed out that Kaspar Zeuss, *Die Deutschen und die Nachbarstämme* (München, 1837), 703, believed that the Alani were the same people as the Budini: ". . . die Vermuthung nicht abweisen kann, dass die Budinen . . . ein und dasselbe Volk mit den späteren Alanen . . ."

Within a few years of the time to which the data provided by Pliny and Ptolemy refer, the Abzoae or Yen-ts'ai became identified with the confederacy of the Alani (before A.D. 55), and this information, supplied by the Chinese historians, reveals one of the steps in the remarkable expansion of the Alani during the third quarter of the first century. So Ammianus directs attention to the existence not only of "European" but also of "Asiatic" Alani. Of the former, situated beyond the Danube, he says that, "like the Persians, they have gradually subdued the neighboring nations by repeated victories, have united them to themselves, and comprehended them under their own name." Of the latter, he remarks that they extend to the east, and "are spread out among many populous and wealthy nations, stretching to the parts of Asia which, as I am told, extend up to the Ganges." To Ammianus it was a striking fact that these peoples were called by one name although they were divided between two continents and separated by vast distances.[70]

The conditions under which the great expansion of the Alani in the middle of the first century took place are not obscure. First, the war which the Romans carried on against Mithridates III of Bosporus (46 to 49) interrupted (1) the trade of the Siraci and Thali with the Abzoae, (2) the trade of the Aorsi with the Medes and Armenians, (3) the trade of the Aorsi-Iaxamatae with the peoples north of the lower Don. It was within these years that the Jazyges moved from South Russia to the Theiss, in Hungary. Second, the disruption of the Hsiung-nu in A.D. 48–49 resulted in an interruption of trade which affected the Alani in the region of the Kama, and hence the "Alauni" in central Russia. Third, the war between Hsien of Yarkand and the K'ang-chü, about A.D. 50, resulted in an interruption of trade which directly affected the Yen-ts'ai–Abzoae, on the Emba, and led to a new alignment of this people, on the one hand with the Alani of the Kama and, on the other, with the K'ang-chü and the king-

[70] Ammianus Marcellinus xxxi. 2. 13, 16, 17, tr. C. D. Yonge.

dom of the Kushans. Moreover, owing to the wars south of the Caucasus, including Corbulo's invasion of Armenia, the interruptions must have continued until the end of A.D. 63.

In the situation thus briefly described, it is not remarkable that occurrences in Central Europe about A.D. 50 are out of the common, or that occurrences in South Russia up to A.D. 63 exhibit unusual features. Thus the Romans, in 54, occupied Chersonesus, in the Crimea; in 56 occupied and rebuilt Tyras, at the mouth of the Dniester; in 62 or 63 defended Chersonesus from barbarian attacks, and at the same time took over the administration of the Bosporan kingdom. Moreover, within the same period Ti. Plautius Silvanus Aelianus carried on the remarkable activities which are so inadequately described on his monument. The inscription records, indeed, that the governor of Moesia gave refuge in his province to a great number of people from beyond the Danube, that he subdued kings hitherto unknown to the Romans, and that he rendered services to the Bastarnae, Roxolani, and Dacians when they had suffered at the hands of enemies who are not specified. It is singularly unfortunate that the names of the more remote participants in these wars are not mentioned; yet it appears certain from the contemporary reference in the *Thyestes* (630) of Seneca, the prime minister of Nero, that the Alani were the enemy before whom the trans-Danubians had fled. Southwestward, then, the Alani attacked the Bastarnae and Dacians; westward, according to Ammianus (xxxi. 2. 13), they conquered the Neuri (probably between the river Pripet and the Carpathians); southeastward they dislodged the Roxolani from their old habitation north of the Sea of Azov, between the Dnieper and the Don.

The precise time at which the Alani crossed the Don and appeared in the region of the Caucasus is not known.

The supposition that they were the Sarmatians who were called in by Pharasmanes of Iberia in A.D. 36 has a foundation only in a particularly doubtful reading of a passage in Josephus.[71] It should not be overlooked in this connection that Strabo, a generation earlier, had said (xi. 500) that the Iberians "assemble many tens of thousands, both from their own people and from [their neighbors and kinsmen] the Scythians and Sarmatians, whenever anything alarming occurs"; and (xi. 502) that "against outsiders the nomads join with the Albanians in war, just as they do with the Iberians." Again, it cannot be said that the Alani were participants in the disturbances south of the Caucasus in or about A.D. 50, when Pharasmanes of Iberia was engaged in war with the king of the Albani,[72] for the possibility here rests only on the supposition that Tacitus was in error.

On the other hand, it seems probable that the reference to the Alani in Lucan's *Pharsalia* (viii. 223), though a palpable anachronism, may be taken as evidence that they had made their appearance south of the Caucasus by A.D. 63. But the first cross-

[71] In his account of the events of A.D. 35–36, Gutschmid, *Geschichte Irans*, 121, follows Tacitus in speaking of "Sarmaten," but adds parenthetically that "eine andere Quelle nennt sie Alanen"; in his note he specifies this other source as Josephus *Antiq.* xviii. 4. 4 (97)—"nach den Handschriften," and remarks further that Σκύθas, the reading of the text as printed, "ist blosse Interpolation." In 1890 Niese (*Flavii Josephi Opera*, IV, 158) introduced the name of the Alani, for the first time, into the printed text, because of a preponderance of manuscript evidence in favor of this reading. In 1904 Eugen Täubler, in his dissertation, *Die Parthernachrichten bei Josephus*, 31, 58–61, sought, on the basis of Niese's emendation, to establish A.D. 35 as the date of the first appearance of the Alani, and elaborated his argument in *Klio*, 9 (1909), 14–17. On the other hand, against Gutschmid, Marquart contended, *Philologus,* Supptbd. 10 (1905), 83, that the reading 'Αλανοί of the Greek MSS. was, in all probability, an emendation suggested by a passage in the *Jewish War*. In this work, vii. 7. 4 (244–251), Josephus gives an account of a later invasion of the Alani and designates them "a race of Scythians, as we have somewhere previously remarked, inhabiting the banks of the river Tanais and the lake Maeotis." The allusion cannot have reference to any statement in the *Antiquities*, which was written subsequently, but it would have incited almost any reader to search for the suggested (chronologically) earlier passage in which Scythians were mentioned, and hence to identify the Scythians of *Antiq.* xviii. 4. 4 with the Alani. H. St. John Thackeray thought that "the allusion [in the *Jewish War*] to a previous remark has possibly been carelessly taken over by Josephus from the source from which the section, irrelevant to Jewish history, has been derived" (note to his translation, Loeb Classical Library). On the composition of the later books of the *Jewish Antiquities*, see Thackeray's *Josephus, the Man and the Historian* (New York, 1929), 51–74, and *Proceedings of the British Academy*, 1930, 15–18.

[72] Tacitus *Ann.* xii. 45.

ing of the Caucasus by the Alani for which the evidence is not open to doubt was in 73–74, and in association with this event Josephus (*Jewish War* vii. 244) makes the statement that at the time spoken of they inhabited the banks of the river Tanais and the lake Maeotis.

The information obtainable concerning the Alani leaves no doubt, then, that they had occupied a central position in Russia for possibly a century and a half before the disturbances of A.D. 50. After the interruptions of trade which these disturbances occasioned on all the major routes with which they were connected, the Alani carried on wars to both the southwest and the southeast until A.D. 63. The peace established in that year by Domitius Corbulo (made possible by the death of Hsien in 61) extended to the northern world, but the expansion of the Alani which had taken place brought new danger to the Roman frontier, so that, with new interruptions, the Romans in 89 and 92 were called upon to resist invasions of Pannonia.

The conclusion to which the evidence concerning the Alani points is not only that there were connections between the peoples of northern Eurasia from the T'ien Shan to the Ural Mountains, but also that there existed in central Russia a great tribal organization comparable to that of the Hsiung-nu in Mongolia. In the East, the Hsiung-nu dominated Inner and Outer Mongolia (up to A.D. 90) and extended to the river Ili and the Irtish. In the West, the Alani reached out (after A.D. 50) toward the Vistula and the lower Danube, the Don and the Caucasus.

The geographical data available thus show that the connections of the peoples of northern Eurasia were such as to make possible the transmission of disturbances from the borders of the Chinese empire to the borders of the Roman province of Pannonia. The historical data accessible in Roman and Chinese sources give evidence that events of a clearly defined type in the eastern T'ien Shan were followed always by outbreaks of a uniform character in Central Europe.

CONCLUSION

T
HE INQUIRY of which the results have now been presented took as its point of departure the observation that historians have long recognized in the occurrences designated barbarian invasions a problem for historical investigation, and have commonly accepted the responsibility of formulating theories to account for the recurrence of these events. Consequently it seems desirable, before a summary is offered of the facts which have here been brought together, that the explanations of the invasions which are discoverable in modern literature should be passed in review.

Explanations of Barbarian Invasions

In the first place, it is to be observed that the explanations of barbarian invasions commonly take the form of theories designed to account for the antecedent occurrence of barbarian "migrations."

The theories put forward in regard to the migrations of the Germanic peoples owe their form and content to statements embodied in the writings of classical authors. Now, of the authorities to whose testimony appeal is commonly made, Caesar is the most distinguished, and his remark that a certain movement took place "because of the number of the people and the lack of land" has been adopted without hesitation as the conclusion reached by a qualified and circumspect observer; consequently the view that the Germanic migrations were due to "overpopulation"[1] has, at all times been accorded a position of prestige.

[1] For some recent examples, see Ernest Barker, "Italy and the West, 410–476," in *The Cambridge Medieval History*, I (New York, 1911), 393. A. C. Haddon, *The Wanderings of Peoples* (Cambridge, 1911), 1. E. C. Semple, *Influences of*

Notwithstanding the favor in which it has been held, this solution of the problem has persistently been called in question;[2] but the debate continues without prospect of termination, for the reason that the arguments on the one side and the other are concerned with the possibility or impossibility of a condition for which there is no direct historical evidence. In presence of the dilemma created by this situation, it would appear necessary to reëxamine the sources from which the theory of overpopulation has been derived, and specifically to inquire whether the words of Caesar justify the confidence which has been reposed in them.

In considering the statements contained in historical sources, it is of importance to discriminate between those which relate to occurrences at some time far in the past, judged from the standpoint of the particular author, and those which refer to events in which the author himself was a participant or for which he may have had the testimony of witnesses. If the narrative of Caesar be examined, a marked difference will be found between the accounts he gives of movements which had taken place before the period of his own activities in Gaul and the information he provides concerning those which he himself was called

Geographic Environment (New York, [1911]), 75. C. R. L. Fletcher, *The Making of Western Europe*, I (London, 1912), 44. Hutton Webster, *Ancient History* (New York, [1913]), 536. Ernest Babelon, *Le Rhin dans l'histoire; l'antiquité* (Paris, 1916), 206. C. W. Previté Orton, *Outlines of Medieval History* (Cambridge, 1916), 26. Theodor Arldt, *Germanische Völkerwellen* (Leipzig, 1917), 4. Ludwig Wilser, *Deutsche Vorzeit* (2. Aufl., Steglitz, 1918), 93. Pierre Imbart de la Tour, in Gabriel Hanotaux, *Histoire de la nation française*, III (Paris, [1920]), 112. Otto Seeck, *Geschichte des Untergangs der antiken Welt*, I (4. Aufl., Stuttgart, 1921), 395. J. B. Bury, *History of the Later Roman Empire*, I (London, 1923), 97. Alfred Hettner, *Der Gang der Kultur über die Erde* (Leipzig, 1923), 17. Johannes Bühler, *Die Germanen in der Völkerwanderung* (Leipzig, 1925), 30: "Der eigentliche Grund hierfür war Übervölkerung und Landnot." Otto Maull, *Politische Geographie* (Berlin, 1925), 457. B. W. Henderson, *Five Roman Emperors* (Cambridge, 1927), 84: "Over-population, the greed for land, the very love of roaming, all bid mankind go wandering." J. B. Bury, *The Invasion of Europe by the Barbarians* (London, 1928), 6–9. J. A. Field, *Essays on Population, and Other Papers*, ed. by H. F. Hohman (Chicago, [1931]), 301–302.

[2] A. M. Carr-Saunders, *The Population Problem* (Oxford, 1922), 297–304. See below notes 16–18.

upon to oppose. Thus, indicating in each instance that the occurrence had taken place at a much earlier time, he says that the Belgae had settled in Gaul "by reason of the fruitfulness of the soil"; that tribes from Belgium had invaded Britain "to seek booty";[3] and, notably, that once upon a time, when the Gauls were superior to the Germans, they had sent colonies across the Rhine "because of the number of the people and the lack of land."[4] The statements which Caesar makes from his own knowledge and observation are altogether different in character. In his narrative of the migration of the Helvetii, he recites the antecedent circumstances in detail, and attributes the movement, first and chiefly, to the persuasion of Orgetorix. Again, to account for the presence in Gaul of the Germans under Ariovistus, he relates that the Arverni and Sequani had hired Ariovistus to aid them against the Aedui, and that when, from living in their new surroundings, the barbarians "had got a liking for the farmsteads, the civilization, and the wealth of the Gauls, more were brought over." Once again, speaking of the migration of the Usipetes and Tencteri across the Rhine, he records their own statement "that they had come against their will, having been driven out of their homes" by the Suebi. The Ubii also told Caesar that they had been grievously hard pressed by the Suebi.[5] If, then, the testimony of Caesar is to be accepted, there can be no question concerning which of the two accounts is to be admitted in evidence.

The use made by modern writers of the more general statements included in Caesar's narrative might conceivably be defended by recourse to the argument that, in these passages, he

---

[3] Caesar *BG* ii. 4; v. 12.

[4] Caesar *BG* vi. 24. Eduard Norden, *Die germanische Urgeschichte in Tacitus Germania* (2. Abdr., Leipzig, 1922), 469, accepts the overpopulation theory: "Einen entscheidenden Grund zu deren Preisgabe," he says, "haben zu allen Zeiten nur Ernährungsschwierigkeiten gebildet, die, durch Übervölkerung hervorgerufen,..."; in support of this opinion he cites only Caesar *BG* vi. 24, which he interprets as being "richtiger Angabe des Grundes, aber falscher Orientierung."

[5] Caesar *BG* i. 2–5, 31; iv. 1, 4, 7, 16.

was relying upon tribal tradition. Apart from the fact that the author himself makes no appeal to this source of information, further consideration suggests that, where his own knowledge fails, Caesar falls back upon the literary tradition of Roman historians.[6] Evidence in regard to the content of this tradition is amply provided by Livy, who has much to say concerning invasions of Italy by the Gauls. In the time of Tarquinius Priscus, he says, Ambigatus, king of the Celts, "anxious to relieve his realm from the burden of overpopulation," sent out two bodies of his people, under his nephews Bellovesus and Segovesus; the latter, with "the surplus population" of divers tribes, crossed the Alps and defeated the Etruscans. Again, "the tradition is" that the Gauls who crossed the Alps in the time of Camillus were "attracted by the report of the delicious fruits and especially of the wine," a report which had been spread by one Arruns of Clusium "in order to allure them into Italy."[7] Pliny also relates the incident, but says that the person who provided the enticement was Helico, an Helvetian.[8] According to Livy, the Gauls who settled in Galatia were induced to make their way eastward "either by want of room or desire for plunder," and crossed over into Asia when they heard "reports of the fertility of its soil." Other Gauls, who attempted to establish themselves in Italy, gave as their reason, he says, that, "owing to overpopulation, want of land and general destitution, they had been compelled to seek a home across the Alps."[9] The explanations given by Livy, it will be observed, relate to occurrences which had taken place from three to six centuries before his own time; they are frankly traditional, and not of his own invention.

Strabo, as a geographer, was directly interested in the subject of migrations;[10] he, however, makes no reference to the

[6] See Georges Dottin, *Manuel pour servir à l'étude de l'antiquité celtique* (Paris, 1906), 179.

[7] Livy v. 33–34. Plutarch *Camillus* xv.   [8] Pliny *NH* xii. 1 (2).

[9] Livy xxxviii. 16; xxxix. 54.

[10] Strabo i. 3. 21; iii. 4. 19; vii. 1. 3; vii. 3. 13; vii. 4. 5.

"overpopulation" theory which is prominent in the history of Livy, his contemporary. On the contrary, he says that the Tectosages who made their way to Galatia had been expelled from the parent tribe in Gaul, and that the Boii who migrated from the valley of the Po to the Danube had been driven out of the region they occupied. He remarks that, in his own day, various German tribes had been driven by the Suebi across the Rhine, while others, such as the Marsi, had migrated "deep into the country" to escape the Romans; the Marcomanni had been "caused to migrate" by their leader Maroboduus; the Langobardi had, "to the last man, been driven in flight out of their country."[11]

The conflicting explanations of tribal movements which Caesar incorporated into his narrative of the Gallic War are found also in the *Compendium of Roman History* written by Velleius Paterculus. In that part of his work which deals with the remote past, Velleius tells how Lydus and Tyrrhenus, who were joint kings in Lydia, were "hard pressed by the unproductiveness of their crops and drew lots to see which should leave his country with part of the population"; the lot fell upon Tyrrhenus, and he sailed to Italy. Again, he says that, later on, " a great number of young Greeks, seeking new abodes because of an excess of population at home, poured into Asia."[12] On the other hand, when he comes to speak of the Marcomanni, against whom he fought, Velleius says that they moved "at the summons of their leader Maroboduus."[13]

It is evident, then, that the classical sources offer two contrasting reasons for the movements of barbarian peoples: one, of unknown authorship, lays emphasis upon overpopulation and the need of land; the other sets forth the factual details of recent historical happenings. Notwithstanding the character of the first of these categories, it has been accorded a wide currency, and

[11] Strabo iv. 1. 13; v. 1. 6; iv. 3. 4; vii. 1. 3.
[12] Velleius i. 1. 4; i. 4. 3.   [13] Velleius ii. 108. 1–2.

has even been taken as the point of departure for extended speculation. Thus investigators have elaborated theories to show how the stipulated overpopulation could have been brought about, and to demonstrate how the presumed need of land could have arisen. It has been argued, for example, that overpopulation would be a natural consequence of a change from pastoral life to agricultural pursuits;[14] similarly, it has been maintained that the need of land would follow from the exhaustion of the soil brought about by a rudimentary system of agriculture.[15] Since, however, the literary tradition cannot be regarded as an acceptable ground for the investigation of the problem, there will be no reason to discuss these secondary elaborations.

When, for any reason, historians have been led to reject the overpopulation theory, they have usually adopted another suggestion from the Roman literary tradition and discovered the origin of migrations in the psychological traits of barbarian peoples. William Robertson, for example, thought that the impulse came from "the martial spirit" of the Germans, and expressed the opinion that "their first inroads into the empire proceeded rather from the love of plunder, than from the desire of new settlements."[16] In this opinion he has had many followers,[17]

[14] Felix Dahn, *Urgeschichte der germanischen und romanischen Völker*, I (Berlin, 1881), 76: "Der letzte Grund dieser unwiderstehlichen Bewegung lag in der bei allen Germanenstämmen seit dem Uebergange von überwiegendem Nomadenthume mit Jagd und Viehzucht zu überwiegendem sesshaften Ackerbau eintretenden raschen Zunahme der Bevölkerung." Georg Waitz, *Deutsche Verfassungsgeschichte*, II (3. Aufl., Kiel, 1882), 12.

[15] Ludwig Schmidt, "Die Ursachen der Völkerwanderung," *NJKA*, 11 (1903), 344–345. Georg Grupp, *Kulturgeschichte des Mittelalters*, I (2. Bearb., Paderborn, 1907), 3. L. M. Hartmann, "Der Untergang der antiken Welt," in L. M. Hartmann & Johann Kromayer, *Römische Geschichte* (2. Aufl., Gotha, 1921), 263. D. C. Munro, *The Middle Ages* (New York, 1921), 36. Frantz Funck-Brentano, *L'histoire de France racontée à tous: Les origines* (3e éd., Paris, [1925]), 170. J. W. Thompson, *An Economic and Social History of the Middle Ages* (New York, [1928]), 98.

[16] William Robertson, *The History of the Reign of the Emperor Charles V.* [1769], in his *Works*, III (London, 1840), 4–5.

[17] Friedrich Ratzel, "Über geographische Bedingungen und ethnographische Folgen der Völkerwanderungen" [1880], in his *Kleine Schriften*, hrsg. von Hans Helmolt, II (München, 1906), 55: "Eroberungs- und Raublust, gepaart mit unbestimmter Sehnsucht nach einem fremden besseren Lande." Hans Delbrück, *Ge-*

though, more recently, the militaristic motive has been transmuted into "the desire for change," "the longing for adventure," "the attraction of the unknown," and even "the hope of enjoying some of the advantages of their civilized neighbors."[18]

The views which have been put forward in modern times to account for the movements of Asiatic tribes have their point of departure, about the middle of the eighteenth century, in the publication of the *Histoire générale des Huns, desTurcs, des Mogols, et des autres Tartares occidentaux*, by Joseph de Guignes. The importance of this work lies in the fact that it connected the irruptions of Asiatic peoples into Europe with events in Central Asia,[19] and thus, as Gibbon remarked, "laid open new and

---

schichte der Kriegskunst, II (Berlin, 1902), 267: "Nicht, wie man wohl gemeint, weil die alten Gebiete die wachsende Menge nicht mehr zu fassen vermochten, sondern als Kriegsschaaren, begierig nach Sold, Beute, Abenteuren und Würden, sind die Germanen in die Völkerwanderung eingetreten." Ferdinand von Richthofen, *Vorlesungen über allgemeine Siedlungs- und Verkehrsgeographie*, hrsg. von Otto Schlüter (Berlin, 1908), 70–73. Johannes Hoops, *RGA*, I (Strassburg, 1911–13), 44. Gerhard Seelinger, *Same*, IV (Strassburg, 1918–19), 212: "Kriegslust und Wandertrieb." J. H. Breasted, *The Conquest of Civilization* (New York, [1926]), 681: "their native fearlessness and love of war and plunder."

[18] C. H. Hayes, *An Introduction to the Sources Relating to the Germanic Invasions* (New York, 1909), 84. Leon Dominian, *The Frontiers of Language and Nationality in Europe* (New York, 1917), 5: "a single determining cause, definable as the quest after comfort." W. H. Barker & William Rees, *The Making of Europe* (London, 1920), 15. William McDougall, *The Group Mind* (Cambridge, 1920), 223: "it must have been the love of activity and enterprise that led these peoples perpetually to wander." Henri Berr, "Race et migrations," in Eugène Pittard, *Les races et l'histoire* (Paris, 1924), x–xi. J. H. Robinson, *An Introduction to the History of Western Europe*, I (revised ed., Boston, 1924), 39. A. W. Brøgger, *Ancient Emigrants* (Oxford, 1929), 19. Charles Guignebert, *A Short History of the French People*; tr. by F. G. Richmond, I (New York, 1930), 88: "a mania for movement and adventure."

[19] De Guignes, I. 2 (Paris, 1756), 288: "Le refoulement de toutes ces Nations orientales vers l'ouest & le nord-ouest a dû occasionner dans l'Empire Romain ces grandes irruptions dont il est parlé dans l'histoire & qui furent la cause de sa ruine." Note, however, the view expressed in the twentieth century by Louis Halphen, "La place de l'Asie dans l'histoire du monde," *Revue historique*, 142 (1923), 1–13; "Les origines asiatiques des 'Grandes invasions'," *Revue belge de philologie et d'histoire*, 2 (1923), 453–460; also *Compte rendu du V⁰ Congrès international des sciences historiques* (Bruxelles, 1923), 94: "L'histoire de l'Asie semble n'avoir pas été jusqu'ici étudiée d'assez près par les historiens de l'Europe. En fait, cependant, l'Asie et l'Europe ne font qu'un et l'histoire de notre 'continent' ne saurait être sans inconvénient isolée de celle des pays asiatiques."

important scenes in the history of mankind." Gibbon himself
sought to reach an understanding of these movements through
inquiry into the conditions of life of nomadic tribes, and came
to the conclusion that "the thirst of rapine, the fear or the resentment of injury, the impatience of servitude, have, in every
age, been sufficient causes to urge the tribes of Scythia boldly to
advance into some unknown countries, where they might hope
to find a more plentiful subsistence or a less formidable enemy."
Following de Guignes, he directed attention to the fact that,
about the end of the first century of our era, the Huns had been
overthrown by the "Sienpi" and had moved westward; but he
gave his own interpretation of the later events in saying that
"the most warlike and powerful tribes of the Huns . . . resolved,
under the conduct of their hereditary chieftains, to discover and
subdue some remote country, which was still inaccessible to the
arms of the Sienpi and to the laws of China."[20]

Since the eighteenth century, speculation has ranged widely
in the endeavor to discover a general theory explanatory of the
migrations from Mongolia. It has been suggested that the movements were due to the domestication of the horse;[21] that they
were occasioned by the building of the Chinese Wall;[22] that they

---

[20] Gibbon, ed. Bury, III, 75; 75 note 10; 87.

[21] Paul Vidal de la Blache, "The Geographical Evolution of Communications,"
Report of the 77th Meeting of the British Association, 1907 (London, 1908), 576.
See also Harold Peake and H. J. Fleure, *The Steppe & the Sown* (New Haven,
1928), 17, 51.

[22] Adolf Bastian, "Ueber die Beziehungen der indischen Halbinsel zu Inner-
Asien," *VGEB,* 1 (1874), 141. Ferdinand von Richthofen, *China,* I (Berlin, 1877),
445. K. J. Ujfalvy de Mezö-Kövesd, *Les Aryens au nord et au sud de l'Hindou-
Kouch* (Paris, 1896), 24: "La construction de la grande muraille de Chine fut
un des événements les plus gros de conséquences, et on peut dire, sans être taxé
d'exagération, que cet événement contribua puissamment à la chute prématurée de
l'empire de Rome." E. H. Minns, *Scythians and Greeks* (Cambridge, 1913), 121.
Edward Foord, "China and the Destruction of the Roman Empire," *Contemporary
Review,* 94 (1908), 207–208. Raphael Pumpelly, *My Reminiscences,* II (New York,
1918), 451. Fritz Machatschek, *Landeskunde von Russisch-Turkestan* (Stuttgart,
1921), 113. M. I. Rostovtzeff, *Iranians and Greeks in South Russia* (Oxford, 1922),
114–115. Ludwig Schmidt, *Geschichte der germanischen Frühzeit* (Bonn, 1925),
205. Owen Lattimore, "Caravan Routes of Inner Asia," *Geographical Journal,* 72

followed upon the rise, from time to time, of military leaders;[23] that they were the outcome of struggles for the possession of pastures—struggles in which "the relatively weakest horde" was forced out of the steppe and driven to conquer a new home.[24] Concurrently, a strong predilection has manifested itself to establish some hypothesis which would link these Asiatic migrations with changes in the physical environment of the nomadic peoples. The idea was put forward that the nomads had been "rendered waterless, and thus driven into a forced emigration" by reason of topographical changes, due to the slow upward movement of the earth's crust, which converted the Gobi from the bed of a sea to its present condition as a great sandy desert.[25] The suggestion met with favor and, as modified in the course of transmission, is represented in current literature by the theory that the Asiatic migrations were brought about by "change of

---

(1928), 523. Sir E. D. Ross, "The Invasions and Immigrations of the Tatars," *JCAS*, 15 (1928), 133: "It may even be asserted that the construction of the Great Wall of China contributed very largely to the fall of the Roman Empire"; see also "Nomadic Movements in Asia," *JRSA*, 77 (1929), 1077.

[23] Sir H. J. Mackinder, *Geographical Journal*, 23 (1904), 735: "An adequate reason for the descents may surely be found in the opportunity of rich booty in the surrounding countries, and the leadership of such chiefs as Attila and Ghenghiz Khan." A. R. Cowan, *A Guide to World-history* (London, 1923), 229. J. B. Bury, *The Invasion of Europe by the Barbarians* (London, 1928), 50.

[24] T. Peisker, "The Asiatic Background," in *The Cambridge Medieval History*, I (New York, 1911), 349.

[25] J. W. Draper, *History of the Intellectual Development of Europe*, I (rev. ed., New York, 1876), 28–29. Draper may have derived the idea from Raphael Pumpelly, "Geological Researches in China, Mongolia, and Japan, during the Years 1862 to 1865," *Smithsonian Contributions to Knowledge*, 202 (1866), 77. The suggestion that the Gobi was the dry bed of an ancient sea was made by Julius Klaproth, *Tableaux historiques de l'Asie* (Paris, 1826), 181–182. Ferdinand von Richthofen, *China*, I (Berlin, 1877), 24–25, gave the name *Han-hai* to this "dry sea." Emil Bretschneider, *Mediaeval Researches from Eastern Asiatic Sources*, I (London, 1888), 15 note 9, pointed out, however, that Richthofen was "wrong in translating these two characters by 'dry sea' . . . Notwithstanding the fact that a Chinese commentator translated *han hai* by northern sea, there is no evidence from Chinese history that this term has ever been applied to an inland sea."
See also Richthofen, 43–55: "Die Völkerströmungen Central-Asiens in ihren Beziehungen zur Bodengestaltung." Franz von Schwarz, *Sintfluth und Völkerwanderungen* (Stuttgart, 1894), 496–497. Pumpelly, *Explorations in Turkestan: Expedition of 1904*, I (Washington, 1908), xxiv.

climate" in the form of "progressive desiccation,"[26] "climatic pulsations,"[27] "climatic cycles,"[28] or merely a succession of dry seasons.[29] It may be that "the geographer who believes in pulsatory changes of climate can scarcely avoid the conclusion that great movements of peoples have been induced by such causes,"[30]

[26] The use of the term 'desiccation' becomes exceedingly common after the appearance of Prince Kropotkin's article, "The Desiccation of Eur-Asia," *Geographical Journal*, 23 (1904), 722–734. "Altogether," he says, "it is quite certain that within historical times East Turkestan and Central Mongolia have not been the deserts they are now. They have had a numerous population, advanced in civilization, which stood in a lively intercourse with different parts of Asia. All this is gone now, and it must have been the rapid desiccation of this region which compelled its inhabitants to rush down to the Jungarian Gate, . . ." (723).

[27] The theory of "climatic pulsations" is distinctively that of Ellsworth Huntington, and was stated originally in *The Pulse of Asia* (Boston, 1907). For the extensive bibliography of the author, see his *Civilization and Climate* (3d ed., New Haven, 1924), xvii–xix; for an account of the changes in his opinions, see the chapter entitled: "The Pulsatory Hypothesis and its Critics," 335–346. See also the survey of the literature given by J. W. Gregory, "Is the Earth Drying Up?" *Geographical Journal*, 43 (1914), 148–172, 293–318.

[28] Eduard Brückner, "Klimaschwankungen und Völkerwanderungen in der alten Welt," *MGGW*, 58 (1915), 210: "So erteilen Klimaschwankungen der Menschheit Impulse, die im Ebben und Fluten der Völkerwanderungen zum Ausdrucke kommen." C. J. Curry, "Climate and Migrations," *Antiquity*, 2 (1928), 292–307, reaches the conclusion that "A regular succession of climatic cycles approximately 640 years in duration, each including on the average something like 300 years of increasing aridity, has produced a series of alternating periods of migration and consolidation in Europe and Asia, where the effects can be traced between the years 2300 B.C. and 1600 A.D." (303).

[29] Sir H. J. Mackinder, *Democratic Ideals and Reality* (New York, 1919), 121: "it may have been owing to spells of droughty years." For other variations of the explanation, see, for example, Owen Lattimore, *High Tartary* (Boston, 1930), 110: "All Mongolia, the breeding ground of warlike migrations, was then restless, whether by pressure of a natural increase of population or because some fluctuation of climate had tended to dry up pastures and forced the nomads to look for fresh grounds." A. J. Toynbee, *A Study of History*, III (London, 1934), 396: ". . . These eruptions are not, as a matter of fact, the spontaneous expressions of the Nomads' human initiative, but are all produced mechanically by the action upon the Nomads of either one or other of two alternative external forces: either a pull exerted by one of the sedentary societies in the neighbourhood of the Steppes, or else a push exerted by the climate of the Steppes themselves."

[30] Ellsworth Huntington, "Changes of Climate and History," *AHR*, 18 (1913), 215; but he also goes on to say: "Possibly and indeed probably a certain number of migrations of this sort might have occurred had there been no changes of climate, for the mere pressure of increasing population would sometimes start them, but that they would have been so severe or prolonged as they were seems hardly probable" (225).

but it is evident from the literature that there are many investigators[31] who have not been convinced that the effects in question
have followed from pulsatory or other changes of climate; it
may also be added that no instance has been adduced in which
the postulated impulse was followed demonstrably by the corresponding exodus.

The survey which has been made shows that the theories advanced to account for "migrations," Asiatic as well as Germanic,
are inconclusive,[32] and indicates the reason for the inadequacy
of the explanations in regard to the barbarian invasions. The
reason is, in short, that theories once suggested have been retained and repeated with endless variations and elaborations,
but without critical examination. Since, then, the older views
are unsatisfactory, the necessity has arisen for an examination
of all the historical data in regard to the activities and relations
of barbarian peoples for a period of some length, without geographical restriction to Europe, and without predilection in favor of European history.

Correlations in Historical Events

It will be evident from the foregoing discussion that historians
have fully accepted the barbarian invasions of the Roman
empire as a problem for historical investigation, and have ad-

---

[31] See especially the conclusions of Sir Aurel Stein, "Innermost Asia: its Geography as a Factor in History," *Geographical Journal*, 65 (1925), 487–490; he ends
his discussion of the problem by saying: "It would obviously be a mistake to assume the *post hoc* as implying a *propter hoc* and then on the basis of such an assumption to try and interpret developments in the history of the Tarim basin or
of Central Asia in general, mainly by conjecturally determined changes of climate."
See also his comments, *Serindia*, I (Oxford, 1921), 246, and *Innermost Asia*, II
(Oxford, 1928), 778–781. R. C. F. Schomberg, *Geographical Journal*, 80 (1932),
140, remarks: "It has even been alleged that the climatic changes of southern
Sinkiang have affected or indeed caused the great human migrations of Central
Asia. Both premise and hypothesis seem fantastic."

[32] The most recent tendency in opinion is expressed in the statement of T. D.
Kendrick, *A History of the Vikings* (London, [1930]), 23: "In short," he says,
"since there is no solution of the problem the historian must perforce accept the
phenomenon of the viking movement without further questioning, just as the
earlier and unexplained movements of the Migration Period are accepted."

vanced numerous theories in the attempt to account for the recurrence of these outbreaks. Even a rapid survey, however, reveals the fact that the theories referred to are not conclusions which have been reached through examination and comparison of the happenings incident to a number of different invasions, or arrived at by the employment of a clearly defined procedure which has been adopted in the endeavor to reach verifiable results.

In the present investigation it has been taken for granted that inquiry into a historical problem must necessarily begin with the collection of data having reference to a given class of events, and proceed by making comparison of the different happenings in a consecutive series of occurrences. In practice, this procedure has led to unexpected and hitherto unnoticed results. Thus it has been found that between 58 B.C. and A.D. 107 barbarian uprisings in Europe were preceded invariably by the outbreak of war either on the eastern frontiers of the Roman empire or in the "Western Regions" of the Chinese. Also it has been found that the invasions which followed disturbances in the Roman East occurred both on the lower Danube and on the Rhine, whereas the uprisings which followed disturbances in the T'ien Shan affected only the upper Danube. Further, there were no uprisings in Europe which were not preceded by the respective disturbances in the Near or Far East, and there were no wars in the Roman East or the T'ien Shan which were not followed by the respective outbreaks in Europe. These two-way correspondences represent Correlations in Historical Events.

The extent to which the foregoing statement concerning the correspondence of events is borne out by the evidence will be more readily appreciated if expressed in numerical terms. Simple enumeration, indeed, can never be accepted as a substitute for historical detail; it is, nevertheless, warrantable so far as it provides a means for summarizing occurrences which have already been described, and for displaying the relationship of events in different parts of the world. With this proviso, then, it may be stated that, during the period under consideration, wars in the eastern T'ien Shan (Turfan and Guchen) were followed on four occasions by invasions of Pannonia, and on five earlier occasions by disturbances beyond the upper Danube which called for defensive measures on the Pannonian frontier. During the same period the thirty-one occasions on which conflicts took place in the Roman East were followed by uprisings on the lower Danube twenty-eight, and on the Rhine twenty-six, times; so that, in spite of the unsystematic character of the Roman sources and their imperfect preservation, evidence is lacking for correspondent events on the Rhine in only five, and on the lower Danube in only three occurrences out of thirty-one. Furthermore, it may be pointed out that eighteen times the disturbances on the eastern borders of the Roman empire occurred in correspondence with wars in Kashgaria; consequently, out of a total of forty occasions on which uprisings took place in Europe, twenty-seven are to be attributed to the influence of events in the "Western Regions," and about half that number to the aggressions of the Romans in the Near East.

In certain particulars, the details which have just been given invite further comment. Thus it is noticeable that, whereas the invasions of Pannonia in A.D. 89, 92, 97, and 107 were preceded uniformly by disturbances at Guchen and Turfan, earlier conflicts at these places had not been followed by the same results. But from the time the Romans reached the upper Danube (between 15 and 8 B.C.) all wars in the T'ien Shan were followed by outbreaks among the peoples north of the river, and it is a fact of exceptional interest that the invasions of Pannonia followed upon the construction by the Romans of forts on the Raetian limes.

In succession to wars on the eastern frontiers of the Roman empire, outbreaks took place on the lower Danube in twenty-eight out of thirty-one disturbances, and, until the conquest of Pannonia in 8 B.C., all these outbreaks extended (as also in A.D. 6) to the region of the Save, and even into the Alps. While a high degree of correspondence is thus indicated, it may also be pointed out that even the three exceptions are not necessarily to be regarded as occasions when no outbreak occurred on the lower Danube. The situation is that, in his account of the reigns of Gaius, Claudius, and Nero, Tacitus makes no reference to affairs in Moesia, and for the years A.D. 39, 42, and 50 no other information concerning the region under discussion has been preserved. Since, then, Tacitus does not mention the important events in which Plautius Silvanus Aelianus took a leading part in and about 58, his silence cannot be construed as evidence against the possibility of disturbances on the three earlier occasions.

On the Rhine frontier, twenty-six uprisings are known which occurred in correspondence with events in the Roman East; contrariwise, there are five in which the sources give no hint of outbreaks among the German tribes. With reference to two items in the latter group, it appears all but certain that in 48–47 and 45–44 B.C. the Germans engaged in no acts of hostility, though for a short time in 44 Cicero was apprehensive of an invasion. The exceptional circumstance on these occasions seems to have been that the German cavalry employed by Caesar constituted a guaranty for the continuance of peace.

In regard to the frontier disturbances in Europe, it need only be added that, in the reckoning given, insurrections within territory held by the Romans and wars undertaken by the Roman government on its own initiative have not been included. In the first of these groups, the Pannonian-Dalmatian war (A.D. 6–9), the rising under Arminius (A.D. 9), and the rebellion of the Frisii (A.D. 28), though occurrences of great interest, cannot be classed as invasions. In the second group, only the campaigns against Maroboduus in A.D. 6 and against Decebalus in A.D. 101 appear to have been undertaken without immediate and direct provocation.

The wars on the eastern frontiers of the Roman empire, though they were followed uniformly by outbreaks on the lower Danube and the Rhine, were not restricted to one special region, and the term "Roman East," which has here been freely employed, has reference not only to the province of Syria but also to the kingdoms of Bosporus and Armenia. Thus, of the disturbances in these areas which have been described, three had their center in Bosporus, three in Pontus or Iberia, thirteen in Armenia, and twelve in Syria. In further detail, it may be pointed out that the wars in Bosporus arose from the determination of Augustus and Claudius to impose rulers satisfactory to themselves upon the kingdom. On the other hand, all but two or three of the wars in Armenia (though at first sight they also turned upon questions of succession) followed disturbances in the Tarim basin, first, in the time of Wang Mang and, second, in that of Hsien of Yarkand. When, however, after the settlement effected by Corbulo in A.D. 63, Armenia was governed by Parthian princes, wars in Kashgaria, as in the time of Pan Ch'ao, were followed by disturbances on the Syrian frontier. More often than not, then, the disturbances in Armenia and Syria (seventeen out of twenty-eight) followed the occurrence of war in the Tarim basin; of the rest (eleven), all but two fall in the later half of the first century B.C., when the example of Pompey seems to have inspired Gabinius, Crassus, Antony, and Augustus to renewed assertions of Roman power in the East.

The significance of the results stated is that the investigation has brought to light a relation in certain specified events such that, when the first occurred (in the T'ien Shan or the Roman East), the second occurred (on the Pannonian Danube or the lower Danube and the Rhine), and that, when the first did not occur, the second did not occur. Hence it becomes evident that the events in Asia and Europe are co-related. The discovery, however, that certain sets of events—wars in Asia and barbarian invasions in Europe—are correlated is a matter of signal importance, for it demonstrates the existence of a type or order of historical facts which has not hitherto received attention, and in an impressive manner enlarges the scope of historical inquiry.

So far, then, the procedure adopted in the investigation has been justified by the results. Nevertheless, even the positive conclusion that the barbarian invasions were occasioned by wars either on the western borders of the Chinese or the eastern borders of the Roman empire does not bring the inquiry to an end. On the contrary, it at once sets a new problem for investigation by raising the question of how the correspondences in events are to be accounted for. Stated in this obvious form, however, the new question lacks precision and a clear focus. On the other hand, when it is recognized that the initial events recorded are wars, it follows that the explanation of the circumstances must lie in some characteristic aspect of the effects which wars produce.

Certain clearly defined antecedents in Asia were followed forty times by characteristic results in Europe, and no occasion is known on which the results appeared except in succession to the antecedents. It may therefore be said without qualification that the barbarian outbreaks were consequent upon wars in the T'ien Shan or the Roman East. Now, wars at all times break in upon the established routine of orderly existence and interfere with the everyday activities of the peoples in conflict, and more especially they put a stop to usual forms of intercourse between the inhabitants of the opposing countries. Hence, when China initiated war in Mongolia or against the kingdoms in the Tarim basin, and when Rome invaded Parthia or Armenia, the inception of hostilities automatically interrupted communications, however well established, across the border. It follows, therefore, that the problem of the relationship between wars in the Far or the Near East and barbarian uprisings in Europe calls for the identification of some usual activity of men which would be subject to immediate interruption in the event of war, and which also might be resumed promptly on the return of peace. The activity which at once suggests itself as complying with these requirements or conditions is that of trade or commerce.

In detail, it is well known that the Chinese carried on trade with the kingdoms in the Tarim basin and, through these and other intermediaries, with Syria. Also it has been shown in the course of this investigation that, when war occurred on the routes in the Tarim basin, disturbances broke out in Parthia and either in Armenia or on the borders of Syria. Evidently, then, war in the Tarim occasioned an interruption of traffic on the silk route, and this interruption aroused hostilities at points along the route as far west as the Euphrates. It seems highly probable, for example, that the invasions of Armenia by the Parthians, while Armenia was controlled by Rome, were inspired by the suspicion that the Romans had succeeded in diverting the movement of commodities from Central Asia to some route which avoided Parthian territory. But these secondary or derivative wars, that is, the conflicts between Parthia and Rome for control of Armenia, brought about new interruptions of trade, and thus led to new wars in more and more distant areas. So interruptions of traffic on the Black Sea stirred up peoples north of the (lower) Danube, and the long train of disturbances ended finally in collisions of the barbarians with the Roman legions on the Rhine. Consequently it is to be seen that peoples in no way concerned with the silk route might yet be connected with the interruptions of trade on that route through the hostilities which the interruptions precipitated between Parthia and Rome. North of the Caspian, though the operations of the fur trade differed widely from the traffic in silk, similar results ensued when the Chinese made war on the Hsiung-nu, and the disturbances extended into Central Europe, and into Media and Armenia.

Observations and Comments

The details on the preceding pages indicate that wars which were undertaken by the governments of China and Rome in pursuit of what were conceived to be important national aims led inevitably to conflicts among the peoples of northern Europe and to invasions of the Roman empire. It is of some importance to note that the statesmen who were responsible for or advocated the resort to war, on each of forty occasions, were entirely unaware of the consequences which this policy entailed. The wars of the Chinese, indeed, were initiated only after lengthy discussions at the imperial court by ministers who were well versed in Chinese history, and who reasoned from historical experience no less than from moral principles and from expediency. But the Chinese emperors and their advisors were unconscious of the fact that their decisions were the prelude to conflicts and devastations in regions of which they had never heard. The Romans were equally in the dark with respect to the consequences of their wars in Bosporus, Armenia, and Syria, but here the fact is striking, for the reason that their wars in the East were followed invariably by outbreaks in Europe. Even though, time after time, disturbances in the East and attacks by the northern barbarians are mentioned in the same context by poets (including Virgil) and historians, there is no intimation in the sources that the conjunction ever provoked comment or inspired reflection. So Augustus persisted in his attempts to dominate Armenia, though the actual results on the Danube and the Rhine might have been unerringly predicted.

The conduct of affairs by Augustus is typical of statesmanship in every age. In justice, it must be said that rulers have been and still are dependent upon the state of knowledge in their own generation. Their concern is always with an immediate present, and the decisions called for in a crisis give no opportunity for prolonged and exacting investigation. The hope of the future, therefore, is dependent upon the efforts of individuals in private life; for, if the actions of those in positions of authority are not to continue to be a major cause of misfortunes to the world, some new form of knowledge must be elicited from the experience of men. The objective may seem unattainable. The record of human experience is History, and the assiduous cultivation of historical inquiry for a century has led only to increased tension in the relations of national groups. Nevertheless, because historians have adhered to the beaten paths and settled conventions of historical writing, it should not hastily be assumed that the possibilities of historical investigation have been exhausted, or that the only expectation of new knowledge concerning "what has actually happened" lies in the discovery of unused documents. As has now been shown, historians, though they have been careful to examine the contents of archives and to base their narratives on documentary sources, have left entirely unexplored means of acquiring information which have been accessible since the beginning of the Christian era.

All histories of the Roman empire make reference to the frontier wars in Europe and present these occurrences in their proper chronological sequence. In practice, however, events on the Rhine, on the Danube, and in the Near East are described under separate headings; and the accounts are dominated by the localized interest of specialists (as are the accounts of wars on the Rhine), rather than by awareness of the concurrence of events in different regions. Since it is now evident that on many successive occasions the wars of Rome in the Near East, on the lower Danube, and on the Rhine followed a well-defined pattern, the convenience of dealing with occurrences on the Rhine or on the Danube in isolation must give place to a presentation which exhibits the relationship between contemporaneous disturbances in the several areas. A knowledge of the relationship of these events is essential to the organization of any history of the empire, and this knowledge can be obtained only by making comparison of events on the eastern and northern frontiers. Yet even this procedure will not enable the investigator to discriminate between the antecedents of invasions on the lower and the upper Danube. It follows, therefore, that knowledge which is indispensable for an historical account of Roman affairs, for an understanding of the situation on the northern frontiers, and even for a just estimate of the character and abilities of emperors can be obtained in no other way than by the comparison of events throughout Eurasia. Thus, apart altogether from any wider interest, the comparison of histories is necessary for a comprehension of what has actually happened within the borders of any national state.

The procedure of comparing histories has other and more vital claims upon attention than the service it may render in the composition of historical narratives. Inquiry has demonstrated beyond the possibility of doubt that in the affairs of nations causes have effects, and that a given cause will produce a characteristic effect. The invariability of this relationship has been shown in forty consecutive instances of barbarian uprisings during a period of 165 years. In thirty-one of these the Romans might readily have foreseen the results which followed their wars in the East, and the adherence of Augustus to a policy of interference in Bosporus and Armenia was responsible for most of the wars which were fought during his reign on the Danube and the Rhine. Here but one series of events has been examined. Yet the results arrived at are such as to make manifest that the knowledge to be derived from similar comparisons of human experience in different regions must be cultivated if rulers and peoples are not to be left in ignorance concerning the determinable effects of proposed modes of action.

At this point it may, indeed, be argued that, although in the ancient world causes were followed uniformly by effects, such correlations in historical events are not to be expected in modern times. It is true that at the beginning of the modern period Western Europe turned from the continental land routes to the outer seaways and skirted the coasts of Africa and Asia; it is true that the seamen of the fifteenth and sixteenth centuries changed the pattern of events, which up to their time had been set by the policies and interests of the Far East. So it may be imagined that the new situation in the world is altogether distinct from the old. Yet the activities of the merchant adventurers were of the same kind and were directed to the same ends as those of their Chinese, Persian, and Arabian predecessors. The actual character of the changes wrought by the seamen of western Europe can be determined by comparing the new situation with the old, or, more specifically, by comparing the correlations in events characteristic of different periods of time both before and after the West embarked upon the exploitation of the world. And since, unfortunately, it is obvious that even the data necessary for the discovery of these correlations have not been assembled, it must be admitted that the essential consequences of Europe's bid for mastery remain hidden at the moment when the Far East offers to resume its former position as the protagonist in the drama of civilization.

There is no reason to doubt that both historians and their public are content with that form of literature which has for its object the appreciative description of the successes of some particular national state. Nevertheless no enthusiasm for the greater moments and more distinctive characters in the history of one's country, no interpretation of the course of world events in terms of some philosophy of history, no insight of practical statesmanship can make available for the guidance of men the resources of human experience. The study of the past can become effective only when it is fully realized that all peoples have histories, that these histories run concurrently and in the same world, and that the act of comparing is the beginning of knowledge. Thus, only by facing an undertaking of new scope and of significant difficulty can history fulfill its obligation of making inquiry, not merely into what has happened, but into the way things actually work in the affairs of men.

ABBREVIATIONS

AAWB	Abhandlungen der preussischen Akademie der Wissenschaften, Berlin
AAWL	Abhandlungen der sächsischen Gesellschaft der Wissenschaften, Leipzig
ABSA	Annual of the British School at Athens
AEM	Archaeologisch-epigraphische Mittheilungen aus Oesterreich-Ungarn
AGWG	Abhandlungen der Gesellschaft der Wissenschaften zu Göttingen
AHR	American Historical Review
AJA	American Journal of Archaeology
AJP	American Journal of Philology
AQR	Asiatic Quarterly Review
CAH	Cambridge Ancient History
CHI	Cambridge History of India
CHJ	Cambridge Historical Journal
CIL	Corpus Inscriptionum Latinarum
CRAI	Comptes rendus de l'Académie des inscriptions et belles-lettres
DAWW	Denkschriften der Akademie der Wissenschaften in Wien
DER	Dizionario epigrafico di antichità romane di Ettore de Ruggiero
EHR	English Historical Review
ESA	Eurasia Septentrionalis Antiqua
FDG	Forschungen zur deutschen Geschichte
FHG	Fragmenta Historicorum Graecorum
HSCP	Harvard Studies in Classical Philology
JAI	Journal of the Royal Anthropographical Institute
JAOS	Journal of the American Oriental Society
JASB	Journal of the Asiatic Society of Bengal
JCAS	Journal of the Royal Central Asian Society
JHS	Journal of Hellenic Studies
JNCB	Journal of the North China Branch of the Royal Asiatic Society
JOAI	Jahreshefte des österreichischen archäologischen Instituts in Wien
JRAS	Journal of the Royal Asiatic Society
JRGS	Journal of the Royal Geographical Society
JRS	Journal of Roman Studies
JRSA	Journal of the Royal Society of Arts
MEFR	Mélanges d'archéologie et d'histoire, École française de Rome
MAI	Mémoires de l'Académie des inscriptions et belles-lettres

MGGW Mittheilungen der geographischen Gesellschaft in Wien
MSOS Mittheilungen des Seminars für orientalische Sprachen zu Berlin
NGWG Nachrichten von der Gesellschaft der Wissenschaften zu Göttingen
NHJ Neue Heidelberger Jahrbücher
NJKA Neue Jahrbücher für das klassische Altertum
NJWJ Neue Jahrbücher für Wissenschaft und Jugendbildung
PBA Proceedings of the British Academy
PBSR Papers of the British School at Rome
PIR Prosopographia Imperii Romani
PRGS Proceedings of the Royal Geographical Society
REA Revue des études anciennes
RECA Paulys Real-Encyclopädie der classischen Altertumswissenschaft, hrsg.
 von Wissowa, Kroll, Witte, Mittelhaus
REO Revue de l'Extrême-Orient
RGA Reallexikon der germanischen Altertumskunde, hrsg. von Hoops
RGK Römisch-germanisches Korrespondenzblatt
RMP Rheinisches Museum für Philologie
SAWB Sitzungsberichte der preussischen Akademie der Wissenschaften, Berlin
SAWM Sitzungsberichte der bayerischen Akademie der Wissenschaften,
 München
SAWW Sitzungsberichte der Akademie der Wissenschaften in Wien
TAPA Transactions of the American Philological Association
VGEB Verhandlungen der Gesellschaft für Erdkunde zu Berlin
WDZ Westdeutsche Zeitschrift für Geschichte und Kunst
ZDA Zeitschrift für deutsches Altertum
ZDMG Zeitschrift der Deutschen Morgenländischen Gesellschaft
ZGEB Zeitschrift der Gesellschaft für Erdkunde zu Berlin

GENERAL BIBLIOGRAPHY

THE TITLES given are intended to present a general view of the published material available in regard to the history of the Roman, the Parthian, and the Chinese empires for the period under consideration, and of the standard works which may be utilized to check the statements in the text. Contributions which have reference to more restricted periods and topics and which have been mentioned in the footnotes are not included.

I. THE ROMAN EMPIRE

ALBERTINI, EUGÈNE. L'empire romain. Paris, 1929. (Peuples et civilisations. Histoire générale publiée sous la direction de Louis Halphen et Philippe Sagnac. IV.)

ARNOLD, WILLIAM THOMAS. The Roman System of Provincial Administration to the Accession of Constantine the Great. 3d ed., rev. by E. S. Bouchier. Oxford, 1914.

—— Studies of Roman Imperialism, ed. by Edward Fiddes. Manchester, 1906.

BERNHART, MAX. Handbuch zur Münzkunde der römischen Kaiserzeit. Halle a. S., 1926. 2 vols.

BESNIER, MAURICE. Lexique de géographie ancienne. Paris, 1914.

BLOCH, GUSTAVE. L'empire romain; évolution et décadence. Paris, 1922.

BOAK, ARTHUR EDWARD ROMILLY. A History of Rome to 565 A.D. New York, 1921. Rev. ed., 1929.

BURY, JOHN BAGNELL. A History of the Roman Empire . . . to the Death of Marcus Aurelius (27 B.C.–A.D. 180). London, 1893.

CAVAIGNAC, EUGÈNE. La paix romaine. Paris, 1928. (Histoire du monde. V.)

CHAPOT, VICTOR. Le monde romain. Paris, 1927. (L'évolution de l'humanité. Synthèse collective.) The Roman World, [tr. by E. A. Parker]. New York, 1928.

CHARLESWORTH, MARTIN PERCIVAL. Trade-routes and Commerce of the Roman Empire. Cambridge, 1924. 2d ed., 1926.

CHEESMAN, GEORGE LEONARD. The Auxilia of the Roman Imperial Army. Oxford, 1914.

CLINTON, HENRY FYNES. Fasti Romani: the Civil and Literary Chronology of Rome and Constantinople from the Death of Augustus to the Death of Justin II. Oxford, 1845–1850. 2 vols.

COHEN, HENRY. Description historique des monnaies frappées sous l'empire romain. 2ᵉ éd. Paris, 1880–1892. 8 vols.

COOK, STANLEY ARTHUR, and others, eds. The Cambridge Ancient History, IX–XI. New York, 1932–1936.

DAREMBERG, CHARLES and SAGLIO, EDMOND. Dictionnaire des antiquités grecques et romaines. Paris, 1877–1919. 5 vols.

DESSAU, HERMANN. Geschichte der römischen Kaiserzeit. Berlin, 1924–1930. 3 vols.

DOMASZEWSKI, ALFRED VON. Geschichte der römischen Kaiser. Leipzig, 1909. 2 vols. 3. Aufl., 1922.

—— "Die Rangordnung des römischen Heeres." *Bonner Jahrbücher*, 117 (1908), pp. 1–278.

—— "Zur Geschichte der römischen Provinzialverwaltung." *RMP*, N.F. 45 (1890), pp. 1–10, 203–211; 46 (1891), pp. 599–605; 48 (1893), pp. 240–247.

DRUMANN, WILHELM. Geschichte Roms in seinem Übergange von der republikanischen zur monarchischen Verfassung. 2. Aufl., hrsg. von P. Groebe. Berlin, 1899–1929. 6 vols.

DURUY, VICTOR. History of Rome and the Roman People, tr. by M. M. Ripley and W. J. Clarke. Boston, 1883–1886. 6 vols.

ECKHEL, JOSEPH. Doctrina numorum veterum. Vindobonae, 1792–1839. 9 vols.

FERRERO, GUGLIELMO. The Greatness and Decline of Rome, tr. by A. E. Zimmern and H. J. Chaytor. London, 1907–1909. 5 vols.

FRANK, TENNEY. An Economic History of Rome. 2d ed., rev. Baltimore, 1927.

—— A History of Rome. New York, [1923].

—— Roman Imperialism. 2d ed. New York, 1925.

GARDTHAUSEN, VICTOR EMIL. Augustus und seine Zeit. Leipzig, 1891–1904. 2 pts. in 6 vols.

GIBBON, EDWARD. The History of the Decline and Fall of the Roman Empire. London, 1776–1788. 6 vols. Ed. by J. B. Bury, 1896–1900. 7 vols.

GOYAU, GEORGES. Chronologie de l'empire romain. Paris, 1891.

GRUNDY, GEORGE BEARDOE. A History of the Greek and Roman World. London, [1926].

HEAD, SIR BARCLAY VINCENT. Historia numorum; a manual of Greek numismatics. New ed. Oxford, 1911.

HEITLAND, WILLIAM EMERTON. The Roman Republic. Cambridge, 1909. 3 vols.

HENDERSON, BERNARD WILLIAM. The Life and Principate of the Emperor Nero. London, 1903.

—— Civil War and Rebellion in the Roman Empire, A.D. 69–70. London, 1908.

—— Five Roman Emperors: Vespasian, Titus, Domitian, Nerva, Trajan, A.D. 69–117. Cambridge, 1927.

HIRSCHFELD, OTTO. Die kaiserlichen Verwaltungsbeamten bis auf Diocletian. 2. Aufl. Berlin, 1905.

HOLMES, THOMAS RICE EDWARD. The Roman Republic and the Founder of the Empire. Oxford, 1923. 3 vols.

—— The Architect of the Roman Empire. Oxford, 1928–1931. 2 vols.

HOMO, LÉON. L'empire romain. Le gouvernement du monde. La défense du monde. L'exploitation du monde. Paris, 1925.

—— Le haut-empire. Paris, 1933. (Histoire générale publiée sous la direction de Gustave Glotz ... Histoire romaine. III.)

JONES, SIR HENRY STUART. Companion to Roman History. Oxford, 1912.

—— The Roman Empire, B.C. 29–A.D. 476. London, 1908.

KLEBS, ELIMAR, and others. Prosopographia imperii romani saec. I, II, III. Berolini, 1897–1898. 3 vols.

KORNEMANN, ERNST. "Die römische Kaiserzeit," in Alfred Gercke and Eduard Norden, Einleitung in die Altertumswissenschaft. 3. Bd. 2. Aufl. Leipzig, 1914. pp. 210–306.

—— Staaten, Völker, Männer aus der Geschichte des Altertums. Leipzig, 1934.

KROMAYER, JOHANNES and VEITH, GEORG. Heerwesen und Kriegführung der Griechen und Römer, unter Mitarbeit von A. Köster, E. v. Nischer und E. Schramm. München, 1928.

—— Schlachten-Atlas zur antiken Kriegsgeschichte. Römische Abteilung, III–IV. Leipzig, 1924–1929.

LIEBENAM, WILHELM. Fasti consulares imperii romani von 30 v. Chr. bis 565 n. Chr. Bonn, 1909.

—— Die Legaten in den römischen Provinzen von Augustus bis Diocletian. Leipzig, 1888.

MARQUARDT, JOACHIM. Römische Staatsverwaltung. 2. Aufl. Leipzig, 1881–1885. 3 vols.

MARSH, FRANK BURR. A History of the Roman World from 146 to 30 B.C. London, [1935].

MATTINGLY, HAROLD. Coins of the Roman Empire in the British Museum. I–III. London, 1923–1936.

—— Roman Coins from the Earliest Times to the Fall of the Western Empire. London, [1928].

—— and SYDENHAM, EDWARD ALLEN. The Roman Imperial Coinage. I–III. London, 1923–1930.

MILLER, STEUART NAPIER. "The Roman Empire in the First Three Centuries," in Edward Eyre, European Civilization, Its Origin and Development. II. London, 1935. pp. 279–521.

MOMMSEN, THEODOR. The Provinces of the Roman Empire from Caesar to Diocletian, tr. by W. P. Dickson. London, 1886. 2 vols. Reprinted with corrections, 1909.

MUIR, RAMSAY and PHILIP, GEORGE. Philips' Atlas of Ancient and Classical History. London, 1938.

NIESE, BENEDICTUS. Grundriss der römischen Geschichte nebst Quellenkunde. 5. Aufl., neubearbeitet von E. Hohl. München, 1923.

NILSSON, MARTIN PERSSON. Imperial Rome, tr. by G. C. Richards. London, 1926.

PAIS, ETTORE, ed. Fasti trivmphales popvli romani. Roma, 1920. 2 vols.

PARKER, HENRY MICHAEL DENNE. The Roman Legions. Oxford, 1928.

PELHAM, HENRY FRANCIS. Outlines of Roman History. New York, [1893]. 4th ed., [1905].

PETER, CARL. Zeittafeln der römischen Geschichte. 6. Aufl. Halle a. S., 1882.

PIGANIOL, ANDRÉ. La conquête romaine. Paris, 1927. (Peuples et civilisations. Histoire générale publiée sous la direction de Louis Halphen et Philippe Sagnac. III.)

RITTERLING, EMIL. "Legio." RECA, XII (1924–1925), pp. 1186–1829.

ROSTOVTZEFF, MICHAEL IVANOVICH. A History of the Ancient World. II. Rome, tr. by J. D. Duff. Oxford, 1927.

—— The Social and Economic History of the Roman Empire. Oxford, 1926.

RUGGIERO, ETTORE DE, ed. Dizionario epigrafico di antichità romane. Roma, Spoleta, 1895 ff.

SANDS, PERCY COOPER. The Client Princes of the Roman Empire under the Republic. Cambridge, 1908.

SANDYS, SIR JOHN EDWIN, ed. A Companion to Latin Studies. Cambridge, 1910. 3d ed., 1921.

SCHILLER, HERMANN. Geschichte der römischen Kaiserzeit. Gotha, 1883–1887. 2 vols. in 3.

STEVENSON, GEORGE HOPE. The Roman Empire. London, [1930].

THIERSCH, HERMANN. An den Rändern des Römischen Reichs; sechs Vorträge über antike Kultur. München, 1911.

TOUTAIN, JULES. L'économie antique. Paris, 1927. (L'évolution de l'humanité. Synthèse collective.) The Economic Life of the Ancient World, [tr. by M. R. Dobie]. New York, 1930.

VOGT, JOSEPH. Die alexandrinischen Münzen. Stuttgart, 1924. 2 pts.

WARMINGTON, ERIC HERBERT. The Commerce between the Roman Empire and India. Cambridge, 1928.

WELLS, JOSEPH and BARROW, REGINALD HAYNES. A Short History of the Roman Empire to the Death of Marcus Aurelius. London, 1931.

WISSOWA, GEORG, and others, eds. Paulys Real-Encyclopädie der classischen Altertumswissenschaft. Neue Bearbeitung. Stuttgart, 1894 ff.

WOLF, JULIUS. Die römische Kaiserzeit. Freiburg i. B., 1932.

WRUCK, WALDEMAR. Die syrische Provinzialprägung von Augustus bis Trajan. Stuttgart, 1931.

A. ROMAN FRONTIER PROVINCES

1. GAUL AND THE RHINE

BLOCH, GUSTAVE. "Les origines. La Gaule indépendante et la Gaule romaine," in Ernest Lavisse, Histoire de France depuis les origines jusqu'à la Révolution. I. Paris, 1904.

CRAMER, FRANZ. Deutschland in römischer Zeit. Berlin, Leipzig, 1912.

—— Römisch-germanische Studien. Gesammelte Beiträge zur römisch-germanischen Altertumskunde. Breslau, 1914.

CUMONT, FRANZ. "Comment la Belgique fut romanisée." Annales de la Société royale d'archéologie de Bruxelles, 28 (1919), pp. 77–181.

DELBRÜCK, HANS. Geschichte der Kriegskunst im Rahmen der politischen Geschichte. I. Das Alterthum. [II. Die Germanen.] Berlin, 1900–1902. 3. Aufl., 1920–1921.

DESJARDINS, ERNEST. Géographie historique et administrative de la Gaule romaine. Paris, 1876–1893. 4 vols.

DRAGENDORFF, HANS. Westdeutschland zur Römerzeit. Leipzig, 1912. 2. Aufl., 1919.

FORRER, ROBERT. L'Alsace romaine. Paris, 1935.

GRENIER, ALBERT. Etudes d'archéologie rhénane. Quatre villes romaines de Rhénanie: Trèves, Mayence, Bonn, Cologne. Paris, 1925.

—— Manuel d'archéologie gallo-romaine. Paris, 1931–1934. 3 vols. (Manuel d'archéologie préhistorique, celtique et gallo-romaine par Joseph Déchelette. V–VI.)

HAGEN, JOSEPH. Römerstrassen der Rheinprovinz. Bonn, 1923. 2. Aufl., 1931.

HOLMES, THOMAS RICE EDWARD. Caesar's Conquest of Gaul. London, 1899. 2d ed., Oxford, 1911.

JULLIAN, CAMILLE. De la Gaule à la France; nos origines historiques. Paris, 1922.

—— Histoire de la Gaule. Paris, 1908–1926. 8 vols.

KOEPP, FRIEDRICH. Die Römer in Deutschland. Bielefeld und Leipzig, 1905. 2. Aufl., 1912.

—— and WOLFF, GEORG. Römisch-germanische Forschungen. Berlin, Leipzig, 1922.

LONGNON, AUGUSTE. Géographie de la Gaule au vi° siècle. Paris, 1878.

RIESE, ALEXANDER. Das rheinische Germanien in der antiken Litteratur. Leipzig, 1892.

—— Das rheinische Germanien in den antiken Inschriften. Leipzig, 1914.

RITTERLING, EMIL. Fasti des römischen Deutschland unter dem Prinzipat, mit Beiträgen von Edmund Groag, hrsg. von Ernst Stein. Wien, 1932.

SADÉE, EMIL. Römer und Germanen. II. Berlin, 1911.

—— "Rom und Deutschland vor 1900 Jahren. Weshalb hat das römische Reich auf die Eroberung Germaniens verzichtet?" *Bonner Jahrbücher*, 124 (1917), pp. 1–16.

SCHUMACHER, KARL. Siedelungs- und Kulturgeschichte der Rheinlande von der Urzeit bis in das Mittelalter. II. Die römische Periode. Mainz, 1923.

STEIN, ERNST. Die kaiserlichen Beamten und Truppenkörper im römischen Deutschland unter dem Prinzipat. Wien, 1932.

2. THE UPPER RHINE AND THE UPPER DANUBE

For publications relating to the Roman limes in Germany,
see above, page 125, note 11.

CARTELLIERI, WALTHER. Die römischen Alpenstrassen über den Brenner, Reschen-Scheideck und Plöckenpass, mit ihren Nebenlinien. Leipzig, 1926. (*Philologus*, Supptbd. 18, Heft 1.)

FABRICIUS, ERNST. Die Besitznahme Badens durch die Römer. Heidelberg, 1905.

—— "Das römische Heer in Obergermanien und Rätien." *Historische Zeitschrift*, 98 (1906), pp. 1–29.

FRANZISS, FRANZ. Bayern zur Römerzeit. Regensburg, 1905.

GNIRS, ANTON. Die römischen Schutzbezirke an der Oberen Donau. Augsburg, 1929.

GRAF, ANDREAS. Übersicht der antiken Geographie von Pannonien. Budapest, 1936. (Dissertationes Pannonicae, ser. I, fasc. 5.)

HAUG, FERDINAND. "Raetia." *RECA*, 2. Reihe, I (1914), pp. 46–62.

HERTLEIN, FRIEDRICH. Die Geschichte der Besetzung des römischen Württemberg. Stuttgart, 1928. (Die Römer in Württemberg. I.)

HEUBERGER, RICHARD. Rätien im Altertum und Frühmittelalter. I. Innsbruck, 1932.

—— "Zur Geschichte der römischen Brennerstrasse." *Klio*, 27 (1934), pp. 311–336.

HYDE, WALTER WOODBURN. Roman Alpine Routes. Philadelphia, 1935. (Memoirs of the American Philosophical Society, vol. 2.)

KAHRSTEDT, ULRICH. "Studien zur politischen und Wirtschafts-Geschichte der Ost- und Zentralalpen vor Augustus." *NGWG*, 1927, pp. 1–36.

KUBITSCHEK, WILHELM. "Ältere Berichte über den römischen Limes in Pannonien." *SAWW*, 209 (1931), 1. Abh.

—— Die Römerzeit. Wien, [1921]. (Heimatkunde von Nieder-Oesterreich. 8.)

NISCHER, ERNST. Die Römer im Gebiete des ehemaligen Österreich-Ungarn. Wien, 1923.

OHLENSCHLAGER, FRIEDRICH. Römische Ueberreste in Bayern. München, 1902–1910. 3 pts.

PARET, OSKAR. Urgeschichte Württembergs mit besonderer Berücksichtigung des mittleren Neckarlandes. Stuttgart, 1921.

PEAKS, MARY BRADFORD. The General Civil and Military Administration of Noricum and Raetia. Chicago, 1907.

PFISTER, JOSEF. "Pannonien in politisch-geographischer Betrachtung." *Ungarische Jahrbücher*, 8 (1928), pp. 114–163.

POLASCHEK, E. "Noricum." *RECA*, XVII (1936), pp. 971–1048.

RITTERLING, EMIL. "Die Statthalter der pannonischen Provinzen." *AEM*, 20 (1897), pp. 1–40.

Scheffel, Paul Hugo. Die Brennerstrasse zur Römerzeit. Berlin, 1912.

Stähelin, Felix. Die Schweiz in römischer Zeit. 2. Aufl. Basel, 1931.

Wagner, Friedrich. Die Römer in Bayern. München, 1924. 4. Aufl., 1928.

3. ILLYRICUM, MACEDONIA, AND MOESIA

Ballif, Philipp. Römische Strassen in Bosnien und der Hercegovina. Wien, 1893.

Cons, Henri. La province romaine de Dalmatie. Paris, 1881.

Desdevises du Dezert, Théophile Alphonse. Géographie ancienne de la Macédoine. Paris, 1863.

Dessau, Hermann. "Zur Reihenfolge der Statthalter Moesiens." JOAI, 23 (1926), Beiblatt, pp. 345–358.

Domaszewski, Alfred von. "Die Entwicklung der Provinz Moesia." NHJ, 1 (1891), pp. 190–200.

—— "Die Beneficiarierposten und die römischen Strassennetze." WDZ, 21 (1902), pp. 158–211.

—— "Die Grenzen von Moesia superior und der illyrische Grenzzoll." AEM, 13 (1890), pp. 129–154.

Evans, Sir Arthur John. "Antiquarian researches in Illyricum." Archaeologia, 48 (1885), pp. 1–105; 49 (1885), pp. 1–167.

Filow, Bogdan. Die Legionen der Provinz Moesia von Augustus bis auf Diokletian. Leipzig, 1906. (Klio, VI. Beiheft.)

Fluss, Max. "Moesia." RECA, XV (1932), pp. 2350–2411.

Grégoire, Henri. "La romanisation aux [des] bouches du Danube." Revue belge de philologie et d'histoire, 4 (1925), pp. 317–331; 11 (1932), pp. 599–625.

Henry, P. "Une histoire des Gètes avant la conquête de la Dacie par les Romains." Revue historique, 156 (1927), pp. 269–293.

Jireček, Constantin. Die Heerstrasse von Belgrad nach Constantinopel und die Balkanpässe. Prag, 1877.

Jung, Julius. Roemer und Romanen in den Donaulaendern; historisch-ethnographische Studien. Innsbruck, 1877. 2. Aufl., 1887.

—— Die romanischen Landschaften des roemischen Reiches. Innsbruck, 1881.

Pârvan, Vasile. Dacia, [tr. by I. L. Evans and M. P. Charlesworth.] Cambridge, 1928.

—— Getica, o protoistorie a Daciei. Bucureşti, 1926.

—— "I primordi della civiltà romana alle foci del Danubio." Ausonia, 10 (1921), pp. 187–209.

——, ed. Dacia: recherches et découvertes archéologiques en Roumanie, I–IV. Bucarest, 1927–1933.

Patsch, Carl Ludwig. Beiträge zur Völkerkunde von Südosteuropa. V. Aus 500 Jahren vorrömischer und römischer Geschichte Südosteuropas. I. Bis zur Festsetzung der Römer in Transdanuvien. Wien, 1932. (SAWW, 214.)

—— Bosnien und Herzegowina in römischer Zeit. Sarajevo, 1911.

—— Historische Wanderungen im Karst und an der Adria. I. Die Herzegowina einst und jetzt. Wien, 1922.

Pick, Behrendt and Regling, Kurt. Die antiken Münzen von Dacien und Moesien. Berlin, 1898–1910. (Die antiken Münzen Nord-Griechenlands, unter Leitung von Friedrich Imhoof-Blumer. I.)

Premerstein, Anton von. "Die Anfänge der Provinz Moesien." JOAI, 1 (1898), Beiblatt, pp. 145–196.

Sehmsdorf, Erich. Die Germanen in den Balkanländern bis zum Auftreten der Goten. Leipzig, 1899.

STOUT, SELATIE EDGAR. The Governors of Moesia. Princeton, 1911.

TOMASCHEK, WILHELM. "Die vorslawische Topographie der Bosna, Herzegowina, Crnagora und der angrenzenden Gebiete." *MGGW*, 23 (1880), pp. 497–528, 545–567.

WEERD, HUBERT VAN DE. Etude historique sur trois légions romaines du Bas-Danube (Vᵉ Macedonica, XIᵉ Claudia, Iᵉ Italica), suivie d'un aperçu général sur l'armée romaine de la province de Mésie inférieure sous le haut-empire. Louvain, 1907.

WEISS, JAKOB. Die Dobrudscha im Altertum; historische Landschaftskunde. Sarajevo, 1911.

ZIPPEL, GUSTAV. Die römische Herrschaft in Illyrien bis auf Augustus. Leipzig, 1877.

4. EASTERN FRONTIER PROVINCES

ANDERSON, JOHN GEORGE CLARKE. "The Road-system of Eastern Asia Minor." *JHS*, 17 (1897), pp. 22–44.

BOUCHIER, EDMUND SPENSER. Syria as a Roman Province. Oxford, 1916.

CHAPOT, VICTOR. La frontière de l'Euphrate de Pompée à la conquête arabe. Paris, 1907. (Bibliothèque des Ecoles françaises d'Athènes et de Rome, 99.)

CUMONT, FRANZ. Etudes syriennes. Paris, 1917.

DOBIÁŠ, JOSEF. "Les premiers rapports des Romains avec les Parthes et l'occupation de la Syrie." *Archiv orientální*, 3 (1931), pp. 215–256.

DUSSAUD, RENÉ. Les Arabes en Syrie avant l'Islam. Paris, 1907.

—— Topographie historique de la Syrie antique et médiévale. Paris, 1927.

FÉVRIER, JAMES GERMAIN. Essai sur l'histoire politique et économique de Palmyre. Paris, 1931.

GWATKIN, WILLIAM EMMETT. Cappadocia as a Roman Procuratorial Province. Columbia, Missouri, 1930. (University of Missouri studies, vol. 5. no. 4.)

HARRER, GUSTAVE ADOLPHUS. Studies in the History of the Roman Province of Syria. Princeton, 1915.

HOGARTH, DAVID GEORGE and MUNRO, J. A. R. "Modern and Ancient Roads in Eastern Asia Minor." Royal Geographical Society, Supplementary Papers, 3 (1893), pp. 639–739.

HONIGMANN, ERNST. "Historische Topographie von Nordsyrien im Altertum." *Zeitschrift des Deutschen Palästina-Vereins*, 46 (1923), pp. 149–193; 47 (1924), pp. 1–64.

—— "Syria." *RECA*, 2. Reihe, IV (1932), pp. 1549–1727.

JONES, ARNOLD HUGH MARTIN. The Cities of the Eastern Roman Provinces. Oxford, 1937.

KAHRSTEDT, ULRICH. Syrische Territorien in hellenistischer Zeit. Berlin, 1926. (*AGWG*, N.F. Bd. 19.)

KAMMERER, ALBERT. Pétra et la Nabatène. L'Arabie Pétrée et les Arabes du Nord dans leurs rapports avec la Syrie et la Palestine jusqu'à l'Islam. Paris, 1929–1930. 2 vols.

MUNRO, JOHN ARTHUR RUSKIN. "Roads in Pontus, Royal and Roman." *JHS*, 21 (1901), pp. 52–66.

RAMSAY, SIR WILLIAM MITCHELL. The Historical Geography of Asia Minor. London, 1890. (Royal Geographical Society, Supplementary Papers, 4.)

ROSTOVTZEFF, MICHAEL IVANOVICH. Caravan Cities, tr. by D. and T. Talbot Rice. Oxford, 1932.

—— "La Syrie romaine." *Revue historique*, 175 (1935), pp. 1–40.

SCHÜRER, EMIL. Geschichte des jüdischen Volkes im Zeitalter Jesu Christi. 3.–4. Aufl. Leipzig, 1901.

WROTH, WARWICK WILLIAM. Catalogue of the Greek Coins of Galatia, Cappadocia, and Syria. London, 1899. (A Catalogue of the Greek Coins in the British Museum.)

B. PEOPLES AND STATES ON THE BORDERS OF THE ROMAN EMPIRE

1. GERMANS

BANG, MARTIN. Die Germanen im römischen Dienst bis zum Regierungsantritt Constantins I. Berlin, 1906.

BLUME, ERICH. Die germanischen Stämme und die Kulturen zwischen Oder und Passarge zur römischen Kaiserzeit. Würzburg, 1912–1915. 2 vols. (Mannus-Bibliothek. 8, 14.)

BREMER, OTTO. Ethnographie der germanischen Stämme [1899]. 2. Abdruck. Strassburg, 1904. "Sonderabdruck aus der zweiten Auflage von Pauls Grundriss der germanischen Philologie."

CAPELLE, WILHELM, ed. Das alte Germanien: die Nachrichten der griechischen und römischen Schriftsteller. Jena, 1929.

DETLEFSEN, DETLEF. Die Entdeckung des germanischen Nordens im Altertum. Berlin, 1904. (Quellen und Forschungen zur alten Geschichte und Geographie, hrsg. von W. Sieglin. 8.)

EBERT, MAX, ed. Reallexikon der Vorgeschichte. Berlin, 1924–1932. 15 vols.

FIEBIGER, OTTO and SCHMIDT, LUDWIG. Inschriftensammlung zur Geschichte der Ostgermanen. Wien, 1917. (*DAWW*, 60. Bd., 3. Abh.)

GNIRS, ANTON. Das östliche Germanien und seine Verkehrswege in der Darstellung des Ptolemaeus. Prag, 1898.

HAYES, CARLTON HUNTLEY. An Introduction to the Sources Relating to the Germanic Invasions. New York, 1909. (Studies in History, Economics and Public Law, Columbia University, vol. 33, no. 3.)

HOOPS, JOHANNES, ed. Reallexikon der germanischen Altertumskunde. Strassburg, 1911–1919. 4 vols.

KAUFFMANN, FRIEDRICH. Deutsche Altertumskunde. I. Von der Urzeit bis zur Völkerwanderung. München, 1913.

KLOSE, JOHANNES. Roms Klientel-Randstaaten am Rhein und an der Donau. Breslau, 1934.

KOSSINNA, GUSTAF. Germanische Kultur im 1. Jahrtausend nach Christus. Leipzig, 1932. (Mannus-Bibliothek. 50.)

—— Ursprung und Verbreitung der Germanen in vor und frühgeschichtlicher Zeit. Berlin, 1926–1927. 2 vols.

KRÁLIČEK, ANTON. Die Donauvölker Altgermaniens nach Cornelius Tacitus und Claudius Ptolemaeus: ein Beitrag zur Geschichte der deutschen Völkerbewegung. Brünn, [1897].

MUCH, RUDOLF. Deutsche Stammsitze: ein Beitrag zur ältesten Geschichte Deutschlands. Halle, 1892.

—— Deutsche Stammeskunde. Leipzig, 1900. 2. Aufl., 1905.

—— "Germani." *RECA*, 3. Suppbd. (1918), pp. 545–585.

——, ed. Die Germania des Tacitus. Heidelberg, 1937. (Germanische Bibliothek. I. Abt., V. Reihe, 3. Bd.)

Müllenhoff, Karl. Deutsche Altertumskunde. Berlin, 1870–1900. 5 vols. Neuer vermehrter Abdruck besorgt durch Max Roediger. Bd. 1, 2, 4, 5. Berlin, 1890–1920.

Nerman, Birger. Die Herkunft und die frühesten Auswanderungen der Germanen. Stockholm, 1924.

Norden, Eduard. Die germanische Urgeschichte in Tacitus Germania. Leipzig, 1920. 3. Abdruck, 1923.

Reeb, Wilhelm, ed. Tacitus Germania, mit Beiträgen von A. Dopsch, H. Reis, K. Schumacher, unter Mitarbeit von H. Klenk. Leipzig, 1930.

Schmidt, Ludwig. Allgemeine Geschichte der germanischen Völker bis zur Mitte des sechsten Jahrhunderts. München und Berlin, 1909. (Handbuch der Mittel-alterlichen und Neueren Geschichte, hrsg. von G. v. Below und F. Meinecke. Abt. II.)

—— Geschichte der deutschen Stämme. I–II. Berlin, 1904–1918. (Quellen und Forschungen zur alten Geschichte und Geographie, hrsg. von W. Sieglin. 7, 10, 12, 22, 24, 27, 29, 30.) [I] Die Ostgermanen. 2. Aufl. München, 1934.

—— Geschichte der germanischen Frühzeit. Bonn, 1925.

Schönfeld, Moritz. Wörterbuch der altgermanischen Personen- und Völkernamen. Heidelberg, 1911. (Germanische Bibliothek. I. Sammlung. IV. Reihe, 2. Bd.)

Schránil, Josef. Die Vorgeschichte Böhmens und Mährens. Berlin, 1928.

Schulz, Otto Theodor. "Ueber die wirtschaftlichen und politischen Verhältnisse bei den Germanen zur Zeit des C. Julius Caesar." *Klio*, 11 (1911), pp. 48–82.

Zeuss, Kaspar. Die Deutschen und die Nachbarstämme. München, 1837. [Reprint], Heidelberg, 1925. (Germanische Bibliothek. 2. Abt., 18. Bd.)

2. SARMATIANS AND THE KINGDOM OF BOSPORUS

Bonnell, Ernst. Beiträge zur Alterthumskunde Russlands, von den ältesten Zeiten bis um das Jahr 400 n. Chr. St. Petersburg, 1882–1897. 2 vols.

—— "Einige Nachrichten der alten griechischen und römischen Schriftsteller über die Skythen, Sarmaten, Kimmerier, Perser, und andere Völker." *Travaux de la 3e session du Congrès international des Orientalistes*. II. St.-Pétersbourg, 1879. pp. 371–387.

Brandis, Carl G. "Bosporos" (3). *RECA*, III (1899), pp. 757–789.

Burachkov, P. O. General Catalogue of Coins Belonging to the Greek Colonies ... within the Bounds of What Is Now South Russia. [In Russian.] Odessa, 1884.

Diehl, Erich. "Olbia" (4). *RECA*, XVII (1937), pp. 2405–23.

Ebert, Max. Südrussland im Altertum. Bonn, 1921.

Herrmann, Albert. "Tanais." *RECA*, 2. Reihe, IV (1932), pp. 2162–69.

Kretschmer, Konrad. "Sarmatia," "Scythae," "Scythia." *RECA*, 2. Reihe, II (1921), pp. 1–12, 923–946.

Latyschev, Basilius. Inscriptiones antiquae orae septentrionalis Ponti Euxini. I, II, IV. St. Petersburg, 1885–1901.

—— Scythica et Caucasica e veteribus scriptoribus Graecis et Latinis, cum versione Rossica. St. Petersburg, 1890–1906.

Mannert, Konrad. Der Norden der Erde von der Weichsel bis nach China. Nürnberg, 1795. (Geographie der Griechen und Römer. IV. Theil.)

Minns Ellis Hovell. Scythians and Greeks: a Survey of Ancient History and Archaeology on the North Coast of the Euxine from the Danube to the Caucasus. Cambridge, 1913.

—— "The Scythians and the Northern Nomads." *CAH*, III (New York, 1925), pp. 187–205.

Morgan, Jacques de. Manuel de numismatique orientale. I. Paris, 1923. pp. 176–188.

Müllenhoff, Karl. Deutsche Altertumskunde. III. Berlin, 1892.

Neumann, Karl. Die Hellenen im Skythenlande: ein Beitrag zur alten Geographie, Ethnographie und Handelsgeschichte. I. Bd. Berlin, 1855.

Potocki, Ian. Fragments historiques et géographiques sur la Scythie, la Sarmatie et les Slaves. Brunswick, 1795. 4 vols.

Rostovtzeff, Michael Ivanovich. Iranians and Greeks in South Russia. Oxford, 1922.

——— Skythien und der Bosporus. I. Kritische Übersicht der schriftlichen und archäologischen Quellen. Berlin, 1931.

Sadowski, Jan Nepomucen. Die Handelsstrassen der Griechen und Römer durch das Flussgebiet der Oder, Weichsel, des Dniepr und Niemen an die Gestade des Baltischen Meeres. . . . Aus dem Polnischen von Albin Kohn. Jena, 1877.

Sallet, Alfred von. Beiträge zur Geschichte und Numismatik der Könige des cimmerischen Bosporus und des Pontus von der Schlacht bei Zela bis zur Abdankung Polemo II. Berlin, 1866.

Stern, Ernst von. "Die politische und sociale Struktur der Griechencolonien am Nordufer des Schwarzmeergebietes." Hermes, 50 (1915), pp. 161–224.

Wroth, Warwick William. Catalogue of Greek Coins [in the British Museum]. Pontus, Paphlagonia, Bithynia, and the Kingdom of Bosporus. London, 1889.

3. ARMENIA

Abbruzzese, Antonio. "Le relazioni fra l'impero romano e l'Armenia a tempo di Augusto." Rivista di storia antica, n.s. 7 (1903), pp. 505–521, 722–734; 8 (1904), pp. 32–61. "Le relazioni fra l'impero romano e l'Armenia a tempo di Tiberio e di Caligola." Bessarione, 3 ser., 2 (1907), pp. 63–106. "Le relazioni politiche fra l'impero romano e l'Armenia da Claudio a Traiano." Bessarione, 8 (1911), pp. 389–434.

Asdourian, Pascal. Die politischen Beziehungen zwischen Armenien und Rom von 190 v. Chr. bis 428 n. Chr. Venedig, 1911.

Aslan, Kévork. Etudes historiques sur le peuple arménien. Paris, 1909. Nouvelle éd., 1928.

Babelon, Ernest. Les rois de Syrie, d'Arménie et de Commagène. Paris, 1890. (Catalogue des monnaies grecques de la Bibliothèque Nationale.)

Basmadjian, K. J. "Chronologie de l'histoire d'Arménie." Revue de l'orient chrétien, 19 (1914), pp. 290–301, 358–377.

Brosset, Marie Félicité, tr. Collection d'historiens arméniens. S.-Pétersbourg, 1874–1876. 2 vols.

Hübschmann, Heinrich. "Die altarmenischen Ortsnamen, mit Beiträgen zur historischen Topographie Armeniens und einer Karte." Indogermanische Forschungen, 16 (1904), pp. 197–490.

Langlois, Victor, tr. Collection des historiens anciens et modernes de l'Arménie. Paris, 1867–1869. 2 vols.

Lehmann-Haupt, Ferdinand Friedrich Carl. Armenien einst und jetzt. Berlin, 1910–1931. 2 vols. in 3.

——— "Tigranokerta," RECA, 2. Reihe, VI (1936), 981–1007.

Lynch, Harry Finnis Bloss. Armenia: Travels and Studies. London, 1901. 2 vols.

Markwart, Joseph. Südarmenien und die Tigrisquellen nach griechischen und arabischen Geographen. Wien, 1930. (Studien zur armenischen Geschichte. IV.)

MORGAN, JACQUES DE. Histoire du peuple arménien, depuis les temps les plus re-
culés de ses annales jusqu'à nos jours. Paris, 1919.

SAINT-MARTIN, JEAN. Mémoires historiques et géographiques sur l'Arménie. Paris,
1818–1819. 2 vols.

SANDALGIAN, JOSEPH. Histoire documentaire de l'Arménie des âges du paganisme,
1410 av.–305 apr. J.-C. Rome, 1917. 2 vols.

TOURNEBIZE, HENRI FRANÇOIS. Histoire politique et religieuse de l'Arménie. I.
Depuis les origines des Arméniens jusqu'à la mort de leur dernier roi, l'an 1393.
Paris, 1910.

II. THE PARTHIAN EMPIRE

ALLOTTE DE LA FUŸE, FRANÇOIS MAURICE. "Nouveau classement des monnaies arsacides." *Revue numismatique,* 4. sér., 8 (1904), pp. 317–371.

DEBEVOISE, NEILSON CAREL. A Political History of Parthia. Chicago, [1938].

DOBIÁŠ, JOSEPH. "Séleucie sur l'Euphrate." *Syria,* 6 (1925), pp. 253–267.

DROUIN, EDME. "Onomastique arsacide: essai d'explication des noms des rois parthes." *Revue numismatique,* 3. sér., 13 (1895), pp. 360–388.

DUVAL, RUBENS. Histoire politique, religieuse et littéraire d'Edesse jusqu'à la
première croisade. Paris, 1892.

ENSSLIN, WILHELM. "Die weltgeschichtliche Bedeutung der Kämpfe zwischen Rom
und Persien." *NJWJ,* 4 (1928), pp. 399–415.

FURNEAUX, HENRY. "The Roman Relations with Parthia and Armenia from the
Time of Augustus to the Death of Nero," in his The Annals of Tacitus. Oxford,
1891. pp. 96–126.

GARDNER, PERCY. The Parthian Coinage. London, 1877.

GÜNTHER, ADOLF. Beiträge zur Geschichte der Kriege zwischen Römern und Parthern. Berlin, 1922.

GUTSCHMID, ALFRED VON. "Persia. II. Greek and Parthian empires." *Encyclopaedia
Britannica,* 9th ed., XVIII (New York, 1885), pp. 582–607. German translation:
Geschichte Irans und seiner Nachbarländer von Alexander dem Grossen bis zum
Untergang der Arsaciden. Tübingen, 1888.

—— Untersuchungen über die Geschichte des Königreichs Osroëne. St.-Péters-
bourg, 1887. (Mémoires de l'Académie impériale des sciences de St.-Pétersbourg,
7. sér., t. 35.)

HERRMANN, ALBERT. "Sacaraucae," "Sakai," "Sakastane," *RECA,* 2. Reihe, I (1920),
1611–20, 1770–1812.

HERZFELD, ERNST. Archaeological History of Iran. London, 1935.

—— "Sakastan." *Archaeologische Mitteilungen aus Iran,* 4 (1931–1932), pp. 1–116.

HILL, GEORGE FRANCIS. Catalogue of the Greek Coins of Arabia, Mesopotamia, and
Persia. London, 1922. (A Catalogue of the Greek Coins in the British Museum.)

HONIGMANN, ERNST. "Ktesiphon." *RECA,* IV. Supptbd. (1924), pp. 1102–1119.

HUART, CLÉMENT IMBAULT. La Perse antique et la civilisation iranienne. Paris,
1925. (L'évolution de l'humanité. Synthèse collective.) Ancient Persia and
Iranian Civilization, [tr. by M. R. Dobie]. London, 1927.

JUSTI, FERDINAND. Geschichte des alten Persiens. Berlin, 1879. (Allgemeine Geschichte in Einzeldarstellungen, hrsg. von Wilhelm Oncken.)

—— "Geschichte Irans von den ältesten Zeiten bis zum Ausgang der Sāsāniden,"
in Wilhelm Geiger and Ernst Kuhn, Grundriss der iranischen Philologie. II.
Strassburg, 1896–1904. pp. 395–550.

KIAN, GHOLAM REZA. Introduction à l'histoire de la monnaie et histoire monétaire de la Perse des origines à la fin de la période parthe. Paris, 1934.

KIESSLING, MAX. "Hyrkania." *RECA*, IX (1914), pp. 454–526.

LINDSAY, JOHN. A View of the History and Coinage of the Parthians. Cork, 1852.

LONGPÉRIER, ADRIEN PRÉVOST DE. Mémoires sur la chronologie et l'iconographie des rois parthes arsacides. Paris, 1853–1882.

McDOWELL, ROBERT HARBOLD. Coins from Seleucia on the Tigris. Ann Arbor, 1935. (University of Michigan Studies. Humanistic Series. XXXVII.)

MANFRIN, PIETRO, CONTE. La cavalleria dei Parthi nelle guerre contro i Romani. Roma, 1893.

MARQUART, JOSEF. "Beiträge zur Geschichte und Sage von Erān." *ZDMG*, 49 (1895), pp. 628–672.

—— Ērānšahr nach der Geographie des Ps. Moses Xorenac'i. Berlin, 1901. (*AGWG*, N.F. Bd. 3.)

—— "Untersuchungen zur Geschichte von Eran." *Philologus*, 54 (1895), pp. 489–527; 55 (1896), pp. 213–244; Supptbd. 10 (1905), pp. 1–258.

MEYER, EDUARD. "Edessa in Osroene." *RECA*, V (1905), pp. 1933–38.

—— "Parthia," "Parthian Empire." *Encyclopaedia Britannica*, 14th ed., XVII (New York, 1929), pp. 344–345, 575–580.

MORGAN, JACQUES DE. Manuel de numismatique orientale de l'antiquité et du moyen-âge. I. Paris, 1923.

PETROWICZ, ALEXANDER VON. Sammlung Petrowicz. Arsaciden-Münzen. Katalog. Wien, 1904.

RAWLINSON, GEORGE. The Sixth Great Oriental Monarchy; or, The Geography, History, and Antiquities of Parthia. London, 1873.

—— The story of Parthia. New York, 1893.

REGLING, KURT LUDWIG. "Zur historischen Geographie des mesopotamischen Parallelogramms." *Klio*, 1 (1902), pp. 443–476.

SAINT-MARTIN, JEAN. Fragments d'une histoire des Arsacides. Paris, 1850. 2 vols.

SCHACHERMEYR, FRITZ. "Mesopotamien." *RECA*, XV (1931), pp. 1105–63.

SCHNEIDERWIRTH, JOHANN HERMANN. Die Parther; oder, Das neupersische Reich unter den Arsaciden, nach griechisch-römischen Quellen. Heiligenstadt, 1874.

SCHUR, WERNER. "Die orientalische Frage im römischen Reiche." *NJWJ*, 2 (1926), pp. 270–282.

—— Die Orientpolitik des Kaisers Nero. Leipzig, 1923. (*Klio*, XV. Beiheft.)

SPIEGEL, FRIEDRICH. Ērân, das Land zwischen dem Indus und Tigris. Berlin, 1863.

—— Erânische Alterthumskunde. Leipzig, 1871–1878. 3 vols.

STEINMANN, ADOLF BERNHARD. De Parthis ab Horatio memoratis: quaestiones chronologicae. Berolini, 1898.

STRECK, MAXIMILIAN. "Seleukeia am Tigris." *RECA*, 2. Reihe, II (1921), pp. 1149–84.

—— Seleucia und Ktesiphon. Leipzig, 1917. (Der alte Orient. 16. Jahrg.)

SYKES, SIR PERCY MOLESWORTH. A History of Persia. London, 1915. 2 vols. 3d ed., 1930.

TARN, WILLIAM WOODTHORPE. The Greeks in Bactria & India. Cambridge, 1938.

—— "Seleucid-Parthian Studies." *PBA*, 16 (1930), pp. 105–135.

TEN CATE FENNEMA, HENRICUS. Quaestiones Parthicae. Neomagi, 1882.

TOMASCHEK, WILHELM. "Zur historischen Topographie von Persien." *SAWW*, 102 (1883), pp. 145–231; 108 (1885), pp. 561–652.

WEISSBACH, FRANZ HEINRICH. "Mesene." *RECA*, XV (1931), pp. 1082–95.

WROTH, WARWICK WILLIAM. Catalogue of the Coins of Parthia. London, 1903. (A Catalogue of the Greek Coins in the British Museum.)

III. THE CHINESE EMPIRE

AMIOT, JOSEPH MARIE, and others. Mémoires concernant l'histoire, les sciences, les arts, les mœurs, les usages, &c. des Chinois, par les Missionnaires de Pékin. Paris, 1776–1791. 15 vols.

ARENDT, CARL. "Synchronistische Regententabellen zur Geschichte der chinesischen Dynastien." *MSOS*, Jahrg. 2 (1899), I, pp. 152–250; Jahrg. 3 (1900), I, pp. 1–164; Jahrg. 4 (1901), I, pp. 114–170.

BIOT, EDOUARD. Dictionnaire des noms anciens et modernes des villes et arrondissements . . . compris dans l'empire chinois. Paris, 1842.

—— "Mémoire sur les colonies militaires et agricoles des Chinois." *Journal asiatique*, 4. sér., 15 (1850), pp. 338–370, 529–595.

BOULGER, DEMETRIUS CHARLES DE KAVANAGH. History of China. London, 1881–1884. 3 vols. 2d ed., 1898.

CHAVANNES, EDOUARD, tr. Les mémoires historiques de Se-ma Ts'ien. Paris, 1895–1905. 5 vols.

CLAPP, FREDERICK GARDNER. "Along and Across the Great Wall of China." *Geographical Review*, 9 (1920), pp. 221–249.

CONRADY, AUGUST. "China," in Julius von Pflugk-Harttung, Weltgeschichte. [Bd. III. Geschichte des Orients]. Berlin, [1910]. pp. 459–567.

CORDIER, HENRI. Aperçu sur l'histoire de l'Asie en général et de la Chine en particulier. Paris, [1904].

—— Bibliotheca Sinica: dictionnaire bibliographique des ouvrages relatifs à l'empire chinois. 2ᵉ éd. Paris, 1904–1908. 4 vols. Supplément. Paris, 1922–1924. 4 pts.

—— Histoire générale de la Chine et de ses relations avec les pays étrangers depuis les temps les plus anciens jusqu'à la chute de la dynastie mandchoue. Paris, 1920–1921. 4 vols.

—— Mélanges d'histoire et de géographie orientales. Paris, 1914–1923. 4 vols.

COUVREUR, SÉRAPHIN. Géographie ancienne et moderne de la Chine. Hien Hien, 1917.

DOUGLAS, SIR ROBERT KENNAWAY. China. London, 1882. 2d ed., rev., 1887.

DU HALDE, JEAN BAPTISTE. Description géographique, historique, chronologique, politique, et physique de l'empire de la Chine et de la Tartarie chinoise. Paris, 1735. 4 vols. Nouvelle éd., La Haye, 1736. 4 vols.

—— The General History of China, Containing a Geographical, Historical, Chronological, Political and Physical Description of China, Chinese-Tartary, Corea and Tibet, [tr. by Richard Brookes]. London, 1736. 4 vols. 3d ed., 1741. 4 vols.

FRANKE, OTTO. Geschichte des chinesischen Reiches. Berlin, 1930–1937. 3 vols.

GARDNER, CHARLES SIDNEY. Chinese Traditional Historiography. Cambridge, Mass., 1938.

GILES, HERBERT ALLEN. A Chinese Biographical Dictionary. Shanghai, 1898.

—— A Chinese-English Dictionary. 2d ed. Shanghai, 1909–1912. 2 vols.

GOWEN, HERBERT HENRY, and HALL, JOSEF WASHINGTON. An Outline History of China. New York, 1926.

GROUSSET, RENÉ. Histoire de l'Asie. Paris, 1921–1922. 3 vols.

—— Histoire de l'Extrême-Orient. Paris, 1929. 2 vols. (Annales du Musée Guimet. Bibliothèque d'études. 39–40.)

HERRMANN, ALBERT. Historical and Commercial Atlas of China. Cambridge, Mass., 1935. (Harvard-Yenching Institute. Monograph Series. I.)

HERVEY DE SAINT-DENYS, MARIE JEAN LÉON, MARQUIS D! Ethnographie des peuples étrangers à la Chine, ouvrage composé au xiii° siècle de notre ère par Ma-touan-lin, traduit pour la première fois du Chinois. Genève, 1876–1883. 2 vols.

KARLGREN, BERNHARD. Analytic Dictionary of Chinese and Sino-Japanese. Paris, 1923.

KRAUSE, FRIEDRICH ERNST AUGUST. Geschichte Ostasiens. Göttingen, 1925. 3 vols.

LATOURETTE, KENNETH SCOTT. The Chinese, their History and Culture. New York, 1934. 2 vols.

—— The Development of China. Boston, 1917. 5th ed., 1937.

MACGOWAN, JOHN. The Imperial History of China, Being a History of the Empire as Compiled by the Chinese Historians. 2d ed. Shanghai, 1906.

MAILLA, JOSEPH ANNE MARIE DE MOYRIAC DE. Histoire générale de la Chine, ou Annales de cet empire, traduites du Tong-kien-kang-mou. Publiées par M. l'Abbé Grosier, et dirigées par M. Le Roux des Hautesrayes. Paris, 1777–1785. 13 vols.

MASPERO, GEORGES. La Chine. Paris, 1918. Nouv. éd., 1925. 2 vols.

MASPERO, HENRI. La Chine antique. Paris, 1927. (Histoire du monde, publiée sous la direction de M. E. Cavaignac. IV.)

MAYERS, WILLIAM FREDERICK. The Chinese Reader's Manual: a Handbook of Biographical, Historical, Mythological, and General Literary Reference. Shanghai, 1874. Reprinted 1910.

OXENHAM, EDWARD LIVINGSTON. Historical Atlas of the Chinese Empire. Shanghai, 1888. 2d ed. London, 1898.

PARKER, EDWARD HARPER. Ancient China Simplified. London, 1908.

—— China: her History, Diplomacy, and Commerce, from the Earliest Times to the Present Day. London, 1901. 2d ed., 1917.

—— China, Past and Present. London, 1903.

PAUTHIER, JEAN PIERRE GUILLAUME. Chine; ou, Description historique, géographique et littéraire de ce vaste empire, d'après des documents chinois. I. Paris, 1837.

PLAYFAIR, GEORGE MACDONALD HOME. The Cities and Towns of China: a Geographical Dictionary. Hongkong, 1879. 2d ed., Shanghai, 1910.

POTT, FRANCIS LISTER HAWKS. A Sketch of Chinese History. Shanghai, 1903. 4th ed., 1923.

RICHTHOFEN, FERDINAND, FREIHERR VON. China. Ergebnisse eigener Reisen und darauf gegründeter Studien. Berlin, 1877–1912. 5 vols. Atlas. 2 vols.

ROSTHORN, ARTHUR VON. Die Ausbreitung der chinesischen Macht in südwestlicher Richtung bis zum vierten Jahrhundert nach Chr.; eine historisch-geographische Studie. Wien, 1895.

—— Geschichte Chinas. Stuttgart, Gotha, 1923. (Weltgeschichte in gemeinverständlicher Darstellung, hrsg. von Ludo Moritz Hartmann.)

TCHANG, MATHIAS. Synchronismes chinois. Chronologie complète et concordance avec l'ère chrétienne de toutes les dates concernant l'histoire de l'Extrême-Orient: Chine, Japon, Corée, Annam, Mongolie, etc. (2357 av. J.-C.–1904 apr. J.-C.). Chang-Hai, 1905. (Variétés sinologiques, 24.)

WIEGER, LÉON. La Chine à travers les âges, hommes et choses. [Hsien Hsien], 1920.

—— Textes historiques. Histoire politique de la Chine. 2° éd., Hsien Hsien, 1922–1923. 2 vols.

WILLIAMS, SAMUEL WELLS. The Middle Kingdom. New York, 1848. 2 vols. Rev. ed., 1899.

YANAI, WATARU, and others. Beiträge zur historischen Geographie der Mandschurei. Tokio, 1912–1914. 2 vols. (Veröffentlichungen der historisch-geographischen Studien-Abteilung der Südmandschurischen Eisenbahn A.G., hrsg. von Kurakichi Shiratori. 1.)

—— Toyo Tokushi Chizu [Historical Atlas of Asia]. Tokyo, 1926.

A. THE "WESTERN REGIONS"

BELL, MARK SEVER. "The Great Central Asian Trade Route from Peking to Kashgaria." PRGS, n.s. 12 (1890), pp. 57–93.

BROSSET, MARIE FÉLICITÉ. "Relation du pays de Ta ouan, traduite du chinois." Journal asiatique, 2. sér., 2 (1828), pp. 418–450.

CHAVANNES, EDOUARD. Les documents chinois découverts par Aurel Stein dans les sables du Turkestan oriental. Oxford, 1913. "Introduction," tr. by Madame Edouard Chavannes and H. Wilfred House. New China Review, 4 (1922), pp. 341–359, 427–442.

—— "Les pays d'Occident d'après le Heou Han chou." T'oung pao, 2. sér., 8 (1907), pp. 149–234.

—— "Les pays d'Occident d'après le Wei lio." T'oung pao, 2. sér., 6 (1905), pp. 519–571.

—— "Trois généraux chinois de la dynastie des Han orientaux. . . . Chapitre LXXVII du Heou Han chou." T'oung pao, 2. sér., 7 (1906), pp. 210–269.

CONRADY, AUGUST. Die chinesischen Handschriften- und sonstigen Kleinfunde Sven Hedins in Lou-lan. Stockholm, 1920.

DRAKE, F. S. "China's North-west Passage." [1] A chapter in its opening. [2. The struggle for the Tarim basin in the Later Han dynasty.] JNCB, 66 (1935), pp. 42–49; 67 (1936), pp. 147–159.

FORSYTH, SIR THOMAS DOUGLAS. "On the Buried Cities in the Shifting Sands of the Great Desert of Gobi." PRGS, 21 (1877), pp. 27–46.

GRENARD, FERNAND. "Sur quelques routes anciennes et modernes," in Jules Léon Dutreuil de Rhins, Mission scientifique dans la Haute Asie, 1890–1895. Paris, 1898. pp. 212–249.

GROOT, JAN JAKOB MARIA DE. Chinesische Urkunden zur Geschichte Asiens. II. Die Westlande Chinas in der vorchristlichen Zeit, hrsg. von O. Franke. Berlin, Leipzig, 1926.

HEDIN, SVEN ANDERS. Central Asia and Tibet towards the Holy City of Lassa, [tr. by J. T. Bealby]. London, 1903. 2 vols.

—— Scientific Results of a Journey in Central Asia, 1899–1902. Stockholm, 1904–1907. 6 vols. in 7.

—— Through Asia, [tr. by J. T. Bealby]. New York, 1899 [1898]. 2 vols.

HERRMANN, ALBERT. "Die ältesten chinesischen Karten von Zentral- und Westasien." Ostasiatische Zeitschrift, 8 (1920), pp. 185–198.

—— "Die Westländer in der chinesischen Kartographie," in Sven Hedin, Southern Tibet. VIII. Stockholm, 1922. pp. 91–406.

HIMLY, KARL. "Ein chinesisches Werk über das westliche Inner-Asien." Ethnologisches Notizblatt, 3 (1902), pp. 1–77. An account of Chinese exploration carried out in 1817.

RÉMUSAT, ABEL. "Remarques sur l'extension de l'empire chinois du côté de l'Occident." *MAI*, 8 (1827), pp. 60–130.

—— "Sur quelques peuples du Tibet et de la Boukharie, tiré de l'ouvrage de Ma-touan-lin, et traduit du chinois," in his Nouveaux mélanges asiatiques. I. Paris, 1829. pp. 186–257.

RITTER, CARL. Die Erdkunde von Asien. V, 3: West-Asien. Berlin, 1837.

STEIN, SIR MARC AUREL. Ancient Khotan: Detailed Report of Archaeological Explorations in Chinese Turkestan. Oxford, 1907. 2 vols.

—— "Central-Asian Relics of China's Ancient Silk Trade." *Asia Major*, Introductory volume (London, [1922]), pp. 367–374. See also *T'oung pao*, 20 (1921), pp. 130–141.

—— "Innermost Asia: its Geography as a Factor in History." *Geographical Journal*, 65 (1925), pp. 377–403, 473–501.

—— Innermost Asia: Detailed Report of Explorations in Central Asia, Kan-su, and Eastern Īrān. Oxford, 1928. 4 vols.

—— On Ancient Central-Asian Tracks. London, 1933.

—— Ruins of Desert Cathay; Personal Narrative of Exploration in Central Asia and Westernmost China. London, 1912. 2 vols.

—— Sand-buried Ruins of Khotan; Personal Narrative of a Journey of Archaeological and Geographical Exploration in Chinese Turkistan. London, 1903.

—— Serindia: Detailed Report of Explorations in Central Asia and Westernmost China. Oxford, 1921. 5 vols.

WYLIE, ALEXANDER. "Notes on the Western Regions, tr. from the 'Tseën Han Shoo.'" *JAI*, 10 (1881), pp. 20–73; 11 (1882), pp. 83–115.

The extensive philological literature which has arisen since the discovery in the Tarim basin of documents in hitherto unknown languages is not represented in the foregoing list.

B. MONGOLIA AND THE HSIUNG-NU

BICHURIN, IAKINTH. Denkwürdigkeiten über die Mongolei, von dem Mönch Hyakinth, aus dem Russischen übersetzt von Karl Friedrich von der Borg. Berlin, 1832.

CAHUN, LÉON. Introduction à l'histoire de l'Asie. Turcs et Mongols des origines à 1405. Paris, 1896.

CHAVANNES, EDOUARD. Documents sur les Tou-kiue (Turcs) occidentaux. St.-Pétersbourg, 1903. "Notes additionnelles," *T'oung pao*, 2. sér., 5 (1904), pp. 1–110.

CONSTEN, HERMANN. Weideplätze der Mongolen im Reiche der Chalcha. Berlin, 1919–1920. 2 vols.

DROUIN, EDMÉ. "Huns et Hioung-nou," in La grande encyclopédie. XX. Paris, [1894].

FRANKE, OTTO. Beiträge aus chinesischen Quellen zur Kenntnis der Türkvölker und Skythen Zentralasiens. Berlin, 1904. (*AAWB*, 1904).

GROOT, JAN JAKOB MARIA DE. Chinesische Urkunden zur Geschichte Asiens. I. Die Hunnen der vorchristlichen Zeit. Berlin, Leipzig, 1921.

GUIGNES, JOSEPH DE. Histoire générale des Huns, des Turcs, des Mogols, et des autres Tartares occidentaux, &c. avant et depuis Jésus-Christ jusqu'à présent. Paris, 1756–1758. 4 vols. in 5.

HALPHEN, LOUIS. "Les origines asiatiques des 'grandes invasions.'" *Revue belge de philologie et d'histoire*, 2 (1923), pp. 453–460.

HALPHEN, LOUIS. "La place de l'Asie dans l'histoire du monde." *Revue historique,* 142 (1923), pp. 1–13.

HERRMANN, ALBERT. "Die Gobi im Zeitalter der Hunnen-Herrschaft," *Geografiska Annaler,* 17 (1935), Suppt., pp. 130–143.

HIRTH, FRIEDRICH. "Hunnenforschungen." *Keleti szemle (Revue orientale pour les études ouralo-altaïques),* 2 (1901), pp. 81–91.

—— "Sinologische Beiträge zur Geschichte der Türk-Völker. I. Die Ahnentafel Attila's nach Johannes von Thurócz." *Bulletin de l'Académie impériale des sciences de St.-Pétersbourg,* 5. sér., 13 (1900), pp. 221–261.

—— "Ueber Wolga-Hunnen und Hiung-nu." *SAWM,* 1899, II, pp. 245–278.

KIESSLING, MAX. "Hunni." *RECA,* VIII (1913), pp. 2583–2615.

LATTIMORE, OWEN. "Caravan Routes of Inner Asia." *Geographical Journal,* 72 (1928), pp. 497–528.

—— "The Geographical Factor in Mongol History." *Geographical Journal,* 91 (1938), pp. 1–16.

—— The Mongols of Manchuria. New York, 1934.

NÉMÄTI, KÁLMÁN. "The Historic-geographical Proofs of the Hiung-nu–Hun Identity." *AQR,* 3d ser., 29 (1910), pp. 352–369.

PARKER, EDWARD HARPER. "Chinese Relations with the Tartar and Tibetan Tribes." *Chinese Recorder,* 15 (1884), pp. 262–266, 351–360.

—— "The History of the Wu-wan or Wu-hwan Tunguses of the First Century; Followed by That of their Kinsmen the Sien-pi." *China Review,* 20 (1892–1893), pp. 71–100.

—— A Thousand Years of the Tartars. London, [Shanghai], 1895. 2d ed., New York, 1924.

—— "The Turko-Scythian tribes." *China Review,* 20 (1892–1893), pp. 1–24, 109–125; 21 (1894–1895), pp. 100–119, 129–137, 253–267, 291–301.

PEISKER, T. "The Asiatic Background," in Cambridge Medieval History. I. New York, 1911, pp. 323–359, 660–664.

ROSTHORN, ARTHUR VON. Die Hochburg von Zentralasien. *Asia Major,* Introductory volume (London, [1922]), pp. 286–297.

SCHURTZ, HEINRICH. "Central Asia and Siberia," in Hans Ferdinand Helmolt, ed., The History of the World. II. New York, 1904. pp. 122–229.

SHIRATORI, KURAKICHI. "Über den Wu-sun-Stamm in Centralasien." *Keleti Szemle,* 3 (1902), pp. 103–140.

SOULIÉ, GEORGES. "Les Mongols, leur organisation administrative d'après des documents chinois." *Actes du xivᵉ Congrès international des Orientalistes,* I (Paris, 1906), pp. 64–83.

TAKÁCS, ZOLTÁN DE. "Huns et Chinois." *Túrán,* 1918, pp. 273–285.

THOMASSON, H. W. "The Origin of the Huns," *Journal of the Manchester Egyptian and Oriental Society,* 13 (1927), pp. 51–59.

WIRTH, ALBRECHT. Geschichte Asiens und Osteuropas. Halle a. S., 1905.

WYLIE, ALEXANDER. "History of the Heung-noo in their Relations with China, tr. from the Tseen-Han-shoo." *JAI,* 3 (1874), pp. 401–452; 5 (1876), pp. 41–80.

THE ART OF THE PEOPLES OF NORTHERN EURASIA

ANDERSSON, JOHAN GUNNAR. "The Highway of Europe and Asia." *JRAS,* 1929, pp. 422–425.

—— "Hunting Magic in the Animal Style." Museum of Far Eastern Antiquities, Stockholm, *Bulletin,* 4 (1932), 221–317.

ANDERSSON, JOHAN GUNNAR. "Der Weg über die Steppen." Museum of Far Eastern Antiquities, Stockholm, *Bulletin*, 1 (1929), pp. 143–163.

ARDENNE DE TIZAC, HENRI D'. Animals in Chinese Art, tr. by Henry Stuart. New York, [1923].

BOROVKA, GREGORY. "Die Funde der Expedition Koslow in der Mongolei 1924/25. Der skythische Tierstil." *Archäologischer Anzeiger*, 1926, pp. 341–386.

—— Scythian Art, tr. by V. G. Childe. London, 1928.

DALTON, ORMONDE MADDOCK. The Treasure of the Oxus, with Other Examples of Early Oriental Metal-work. 2d ed. London, 1926.

GLÜCK, HEINRICH. "Die Weltstellung der Türken in der Kunst." *Wiener Beiträge zur Kunst- und Kulturgeschichte Asiens*, 2 (1927), pp. 7–34.

HENTZE, CARL. "Beiträge zu den Problemen des eurasischen Tierstyles." *Ostasiatische Zeitschrift*, 16 (1930), 150–169.

JANSE, OLOV. "L'empire des steppes et les relations entre l'Europe et l'Extrême-Orient dans l'antiquité." *Revue des arts asiatiques*, 9 (1935), pp. 9–26.

KOZLOV, PETR KUZ'MICH. Comptes rendus des expéditions pour l'exploration du nord de la Mongolie rattachées à l'expédition Mongolo-Tibétaine de P. K. Kozlov. [In Russian.] Leningrad, 1925.

MARTIN, FREDRIK ROBERT. L'âge du bronze au Musée de Minoussinsk. Stockholm, 1893.

MERHART, GERO VON. Bronzezeit am Jenissei; ein Beitrag zur Urgeschichte Sibiriens. Wien, 1926.

MINNS, ELLIS HOVELL. Scythians and Greeks: a Survey of Ancient History and Archaeology on the North Coast of the Euxine from the Danube to the Caucasus. Cambridge, 1913.

—— "The Baron de Baye's Antiquities from North-east Russia and Siberia." *Antiquaries Journal*, 3 (1923), pp. 52–60.

—— "Small Bronzes from Northern Asia." *Antiquaries Journal*, 10 (1930), pp. 1–23.

RADLOFF, WILHELM. "Sibirische Alterthümer," in his Aus Sibirien. II. 2. Ausgabe. Leipzig, 1893. pp. 68–143.

REINACH, SALOMON. "La représentation du galop dans l'art ancien et moderne." *Revue archéologique*, 3. sér., 36–39 (1900–1901), passim. Nouvelle éd. Paris, 1925.

REINECKE, PAUL. "Ueber einige Beziehungen der Alterthümer China's zu denen des skythisch-sibirischen Völkerkreises." *Zeitschrift für Ethnologie*, 29 (1897), pp. 141–163.

ROSTOVTZEFF, MICHAEL IVANOVICH. The Animal Style in South Russia and China. Princeton, 1929. (Princeton Monographs in Art and Archaeology. XIV.)

—— "L'art gréco-sarmate et l'art chinois de l'époque des Han." *Aréthuse*, 1 (1924), pp. 81–94.

—— Le centre de l'Asie, la Russie, la Chine et le style animal. Prague, 1929.

—— Iranians and Greeks in South Russia. Oxford, 1922.

SALMONY, ALFRED. Sino-Siberian Art in the Collection of C. T. Loo. Paris, 1933.

TAKÁCS, ZOLTÁN DE. "Some Irano-Hellenistic and Sino-Hunnic Art Forms." *Ostasiatische Zeitschrift*, 15 (1929), pp. 142–148.

TALLGREN, AARNE MICHAËL. Collection Tovostine des antiquités préhistoriques de Minoussinsk. Helsingfors, 1917. (Société finlandaise d'archéologie.)

—— "Zum Ursprungsgebiet des sog. skythischen Tierstils." *Acta archaeologica*, 4 (1933), 258–264.

——, ed. Eurasia septentrionalis antiqua. Helsingfors. 1 (1926)–12 (1938).

YETTS, W. PERCIVAL. "Discoveries of the Kozlóv expedition." *Burlington Magazine*, 48 (1926), pp. 168–185.

—— "Links between Ancient China and the West." *Geographical Review*, 16 (1926), pp. 614–622.

IV. COMMUNICATIONS EAST AND WEST

On the knowledge which the Romans had of China and India and which the Chinese had of India, Parthia, and Syria, and on overland communications in the first century.

ANVILLE, JEAN BAPTISTE BOURGUIGNON D. "Recherches géographiques et historiques sur la Sérique des anciens." *MAI*, 32 (1768), pp. 573–603.

BAER, KARL ERNST VON. Historische Fragen mit Hülfe der Naturwissenschaften beantwortet. St. Petersburg, 1873. 2. Aufl., Braunschweig, 1886. pp. 288–340.

BANERJEE, GAURANGANATH. India as Known to the Ancient World, or India's Intercourse in Ancient Times with her Neighbours, Egypt, Western Asia, Greece, Rome, Central Asia, China, Further India, and Indonesia. London, 1921.

BARNETT, LIONEL DAVID. "Commercial and Political Connexions of Ancient India with the West." *Bulletin of the School of Oriental Studies*, 1 (1917), pp. 101–105.

BERGER, HUGO. "Erythraeum mare." *RECA*, VI (1907), pp. 592–601.

BERTHELOT, ANDRÉ. L'Asie ancienne, centrale et sud-orientale d'après Ptolémée. Paris, 1930.

BISHOP, CARL WHITING. "The Geographical Factor in the Development of Chinese Civilization." *Geographical Review*, 12 (1922), pp. 19–41.

—— "The Rise of Civilization in China with Reference to its Geographical Aspects." *Geographical Review*, 22 (1932), pp. 617–631.

BLÜMNER, HUGO. "Serica." *RECA*, 2. Reihe, II (1923), pp. 1724–27.

CHARLESWORTH, MARTIN PERCIVAL. "Some Notes on the Periplus Maris Erythraei." *Classical Quarterly*, 22 (1928), pp. 92–100.

—— Trade-routes and Commerce of the Roman Empire. Cambridge, 1924. 2d ed., 1926.

COEDÈS, GEORGE, ed. Textes d'auteurs grecs et latins relatifs à l'Extrême-Orient depuis le iv⁰ siècle av. J.-C. jusqu'au xiv⁰ siècle. Paris, 1910.

EDKINS, JOSEPH. "What Did the Ancient Chinese Know of the Greeks and Romans?" *JNCB*, n.s. 18 (1884), pp. 1–19.

FORKE, ALFRED. "Ta-ts'in das römische Reich." *Ostasiatische Zeitschrift*, 14 (1927), pp. 48–60.

GISINGER, FRIEDRICH. "Geographie." *RECA*, 4. Supptbd. (1924), pp. 521–685.

GÖTZ, WILHELM. Die Verkehrswege im Dienste des Welthandels: eine historisch-geographische Untersuchung. Stuttgart, 1888.

GOSSELLIN, PASCAL FRANÇOIS JOSEPH. "Recherches sur la Sérique des anciens, et sur les limites de leurs connoissances dans la Haut-Asie." *MAI*, 49 (1808), pp. 713–749.

GUIGNES, JOSEPH DE. "Idée générale du commerce & des liaisons que les Chinois ont eus avec les nations occidentales." *MAI*, 46 (1793), pp. 534–579.

—— "Réflexions générales sur les liaisons & le commerce des Romains avec les Tartares & les Chinois." *MAI*, 32 (1768), pp. 355–369.

HEEREN, ARNOLD HERMANN LUDWIG. "Commentatio de Romanorum de India notitia et cum Indis commerciis." Gesellschaft der Wissenschaften zu Göttingen, *Commentationes*, 11 (1793), pp. 91–111.

HENNIG, RICHARD. "Der Begriff der Serer in der antiken Literatur." *Zeitschrift für Rassenkunde*, 2 (1935), pp. 90–92.

—— Terrae incognitae, I. Altertum bis Ptolemäus. Leiden, 1936.

—— "Thin und Cattigara," in his Von rätselhaften Ländern, versunkene Stätten der Geschichte. München, [1925]. pp. 153–158.

—— "Der Weltverkehr der Vorzeit und des Altertums." *Prometheus*, 23 (1911), pp. 65–69, 81–85, 101–104.

—— Zur Frühgeschichte des Seeverkehrs im indischen Ozean. Berlin, 1919.

HERRMANN, ALBERT. "Die ältesten chinesischen Weltkarten." *Ostasiatische Zeitschrift*, 11 (1924), pp. 97–118.

—— Die alten Seidenstrassen zwischen China und Syrien: Beiträge zur alten Geographie Asiens. I. Berlin, 1910. (Quellen und Forschungen zur alten Geschichte und Geographie, hrsg. von W. Sieglin. 21.)

—— "Die alten Verkehrswege zwischen Indien und Süd-China nach Ptolemäus." *ZGEB*, 1913, pp. 771–787.

—— "Ein alter Seeverkehr zwischen Abessinien und Süd-China bis zum Beginn unserer Zeitrechnung." *ZGEB*, 1913, pp. 553–561.

—— "Die Lage des Landes Ta Ts'in." *Ostasiatische Zeitschrift*, 14 (1927), pp. 196–202.

—— Lou-lan: China, Indien und Rom im Lichte der Ausgrabungen am Lobnor. Leipzig, 1931.

—— "Die Seidenstrassen vom alten China nach dem römischen Reich." *MGGW*, 58 (1915), pp. 472–500.

—— "Seres." *RECA*, 2. Reihe, II (1923), pp. 1678–83.

—— Die Verkehrswege zwischen China, Indien und Rom um 100 nach Chr. Geb. Leipzig, 1922.

—— "Zur alten Geographie Zentralasiens." *Petermanns Mitteilungen*, 57 (1911), I, pp. 12–15.

HIRTH, FRIEDRICH. China and the Roman Orient: Researches into their Ancient and Mediaeval Relations as Represented in Old Chinese Records. Shanghai, Hongkong, 1885.

—— "The Story of Chang K'ién, China's Pioneer in Western Asia. Text and translation of chapter 123 of Ssï-ma Ts'ién's Shï-ki." *JAOS*, 37 (1917), pp. 89–152.

—— "Syrisch-chinesische Beziehungen im Anfang unserer Zeitrechnung," in Roman Oberhummer and Heinrich Zimmerer, Durch Syrien und Kleinasien: Reiseschilderung und Studien. Berlin, 1899. pp. 436–449.

—— "Zur Geschichte des antiken Orienthandels," in his Chinesische Studien. I. München, 1890. pp. 1–24.

HORNELL, JAMES. "A Review of our Knowledge of Ancient Sea-trade with India," in his "The Origins and Ethnological Significance of Indian Boat Designs." *Memoirs of the Asiatic Society of Bengal*, 7 (1920), pp. 191–206.

HUDSON, GEOFFREY FRANCIS. Europe and China: a Survey of their Relations from the Earliest Times to 1800. London, [1931].

KINGSMILL, THOMAS WILLIAM. "The Sêrica of Ptolemy and its Inhabitants." *JNCB*, n.s. 19 (1886), pp. 43–60.

LASSEN, CHRISTIAN. "Geschichte des Handels und des griechisch-römischen Wissens von Indien," in his Indische Alterthumskunde, III. Leipzig, 1858. pp. 1–301.

LAUFER, BERTHOLD. "Chinesische Altertümer in der römischen Epoche der Rheinlande." *Globus*, 88 (1905), pp. 45–49.

—— Sino-Iranica: Chinese Contributions to the History of Civilization in Ancient Iran. Chicago, 1919. (Field Museum of Natural History. Publication, 201.)

Lévi, Sylvain. "La Grèce et l'Inde d'après les documents indiens." *Revue des études grecques,* 4 (1891), pp 24–45.

M'Crindle, John Watson. Ancient India as Described by Ptolemy. Calcutta, Bombay, 1885.

—— Ancient India as Described in Classical Literature. Westminster, 1901.

—— The Commerce and Navigation of the Erythraean Sea: being a Translation of the Periplus Maris Erythraei. Calcutta, Bombay, 1879.

Michell, Robert. "Ancient Imaus, or Bam-i-Dunia, and the Way to Serica." *Scottish Geographical Magazine,* 8 (1892), pp. 591–605, 643–654.

Neumann, Carl Friedrich. "Handelsstrassen von China nach dem Westen," in his Asiatische Studien. I. Leipzig, 1837. pp. 187–202.

Nissen, Heinrich. "Der Verkehr zwischen China und dem römischen Reiche." *Bonner Jahrbücher,* 95 (1894), pp. 1–28.

Pardessus, Jean Marie. Mémoire sur le commerce de la soie chez les anciens antérieurement au vi⁰ siècle de l'ère chrétienne. Paris, 1841.

Pariset, Ernest. Histoire de la soie. Paris, 1862–1865. 2 vols.

Parker, Edward Harper. China: her History, Diplomacy, and Commerce. London, 1901. 2d ed., 1917. "Trade Routes," pp. 59–86.

—— "Chinese Knowledge of Ancient Persia." *AQR,* 3d ser., 15 (1902), pp. 144–169.

Pauthier, Jean Pierre Guillaume. Histoire des relations politiques de la Chine avec les puissances occidentales, depuis les temps les plus anciens jusqu'à nos jours. Paris, 1859.

Pelliot, Paul. "Li-kien, autre nom du Ta-ts'in (Orient méditerranéen)." *T'oung pao,* 2. sér., 16 (1915), pp. 690–691.

—— "Note sur les anciens itinéraires chinois dans l'Orient romain." *Journal asiatique,* 11. sér., 17 (1921), pp. 139–145.

Priaulx, Osmond de Beauvoir. The Indian Travels of Apollonius of Tyana, and the Indian Embassies to Rome from the Reign of Augustus to the Death of Justinian. London, 1873.

Rawlinson, Hugh George. Intercourse between India and the Western World from the Earliest Times to the Fall of Rome. Cambridge, 1916. 2d ed., 1926.

Reinaud, Joseph. "Relations politiques et commerciales de l'empire romain avec l'Asie orientale (l'Hyrcanie, l'Inde, la Bactriane et la Chine), pendant les cinq premiers siècles de l'ère chrétienne, d'après les témoignages latins, grecs, arabes, persans, indiens et chinois." *Journal asiatique,* 6. sér., 1 (1863), pp. 93–234, 297–441.

Richthofen, Ferdinand von. "Entwickelung der Kenntniss von China," in his China. I. Berlin, 1877. pp. 273–733.

—— "Ueber den Seeverkehr nach und von China in Alterthum und Mittelalter." *VGEB,* 1876, pp. 86–97.

—— "Ueber die centralasiatischen Seidenstrassen bis zum 2. Jahrhundert n. Chr." *VGEB,* 1877, pp. 96–122.

Robertson, William. An Historical Disquisition concerning the Knowledge which the Ancients Had of India. London, 1791.

Schoff, Wilfred Harvey. Early Communication between China and the Mediterranean. [Philadelphia, 1921.]

—— "The Eastern Iron Trade of the Roman Empire." *JAOS,* 35 (1915), pp. 224–239.

—— "Navigation to the Far East under the Roman Empire." *JAOS,* 37 (1917), pp. 240–249.

SCHOFF, WILFRED HARVEY. "Some Aspects of the Overland Oriental Trade at the Christian Era." *JAOS*, 35 (1915), pp. 31–41.

——, ed. Parthian Stations by Isidore of Charax; an Account of the Overland Trade Route between the Levant and India in the First Century B.C. Philadelphia, 1914.

—— ed. The Periplus of the Erythraean Sea: Travel and Trade in the Indian Ocean by a Merchant of the First Century. New York, 1912.

SELIGMAN, CHARLES GABRIEL. "The Roman Orient and the Far East." *Antiquity*, 11 (1937), pp. 5–30.

SEVERTZOW, NICOLAS. "Etudes de géographie historique sur les anciens itinéraires à travers le Pamir." *Bulletin de la Société de Géographie,* 7. sér., 11 (1890), pp. 417–467, 553–610.

SPECK, ERNST. Handelsgeschichte des Altertums. I. Leipzig, 1900. pp. 139–209.

SYKES, SIR PERCY. The Quest for Cathay. London, 1936.

TARN, WILLIAM WOODTHORPE. Hellenistic Civilisation. London, 1927. "Trade and Exploration," pp. 193–214.

—— "Notes on Hellenism in Bactria and India." *JHS*, 22 (1902), pp. 268–293.

THOMSON, J. OLIVER. "The Silk Routes and Ancient Geography." Classical Association, *Proceedings*, 30 (1933), pp. 28–30.

VIDAL DE LA BLACHE, PAUL. "Note sur l'origine du commerce de la soie par voie de mer." *CRAI*, 4. sér., 25 (1897), pp. 520–527.

—— "Les voies de commerce dans la Géographie de Ptolémée." *CRAI*, 4. sér., 24 (1896), pp. 456–483.

VINCENT, WILLIAM. The Commerce and Navigation of the Ancients in the Indian Ocean. London, 1807. 2 vols.

WARMINGTON, ERIC HERBERT. The Commerce between the Roman Empire and India. Cambridge, 1928.

—— "Indian Waters," in Max Cary and E. H. Warmington, The Ancient Explorers. New York, 1929. pp. 56–85.

YULE, SIR HENRY. Cathay and the Way Thither: being a Collection of Medieval Notices of China. With a Preliminary Essay on the Intercourse between China and the Western Nations Previous to the Discovery of the Cape Route. London, 1866. 2 vols. (Works issued by the Hakluyt Society. 36, 37.)

—— Cathay and the Way Thither: being a Collection of Medieval Notices of China. New ed., revised by Henri Cordier. London, 1913–1916. 4 vols. (Works issued by the Hakluyt Society. 2d series. 33, 37, 38, 41.)

—— "Notes on the Oldest Records of the Sea-route to China from Western Asia." *PRGS*, n.s. 4 (1882), pp. 649–660.

INDEX

A-lan (Yen-ts'ai), 159 *and note* 5, 199, 200, 204, 205

A-lan-liau, 199

Abdageses, Parthian conspirator, 65

Abdus, Parthian conspirator, 64

Abeacus, king of the Siraci, 17, 153

Abgar V of Osroëne, 93

Abzoae, 183, 197, 200–205, 211, 220. *See also* Ho-su and Yen-ts'ai

Achardeus (Yegorlyk) River, 176

Acibi, 175, 185

Adiabene, 97, 119

Aedui, 3, 9, 10, 63, 227

Aegissus, 58

Aelius Gallus, 31

Aelius Hadrianus, P., 134, 169

Aelius Catus, Sex., 49 *and note* 9, 82

Aelius Lamia, L., 156, 157

Aemilius Scaurus, M., 6

Agricola. *See* Julius

Agrippa. *See* Vipsanius

Ahenobarbus. *See* Domitius

Ak-su (Ku-mo), 110, 138, 139, 143

Akmolinsk, 206

Alani, 101 *note* 2, 135, 136 *note* 6, 152 *note* 5, 159, 161–164, 166 *note* 2, 174, 175, 185, 186, 191, 192, 204, 205; position in eastern Europe, 217–223. *See also* A-lan and Yen-ts'ai

Alani Mountains, in Scythia within Imaus, 191, 219 *note* 68

Alani Scythae, 175, 191, 192, 205, 208, 219 *and note* 68

Alanorsi, 177 *note* 3, 191, 205, 208, 209, 211

Alanus *or* Alaunus Mountains, in European Sarmatia, 218

Alauni, 175, 185, 191, 218–220

Albani, Albania, 3, 26, 37, 65, 101, 160, 163, 222

Aliso, 56

Allobroges, 9, 149

Altai Mountains, 205, 209–213

Aluta River, 129, 133

Am-ts'ai (Yen-ts'ai), 202, 203, 205

Amanus Mountain, 16

Ambiorix, king of the Eburones, 15, 16

Amisus, 17, 71

Ammianus Marcellinus, on Alani, 204, 218–221

Ampsivarii, 44, 99

Amyntas, king of Galatia, 31

An, king of Shan-shan, 113, 114

An-hou River, 166, 167

An-hsi (Parthia), 117, 141, 145, 153, 197

An-ts'ai, 152 *note* 5, 202

Ananyino, 192, 213 *note* 51

Anarei, 205, 211; Mountains, 205–208

Anartii, 49, 73 *note* 15, 78, 79, 156

Angrivarii, 132

Anicetus, 102

Anilai, 64 *note* 5

Antioch (Syria), 13, 120

Antiochus I of Commagene, 23

Antiochus IV of Commagene, 134, 135

Antistius Vetus, C., 20, 27

Antonius, C., 19

Antonius, L., 22

Antonius (Antony), M., 23 *and note* 1, 25–28, 29 *note* 6, 31, 239

Antonius Hybrida, C., governor of Macedonia, 7

Antonius Saturninus, L., governor of Upper Germany, 130, 143

Aorsi, 17, 90, 153, 159, 162, 163, 171, 176, 177, 180, 181, 185, 187, 192, 193, 196, 220; discussion of identification with the Yen-ts'ai, 201–203; "upper Aorsi," 162, 163, 176, 201, 202; in northern part of European Sarmatia, 185, 187; north of the Caspian Sea, 192, 193, 196

Apamea (Syria), 20

Apollonia (Macedonia), 21

Appianus, *quoted*, 15, 20, 29

Appius Maximus Norbanus, L., governor of Lower Germany, 130

Appuleius, Sex., 45

Apronius, L., governor of Lower Germany, 56, 64